AMERICAN LABOR

FROM CONSPIRACY
TO
COLLECTIVE BARGAINING

THE MAKING OF AMERICA
LABOR

Edited by Robert Marion La Follette

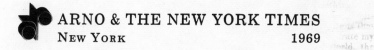
ARNO & THE NEW YORK TIMES

NEW YORK   1969

THE MAKING OF AMERICA
LABOR

AVERAGE WAGES PER HOUR

CENTS PER HOUR

	5	10	15	20	25	30	35	40

BLACKSMITHS

BOILER MAKERS

BRICKLAYERS

CARPENTERS

COMPOSITORS

HODCARRIERS

IRONMOLDERS

LABORERS-GENERAL

MACHINISTS

PAINTERS

PLUMBERS

STONECUTTERS

STONEMASONS

——— UNITED STATES   - - - - - BELGIUM

· · · · · · · · GREAT BRITAIN

UNITED STATES AND EUROPE

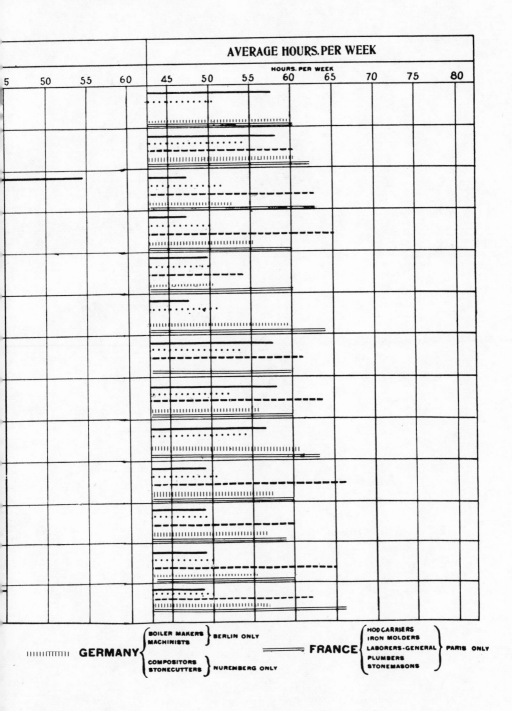

	AVERAGE HOURS. PER WEEK

HOURS. PER WEEK

5   50   55   60   45   50   55   60   65   70   75   80

GERMANY { BOILER MAKERS / MACHINISTS } BERLIN ONLY   { COMPOSITORS / STONECUTTERS } NUREMBERG ONLY   ═══ FRANCE { HOD CARRIERS / IRON MOLDERS / LABORERS-GENERAL / PLUMBERS / STONEMASONS } PARIS ONLY

The MAKING OF AMERICA

Editorial Edition

limited to one thousand copies
of which this is No. _____

Robert Marion La Follette

Editor-in-Chief

William M. Handy
Charles Higgins
Managing Editors

VOL. VIII

Labor

The Making of America Co.

Chicago

CONTENTS

VOLUME VIII

LABOR.

CONTENTS

THE AMERICAN WORKMAN.

BY THOMAS I. KIDD.

[Thomas I. Kidd, fifth vice-president American Federation of Labor; born Edinburgh, Scotland, and educated in the schools of that city; became identified with the labor movement in America shortly after his arrival in this country, and was general secretary of the Amalgamated Woodworkers from Aug. 5, 1890, to Jan. 1, 1905; has been editor of the International Woodworker since 1891.]

In fifty years the working power, the exerted energy, of the nations of christendom has more than doubled. That of Europe has increased fourfold. That of the United States tenfold. All signs point toward the United States as the country which for the next half century must sustain and surpass this enormous increase of the world's productivity.

The last half century's great increase in the working energy of the world was due mainly to the development of steam. In the adoption of modern machinery this country surpassed the world in promptness and in the productive consequences. Its expansion in applied energy was greater than that of all Europe put together.

Students of industrial evolution attribute the waxing pre-eminence of the United States in all lines of productivity, first, to its freedom from overpopulation; second, its favorable system of government and society; third, the superiority of its workmen and its facilities—the latter including raw material, fuel, transportation, and mechanical appliances. Ten years ago, figuring on the accepted basis by which there should not be more than fifty people to every 100 productive acres, seven European countries were overpopulated—viz.: England, Scotland, Germany, Belgium, Holland, Italy, and Switzerland.

The American workman himself may fairly be regarded as the principal factor in the surpassing excellence of his country's manual and manufacturing performances, since he is chiefly responsible for the existing industrial system, a powerful influence in the governmental attitude toward labor, the operator and in many cases the author of the best of modern machinery, and, in the last analysis, the director and governor of that energy which makes things.

Fifty years ago the United States held lowest rank among the four great textile manufacturing nations. To-day it has almost equaled Great Britain and surpassed all the others. In the making of hardware this country has excelled, in the quantity and value of its output, all the other nations except England. It makes one third of the hardware used in the world, although it consumes not more than one seventh.

The superiority of the American workman to all others is not longer a doubtful proposition even in England, where both prejudice and rivalry help to put every claim of American pre-eminence in the category of brag. But when it is said that the American workman is the best the world has known, it should be understood that his unequaled excellence as a class is what is meant. There are individual mechanics and artisans in different countries of Europe who have not been surpassed in skill and ingenuity by the workmen of any country. Yet in summing up their productive abilities, who have not been surpassed in skill or influences for the betterment of their class, they are outnumbered and outweighed by their peers in the United States.

In cataloguing the points of excellence of the American workman over his English contemporary, the first should be, perhaps, the superior volume of his output, whether manual or mechanical. It has been estimated that, in purely manual efficiency, the American workingmen, as compared with the English, produce in the ratio of three to two as to quantity. In the United States the productive volume of man run machinery is almost two to one as compared with England, and from this probably accurate estimate it has been inferred that the American mechanic is twice as effective, with the same machine, as his British rival.

In order to be perfectly just, however, it must be stated that the English workingman is to a great extent handicapped by his own established and accepted system of labor regulations, and that his true ability, whether individually or collectively, can hardly be gauged by his performances. For almost half a century the workingmen of England have accepted and acted upon the theory that the less work they did the more work there would remain to do, so that in reckoning their efficiency by the results it should be borne in mind that most of them do as little work as may be compatible with holding their places in shop or factory.

The hostility which European workmen have inveterately and continuously shown to modern machinery is another potent cause of the disparity between the mechanical output of American factories and that of England especially. In one instance a manufacturer installed six machines to be attended by one man, but the English labor union compelled him to employ one man for each machine. In another case a machine capable of increasing the factory output 25 per cent was emplaced. But the union ruled that it should not be permitted to run more than 75 per cent of its capacity.

It would not be accurate, therefore, to finally measure the skill or intelligence of the foreigner by the quantity of his output, though the wisdom or folly of his labor system may be nearly appreciated by the fact that he earns less than his American rival in the same craft and that the factories of the United States successfully compete with his employer in the shadow of the English factory. The foreign workman in his home shop and factory has been an obstructionist rather than a promoter of the quantity phase of effectiveness. The result is that man for man the workers of the old countries have not produced on an average more than two thirds of the output of the Americans in the same lines, and about half as much as the operators of American machinery in similar industries.

Investigation has shown, however, that the questions of piecework, minimum labor rules, and hostility to machinery set aside, the English workman at home is not as effective as his brother in this country. The proportion of illiteracy among foreign workmen is 40 per cent greater than it is among the workmen of the United States, and, it is argued by many observers, that this alone is sufficient explanation of the superiority of our workmen. There is probably a better explanation to be found in the well known physical inferiority of the foreigners, especially the French and English toilers, and some recent British writers on this subject attrib-

ute all of the labor disadvantages of the craftsmen of his
country to bodily, and not to mental depreciation.

It is a famous matter of history that England ceased to
be an agricultural country with the repeal of the corn laws
and essayed at once to be the manufacturing center of the
world. Its factory towns became overcrowded and their
populations in time not only city bred but inbred to a certain
degree. In the United States, with all its growth of manufacture, there has been no sudden hegira from the farms to
the cities and yet the ranks of the city workmen are recruited
constantly and gradually from the yellow farm lands of the
prairies. The new blood of the country boy, his ambition,
his health, his muscular might, have kept alive and growing
the basic vitality of American working enterprise and in no
slight measure account for the admitted pre-eminence of our
workingmen.

Members of the Mosely commission, twenty three representatives of English labor unions, who inspected the conditions and achievements of American workingmen in 1902, were
almost unanimous in depreciating their own circumstances as
compared with what they found here. But they were greatly
at variance in accounting for the palpably surpassing qualities
of the workers here not only as to skill and productivity in
shop and factory but in their dress, bearing, relations to their
employers, and in their home life. One of the commission
admitted that he did not like the business or social conditions
of American industrial life, and attributed the high quality
of the workmen to the fine weather and bright skies, which
he found so exhilarating after the dark, foggy atmosphere of
England.

He expressed the belief that the American workman does
not labor so hard as his English cousin, finding the reason in
the fact that here the whole tendency is to make machinery
relieve the man of as much of the work burden as possible.
The Mosely delegation was astonished at the equality existing
in America between the employers and bosses and the men.
They found that in most shops and factories there is a premium on mere ideas, whereas, in Europe, the workman who
presumed to suggest or dictate a better plan to his superior

would be looked upon as impertinent and, probably, dismissed.

In the report that resulted from that investigation, it is stated that the workmen of the United States are infinitely better in their personal habits than those of England. For instance, it was estimated that English workmen consume four times as much intoxicating liquor per man as do the Americans. The average yearly expenditure of English working people for intoxicants amounts to two months' wages, and drunkenness, as a habit, is the rule rather than the exception. It was found that the British workman, as a rule, squanders one month's wages every year on horse racing, and that the American of the same calling wastes not more than ten days' wages in twelve months in a similar manner.

Here certainly is unbiased testimony to a lofty quality in the workman of the United States as compared with him of England, made by English investigators, which, while speaking loudly in favor of the virtue of the American craftsman, may help to account largely for that high degree of manual and mechanical expertness which places him at the head and front of the workmen of the world.

The self reliance, the ambition, the diligence, the pride with which the American attacks his daily task also struck these foreigners as extraordinary. Some of them were of the belief that this sense of equality with the best of their superiors was the reason for the wonderful efficiency of our workmen. For it is true that in Europe the man who works is looked upon as baser metal in the fabric of society. He is a servant, and he is expected to know and keep his place. He stands for what is left of the old feudal system, and his spirit is hampered with the fetters of caste.

"When you meet an American workman on his way to or from the shop you might take him for a business man," was the surprised comment of one of the Mosely commissioners. "They don't walk the streets here with dirty faces. They dress better than our fellows, and they have a show of pride and independence that one never sees in the workingmen of London, Liverpool, Birmingham, or Manchester."

The sanitary provisions of the big factories here, the familiarity existing between foremen and workmen, the monetary and moral encouragement of the man with an idea, the self assertiveness of the workers, the comfortable, sometimes elegant, manner in which they live at home, all impressed the English examiners, not as evidence of the admitted superiority of the workingmen of this country, but as reasons for it. Some of them, refusing to admit that the American is better paid because he accomplishes more, held that he does more and better work because his wages are higher.

In Lancashire a weaver who runs two looms is regarded as a fair performer. In New England the weaver who cannot run eight looms is looked upon as an apprentice, and paid accordingly. Some statistician having grouped twenty industries in which American workmen excel their European rivals, decided that the craftsmen of the United States produced, in quality and quantity together, 25 per cent more than the same number of workmen of other countries could do. Fifteen per cent of this excellence he attributed to the higher craftsmanship of the American and 10 per cent to his superior facilities.

There is no way of estimating the degree in which drink, gambling, and the discouraging element of caste may hinder or destroy the craftsmanship of a workman, but it is agreed by the best authorities on this subject that in this phase lies one of the nearest explanations of American supremacy in working potentiality. One writer discussing the question of environment and facilities, says: "the British employer has more to learn from America than the British workman."

In explanation of this assertion he cites the instance of the American electric factory at Manchester, which British contractors and architects said would require from three to four years to build. An American builder came along and, with English workmen to do the work at wages so high as to astonish them, and with treatment so generous as to inspire them, completed the entire structure in twelve months. It may be that American labor could have finished the same job in nine months, but the incident seems to point to the fact that the foreigner at home is, at least in some measure, the victim of the system under which he labors.

England did not awaken to the fact of the physical degeneration of her people until it was necessary to form armies for South Africa out of the millions of workmen in the shops and factories of the big cities. The majority of the new soldiers who went to the Boer war came from the huddled sections of the manufacturing districts, and they did not meet two out of four of the physical requirements formerly required of the imperial recruit. The most patriotic public men of England are now alive to this retrograde condition of the working class, and they have accounted for it adequately, if not satisfactorily.

That the foreigner is not intrinsically an inferior workman is almost evident from the fact that, once he takes his place beside an American fellow craftsman in an American shop or factory he rises in most cases to the same high level of skill and effectiveness as his native born comrade. The exceptions—the foreigners who never adapt or arouse themselves to the American pace and the American standard—are almost invariably old or middle aged men or persons of exceptional stupidity—an uncommon fault, by the way, in the workmen from England, Germany, France, or Scandinavia.

It must be that the pride an American has in his work prompts him to give it always a better finish, always an extra polish, for it is a notorious fact that many American made articles of intrinsically inferior quality are preferred even in rival manufacturing countries for no other cause than that the article from the hands of the workman of the United States had some style about it.

In the absolutely manual crafts there are many branches in which the Americans cannot or rather have not equaled the foreigners as to quality. But, except in what may be called the division of manual arts or artistic crafts in which of late years there has been a noticeable revival in America, the output of wholly manual work, whether in factory or shop, is but a small proportion of the manufacturing capacities of the United States. But if he falls behind in quality of his work in many of the handicrafts, the American continues to surpass all others in the quantity of work he does and can do.

Summing it all up in an introduction to the elaborate report of his commission, Mr. Mosely says for the benefit of the British employer:

"I can only say that if we are to hold our own in the commerce of the world, both masters and men must be up and doing. Old methods must be dropped, old machinery abandoned. Practical education of the masses must be instituted and carried out upon a logical basis, and with efficiency. The bulk of our workmen are already both sober and intelligent, but with many of them there is urgent need for them to become more sober, more rational, more ready to adopt new ideas in place of antiquated methods, and improved machinery whenever produced, and to get the best possible results from a day's work. Manufacturers for their part must be prepared to assure their men a piece price that will not be cut when the latter's earnings exceed what has hitherto been considered sufficient for them. Modern machinery must be introduced, co-operation of the workmen sought, and initiative encouraged in every possible way. Without such a modernized system we cannot hope to compete with countries like the United States, which has this advantage, and is moreover blessed with natural resources such as we do not possess. Britain has, however, in the past led the world, and might yet continue to do so. The material is here. It remains for masters and men mutually to decide whether and how far it shall be utilized in the future."

In the reports of the commissioners only a part of them have gone beyond the general field assigned to them. Here and there are pertinent suggestions and observations that are novel and unexpected. The individuality of the commissioner may be marked in most of these reports, but in only two of them are there any marked indications of the man being out of harmony with the general results of the investigation.

Commissioner Walls, speaking of the work of the blast furnace men and of the equipment provided by employing companies, has risen to enthusiasm on several points that strike him as in sharp contrast with British conditions. His tribute to the perfection of the machine in America is almost unbounded. Speaking of a great plant, where every individual piece of the manufactured mechanism has a machine devoted to its production, he says:

"Many of these machines are obviously the product of a marvelous inventive genius, doing their work with more than human ingenuity, and only requiring to be fed through a tube with the brass or steel bar, from which the piece is made. Dayton is an enlarged edition of Bournville. In the rolling mills at South Chicago, Homestead, and Youngstown, the machinery is ahead of anything I have seen in similar works in this country. The American Locomotive company's works at Schenectady, which cover sixty two acres, have a mass of powerful as well as ingenious machines, each having its own special duty. They seem to cut up iron, steel, and brass as wood is cut by a cabinetmaker. We were informed that they could turn out six large locomotives a day, or thirty five a week. Over 10,000 hands are employed."

As to the work of the furnace man, he remarks how the use of machinery has lightened his work over that of the British workman, and says of this machinery: "It has been introduced evidently not so much with a view to dispensing with labor as making it lighter and expediting the work." And of this expeditiousness he says that the output of the American is more than double that of the British furnace.

Of the disposition of the British employer to resent suggestions from workmen, Mr. Walls says that foremen and managers in England almost universally reply to a suggestion with the question, Which of us is gaffer? or the assertion, You are not paid for thinking. "This kind of stupidity kept back progress in the manufacture of pig iron for years. The theoretical man, the manager, insisted on what was known as the open mouth and barring the furnace to make room. The practical workman advised a fast head and leave the furnace to do its own work. This suggestion was looked upon with suspicion because it meant less labor. It was only when it became known that on night shifts, in the absence of the managers, the keeper took his own road and made about 20 per cent more iron than on days, that this suicidal policy was abandoned."

Commissioner Maddison of the foundry men, looking over the Allis-Chalmers plant in Chicago, after saying that it was the best of the type he had seen in America, remarks: It was also provided with apparatus for cooling the shop in summer and heating in winter. Fancy any English firm being asked to make such provision for the comfort of its employees.

Of the strike which had just been settled at that plant, he says: "During the strike the usual free labor men, what the Americans term scabs, came on the scene. In point of ability they seem to be on a par with those sailing under the same flag in this country, as may be gathered from the foreman's statement, that he hoped never to pass through a similar ordeal. Indeed, he said he would not undergo such another experience for any money, it being no uncommon thing to run down forty tons of iron per day and obtain fifteen tons of castings, whereas with the union men the present percentage of bad work is only 2 per cent. Asked what had become of the scabs, he said they had gone to another shop belonging to the same firm in the town, run with non society men."

In the next paragraph Mr. Maddison makes an excellent reflection upon the type of British manufacturer who keeps to his close communion business affairs, resenting everything from the outside as an impertinence. He says:

"We next made application for admission to Crane's shop, but were denied. Owing to the manager or employer having visited England some time ago and being refused admission into one or more English plants, he had determined to reciprocate the treatment whenever opportunity offered itself. I was much disappointed, as I had a great desire to see through this firm's works, their class of work being pipes. I understand they employ a good number of females under rather unusual circumstances."

This remark and regret are especially significant when it is the burden of the whole report of the commission that the American shop everywhere was open to the members at all times.

As to the condition of labor in America, with reference to pay by the employers, he cites two instances in sharp contrast with those at home. The first was in a Cincinnati shop, where, with four pieces constituting the regular day's work of a man, the man who makes five pieces a day gets a day and a quarter credited to him on the pay roll. Of the other case, in Pittsburg, he writes: "I was shown a job by the young man who made it (an Englishman). Though allowed eight days for making it, he completed it in five, but not the slightest attempt was made on the part of the firm to participate in the three days made by extra effort, the man being paid the full eight days. When a bad casting occurred he was paid the five days he spent in making it, and then paid the full eight days for making it over again, thus simply losing the three days' extra effort."

Commissioner Cox of the Associated Iron and Steel workers has been inclined to knock some things that are not down on the lists of his research. For instance: "I had been led to expect one eternal, perpetual rush and bustle pervading every aspect of life, whether in the office, in the street, or in the dining room, quite bewildering to the average Englishman. I have walked the principal streets of the leading cities, I have visited all kinds of hotels and restaurants, I have seen a great deal of commercial life in the office, but have yet to see anything in the nature of rush or hustle which cannot be met with in any of the great industrial centers of England, though I often thought the American constable might advantageously take a few lessons from our metropolitan police in the regulation of city traffic."

At Albany, N. Y., he made a mental note of something which seems to have impressed him at many turns. He was in the statehouse. "I had been admiring one of the assembly rooms of the state buildings, and especially what I conceived to be a magnificent oak carved ceiling. I remarked to one of the attendants my admiration of it. 'Yes sir,' he replied, 'but that is not oak carved, it is a papier maché ceiling.' On recounting this to a prominent American and an extensive traveler, he remarked, 'I know of no country where it may be more forcibly or accurately said, "All is not gold that glitters," ' and so I subsequently realized."

In the gigantic corporations in America, however, Mr. Cox sees something infinitely better than he had seen in Great Britain. Referring to 1899, when American output winded the British manufacturer, he says: "The pity is that several of them ever recovered. The British iron trade and the workmen engaged in it would be infinitely better off if an earthquake could swallow up many of the obsolete works of manufacturers who bleed their works to death in times of good trade and grind their workmen in periods of adversity. Large trusts have their inherent defects, but I am convinced from my investigations that the workman has less to fear in the long run from the operations of concentrated capital than he has from the impecunious employer with his frantic efforts to dip into the wages of his already underpaid workmen."

Mr. Cox is an enthusiast over the machinery equipment of the American iron and steel mills. There is no doubt that the leading mills of American manufacture are far ahead of our own best mills in their arrangement and outputs. I have seen nothing like it in this country—either in the matter of output or labor saving appliances. To the average British iron and steel workers the output of these mills will be incredible. Take the Illinois plate mill of South Chicago, where they have rolled 318 tons of finished plates in twelve hours. The fortnight previous to my visit they had rolled in their one mill 6,060 tons, quite a large percentage of which were down to 3-16 inch thick, and the number of men round the rolls were—one roller, three hookers, one screwer, and one tableman.

Commissioner Barnes, reporting for the Amalgamated Society of Engineers, touches upon the personal side of manufacturing life in the United States. Of Chicago he says in point:

"The Armour school of technology first engaged attention. This school is part of an immense institute, which has been added to from time to time till now there are many activities of a social and educational character. In the school of

PROPORTION OF PERSONS
ENGAGED IN EACH CLASS OF OCCUPATIONS

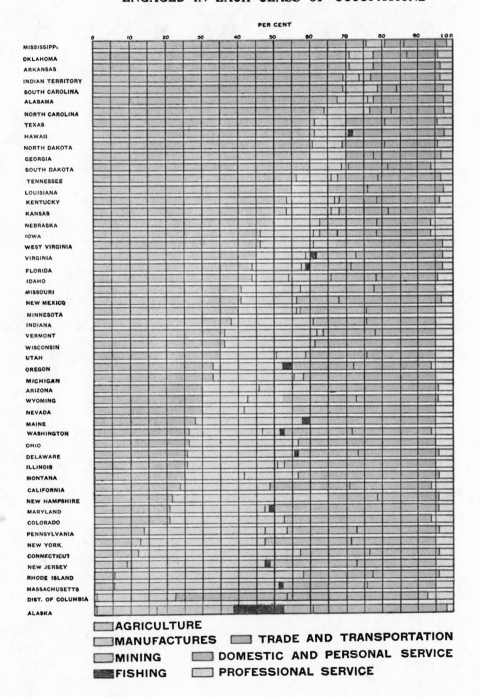

PER CENT

AGRICULTURE

MANUFACTURES ☐ TRADE AND TRANSPORTATION

MINING ☐ DOMESTIC AND PERSONAL SERVICE

FISHING ☐ PROFESSIONAL SERVICE

technology, which is devoted to engineering in all its branches, there are 1,000 students, and these all pay fees ranging from $90 to $120 a year from the day students to $10 per term of ten weeks from the evening students. Notwithstanding fees, the place is not self supporting, and is assisted by the Armour firm to the extent of $80,000 yearly. The engineering classes are fairly well equipped, and I was told that they are successful in training men for office work or superintendence of engineering enterprises. The institute does not, however, contribute much to the education of workmen, excepting to help the more aspiring out of the ranks, and I was told that this had resulted in quite a number of cases of workmen who had attended.

"I also visited while in Chicago another technical school in a poorer district. This is run entirely free as regards technical instruction, but it combines a social club element, for which charge is made. I was not favorably impressed with it, and it seemed to me that all the instruction given there could be given far better in the workshop.

"Car fares throughout America are 5 cents for any distance in city limits. Chicago has a good, although ugly, means of transit, and the result is the spreading out of the place, and probably the keeping down of rents to a point smaller than would otherwise be the case. Coal is $7.50 per ton."

For the shipbuilders and the boiler makers, Commissioner Cummings finds that the American menace to shipbuilding in Great Britain is not nearly as great as he had anticipated. As for the lake yards, he says: "Few pure bred Americans are to be found in the lake shipyards, less than one dozen being employed in Lorain, O., the yard which has put into the water these last two years more tonnage than any other yard in the states, the reason given being that the fairly well educated American workman does not care for the dirty, laborious work of the shipyard."

He is the one observer of the whole commission who has seen the American workman as a confirmed gambler, and more than any other he sees the shortening of the life of the worker in this country.

"Gambling and pleasure seeking appear to be characteristic of the American's life; these, taken in conjunction with his ordinary restless spirit, seem to shorten life, make men prematurely old, and increase insanity. Climatic conditions may be to some extent the cause of the generally unhealthy look of the American people, but the opinion generally expressed to enjoy life while it lasts has also some effect. There is, however, less regard for human life in America than in our own country. Life altogether is held cheaper, and that may be inherited from earlier times when firearms were used on the slightest provocation. Altogether I am of the opinion that a halting time will have to take place in the states. The rush for enjoyment, the disregard of human life, the corruption of local politics, and other immoralities, and the almost continental Sunday, added to which is the disinclination to walk or make any exertion after business hours if it can be avoided, all tend toward the moral and physical deterioration of the people, and must be arrested if disaster is to be avoided."

As to the work of the shipwright in the United States, the opinion of Commissioner Wilkie is that the American workman has little advantage in any way over the British worker. He writes:

"The three outstanding features of American industry appeal to me to be its tendency towards greater centralization, as is evinced by the huge trusts and corporations which are everywhere springing up; the specialization of industry and the subdivision of labor, which are carried on to a much greater extent and with a minuteness which has not yet been reached here, and labor saving machinery, which, so far as the factories are concerned, may be said to be in much greater use than in this country. On the other hand, while there are some workshops which have excellent sanitary arrangements and are clean and well lighted, there are others, as in this country, which are just as insanitary, dirty, and congested. There does not appear to me to be the same regard paid to life and limb of the workmen in America as in this country, which may be attributable, perhaps, to the absence of those factory laws we have here. Generally speaking, therefore, I do not think, as far as the shipbuilding trade is concerned, except in a few instances, the American shipyards are better equipped than those of this country. To speak generally of what I saw on the tour, machinery is in more general use than with us; but, on the other hand, the hours of labor are longer in the week, while the character of the work, its finish, its stability, its permanence, and its durability, is no better than is done in this country. The wages per hour are higher, even having regard to the longer hours worked, and as to the cost of living, generally speaking, I do not think there is much advantage on the side of the United States; and in the shipbuilding industry at least I am satisfied that we can hold our own for years to come."

Commissioner Holmshaw, in his report upon the cutlery business of the country, steps aside for more generally interesting observations. He finds improvement over the cutlery conditions of Sheffield, and then of the American people he adds:

"There is no mistaking native Americans, and as one observes their independent bearing, their shrewd 'cuteness and general air of alertness, one begins to feel prepared for interesting developments in every phase of their national life. Perhaps their most striking characteristic is their intense devotion to everything American—a not unnatural devotion, though perhaps at times emphasized in aggressive character. The finest in the world is a phrase frequently on their lips, but one soon feels so strongly the wonderful fascination of a country which has such superb natural advantages that one can bear the harmless boasting with equanimity. Another characteristic one cannot help noticing is the prevalent desire for making money. Even the children are inspired by it, and perhaps one result of this national ambition strikes us at first as novel, but on second thoughts it is natural enough. This is the absence of any false pride, which, speaking broadly, results in the unconscious recognition of the dignity of labor. Whatever a man can honestly earn money by, no matter what his social position, he counts it no disgrace to do.

"Americans have seen clearly enough that the greatest force to enable them to win their way in the world's markets is education, and they have made wonderful strides of late years to improve this. So far as I could judge, there is little difference in the elementary school life of America and England, save that the former has no religious difficulty to contend with. There is, in fact, no religious education in America, as we understand the term, yet secular education there produces results that outwardly, at any rate, bear comparison with our own. There is a remarkable absence of bad language in the streets; this was particularly noticeable in the Saturday night crowds.

"It struck me that there was an apparent desire on the part of many parents to allow their children to continue at school after the ordinary leaving age, and all who are acquainted with working class homes will know and appreciate the self sacrifice of parents who allow their children to enter on a four years' course in a commercial school after leaving the ordinary elementary school. In one such school at Philadelphia, out of 177 boys, 55 were the sons of workingmen. Technical schools constitute one of the great features of American higher education. Mechanic arts are a form of technical school. These are splendidly equipped, the tools and appliances being of the best and all free. Equal opportunities here are indeed possible. In one fine school at Boston the principal pointed out to me in haphazard fashion a lad who was the son of the richest railway director in the state; on one side of him was the son of a large builder, and on the other a lad who sold newspapers in the street at night."

Commissioner Jones for the Midland Counties' trades federation, makes pleased comment upon most things seen in the shops and works of the United States, and incidentally treats his readers to a pretty little account of a strike upon which he blundered one day.

November 1, I went to Messrs. Plumbs', at Newtown, and was met by men on strike and taken to their room. The men explained that an order came for 200 pairs of tongs, special. These had been made day work, but the employers wanted them made piecework, offering a price based upon what had been made day work. A man made some for half a day and complained he could not get a living at the price. He had another try for half a day with the same result, would not make any more at the price, and was discharged. Messrs. Plumb sent for another man and asked him to make them day work. He happened to be an officer of the society. He declined to make them, got discharged, when the other men left; more than 150 of them out. I told the men who I was, and showed them my card, saying I would see them again. They showed me the work. They said they had good funds; had been out five weeks; result, only small part of work on. Mr. Plumb, jr., asked me to stay to lunch. I thanked him, but went to a saloon. It was 12 o'clock dinner time, when Mr. Plumb, jr., came in and invited me into the back room where lunch was; had some with him. When we came out the men who had brought me stood outside. He said these were some of the men on strike; he showed me a handbill they had printed, asking men to keep away from the works, and admitted they had been partly successful; men could not get lodgings, so he had taken houses for them, but they would not stay.

Commissioner Ashton, for the cotton spinners, saw few advantages possessed by either the operating plants or the operators in American mills. However, he admitted one pleasing feature about the system of working the American cotton mills, and that is the superintendents believe in using a good class of cotton, and by this means they are enabled to run their machinery at quick speeds and get out excellent results. They also act on the principle of having their material well carded and cleaned, and they provide the requisite machines for securing such a result, and by adopting this policy they produce good yarns and avoid making a deal of waste. One of the leading mill superintendents in New Bedford informed me that they made a practice of using three grades better cotton than was used in Lancashire for the spinning of the same counts of yarn, and this statement was confirmed by an experienced cotton buyer and seller, with whom I had a long conversation about the American cotton industry generally.

Concluding his report, he says: "On questions relating to the American trade and commerce, I was surprised at the manner in which the press was used to boom information

which was of a favorable character to American manufacturers and their work people. The journalists make a practice
of writing in an optimistic spirit about everything which is
American, and thereby give encouragement to employers
and work people in their efforts to take the lead in the industrial race for supremacy. As a rule the opposite course is
taken by commercial and other writers in this country, and
this tends to damp the ardor of all concerned in labor and
commerce. I consider it would be better for employers and
work people in England if the policy of the American press
was adopted in this country in the way before referred to."

Commissioner Wilkinson, representing the weavers, found
no great advantages possessed by the American. He found
even shocking conditions in the south, where children 6 years
old were at work in the factories. In no mill anywhere in
this country did he find negroes working inside mills, the
reason being that as a race they objected to the inside work.

"The keen appreciation which Americans have for up to
date machinery ·and the readiness with which they adopt
labor saving machinery of any kind is remarkable. But
whatever part machinery has played in the American cotton
trade, there is no doubt whatever that the great increase of
recent years, especially in fancy cloths, must be attributed to
the American protective tariff."

Writing of the condition of the tailor in America, the report of Commissioner Flynn has in point:

"So far as American employers are concerned, and so
far as we could see, the best kind of relationship exists between them and the people they employ. Whether in day
wage firms or firms using exclusively the piecework system,
every inducement was held out to the employees to combine
their interests with those employing them. On both sides
there was an unmistakable heartiness and good fellowship
which can only arise when the output, wages, and general
working conditions are satisfactory."

American employers believe that machines rather than
men or women ought to be driven, and the clever workman
who by invention or suggestion enables his employer to carry
out this ideal is encouraged in a manner delightfully real and

sincere. Let us illustrate. One firm gives a dollar for every suggestion made by an employee and accepted by the firm. This firm, it may be added, provides a gymnasium for its employees, men and women, and for the latter it also provides a music room and general lounge. Another, abolishing the money prize, gives a week's or a fortnight's holiday at the firm's expense. Another system of encouragement is that of firms which allow a workman who has an idea that will improve the system or method of production a week or a month to work the idea out, pay him his usual wages, and, if need be, tell off a man or gang of men to work under him. Another feature of factory and workshop life in America is the regardless of expense manner in which air, light, all sanitary, bath, and lavatory arrangements are carried out. Better than our best London hotels provide, was the remark of delegates competent to judge. While all were not up to this high standard, it is undoubtedly true that a toil begrimed workingman making his way homewards is a rara avis in America.

Commissioner Hornridge of the British National union of boot and shoe operatives, wrote:

"At Lynn, with one firm I visited, two things struck me as being out of the ordinary: (1) The apparent happiness and contentedness of the people, the familiarity existing between them and their employer, and (2) the fact that quite 40 per cent of them were people ranging from 30 to 63 and 64 years of age. One female, who had worked for the firm twenty nine years, was apparently as happy as could be, and when I congratulated the employer upon the fact that his elderly workers had not been cast into the streets he asked, 'Why should they?' and went on to say that he himself was getting gray and aged, and would not care to be pole axed or starved, and that as long as his workpeople did their work he would rather have around him elderly people on whom he could rely than young ones on whom such reliance could not be placed.

"I took the liberty of asking the lady above referred to what her age might be, as I saw that she was nearly keeping pace in her work of machining uppers with a woman of 28 or

29 years of age who was sitting alongside her. I was astounded on being informed that she was 63 years old."

Commissioner Lapping for the leather workers makes a point of addressing the tanners of his own country in a concluding paragraph in which there is much meaning:

"In conclusion, I must again state that I am of the opinion that we cannot compete with any certainty of success with the states for the markets of the world, as with their great natural advantages they can undersell us, but in these days of chemically tanned goods and the use of extracts, I do not see why we cannot successfully compete with them for the trade of our own country. In my humble opinion the fault does not lie with the British workman in the leather industry, but with the employer. He sticks too much to the old ideas. He does not keep pace with the times. He produces a good article, but that is not all that is required. Let him remodel and refit his factory on an up to date plan, get more in touch with his employees, provide them with a shop that has a degree of comfort about it, and give them a wage that will enable them to live at a higher standard than at present, even if he asks them to do more work for the same; then the time may come when we shall get nearer holding our own with our cousins over the seas. If some of the employers of this country would pay a visit to some of the up to date factories of the states, I feel sure they would learn something that would compensate them for the expense incurred."

"Much as I admire our fellow craftsmen in America," writes Commissioner Taylor of the bricklayers, "I should be sorry indeed to see American methods of building construction (especially as far as brickwork is concerned) adopted in this country, because if they were the workman would be subjected to more risks to life and limb, with little, if any, chance of compensation. Technical knowledge, training, and skill would be at a discount. All that natural pride the real craftsman takes in the strength, durability, and finish of his handicraft would be extinguished and destroyed; all the years of struggle and work we have had to raise the standard of workmanship to its present high standard would have been in vain, and all would be sacrificed in the interests

OCCUPATIONS

PERCENTAGE IN EACH CLASS

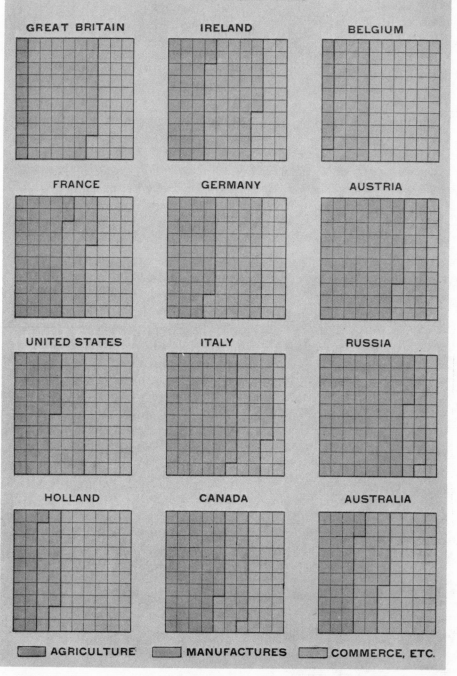

GREAT BRITAIN   IRELAND   BELGIUM

FRANCE   GERMANY   AUSTRIA

UNITED STATES   ITALY   RUSSIA

HOLLAND   CANADA   AUSTRALIA

AGRICULTURE   MANUFACTURES   COMMERCE, ETC.

of present day utility. At the same time I am of opinion that the employers in this country would do well to follow the example set them by the employers in the United States, by keeping in closer touch with those in their employ and meeting them on terms of equality, by forming conciliation boards or branches of the civic federation, by adopting the system of apprenticeship and the eight hour day, and last, but not least, by paying the same rate of wages that are paid in New York."

Slatternly, hurried work in the United States seems to have struck Commissioner Deller, of the plasterers, and he adds to this general arraignment of conditions:

"Speaking generally of the work and workmen in the trade, I can only say that the work is far and away behind that executed in England, and the hampered conditions are anything but pleasant to work under. Were I an employer I should make them better, feeling sure that more work would be the result. The scaffolding was the most crude I ever saw or could have imagined. Poles and ropes are entirely ignored, and the uprights are quartering (called scantling in some parts). If these were not long enough, another piece was put on the end, and the two were merely fastened together by a piece of slab nailed on the one side. On some of those I ventured upon the boards were up and down, so that one had to use much care in walking to prevent a stumble. I was informed by some when remarking upon these defects that few accidents occurred; others said there were plenty, but the press did not report them, so that only those intimately acquainted with the victim, or dependent upon him for subsistence, were aware of the fact. I am inclined to believe the latter in preference to the former. Suffice to say it would be a case of extreme necessity that would induce me to intrust my life upon some of the flimsy scaffolds I saw—uprights as previously shown, stayed by strips no stronger in appearance than a fair slate lath."

W. C. Stedman, representing the parliamentary committee of the trades union congress of Great Britain, has submitted a report covering general observations in all lines of work.

He finds the system of education in the United States
better than that of Great Britain. He did not see the American working at a harder drive than does the average Englishman. A factory at Niagara he is prepared to accept as
the finest industrial building in the world. He found a store
in Chicago which he would urge London merchants to see.

"I thought now was my opportunity to ask a man who
had worked on both sides of the Atlantic, whether the men
worked harder in America than in the old country. His
answer was emphatic: 'The machinery does the work here;
I never worked so hard in all my life as I did in London.
Practically all was hand labor, and what was done by machinery was most imperfectly done. That was not always
the fault of the machinist, but was due to old and not up to
date machinery. Whenever we hear of a new machine coming out, and we find it is better than what we have got, we
chuck the old out and put up the new one at once. Here
is a mortise machine, the best I could get at the time. Now
there is a new one, invented and patented by a Mr. Black of
Milwaukee; I ordered one at once, but I cannot get it, such
is the rush of orders. That is how we get along so fast with
the work here; in the old country they just drag along with
the old machinery, and only when it is worn out, and not
till then, will they think of replacing it.' The men in this
shop were working as comfortably as ever I saw men in all
my experience, for all the hard work was done for them."

Admitting that the machine in the United States is
marvelous in its adaptability to the furniture trades, Commissioner Ham takes a rap at the American product:

"There is no question that if a large hotel required 200
bedroom suits, machine made, and, of course, all of the same
pattern, probably we would be beaten by the Yankees; but
if, on the other hand, a mansion required to be furnished
where a different style and design was desired for each apart-
ment, then I am certain the work could be produced better
and cheaper here than in America. In the states, as far
as furnishing is concerned, everything is sacrificed to turning
out large quantities; there is no chance for indulgence in
individual tastes for a distinctive style, as in England."

But after all there is no comparison between the two countries, he admits. America has natural advantages we have not here. Take her lakes for instance, more like inland seas, and rivers, then compare them with our Thames, Tyne, and Clyde. One can only have admiration for the old country that has been able (and still capable) to do so much out of so little. In New York harbor they have 40 feet of water at low tide, so that the largest ship afloat can always get to its berth without having to wait for the tide.

"The English worker has nothing to learn from America, but the employers have a lot. I do not assume for one moment we are the best, but this I do say, we cannot be beaten in the world for good, solid, well finished work that will stand the test of years to come. Let our employers realize that labor is as much a partner in the business as his capital, and that the success or failure of that business depends upon both; he has the best material to work upon. Treated properly he need have no fear of American competition, or that of any other country in the world, for high wages pay both the employer and the employed. In America they know this, and act up to it; hence the secret of their success."

Whether or no the English workman has nothing to learn from us, there can be no question of the fact that the American workman's high wages are a cause of his efficiency as well as an effect.

A GOVERNMENT INVESTIGATION OF LABOR.

BY RICHARD T. ELY.

[Richard T. Ely, professor political economy and director School of Economics, and political science, University of Wisconsin, since 1892; born Ripley, N. Y., April 13, 1854; graduated from Columbia university 1876; fellow in letters, Columbia, 1876–9; studied abroad, 1877–80; professor political economy, Johns Hopkins, 1881–92; secretary American Economical association, 1885–92; president, 1899–1901. Author of French and German Socialism in Modern Times, Taxation in American States and Cities, Outlines of Economics, Monopolies and Trusts, Labor Movement in America, Introduction to Political Economy, The Social Law of Service, Past and Present of Political Economy, Problems of To-day, etc.]

Although much has been said and written about the progress which has been made in American economics in recent years, we are still more likely to underestimate than to overestimate the advance which has been accomplished, and especially are we apt to forget within how short a space of time this transformation in American economic thought has taken place. The writer of the article in The Nation for January 16, 1902, giving an account of an annual meeting of the American Economic association, speaks about the activity in economics in this country as largely due to men who began their academic work some thirty years ago. Now the truth is that the men whom he had in mind, men prominent in effecting the organization of the American Economic association, were, for the most part, not even undergraduates thirty years ago, but were still engaged in their preparation for college. Most of these men are still on the sunny side of fifty, and some of them are nearer forty than the former age. While the work which was done by men of a still older generation should not be disparaged, while this earlier work was, indeed, a necessary preparation for the more recent work, it is, nevertheless, true that the great change in economic thought in our country, which has given the United States a leading position in economic science, has taken place within twenty years, and that it has been brought about by men who believe that they still have before them the better part of their own work.

Reflections of this kind are especially appropriate as an introduction to those portions of the report of the industrial commission which deal with labor, because the advance which economics has made during the preceding twenty years finds such marked expression in the methods employed and in the conclusions reached by the industrial commission, and especially by the economists who, as experts, were connected with the work of this commission.

It is difficult even for those who have followed with some care the treatment of labor problems for the past fifteen or twenty years to realize the progress which has been made in their discussion, both in respect to positive knowledge and to scientific methods followed. It is now somewhat difficult to do justice to those who, twenty years ago, were actively engaged in a scientific discussion of labor questions in this country, and to realize that a large part of the pioneer work in this field dates back to a period even less remote. The distinction between anarchistic and socialistic movements is now understood by every economist, and even by the general, intelligent public, but it required careful study to discriminate between these two movements in 1885. Every graduate student now understands the difference between the principles underlying the American Federation of Labor and the Knights of Labor, but so careful a student of labor problems as Brentano, twenty years ago, denied the existence of any labor organization based upon the principles underlying the Knights of Labor. These are simply illustrations of the condition of thought and of knowledge even at so recent a period as 1885, when the American Economic association was organized, and serve to show how much work has been done in order to give us that basis of knowledge with which any economist now begins a study of labor.

Another way of getting at the same thing is to contrast the report of the industrial commission, created by act of 1898, with the voluminous report of the senate committee on labor and education, in 1885. This earlier report has some value, because it gives the opinion of all sorts of people on all sorts of questions in any way connected with labor in 1885. It allowed a good many cranks and some thoughtful people an opportunity to express their views, and perhaps served as a safety valve, which is probably the chief purpose which those had in mind who were responsible for the existence of the committee. The American economists are so numerous, and they have made themselves felt to such an extent in every part of the country, that probably we shall see no more federal reports on labor like the one issued by the senate committee of 1885. It is a great thing that it is known that there are in this country a body of economic experts, and that the state of public opinion is such as to demand their employment. The entire character of the report of the industrial commission, the way the work is planned, and the way it is executed, show the constant guidance of the economist. The economists employed belong, for the most part, to those whom we would naturally designate as the younger generation of American economists, a generation younger than those who founded the American Economic association, being, indeed, mostly students of those who were active in the early days of this association. When one considers all the circumstances surrounding their work, it must be said that they did their work remarkably well, and that they have strengthened the position and the influence of economists in this country. The three experts chiefly responsible for that portion of the final report dealing with labor are Dr. E. Dana Durand, the secretary of the commission, Professor John R. Commons, and Mr. Charles E. Edgerton. Other experts employed by the commission whose work fell under the head of labor, are Messrs. J. R. Dodge, for agricultural labor; Samuel M. Lindsay, for railway labor; Victor H. Olmsted and William M. Steuart, for prison labor; Thomas F. Turner, for Asiatic labor on the Pacific coast; F. J. Stimson, for labor legislation, and Eugene Willison, for mine labor legislation. Miss Gail Laughlin also treated the subject of domestic service. It is then seen that, out of twenty seven experts employed by the commission, eleven had to do directly and immediately with various phases of what we broadly designate as labor problems.

While the work of the commission was so broadly outlined in the act which created it that it could take in every subject pertaining to industry, even when industry is most broadly interpreted, it was to be expected that a large part of the report should deal with labor.   There are nineteen volumes in the entire report, and at least ten of them deal directly and immediately with the subject of labor to a large extent.   If there is any one subject which transcended in interest labor in the investigations of the industrial commission, it is the subject of trusts and industrial combinations, and it is in part the influence which these have upon labor that is responsible for the interest in them.

The mass of material furnished in the report is so vast that it is discouraging to the busy man, who would glean from it its practical and scientific teachings, until he discovers how admirably it is all arranged, and how excellent is the review of the whole subject in the final report.   Each volume has its preliminary review of its substance, which is followed by the digest of evidence, the digest giving references to the pages of testimony.   Each volume also has its own index. The final volume has an index covering all the nineteen volumes, as well as the general review, to which reference has been made.   This general review, which covers only a little over two hundred pages, is admirably prepared, covering briefly the most essential points concerning labor in the preceding eighteen volumes.   The one exception to this statement relates to agricultural labor, which is treated too briefly to harmonize with the general plan.   The final review is followed by the recommendations of the commission.

The method of using that part of the report of the industrial commission which deals with labor is then very simple. The student will read, first of all, the entire final review and will find it the best text book as yet written on the labor problem.   After he has read this broad, general survey, quite accurate in its description of the contents of preceding volumes, he will consult these volumes for a further study of particular topics which specially interest him.   If the reader is a legislator, especially concerned in regard to prison labor, he will, if intelligent, desire to read the entire final review, in order to see the relation of prison labor to other kinds of labor.   After he has done this, he will carefully examine the small volume entitled Prison Labor, and ascertain the different arrangements for directing prison labor in the various states of the union. He will also gain some information concerning prison labor in other countries, and will have this knowledge, together with the recommendations of the commission, as a basis for legislation. Those who are interested in various phases of labor legislation will similarly, after having read the final review, consult the volume entitled respectively Labor Legislation and Foreign Labor Laws.

Dr. Durand, the secretary of the commission, has stated that the tone of the final review is progressive. This characterizes it correctly. It is progressive, but at the same time it cannot be called radical. It is based upon a profound knowledge of existing conditions, upon keen analysis, and very evidently upon long continued and fruitful thought. No one else who has written on the subject of labor has given evidence of such careful study and accurate knowledge of the questions at issue as those responsible for this final review. Dr. Durand has stated that the tone of the report is more progressive than the commissioners, as a whole, would be inclined to endorse. It is quite probable that the commissioners did not give so much attention to the part of their report which deals with labor as to other parts, although there seems to be evidence of modifying suggestions received from them in a good many portions of this final review. At the same time, this review is in general harmony with the portions of preceding volumes dealing with labor, and the recommendations of the commissioners themselves could scarcely be characterized otherwise than as progressive.

The final review is divided into four main parts, namely: I. General Conditions and Problems; II. Relations of Employers and Employees; III. Protection of Employees in their Labors; IV. Labor on Public Works.

The first main part, dealing with general conditions and problems, is especially valuable on account of the careful discriminations which are made in this survey. A considerable space is devoted to negative work, which is necessary to clear the ground for profitable discussion. Popular errors must be examined, and the necessary limitations of the investigation must be made clear. It is pointed out under

Profits and Wages that we must sharply distinguish between two different aspects of the problem which they present. One aspect deals with the share of industry which goes to the factors of production, as labor, capital, land, monopolies, etc. The second aspect deals with the income and social welfare of the manual working classes. Every economist knows that here we have two different orders of inquiries, but this fact, important as it is, is often overlooked. Under the head Uncertainty of Statistics we have a correction of errors which are too common; as, for example, that the rate of interest on investments is an indication of the proportion of the product of labor and capital which either one receives. Strange as it may seem, it has been supposed that 10 per cent on an investment indicates that labor receives 90 per cent of the product. On the other hand, there are those who have drawn the conclusion that because of the value of manufactured products the aggregate wages amount to a little less than 25 per cent, that is all that labor receives of the joint product. Manifestly, it is necessary to examine into the cost of raw material used in manufactures, and the portion of that which accrues to labor.

A useful discrimination is made with respect to the earnings of capital, and here we come to something which even economists have not always borne in mind. We have to distinguish between the interest on disposable capital and the profits on established enterprises. The profits on established enterprises include, it is said, such things as good will, trade marks, patent rights, and monopolies of various kinds. The final review continues: "monopoly privileges, for example, wherever they exist, become more and more valuable as population increases, and the net returns are thereby augmented; but, at the same time, the rate of interest on disposable capital, not protected by these privileges, has continually declined." After an examination of the actual decline in the rate of interest since 1865, it is asserted that there is an insurmountable difficulty in the endeavor to discover the rate of profit received in industry, with one exception, namely, national banks; for the reason, it is said, that we cannot ascertain the amount of capital invested, since census returns and statistical inquiries include under capital, not only cash investments, but such factors as those which have just been mentioned, namely, good will, trade marks, franchises, monopoly values, etc.

The treatment of wages which follows is illuminating in its presentation of facts, and in its fine discriminations. Here as elsewhere, what we need is careful analysis, but it requires a great deal of time and effort to educate the general public up to the point where analysis is appreciated. The ordinary man wants what we may term rough and ready conclusions. He wants to know that wages have risen so many per cent, or that they have fallen, and between the two broad statements he finds no middle ground. One of the gains which we may hope will result from the publication of the report of the industrial commission is that it will gradually impress upon the more intelligent portion of the American community the importance of those distinctions which the economist so well understands, but which are too apt to be dismissed by the daily press as merely academic exercises. It is pointed out that the movement of wages is slower than the movement of prices, as a consequence of which, in time of general prosperity the wages do not rise so rapidly as the commodities which the wage earner must purchase; whereas it is affirmed that in time of depression the wage earner suffers from lack of employment and does not enjoy the fruit of low prices. There does not seem to be sufficient support in any part of the report of the industrial commission for this broad statement, and the facts in the case have not received anywhere, so far as the present writer is aware, scientific treatment. Elsewhere in the report it is shown that unemployment is not so great as many have supposed, and probably a good deal of support could be adduced for the thesis that ordinarily the wage earner is most prosperous under a régime of low prices. Wages, however, have risen since 1869, according to the statistics presented, which are based upon a careful examination of a variety of sources. Wholesale prices, however, have fallen in marked degree. The conclusions reached in this particular are of especial interest on account of the fact that we may take it for granted that those who prepared the final report were not seeking to make out a case for existing conditions.

Attention is called, however, to the fact that we must consider not merely or chiefly daily wages but rather yearly wages; to the further fact that the average wages must be higher, on account of the increasing relative proportion of wage earners living in cities, if the wage earner is to be equally well off in his economic well being; and furthermore, mention is made of the increasing intensity of exertion, on account of the introduction of machinery, and the division of labor which must be considered when passing judgment upon relative wages.

Finally, a distinction is made between the earnings of organized men and those unorganized. And it is a difference of importance. It is shown by various illustrations that the organized workingmen have been able to secure a greater relative increase in wages than the unorganized. These conclusions are summed up in the following words, "taking into account these observations, it must be concluded that the daily rate of wages is not a safe measure of the changing conditions of labor, and that in a discussion of the progress of the working population account must be taken of the amount of annual employment, depending on general conditions of prosperity and depression, the life earnings of the worker, depending upon the increasing intensity of exertion and overwork, and the increased necessary expenses of city life."

After a fairly satisfactory treatment of the payment of wages, with respect to time and piece payment, cash payments vs. payments in kind, etc., the sweating system is examined. The most satisfactory results of legislative efforts aimed against sweatshops are found in Massachusetts, and that, not because the legislation itself is most advanced, but because such legislation as there is is rendered effective by excellence of administration, on account of the high grade of inspectors employed, and the civil service laws which give continuity in office and protection to the inspectors. This is only one of several places where the importance of administration as distinguished from legislation is emphasized. In the treatment of child labor it is shown that in addition to good laws there must be a sufficient body of inspectors to enforce the laws effectively. The importance of compulsory school attendance for children is something recognized by the experts employed by the commission, and almost, if not quite unanimously, by the members of the commission themselves. But the District of Columbia offers an illustration of the fact that a compulsory attendance law has little significance unless it is the duty of some specific person to enforce it. It is well that this importance of administration receives emphasis, inasmuch as in the administration of law we Americans have been weak, whereas we have been too inclined to think that mere legislation in itself could accomplish beneficent results.

Unemployment receives especially full treatment, as might be expected from the personnel of the experts who prepared the final report. Again we find that careful analysis, which has been so frequently mentioned. The causes of unemployment are divided into three main classes, namely, personal, climatic, and industrial. Reports of charity organization societies serve as a basis of the treatment of personal causes of unemployment, and this section of the work suggests the admirable treatment upon the same subject found in the late Professor Amos G. Warner's book American Charities.

The climatic causes of unemployment are due either to weather or to changes in consumption on account of the succession of the seasons. Some kinds of seasonal unemployment could, perhaps, without impropriety, be placed under the heading of vacation. The teacher cannot be regarded as unemployed during vacation, and there are seasonal trades which have periods of idleness, which could possibly be treated as rest periods. At the same time, it is interesting to note that with the progress of industries greater regularity in employment is secured. One kind of employment in the summer is followed by another sort in the winter, and certain trades have to a greater extent than heretofore conquered nature. Building is carried on more extensively in winter than formerly. However, after all allowances are made, it is still true that seasonal irregularities are an evil which is keenly felt by large numbers of wage earners.

Under industrial causes of unemployment we find a treatment of strikes, machinery, and employment agencies. The loss of employment through strikes is a serious one, but not so great as we are frequently led to infer by statistical statements. In many cases, the strike means simply a transfer of a period of unemployment from one time to another, and there must be cases where a period of unemployment would, to some extent, coincide with a strike period. The ordinary opinion of experts concerning machinery as a cause of unemployment, is in the main confirmed. An illustration is found in the increasing number of railway employees in the United States, notwithstanding all the improvements and economies of labor which have been introduced. The imperfect and insufficient character, however, of the statistics of unemployment is mentioned, and the conclusion suggests itself that there is an opportunity for various labor bureaus to render service in increasing our knowledge of the facts of the case. More has been done by the New York bureau of labor statistics than by any other, but the researches even of this bureau embrace only organized labor in the state of New York since 1897. The work of the free employment bureaus is described, but they are evidently considered simply a palliative and no real remedy for the evils of unemployment.

The longest section of Part I., dealing with general conditions and problems, is devoted to hours of labor, and this is the final section. The benefits of shorter hours are described and emphasized strongly. The movement to secure shorter hours is favored, and it is insisted that, inasmuch as the tendency of industry requires increasing intensity of exertion, a corresponding shortening of the working day is needed to preserve the health and vigor of the wage earning population. Restrictions of output, on the other hand, are discountenanced as a disadvantage to American industry. Testimony is adduced to show that up to the present time, as a rule, the shortening of the working day has not decreased production, although it is admitted that it is a rule with exceptions. It is also admitted that one part of the American union may be placed at a disadvantage as compared with another section, on account of the more rapid rate in the decrease of the length of the working day in the former. In the matter of foreign competition it is claimed that this disadvantage of American. workmen does not hold, because American labor receives the advantage of the protective tariff.

The efforts of labor organizations to secure shorter hours are described and then there follows a treatment of legislation covering the hours of labor. Emphasis is naturally laid upon the decision of the Supreme court of the United States in the well known Utah mining case, where an eight hour day for the miners was sustained, on the ground that in protecting a large class of employees the state is protecting the community as a whole. The decision of the Supreme court of Massachusetts, sustaining a law limiting the hours of women in certain employments to sixty hours per week, is also cited, as well as the decision of the Supreme court of Illinois, declaring an eight hour law, applying to adult women in factories, unconstitutional. It is interesting to notice the opinion expressed in the final report that legislation upon the subject of hours of labor cannot be general, but must be based upon accurate investigation of the conditions in the several industries. It is urged that the United States department of labor should be furnished with adequate funds to conduct a full investigation of injurious occupations, employing medical and technical experts for this purpose. This is important in view of the tendency of the courts to rule against what is called class legislation; for the question can very well be raised, if effective legislation must not necessarily be based upon a recognition of classes in the community, with needs which vary according to class. A special point is made of the desirability of uniformity of legislation among the states of the union, concerning hours of labor. It is in the main, however, recommended that legislation restricting the hours of labor should be applicable only to those under twenty one. The legislature of New Jersey, limiting the hours of labor in factories to fifty five per week, is recommended as a standard which should be adopted by every state with factory production. It is recognized that federal legislation must be restricted mainly to those engaged in interstate commerce, and to those directly employed by the federal government.

Having treated with such fullness that portion of the final report which gives the general survey, the remaining parts can be passed over much more briefly. The first topic which is discussed under Relations of Employers and Employees is labor organizations. Their growth and membership are briefly described, and it is shown that they are a necessary feature of industrial evolution. As a distinct wage earning class arises, trade unions come into existence, and as industry expands labor organizations expand likewise and become national and international. The two greatest efforts in this country to give unity to the organization of labor are those which have proceeded from the Knights of Labor, and the American Federation of Labor. The Knights of Labor endeavored to secure a unity like that of the republic indivisible, which was the ideal of the leaders of the French revolution, whereas the American Federation of Labor has had as its ideal a large degree of autonomy for the separate organizations, along with unity in important matters of general concern. The founders of the American federation of labor undoubtedly had floating before their minds as a model of organization the political union of the American states. The advantages of labor organizations find sympathetic treatment. If the attitude of labor organizations towards nonunion labor is not justified it is at least explained, and it is needless to dwell upon the importance of understanding the real basis of the antagonism of union labor towards nonunion labor. There are comparatively few people outside the wage earning ranks who understand how much can be said in favor of the position which organized labor assumes in this particular; and this can be admitted even if we are unable to justify the conduct of labor organizations with respect to those outside their ranks. This conduct is undoubtedly frequently reprehensible and sometimes even criminal. But those will not succeed in finding a remedy who do not understand the real nature of the question.

After a brief discussion of the political activities of labor organizations we have an extended treatment of collective bargaining, conciliation, and arbitration. Collective bargaining is defined as a process by which the general labor contract itself is agreed upon by negotiation directly between employers, or employers' associations and organized working men. It is shown that collective bargaining is the necessary outcome of the progress of industry with labor organizations, and that conciliation and arbitration imply organization alike of capital and of labor.

Careful discrimination is made between two main classes of industrial disputes, viz., first, those which concern the interpretation of the existing labor contract or terms of employment, and which usually are of a relatively minor character; second, those which have to do with the general terms of the future labor contract, and which are usually more important. It is shown that conciliation has been far more successful than arbitration. One of the most important features of this part of the final report is the emphasis laid upon the great advantage of conferences composed of relatively large numbers of representatives of employers and employees. It is said that these conferences need not be held at regular intervals, and that when they are held they should be conducted with informality. If disputes cannot be settled by the parties themselves, it is held that they should then be referred to a board, composed of representatives of employers and employees, who, while not directly interested themselves, are nevertheless familiar with trade conditions, and perhaps even personally acquainted with the parties to the dispute. These boards are called trade boards of conciliation and arbitration, and it is maintained that such boards can frequently remove misunderstandings which are so often a cause of industrial strife.

It is shown that the state boards of arbitration in the United States have accomplished important results only in a few states. The states which are mentioned are Massachusetts, New York, Ohio, Indiana, Illinois, and Wisconsin. Perhaps the list would be confined to the first two. The position is taken that the work of state boards must be confined chiefly to disputes in trades where no systematic methods of collective bargaining and of trade conciliation and arbitration exist. Such boards of arbitration frequently lack, it is said, familiarity with local and trade conditions, and are distrusted both by employers and employees. It is evident from the survey of the industrial commission, as well as from the reports of state boards, that they can accomplish no large results unless clothed with sufficient powers to make themselves respected by employers and employees alike. In many states the state boards are so feeble, both in their personnel and in their powers, that they are simply contemptible.

Compulsory conciliation and arbitration, without legal enforceability of decision, meets with sympathetic treatment and is favored, on the whole, on account of the advantages to employers and employees, and also especially on account of the interest of the general public in industrial peace. Compulsory arbitration is briefly described, and its success, up to the present time, in New Zealand noted, although it is pointed out that extreme caution must be displayed in drawing lessons from a small agricultural country like New Zealand for a great industrial country like the United States. Mention is made of the fact that there are persons who believe that compulsory arbitration is desirable as a last resort in the case of those few great disputes which affect with special severity the general public interests. Probably it will be felt by economists that this section, dealing with compulsory arbitration, is one of the least satisfactory in the entire final report. The strength of the argument in favor of compulsory arbitration is found in the gradual extension of legal means for the settlement of disputes in general, and in the superiority of the public interest over the interest of particular persons. A sharp discrimination must be made between various industries, and if compulsory arbitration is to be introduced in a great country like the United States, it must be begun tentatively in those industries, the continuous operation of which is of paramount public concern. It must, in other words, begin with what are called quasi-public industries. A correct line of argument is suggested but not satisfactorily elaborated. One question must, however, be raised, and that is this: does not compulsory arbitration in the final analysis mean that, when everything else fails, government must step in and operate the industry for which compulsory arbitration has been established? President Hadley, in his work on Economics, has some illuminating remarks upon the difficulties of compulsory arbitration.

He points out that compulsory arbitration, even in quasi-public pursuits, may stop the investment of fresh capital and that this investment is important for the general public. We may establish arbitration for coal mines and for railways, but we cannot, consistently with free industry, find a way to compel people to invest their money in the operation of railways and coal mines, if they feel that compulsory arbitration will render these pursuits relatively unprofitable. There can be no doubt that this outcome of compulsory arbitration is a possibility. It would seem necessary, then, in all discussion of compulsory arbitration, to face squarely the fact of a possible temporary, or even permanent, government operation of those industries for which such arbitration is established.

Strikes and lockouts are treated with a considerable degree of thoroughness. The past literature is reviewed instructively, and several points are brought out which, if not new, are at least not very generally understood. The causes of strikes are analyzed, and it is shown that the four chief causes are demands for increase of wages or protests against a decrease; demands for a shorter working day; and finally demands which relate to methods of calculating wages or paying them. These four classes of demands cover four fifths of the entire number of demands by strikers. About half of the strikes, according to the report of the department of labor covering the years from 1881 to 1900, are reported wholly or partially successful. As is well known, the strikes for higher wages are more largely successful than strikes against a reduction of wages, due to the fact that the former are made in times of increasing prosperity. Organized workingmen appear to be more generally successful than unorganized, in their strikes. A comparison of results of strikes between various countries shows that there are more unsuccessful strikes in the United States than in the other leading countries of the world, while Great Britain has the largest percentage of strikes reported as entirely successful. It is pointed out that it is difficult to estimate the final result of strikes, and it is shown why the leaders of organized labor insist that they are, on the whole, beneficial. The claim is made that the fear of strikes has a wholesale influence upon the rate of wages and the conditions of labor, and furthermore that benefits received from strikes continue for indefinite, but very generally long periods of time. While we must deplore strikes and lockouts, we should not overlook the facts to which attention is here called. A strike may last for a few weeks, and the increase in wages or shorter hours thereby secured may continue for something like twenty years, as has happened in the case of a street car strike which took place in Baltimore in the eighties. The very obvious conclusion to be drawn from this part of the report is that we cannot hope to do away with strikes and lockouts unless we substitute other effective methods in their place for the adjustment of industrial disputes. Attention is called to the exaggeration by the press of the influence of the leaders of the workingmen, and it is shown that the actions of trade unions are governed by the vote of their members. Intimidation and violence and picketing are briefly discussed, and then follows a treatment of the boycott. Boycotting is not wholly discountenanced, but a sharp distinction is made between what is called the simple and the compound boycott. The first relates to a voluntary withholding of patronage by workingmen directly concerned in a dispute, or by other persons because of sympathy for them, and compound boycotting is called the coercive boycott. This refers to cases in which workingmen threaten refusal of patronage to those who patronize the employer, thus endeavoring to force them not to do a thing which they have a legal right to do. The compound boycott is pronounced illegitimate.

The subject of injunctions is carefully and, on the whole, conservatively treated. It is held that the right of injunction is to be defended, but that its use is to be restricted. The following quotation expresses the conclusion reached: "It is undoubtedly desirable that this extraordinary process of injunction should be employed with greater conservatism than has been the case during the past decade. However severely the acts of strikers against which injunctions are usually directed, may be condemned, this is, in many cases, scarcely a proper method of checking them. Some injunction orders have gone too far in the scope of acts prohibited, and have been too indiscriminately applied to great bodies of people.

It seems desirable that statutes should be enacted, defining with greater precision the acts of workingmen which are permissible, or which are civilly or criminally unlawful, in order that a clearer indication of the limits of the injunctive process may be given. It would seem more in accordance with legal procedure to limit the application of injunction orders than to provide for jury trial of violation thereof."

The third main section, dealing with the protection of employees in their labor, is one of the most interesting. It reviews the whole body of so-called factory legislation, enabling us to compare the various leading industrial countries of the world with one another, and particularly to institute comparisons between the various states of the union. The four leading states, so far as we may judge from Mr. William F. Willoughby's table upon the duties of factory inspectors, are Massachusetts, New York, New Jersey, and Pennsylvania. Under the duties of factory inspectors to enforce laws there are thirty two points. New Jersey has inspection covering twenty four points; Massachusetts and New York covering twenty two points, and Pennsylvania twenty one points. The position which New Jersey takes will doubtless surprise many readers. On the whole, however, Massachusetts and New York seem to be the leaders, and they are recommended by the commission as models. Probably of all the states, Massachusetts is still the banner state of the union, when we take into account not only the number of points covered, but the methods of carrying out the law and the positive provision made in education and otherwise in behalf of the wage earning population.

One of the most instructively treated topics in this section of the report is that which deals with the employment of women. Here popular and very widely held errors are corrected. It is shown that the increased employment of women is chiefly due to what we may term the socialization of industry. Work which was formerly performed in the house has been taken outside the home into the factories, and the employment of women has largely been transferred. There is no reason to suppose that a larger number of adult women are engaged in toil now than formerly, and still less reason is there to suppose that very generally the women are replacing men. In addition to the fact that industry has been socialized, is the further fact that new employments have arisen, such as typewriting, which have given new work and increased the number of working women, without taking work which was formerly performed by men.

One of the most important topics under the protection of employees relates to employers' liability. Attention is called to the unsatisfactory condition of the law in the United States, and it is shown that not only very few workingmen of the United States receive compensation for accidents but that the number tends to decrease, unless the common law is supplemented by statutes. One great obstacle to the recovery of damages is the doctrine of fellow servant, by which the employer escapes liability for the negligence of his agent in case the injured workingman is a fellow employee of the agent. There is also the further doctrine of contributory negligence, which relieves the employer, although the larger part of the blame may be his. There is also the further doctrine that the employee assumes risk if he was aware of the danger and did not call attention to it, although to have called attention to the danger might have resulted in his discharge. The most instructive part of this portion of the final report is that which establishes the fact that to an increasing extent we have to do in industrial accidents, not with blame attaching either to employee or employer, but with an industrial risk which is part and parcel of modern industrial methods. The ideal then is to make the industry carry the industrial risk rather than to attempt to place the responsibility upon individuals, whether employees or employers. This is the general principle which has received acceptance in Germany in the insurance scheme which provides for employees who suffer from industrial accidents. The difficulty of reaching this ideal in our country is described, and the English employer's liability act is recommended as the present ideal. The English act places the responsibility in a general way upon the employer and prevents contracting out of the liability.

The fourth main section, dealing with labor on public works, is a short one and can be dismissed with a few words. The advantages and disadvantages of public works are discussed. It is shown that in the case of federal public works, production is usually far more costly than in private works, but it is denied that, generally speaking, this is due to defects inherent in public undertakings. So far as this increased costliness is due to better labor conditions it appears to be favored. In a general way it is recommended that government should be a model employer, while maintaining the highest possible degree of efficiency.

Turning now to the formal recommendations of the commission, the reader must again be reminded that these are distinct from the final review, or any other reviews. The recommendations of the commission are the formal official action, whereas the other parts of the report are largely the work of the experts employed by the commission. The commission, first of all, recommend a regulation of the hours of labor in industrial occupations. Uniformity among the states is emphasized as especially important. The opinion is expressed, however, that limitation of the hours of labor should be restricted to persons under twenty one, except in special industries where employment for too many hours becomes positively a menace to the health, safety and well being of the community. It is recommended that no children should be employed under the age of fourteen, and that accompanying labor legislation there should be educational restrictions providing that no child may be employed in factories, shops or stores in large cities, who cannot read and write. In all public work it is recommended that the length of the working day should be fixed at eight hours. It is recognized that this discriminates between public and private employment, but the hope is expressed that private employment may be brought up to the level of public employment in this particular. It is further recommended that the federal government should regulate the hours of labor of employees engaged in interstate commerce.

It is recommended that the states should provide for cash payments and should legislate against company stores.

The careless use of injunctions is pronounced reprehensible, and blanket injunctions against all the world, or against numerous unnamed defendants, as well as the practice of indirectly enforcing the contract for personal service by enjoining employees from quitting work, should be discouraged not only by popular sentiment, but by intelligent judicial opinion. There should be no unnecessary departure from the time honored principle that the contract of personal service can not be specifically enforced, because to do so entails a condition of practical slavery.

Turning to intimidation, the New York statute relative to railway labor is recommended for general adoption. The New York statute, protecting the political rights of laborers, is also recommended as a model.

The practice of giving a preferred lien to employees for debts due for wages and salaries is approved and its extension recommended.

The subject of convict labor, which is treated in a separate volume, is referred to in the recommendations of the commission. In this separate report the New York plan, in accordance with which convicts manufacture goods for the use of state institutions, seems to meet with approval, so far as it is practicable. It is recommended that in all cases the punishment and reformation of the prisoner be placed above revenue considerations, and that a system be devised which should give all prisoners employment in productive labor, with the least possible competition with free labor. In the recommendations of the commission, it is said to be clear that congress should legislate to prevent the importation and sale of convict made goods from one state into another, without the consent of the state into which the goods are imported or where they are sold.

The factory acts of Massachusetts and New York are recommended, as well as the sweat shop laws of New York, Massachusetts, Pennsylvania and Ohio.

The enactment of a code of laws for railway labor is considered to be within the province of congress, as it falls under the interstate powers. It is especially recommended that in such a code there should be a careful definition and regulation of employers' liability and of the hours of labor.

The protection of trade union labels is recommended. It is further recommended that conspiracy should be defined and limited. Laws against blacklisting and the use of private police detectives are approved.

The commission finds that the laws of the states with respect to conciliation and arbitration have been found effective for purposes of conciliation, but that so far as arbitration, strictly defined, is concerned, they have not accomplished any large results. Further efforts in the direction of conciliation and arbitration are recommended, and the commission believe that whoever inaugurates a lockout or strike without first petitioning for arbitration, or assenting to it when offered, should be subjected to an appropriate penalty. It is recommended also that arbitration should not be restricted to a public board, but that the parties to the dispute should be permitted to choose arbitrators if they prefer.

Finally it is recommended that all the states not now having them should establish labor bureaus, and that their duties should be extended, and that they should co-operate with the legislative bodies of the states and with congress in legislation by means of their recommendations.

These recommendations are signed by eleven members of the commission. Another member of the commission cordially endorses them in a supplementary note. Four commissioners dissent from the report. The theory of those who dissent seems to be based upon the eighteenth century philosophy of individual liberty, and to have as its direct, practical purpose the interests, real or supposed, of southern manufacturers. Two of the dissentients are large cotton mill owners, one of them one of the most prominent operators in Charlotte, N. C., and the other the president of the milling corporations of Pelzer, S. C. The former, however, recommends ample school facilities, with compulsory education, co-operative savings institutions under state laws, and the establisnment by the United States government of postal savings banks, and finally, liberal provision for the incorporation of labor organizations.

This review of the portions of the Industrial Commission report dealing with labor, although it has gone beyond the length originally contemplated, is inadequate. This is necessarily so, on account of the largeness of the subject, and the proportion of space devoted to it. It is, however, hoped that what has been said will give an idea, which is correct so far as it goes, of the excellent work which has been done by the commission, and of the character of their report upon the subject of labor.

In a general way it may be said that the report deals with labor in its static rather than in its dynamic aspects. The idea of evolution in labor conditions is suggested here and there, but not consistently developed, and perhaps to do so would not have been in harmony with the character of the work assigned to the commission. The report leaves here, as elsewhere, an unlimited quantity of work for scholars, but the report must be a point of departure for further scientific work concerning labor in the United States. It is a mine of information, and it is also a practical guide for the legislator. It is the most notable achievement of the kind in the history of the United States, and it will compare very favorably with any similar investigation undertaken in any country. Credit must be given to the good sense and judgment of the commission, and especially to the experts they employed.

Perhaps in the whole report nothing is more noteworthy than the extent to which, along with many differences, agreement could be reached in important particulars. Here, as elsewhere, it is seen that ignorance is a cause of dissension, and knowledge a cause of harmony.

THE COURTS AND FACTORY LEGISLATION.

BY GEO. W. ALGER.

[George W. Alger, lawyer and economist; born Burlington, Vt., 1870; educated at the University of Vermont and after graduation began the practice of law and is a member of the New York bar; has always taken an active interest in economic questions and has contributed frequent essays to the magazines and learned reviews chiefly on the legal phases of such topics.]

Within the past twenty years statutes have been enacted in nearly all the great manufacturing states of this country which, under various names, such as factory acts, mine laws, labor laws, railroad laws, building laws, and the like, have for their common object an increase in the safety of working people engaged in dangerous occupations by obviating dangers not necessarily inherent in the trades themselves.

These statutes take various forms; frequently in forbidding the employment of certain classes of workers (as women and children of tender years) in highly dangerous occupations; in directing the manner in which certain work shall be performed, by prescribing the particular precautions for the safety of employees which shall be taken by employers, and by providing for certain safety appliances upon machinery or rolling stock which shall render the chances of personal injury to employees less imminent. The propriety, and even necessity, of what is called factory legislation, in its general principles, is rarely disputed now. The danger of employment in manufacturing establishments increases yearly with the perfection by modern inventive genius of complex, rapidly moving, and dangerous machinery. The number of death cases and cases of serious injury in manufacturing establishments increases yearly in proportion. In New York the report of the factory inspector for 1899 showed that in that state alone the number of workmen killed per annum in industrial establishments was more than twice as large as that of the soldiers killed in the Spanish war; and showed further that, leaving out of consideration the death cases (involving the destruction of some seven hundred lives), the casualties involving crippling, maiming, and wounding would show probably not fewer than forty thousand injuries all told. Under such circumstances, appropriate legislation to reduce the number of casualties by making safer the conditions of employment is amply justified, and statutes having such humanitarian objects in view should be entitled to most favorable consideration and construction by the courts, that the purposes of their enactment should be attained.

This form of legislation is based upon a modern theory of social economy which, long since recognized and followed by the legislatures, is in some states still regarded with concern and suspicion by the courts; a theory which, ordinarily masquerading under the conveniently vague name of police power, justifies class legislation so called, and asserts the right to interfere with the natural laws of the business world, aiming to secure the liberty of one class by curbing the license of another. It is perhaps needless to say that the doctrines of the common law regarding the reciprocal relations of master and servant were formulated and adopted under a totally different conception of economic philosophy—under the old laissez faire theory of extreme individualism. This theory resolutely closed its eyes to common, obvious, social, and economic distinctions between men, either considered as individuals or as classes, and with self imposed blindness imagined rather than saw the servant and his master acting upon a plane of absolute and ideal equality in all matters touching their contractual relation; both were free and equal, and the proper function of government was to let them alone. If the servant was dissatisfied with the conditions of his employment; if the dangers created, not merely by the necessities of the work, but by the master's indifference to the safety of his men, were in the eyes of the latter too great to be endured with prudence, then, being under this theory a free agent to go or to stay, if he choose to stay he must take the possible consequences of personal injury or death. The laissez faire doctrine became firmly imbedded in the law, and upon it the doctrine of assumed risk, in the modern

application of the maxim, Volenti non fit injuria, is unquestionably founded.

Under this theory the rules of the common law regarding
the rights and duties of masters and servants were established
before the commencement of the general legislative movement toward regulative statutes and factory laws. One of
the best known of these rules is the so-called doctrine of assumed risk. There is no practical distinction in principle
between this doctrine and that involved in the Latin maxim,
but in this country the principle involved is more frequently
discussed under the former name than the latter. The principle may be stated thus: A servant, by entering upon and
continuing in a given employment, by the fact of such continuance is presumed to have voluntarily assumed the risk
of personal injuries he may receive, by reason of the ordinary
dangers inherent in the employment, by reason of any defect
not necessarily inherent in the employment which he knew
and understood as a danger before injury received, whether
such defect was occasioned by his master's failure to perform
his common law duty of furnishing his men with a safe place
to work or not. This doctrine is one of the commonest and
most successful defenses interposed by employers in this
country in actions brought against them by their injured
employees. In most of the American states the question
whether the servant assumed the risks of personal injury
from defective appliances has been treated as a matter of
law for the judge to determine, and the continuance in employment with knowledge and comprehension of defects
from which personal injuries are afterward received has been
ordinarily held sufficient to authorize and require the trial
judge to take the case from the jury and dismiss the plaintiff's action. Under the ordinary American rule continuance
at his work by the employee with knowledge of a dangerous
defect in machinery or in his place of employment can mean
but one thing—a conscious, willing assent to the continuance
of the danger to his life or safety, and a voluntary assumption of all chances of personal injury from it, absolving the
master from all responsibility for such injuries, even if this
defect exists by the master's carelessness or indifference to

LEGISLATION RELATING TO LABOR ORGANIZATIONS

Legislation.	U.S.	Ala.	Alaska	Ariz.	Ark.	Cal.	Colo.	Conn.	Del.	D.C.	Fla.	Ga.	Hawaii	Idaho	Ill.	Ind.	Iowa	Kans.	Ky.	La.	Me.	Md.	Mass.	Mich.	Minn.	Miss.	Mo.	Mont.	Nebr.	Nev.	N.H.	N.J.	N.Mex.	N.Y.	N.C.	N.Dak.	Ohio	Okla.	Oreg.	Pa.	P.R.	R.I.	S.C.	S.Dak.	Tenn.	Tex.	Utah	Vt.	Va.	Wash.	W.Va.	Wis.	Wyo.
Legalizing labor organizations:																																																					
Declaring labor combinations lawful																																																						
Providing for incorporation of labor organizations																																																						
Excepting labor organizations from statutes regulating—																																																						
Trusts and industrial combinations																																																						
Insurance corporations and associations																																																						
Protecting members of labor organizations																																																						
Concerning union labels, credentials, or insignia:																																																						
Protecting union labels, credentials, or insignia																																																						
Requiring union label on public printing																																																						
Prohibiting issue or use of false credentials, etc																																																						
Prohibiting unauthorized wearing of insignia																																																						

LEGISLATION RELATING TO BOYCOTTING, BLACKLISTING, CONSPIRACY, INTIMIDATION, ETC.

Legislation.	U.S.	Ala.	Alaska	Ariz.	Ark.	Cal.	Colo.	Conn.	Del.	D.C.	Fla.	Ga.	Hawaii	Idaho	Ill.	Ind.	Iowa	Kans.	Ky.	La.	Me.	Md.	Mass.	Mich.	Minn.	Miss.	Mo.	Mont.	Nebr.	Nev.	N.H.	N.J.	N.Mex.	N.Y.	N.C.	N.Dak.	Ohio	Okla.	Oreg.	Pa.	P.R.	R.I.	S.C.	S.Dak.	Tenn.	Tex.	Utah	Vt.	Va.	Wash.	W.Va.	Wis.	Wyo.
Boycotting																																																					
Blacklisting																																																					
Intimidation of employees																																																					
Interference with employment																																																					
Conspiracy against workingmen																																																					

the employee's safety. Even if the workman protests against the exposure of his life by such defect, if he keeps at work he assumes the risk he protests himself unwilling to assume. A somewhat different rule is adopted in England, where the question whether the workman voluntarily took his chances of being injured is for the jury to say from the circumstances.

Such being the American rule as to the ordinary negligences of the employer to do his legal duty in furnishing his workman a safe place to work, or safe tools and appliances, is there any different rule properly invoked when the master neglects to comply with a specific, definite, statutory duty? In case a statute makes it mandatory upon the employer to take certain precautions, to use certain safety appliances in his business, and he neglects or refuses to comply, does the workman who knows of his employer's neglect to comply with the statute, assume the risk of personal injury which may result from the latter's refusal to obey the law? If he does, then the statute is no protection to the workman, and is utterly worthless as far as its enforcement by ordinary suit at law is concerned. The answer to this question, moreover, will determine whether the courts will recognize and sustain the economic theory upon which such remedial statutes are framed, or will resist and nullify the application of that theory by upholding the laissez faire doctrine upon which the old rule of assumed risk is founded. The modern economic theory which is the justification of factory legislation and laws regulating the hours and conditions of labor for the protection of the working classes, has been recognized and approved by the United States Supreme court, in the great Utah eight hour law case, in which the court, in the opinion by Judge Brown, used the following significant language:

"The legislature has also recognized the fact, which the experience of legislators in many states has corroborated, that the proprietors of these establishments (mining plants) and their operators do not stand upon an equality, and their interests are in a certain extent conflicting. The former naturally desire to obtain as much labor as possible from their employees, while the latter are often induced, by fear of discharge, to conform to regulations which their judgment, fairly exercised, would pronounce detrimental to their health and strength. In other words, the proprietors lay down the rules, and the laborers are practically constrained to obey them. In such cases self interest is often an unsafe guide, and the legislature may properly interpose its authority. . . . . But the fact that both parties are of full age and competent to contract does not necessarily deprive the state of the power to interfere where the parties do not stand upon an equality, or where the public health demands that one party to the contract be protected against himself. The state still retains an interest in his welfare, however reckless he may be. The whole is no greater than the sum of all its parts, and when the individual health, safety, and welfare are sacrificed or neglected, the state must suffer."

Under this theory, it is apparent that the question which we are considering involves an important matter of public policy. In an employment so dangerous (if necessary precautions be not taken) that great numbers of working people are exposed to avoidable dangers to life and limb, and when (recognizing the interest which the state has in the welfare of the citizen) the legislature has interposed its authority in enacting regulative statutes, does not public policy require that such statutes should be mandatory, and not subject to constructive or actual waiver by the persons for whose safety they are framed?

The English courts answer this query in the affirmative. Statutory duties imposed upon the master for the greater protection of the servant may not be waived by the latter. Public policy forbids it. In Baddesley vs. Lord Granville (10 Q. B. 423) an action was brought for the death of a miner caused by a violation of the coal mines regulation act, which requires that a banksman be kept at the mouth of coalpits while miners are going up and down the shaft. The court held that the fact that the deceased knew that no banksman was employed by defendant and yet continued to work at the mine did not constitute a defense. Says Baron Wills:

"There should be no encouragement given to the making of an agreement between A and B that B shall be at liberty to break the law which has been passed for the protection of A. . . . . If the supposed agreement between the deceased and the defendant in consequence of which the principle of volenti non fit injuria is sought to be applied, comes to this, that the master employs the servant on the terms that the latter shall waive the breach by the master of an obligation imposed upon him by the statute, and shall connive at his disregard of the statutory obligation imposed on him for the benefit of others as well as himself—such an agreement would be in violation of public policy and ought not to be listened to."

In New York the question whether the statutory duties imposed on employers to guard cogs, gearings, etc., under the factory act could be waived by the employee continuing his work after he knew of his master's violation of this law, has been considered several times. In the case of Simpson vs. the New York Rubber Co. (80 Hun. 415) the general term of the supreme court held that public policy forbade such waiver.

This decision has been in effect reversed by the court of appeals in a later case involving the same question, and in which it was held that the employee may by entering upon the employment with full knowledge of all the facts waive, under the common law doctrine of obvious risks, the performance by the employer of the duty to furnish the special protection prescribed by the factory act. This case (Knisley vs. Pratt, 148 N. Y. 372) passes lightly over the question of public policy, without giving it consideration, except by saying that to hold that the workman could not waive his master's statutory duty by continuing at work was a new and startling doctrine calculated to establish a measure of liability unknown to the common law, and which is contrary to the decisions of Massachusetts and England under similar statutes. The decision of other states and of England affirming this new and startling doctrine are not considered at all, and the court's attention does not seem to have been called to them by plaintiff's counsel in his brief. The decision is based largely upon supposed analogies between the case at bar and English and Massachusetts

cases on employer's liability acts. These latter cases held
that the English act (that of 1880) and the substantially
similar Massachusetts law of 1887 (neither of which created
or imposed any new statutory duty on the master) were intended to modify the fellow servant doctrine, and not to affect in any way the doctrine of assumed risk. In the Knisley
case the defendant refused or neglected to obey the mandatory provision of the Factory act imposing the specific duty
upon him of placing guards on cogwheels of his machinery.
Owing to the absence of these guards, and apparently not
by reason of any personal carelessness, the plaintiff's arm
was drawn into the cogs and so crushed and torn that it had
to be amputated at the shoulder—a peculiarly distressing
case. In this case the plaintiff was a young woman of full
age. The New York court recognizes no difference in the
rule by reason of infancy, however.

The question of the assumption of statutory risks has
been adjudicated upon in Illinois in several cases, but the
exact question of public policy involved is apparently still
undecided by its highest court. The decisions would make
the final adoption of the English rule more probable. It
has been held in Indiana, Missouri, and Illinois that where
there is a general public ordinance regulating the speed of
railway trains passing near or through cities, enacted for the
benefit of the public, an employee of a railroad who continues
in its employment with knowledge of the violation of the
ordinance (without contributing actively to its violation)
does not assume the risk of injury, nor is he by reason of his
employment deprived of any of the benefits of the ordinance
to which other citizens are entitled.

In Greenlee vs. Southern Railway Co. the plaintiff was
injured by reason of the failure of the railroad company defendant to comply with the federal law requiring self couplers
and air brakes to be placed on all freight and passenger cars
by January 1, 1898. The plaintiff's injuries were due to a defective brake. The plaintiff's recovery, at trial, was affirmed
on appeal, the court using the following language:

"Six years ago this court said it would soon be negligence
per se whenever an action happened for lack of a self coupler.

Congress has enacted that self couplers should be used. For this lack this plaintiff was injured. It is true the defendant replies that the plaintiff remained in its service knowing it did not have self couplers. If that were a defense, no railroad company would ever be liable for failure to put in life saving devices, and the need of bread would force employees to continue the annual sacrifice of thousands of men. But this is not the doctrine of assumption of risk. That is a more reasonable doctrine, and is merely that when a particular machine is defective or injured, and the employee, knowing it, continues to use it, he assumes the risk. That doctrine has no application where the law requires the adoption of new devices to save life or limb (as self couplers), and the employee, either ignorant of that fact or expecting daily compliance with the law, continues in service with the appliances formerly in use."

Two cases illustrative of the diversity of opinion among the courts on this matter of public policy involve statutes requiring railroad companies to fill or block frogs and guard rails on their tracks. In both cases the actions were for recovery of damages for personal injuries from such unblocked frogs received by employees who continued in the railroad service with knowledge that the condition of the rails was contrary to the statute and dangerous. In one decided by the United States Circuit court of appeals, in the opinion of Judge Taft, the learned justice remarks: "In the absence of statute, and upon common law principles, we have no doubt that in this case the plaintiff would be held to have assumed the risk of the absence of blocks in guard rails and switches by defendant." The court held, however, that the plaintiff's rights under the statute could not be waived by continuance:

The only ground for passing such a statute is found in the inequality of terms upon which the railway company and its servants deal in regard to the dangers of their employment. The manifest legislative purpose was to protect the servant by positive law, because he had not previously shown himself capable of protecting himself by contract;

and it would entirely defeat this purpose thus to permit the servant to contract the master out of the statute.

In the other case, the Supreme court of Maine held that the continuing servant assumed the risk of injury from the railway's refusal to obey the law requiring blocked frogs and guard rails.

In Mississippi the state constitution provides (Art. VII., sec. 193):

Knowledge by any employee injured of the defective or unsafe character of any machinery, ways, or appliances shall be no defense to an action for injuries caused thereby, except as to conductors or engineers in charge of dangerous or unsafe cars or engines voluntarily operated by them.

A similar statutory provision appears in the Revised Statutes of Ontario, chap. 160, sec. 6:

Provided, however, that such workman shall not reason only of his continuing in the employment of the employer with knowledge of the defect negligence act or omission which caused his injury be deemed to have voluntarily incurred the risk of the injury.

If the writer may venture a personal opinion, it is that the English rule, in cases where no violation of statute is involved, is fairer, leaving it for the jury to say, from the facts in evidence in a given case, whether the workman who continues to use machinery he knows to be defective should be held to have assumed the risk of injury. It has the merit of flexibility, and is more calculated to meet the requirements of substantial justice in the varying facts of different cases.

As to the violation of regulative statutes framed to secure the safety of the employee, the situation would seem to be simpler. If the conditions of an employment are such as to make such legislation necessary to preserve the lives of employees, such resulting legislation should be supported by the courts instead of being nullified and rendered absurd.

The attitude of the courts toward factory legislation is of importance to others besides the injured litigant. While it has been said on good authority that the courts in the great manufacturing states are desirous of diminishing the constantly increasing flood of negligence litigation by discouraging the injured servant from taking his troubles to court, the public, and particularly the working classes, are interested in obtaining the same result by diminishing the number of accidents from which alone such lawsuits can originate. Any perceptible diminution in the number of accidents can scarcely be expected when the responsibility of the master for his own negligence to his workmen is nominal and not actual. The prospect of verdicts for large damages actually sustained on appeal in actions brought against him by his injured employees would be a most healthful stimulus to vigilance by the master in performing his legal duties to his men and in giving reasonable care to their safety. A reasonable modification of the assumption doctrine would, moreover, make unnecessary the greater part of the regulative statutes applying to particular trades, yearly increasing in bulk and complexity, confusing alike to lawyer and layman—in itself a consummation devoutly to be wished.

CHILD LABOR LEGISLATION.

BY FLORENCE KELLEY.

[Florence Kelley, secretary National Consumer's League since May, 1899; born Philadelphia, September 12, 1859; graduated from Cornell, 1882; writer on social and labor questions; state inspector of factories for Illinois, 1893-7 and did much to enforce the child labor law and brought about many reforms.]

It is most desirable that the present widespread agitation for child labor legislation may achieve permanent results of a uniform character. Such laws as now exist are alike in no two states; they are enforced differently when they are enforced at all; they are uniform only in their failure to afford adequate protection to the rising generation of the working class.

It is the aim of this paper to set forth some essential points of an effectve child labor law efficiently enforced; for whatever the local differences of industrial conditions may be, certain fundamental needs of childhood are constant and child labor legislation must ultimately be framed with regard to these.

This fact is somewhat recognized in the statutes already enacted; for all these begin with a restriction upon the age at which the child may begin to work. This minimal age has varied from ten to fifteen, differing in some states for boys and for girls, while the statutes prescribing it have been weakened in some states by exemptions and strengthened in others by educational requirements. The fundamental provision of all child labor legislation has always been the prohibition of work before a specified birthday.

Akin to the restriction of the age of employment is the restriction of the hours of work. The former secures to the child a fixed modicum of childhood; the latter assures to the adolescent certain leisure, all too little, for growth and development.

No one law can be selected as containing all the provisions needed or even as containing all the provisions now in force. It is not possible to say to students of the subject, the law of Massachusetts should be copied everywhere, for the laws of Ohio and Illinois contain single provisions in advance of that of Massachusetts.

Among the best child labor laws in the United States are those of Illinois and Indiana, which are almost identical. In Illinois no child under the age of fourteen years can be legally employed in any mine, manufacturing establishment, factory or workshop, mercantile institution, office, or laundry. The Indiana law adds, to the foregoing list, renovating works, bakeries, and printing offices. This prohibition is absolute throughout the year, admitting no exemptions or exceptions. Herein lies the superiority of these laws. Under the New York law, children at work in stores are exempt from restrictions during half of December—from December 15 to December 31—and also during the vacations of the public schools, when they may be employed from the age of thirteen years everywhere outside of the factories, which happily they may not enter before the fourteenth birthday. This exemption in New York has been given such elastic construction that children have been employed on Saturday and even on school days out of school hours.

The laws of Illinois and Indiana are humane; they set the highest age limit without exemptions yet attained; they are equitable since they place mine owners, manufacturers, and merchants in the same position in relation to this particular source of cheap labor. The employment of children under fourteen years of age is prohibited to all three sets of employers alike.

Treating these laws as standard or normal, for purposes of comparison, the law of Pennsylvania, for instance, is seen to fall below, because under it children may work in certain mines at twelve years and in factories at thirteen years of age; while lowest in the scale among all the northern and middle states stands New Jersey, whose child labor law permits boys to work at twelve and exempts all children, on grounds of poverty, at discretion of the factory inspectors.

From the foregoing brief statement it is clear that the subject of exemptions is a varied and complicated one. The most insidious form of exemption, and therefore, perhaps, the most dangerous, is that prescribed in the law of Wisconsin. Under it, no child may be employed under the age of fourteen years in manufacture or commerce, unless it is exempted on grounds of poverty by a judge of a local court. In practice, a judge has no time to investigate the economic condition of hundreds of families; hence he follows the recommendation of the deputy factory inspector. This overworked officer is drawn away from his proper duties to perform an economic investigation for which he possesses no special fitness. His own work suffers. Children are exempted from school attendance and permitted to work, who more than any other children in the community need education because of the poverty or shiftlessness of their parents. Too often, drunken fathers are encouraged to further drunkenness because their young children, under exemption, are earning money which the parents spend. Finally, this exemption rests upon the pernicious principle that a young child under fourteen years of age may be burdened with the support of itself or its family.

It is not a legitimate function of the judiciary to investigate the poverty of individual families. It is not a legitimate function of the factory inspectors to investigate family life. Both officers are interrupted in the performance of their legitimate duties by every attempt to perform this alien task. Moreover, children under fourteen years of age are undesirable additions to the body of wage earners, pressing by their competition upon the wages of their seniors and therefore tending to produce in other families the same poverty which serves as a pretext for their own exemption. The number of exempted children, under such a provision, tends to increase continuously, because greedy and pauperized parents are tempted to follow the example of the really needy, in urging applications for exemptions.

Besides being free from all the undermining effects of exemption clauses, the child labor laws of Illinois and Indiana profit by several reinforcing clauses. Chief among these is the requirement that children under sixteen years and over fourteen years must keep on file in the office of the place of employment an affidavit of the parent or guardian, stating

LEGISLATION RELATING TO THE EMPLOYMENT OF WOMEN

Legislation.	U.S.	Ala.	Alaska.	Ariz.	Ark.	Cal.	Colo.	Conn.	Del.	D.C.	Fla.	Ga.	Hawaii.	Idaho.	Ill.	Ind.	Iowa.	Kans.	Ky.	La.	Me.	Md.	Mass.	Mich.	Minn.	Miss.	Mo.	Mont.	Nebr.	Nev.	N.H.	N.J.	N.Mex.	N.Y.	N.C.	N.Dak.	Ohio.	Okla.	Oreg.	Pa.	P.R.	R.I.	S.C.	S.Dak.	Tenn.	Tex.	Utah.	Vt.	Va.	Wash.	W.Va.	Wis.	Wyo.
Prohibiting employment of women in—																																																						
Mines, smelters, etc	◇			◇		◇									◇	◇														◇	◇									◇							◇			◇	◇	◇	◇
Places where intoxicants are made or sold		◇																			◇	◇								◇																						◇	
Cleaning or operating dangerous machinery						◇															◇	◇							◇																								
Regulating working time of women:																																																						
Hours of labor limited						◇	◇								◇													◇	◇					◇																	◇		
Night work prohibited or restricted															◇								◇											◇																			
Requiring for females in factories, etc.																																																						
Seats for rest when not at work	◇				◇	◇		◇	◇		◇	◇			◇	◇	◇			◇	◇	◇	◇	◇	◇		◇		◇		◇	◇		◇			◇			◇		◇	◇		◇					◇	◇	◇	◇
Separate toilet facilities																																																					

LEGISLATION RELATING TO CHILD LABOR

Legislation.	U.S.	Ala.	Alaska.	Ariz.	Ark.	Cal.	Colo.	Conn.	Del.	D.C.	Fla.	Ga.	Hawaii.	Idaho.	Ill.	Ind.	Iowa.	Kans.	Ky.	La.	Me.	Md.	Mass.	Mich.	Minn.	Miss.	Mo.	Mont.	Nebr.	Nev.	N.H.	N.J.	N.Mex.	N.Y.	N.C.	N.Dak.	Ohio.	Okla.	Oreg.	Pa.	P.R.	R.I.	S.C.	S.Dak.	Tenn.	Tex.	Utah.	Vt.	Va.	Wash.	W.Va.	Wis.	Wyo.
Prohibiting employment of children under—																																																					
16 years, in mines							◇					◇			◇						◇			◇			◇					◇		◇			◇		◇							◇					◇		
14 years, in factories, etc.						◇		◇							◇							◇	◇											◇			◇														◇		
14 years, in mercantile establishments															◇																																						
14 years, in mines, smelters, etc.																																							◇														
13 years, in factories, etc.																					◇	◇																															
13 years, in mercantile establishments																															◇					◇		◇						◇							◇	
12 years, in factories, etc						◇																															◇		◇					◇		◇					◇	
12 years, in mercantile establishments																			◇																		◇		◇					◇		◇					◇	
12 years, in mines, smelters, etc.	◇																			◇																	◇									◇						
10 years, in factories, etc																																															◇						
10 years, in mercantile establishments																																															◇						
Prohibiting employment of children under specified age																																																						
During school time						◇	◇	◇		◇					◇						◇			◇	◇			◇			◇						◇			◇						◇					◇	◇	
If illiterate																																																						
Prohibiting employment of children in—																																																						
Places where intoxicants are made or sold		◇		◇			◇	◇				◇			◇							◇	◇							◇	◇			◇			◇			◇						◇					◇	◇	
Gymnastic, mendicant, etc., occupations						◇									◇	◇							◇											◇																		◇	
Running elevators						◇									◇																			◇						◇												◇	
Cleaning or operating dangerous machinery																																															◇						
Regulating working time of children:																																																						
Hours of labor limited					◇	◇	◇	◇				◇			◇						◇	◇	◇					◇			◇	◇		◇			◇			◇		◇				◇					◇	◇	
Night work prohibited or restricted															◇								◇											◇																			

the date and place of birth of the child. In Indiana, this must state also that the child can read and write the English language. While some parents are undoubtedly guilty of perjury, and others carelessly take the oath perfunctorily administered by a notary public, thousands of honest people are deterred by the requirement of the affidavit from sending their children to work before reaching the fourteenth birthday.

Employers must produce, on demand of factory inspectors, affidavits for all children under sixteen years of age in their employ. The penalty prescribed for failure to do this is the same as for employing a child under the age of fourteen years. The value of this provision for the protection of the children depends wholly upon the policy of the inspectors. If every failure to produce the affidavit is followed by immediate prosecution, manufacturers become extremely cautious about employing young children; children under fourteen years of age virtually cease to be employed; and the number of those employed under sixteen years of age diminishes because many employers refuse to be troubled with affidavits, inspections and prosecutions. On the other hand, employers of large numbers of children find it profitable to make one clerk responsible for the presence in the office of an affidavit for every child between the ages of fourteen and sixteen years. In these cases, the children who have affidavits acquire a slight added value, are somewhat less likely to be dismissed for trifling reasons, and become somewhat more stable in their employment.

Where, however, inspectors fear to prosecute systematically, lest they be removed from office, the provision requiring an affidavit to be produced by the employer, on demand of an inspector, is not rigorously enforced; children soon come to be employed upon their verbal assurance that they are fourteen years of age, and the protection which might be derived from this very useful reinforcing clause is lost for the children under fourteen years of age, as well as for the older ones.

A farther reinforcement of the prohibition of employment of children under fourteen years of age is the authority conferred by the Illinois law upon inspectors to demand a certificate of physical fitness for children who may seem unfit

for their work. This provision enforced with energy and discretion can be made, in the case of children, conspicuously
undersized, largely to counteract the tendency to perjury on
the part of parents, besides relieving healthy children from
overstrain of many kinds. The difficulties encountered are
chiefly two:—physicians grant certificates without visiting
the place of employment. This occurs quite uniformly to the
disgrace of the profession. Physicians also grant certificates,
in many cases, without careful examination of eyes, heart,
lungs, and spinal column of the child, simply upon the parent's
statement of poverty. To make this reinforcement thoroughly
effective, every factory inspection staff should include a
physician, preferably two, a man and a woman, appointed
expressly to follow up the children and the conditions under
which they work.

Several states require that children under sixteen years
of age must be able to read and write simple sentences in the
English language before being employed. This is of the highest value in those states which receive large streams of immigration from Europe. In New York, every year, numbers
of children are dismissed from factories by order of factory
inspectors, because the children cannot read; while in Massachusetts, French Canadian children find school attendance at
a high premium because of the difficulty of securing employment without it. The influence of the foreign voting constit-
uency has defeated in several states, for several years past,
the effort to secure a statutory requirement of ability to read
and write English, or a specified attendance at school, as a
prerequisite for work on the part of children under sixteen
years of age   This is conspicuously true of Illinois, where such
a provision was defeated in the legislatures of 1893, 1895, and
1897.

The most powerful reinforcement of the child labor law is
a compulsory school attendance law effectively enforced.
For want of this, the child labor law of Illinois suffers severely.
The school attendance law requires children between the ages
of eight and fourteen years to attend school sixteen weeks, of
which twelve must be consecutive. Children under ten years
of age must enter school in September, children under twelve

must enter school not later than New Year's. Meagre as these provisions are, they are not uniformly and effectively enforced by the local school boards; and the state factory inspectors are therefore burdened with frequent prosecutions of employers because children under fourteen years of age are sent to work by parents who should be rigorously prosecuted by the school attendance officers.

In Indiana, the reinforcement afforded by the state truancy law is of great value, for children must attend school to the age of fourteen years, throughout the term of the school district in which they live, generous provision being made for truant officers. This difference accounts, perhaps, for the fact that Indiana has but three and one half thousand children under the age of sixteen years at work, compared with nineteen thousand such children in Illinois; and this despite the rapid development of the gas belt in Indiana, where the temptation is very great for parents to put excessively young children to work with the help of perjured affidavits. Truant officers, watching young children, from the eighth to the fourteenth birthday, every day of the school term, are the best preventive alike of perjury by parents and of child labor. They constitute the best possible reinforcement of the child labor law.

Among the most advanced restrictions upon the hours of labor of children is that of New Jersey, which prohibits all persons, men, women, and children, alike, from working in manufacturing establishments longer than fifty five hours in any week, or after one o'clock on Saturday. This provision applies throughout the year. Massachusetts and Rhode Island prohibit the employment of women of any age and of youths under eighteen years, longer than fifty four hours in any week, or ten hours in one day, or after nine at night or before six in the morning.

These laws have the advantage of precision. They require that the hours of work of the persons concerned must be posted conspicuously, and that the posted hours shall constitute the working day—work beyond the posted hours constituting a violation of the law—thus rendering the enforcement of the law simple and easy.

The extent to which children are employed at night is not generally recognized. In any state in which such employment is not explicitly prohibited, it is very general in all branches of industry in which children are employed by day. Glassworks, nut and bolt works, tin can factories, furniture factories, cutleries, and scores of miscellaneous industries employ boys regularly at night. Girls are regularly employed in garment and candy factories during the busy season; and in some factories this work continues all through the year, as in the cotton mills of Georgia, Alabama, and the Carolinas. Wherever the prohibition is not explicit and sweeping, the night work of children is the rule, not the exception. In Illinois and Indiana boys are not prohibited from working at night, and are regularly employed in the glassworks in both states under circumstances of great hardship. In Indiana, girls are forbidden to work after ten o'clock; but Illinois, cruelly belated in this respect, merely restricts the work of children under sixteen years of age to sixty hours in any week, and ten hours in one day, failing to proscribe night work even for girls.

Large numbers of working children remain wholly unprotected by legislation. Not only have the four great cotton manufacturing states, Georgia, Alabama, and the Carolinas, defeated all bills presented to their legislatures for the purpose of protecting young children, but in the north, also, newsboys, bootblacks, peddlers, vendors, and the thousands of children employed in the tenement houses of New York and Chicago, and in the sweatshops of Philadelphia, remain wholly outside of the law's protection, so far as statutory regulation of the conditions of their work is concerned. The problem of abolishing the overwork of school children in tenement houses, under the sweating system, appears at present insoluble except by a prohibition of all tenement house work.

To secure the enforcement of child labor legislation, there are needed factory inspectors, both men and women, equipped with ample powers and supplied with adequate funds for traveling and other expenses. These inspectors need good general education, long experience, and vigorous public opinion reinforcing their efforts. Massachusetts enjoys the unique

distinction, among the American states, of possessing a large
staff of factory inspectors meeting all these requirements;
and Massachusetts is, accordingly, the only state of which it
may be confidently asserted that its child labor law is uniformly and effectively enforced at all times and in all its provisions. A faithful officer serving a full quarter century at
the head of the department, with subordinates equally assured
of permanent tenure of office during good behavior, has been
able fearlessly and intelligently to enforce the laws securing
to the children of Massachusetts fourteen full years of childhood, with opportunity for school life, followed by safety of
life, limb and health after entering upon the years of work.

In all of the other states it is extremely difficult for an
inspector who faithfully enforces the law to retain his position.
The interests which oppose such legislation and object to its
enforcement, are enormously powerful and are thoroughly
organized. The people who procure the enactment of child
labor laws are usually working people unacquainted with the
technical details of the work of inspection; busy in the effort
to earn their own living; not able to keep vigilant watch upon
the work of the inspectors, the creation of whose office they
achieve. Thus the officials are subjected to pressure in one
direction only. If they are idly passive, they may be allowed
to vegetate in office several years. If they are aggressively
faithful to the oath of office, enforcing the law by prosecuting
offenders against its provisions, the children who profit by
this are unable to reward their benefactors; the working
people who obtained the creation of the office have no arts
of bringing pressure to bear effectively to reward faithfulness
in public service by appointed officers; while the offending
employers are amply able to punish what they decry as
officious overactivity, if they do not go farther and charge
persecution and blackmail. For these reasons it may almost
be stated as a general proposition that the more lax the
officer, the longer his term of office; and the history of the
departments of factory inspection, the country over, sadly
substantiates the statement.

It is to be borne in mind in all discussions of child labor
laws that they are drawn in the interest of the weakest ele-

ments in the community. It is the recently immigrated family in the north and the poor whites in the south whose children are found at work. It is, therefore, probable that a rigid exclusion of all work of children under the age of sixteen years, while inflicting hardships upon some families already here and involving, perhaps, some need of assistance for them on the part of the community, would act as a check upon the immigration of the least desirable foreigners—those who come in the hope of exploiting their young children—and would somewhat deter the migration of the mountain whites in the south to the mill towns.

In the century since the movement for child labor legislation began with Sir Robert Peel's act of 1802, effort has been devoted chiefly to placing about the labor of children restrictions based upon age or school requirements, and these have been found unsatisfactory by reason of the defective registration of births and the readiness of parents to perjure themselves. It is the tendency of the present to consider the physical fitness of the child itself; and to establish an objective test of fitness for the occupation which the child enters. This has taken primarily the negative form of prohibiting for all children certain specified industries in Massachusetts and New York; and of prohibiting in general, in Ohio, any occupations dangerous to life and limb or whereby its health is likely to be injured or its morals may be depraved. In Illinois, the idea is tentatively expressed in the authority given the factory inspector to require a certificate of physical fitness for any child who may seem physically unfit for the work at which it is engaged. A law enacted by the legislature of New York provides that a child must be of normal development and is in sound health before receiving the certificate of the local board of health enabling it to begin work.

Effective legislation dealing with child labor involves many differing elements, including the child, the parent, the employer, the officials charged with the duty of enforcing the statutes, and finally the community which enacts laws, provides schools for the children when they are prohibited from working, supports and authorizes officers for the enforcement of the laws, prescribes penalties for their violation, assists dependent families in which the children are below the legal age for work. In the long run, the effectiveness of the law depends upon the conscience of the community as a whole far more than upon the parent and the employer acting together.

With the foregoing reservations and qualifications duly emphasized, the following schedules are believed to outline the substance of the effective legislation which it seems reasonable to try to secure in the present and the immediate future. They deal only with provisions for the child as a child, taking for granted the provision for fire escapes, safeguards for machines, toilet facilities and all those things which the child shares with the adult worker.

An effective child labor law rests primarily upon certain definite prohibitions, among which are the following:

LABOR IS PROHIBITED.

(1) For all children under the age of fourteen years.

(2) For all children under sixteen years of age who do not measure sixty inches and weigh eighty pounds.

(3) For all children under sixteen years of age who cannot read fluently and write legibly simple sentences in the English language.

(4) For all children under the age of sixteen years, between the hours of 7 p. m. and 7 a. m., or longer than eight hours in any twenty four hours.

(5) For all children under the age of sixteen years in occupations designated as dangerous by certain responsible officials.

Of the foregoing prohibitions Number 1 is in force in a number of states so far as work in factories, stores, offices, laundries, etc., is concerned. In New York and Massachusetts recent statutes restrict, though they do not yet prohibit outright, work in the street occupations for children under the age of fourteen years. The movement in this direction gained marked headway during the past winter. Number 2 is not yet embraced in any statute, but is vigorously advocated by many physicians and others practically acquainted with working children. Number 3 has long been the law in New York state, and is of the highest value to the immigrant children so far as it is enforced. Number 4 is in force in Ohio. Number 5 is in force in Massachusetts.

Effective legislation requires that before going to work the child satisfy a competent officer appointed for the purpose, that it

(1) Is fourteen years of age, and

(2) Is in good health, and

(3) Measures at least sixty inches and weighs eighty pounds, and

(4) Is able to read fluently and write legibly simple sentences in the English language, and

(5) Has attended school a full school year during the twelve months next preceding going to work.

Effective child labor legislation requires that the parent

(1) Keep the child in school to the age of fourteen years, and

(2) Take oath as to the exact age of the child before letting it begin to work, and

(3) Substantiate the oath by producing a transcript of the official record of the birth of the child, or the record of its baptism, or some other religious record of the time of the birth of the child, and must

(4) Produce the record of the child's school attendance, signed by the principal of the school which the child last attended.

Effective child labor legislation requires that the employer before letting the child begin to work,

(1) Obtain and place on file ready for official inspection papers showing

(a) The place and date of birth of the child, substantiated by

(b) The oath of the parent, corroborated by

(c) A transcript of the official register of births, or by a transcript of the record of baptism, or other religious record of the birth of the child, and by

(d) The school record signed by the principal of the school which the child last attended, and by

(e) The statement of the officer of the board of education designated for the purpose, that he has approved the papers and examined the child.

(2) After permitting the child to begin to work, the employer is required to produce the foregoing papers on demand of the school attendance officer, the health officer and the factory inspectors.

(3) In case the child cease to work, the employer must restore to the child the papers enumerated above.

(4) During the time that the child is at work, the employer must provide suitable seats, and permit their use so far as the nature of the work allows; and must

(5) Post and keep in a conspicuous place, the hours for beginning work in the morning, and for stopping work in the middle of the day; the hours for resuming work and for stopping at the close of the day; and all work done at any time not specified in such posted notice constitutes a violation of the law. The total number of hours must not exceed eight in any one day or forty eight in one week.

Effective legislation for the protection of children requires that the officials entrusted with the duty of enforcing it

(1) Give their whole time, not less than eight hours of every working day, to the performance of their duties, making night inspections whenever this may be necessary to insure that children are not working during the prohibited hours; and

(2) Treat all employers alike, irrespective of political considerations, of race, religion or power in a community;

(3) Prosecute all violations of the law;

(4) Keep records complete and intelligible enough to facilitate the enactment of legislation suitable to the changing conditions of industry.

The best child labor law is a compulsory education law covering forty weeks of the year and requiring the consecutive attendance of all the children to the age of fourteen years. It is never certain that children are not at work, if they are out of school. In order to keep the children, however, it is not enough to compel attendance—the schools must be modified and adapted to the needs of the recent immigrants in the north and of the poor whites in the south, affording instruction which appeals to the parents as worth having, in lieu of the wages which the children are forbidden to earn, and appears to the children as interesting and attractive. These requirements are so insufficiently met in the great manufacturing centers of the north, that truancy is in several of them, at present, an insoluble problem. No system of child labor legislation can be regarded as effective which does not face and deal with these facts.

The evolution of the vacation school and camp promises strong reinforcement of the child labor laws; which are now seriously weakened by the fact that the long vacation leaves idle upon the streets children whom employers covet by reason of the low price of their labor, while parents, greedy for the children's earnings and anxious lest the children suffer from the life of the streets, eagerly seek work for them. Nothing could be worse for the physique of the school child than being compelled to work during the summer; and the development of the vacation school and vacation camp alone seems to promise a satisfactory solution of the problem of the vacation of the city child of the working class.

Effective child labor legislation imposes upon the community many duties, among which are

(1) Maintaining officials—men and women—school attendance officers, health officers, and factory inspectors, all of whom need

   (a) Salary and traveling expenses,
   (b) Access at all reasonable times to the places where children are employed,
   (c) Power to prosecute all violations of the statutes affecting working children,
   (d) Tenure of office so effectively assured that they need not fear removal from office in consequence of prosecuting powerful offenders;

(2) Maintaining schools in which to educate the children who are prohibited from working;

(3) Maintaining vital statistics, especially birth records, such that the real age of native children may be readily ascertained;

(4) Maintaining provision for the adequate relief of dependent families in which the children are not yet of legal age for beginning work.

More important, however, than the enactment of the foregoing provisions is the maintenance in the community of a persistent, lively interest in the enforcement of the child labor statutes. Without such interest, judges do not enforce penalties against offending parents and employers; inspectors become discouraged and demoralized; or faithful officers are removed because they have no organized backing; while some group of powerful industries clamors that the law is injuring its interest. Well meaning employers grow careless, infractions become the rule, and workingmen form the habit of thinking that laws inimical to their interest are enforced, while those framed in their interest are broken with impunity.

Upon parents there presses incessant poverty, urging them to seek opportunities for wage earning even for the youngest children; and upon the employers presses incessant competition, urging them to reduce the pay roll by all means fair and foul. No law enforces itself; and no officials can enforce a law which depends upon them alone. It is only when they are consciously the agents of the will of the people that they can make the law really protect the children effectively,

TENDENCIES OF FACTORY LEGISLATION AND INSPECTION IN THE UNITED STATES.

BY SARAH S. WHITTELSEY.

[Sarah Scovill Whittelsey, educator and economist; born Paris, France, 1872; graduated from Radcliffe college, 1894; Ph. D. Yale, 1898; instructor in economics at Wellesley college since September, 1902; author of Massachusetts Labor Legislation, etc.]

The introduction of the factory system in American industry acted in this country, as it had in England, to develop certain abnormal conditions of labor that in the end required government interference. Thus in the manufacturing states, chiefly in the north and east, there has come into existence a very considerable body of factory law. The enactment of such regulative statutes is the prerogative of each of the several states acting independently and according to the discretion of its own legislature; in consequence there is great variety in these laws and in their scope—from the comparatively complete codes of Massachusetts and New York to absolutely no regulation whatever.

In all, about half the states have so far passed what may be called a factory act; that is, laws for the regulation, mainly sanitary, of conditions in factories and workshops. These include the New England states generally, New York and the northern central and northwestern states following their legislation. There are almost no factory acts in the south nor in the purely agricultural states of the west, but these statutes are being passed rapidly and moreover, in states where they have already been enacted, are being amended every year.

The most usual statutes are those making provision for proper fire escapes, or against use of explosive oils, etc., for the removal of noxious vapors or dust by fans or other contrivances; requiring guards to be placed about dangerous machinery, belting, elevators, wells, air shafts, crucibles, vats, etc.; providing that doors shall open outward; prohibiting the machinery from being cleaned while in motion; laws to prevent overcrowding and to secure sanitary conditions generally. Building laws also re-enforce these measures.

Antedating such factory acts proper, the same states have very generally passed statutes regulating child labor and forbidding employment to those under a stated age. In eleven states this age limit is fourteen years, in nine over twelve, and in four—New Hampshire, Vermont, Nebraska, and California—ten years; eleven also make educational provision for older children and illiterate minors.

The majority of states have further legislated upon the hours of labor of minors, while fifteen limit the working time of women as well, generally to sixty hours per week, but in Massachusetts to fifty eight hours, in New Jersey to fifty five, and in Wisconsin to forty eight. Eight also provides for time for meals, and five prohibit night work. This limitation of hours for women and children, considered wards of the state, very generally necessitates a similar working day for the adult male laborer in the factory, while it in a measure avoids the serious question of constitutionality that a broader statute could not fail to raise.

There is absolutely no limitation for persons of any age or sex only in Iowa, Kansas, Oregon, Nevada, Washington, Idaho, Montana, Wyoming, Utah, Kentucky, Arkansas, Texas, North Carolina, Alabama, Florida, Mississippi, New Mexico, Arizona, Oklahoma, and the District of Columbia.

Besides these statutes, other laws that must be mentioned, as immediately affecting the interests of factory labor, are those which regulate wage payment and fines, also the employers' liability acts which allow recovery of damages for bodily injury sustained in service. Thirteen states have passed laws regulating the period of payment by individuals and corporations, and nine others stipulate weekly or fortnightly payments by corporations. Only Massachusetts, Indiana and Ohio have attempted to prevent the withholding of wages or the imposition of a fine by factory employers for imperfect work.

Outside of the New England states anti-truck acts, similar to the English statute and stipulating a money payment, have been passed in sixteen states, five of which, however, limit its application to corporations. It may be noted in passing that several of these wage regulating laws have already fallen under the ban of the courts.

Employers' liability statutes supplement the factory acts by affording additional reason for care on the part of the employer in guarding dangerous machinery and otherwise providing for the safety of those in his employ. Twenty two states have legislated upon the fellow servant question, and ten make employers liable for injury caused by defective machinery. Of these, however, only six apply in full to factory labor.

The states that have passed factory acts and regulated hours of labor have usually created one or more factory inspectors, charged with the duty of seeing that the statutes are carried out generally with powers to enter personally or by deputy and to inspect all factories at any time.

The child labor laws are variously entrusted for enforcement to the factory inspectors, school committee or board of education, commissioners of labor, or left to the care of the police.

It may seem, perhaps, that such a sketch fails to show the underlying or directive principle of this legislation, but a detailed study of the laws adds confusion rather than enlightenment. Studnitz considered that he had seized upon the real causal force and summed up the situation in the statement that American labor legislation has been determined by the political and social strength of the laborers demanding it, rather than in accordance with the natural needs and varied conditions of industry within the states.

Allowing this explanation, at least as to the immediate agency, we must nevertheless recognize the fact that other forces are at work and that there are traceable tendencies of a natural growth even when arbitrary human action is so apparent. The most casual acquaintance with the history of labor legislation must convince us that the action of economic law has inevitably necessitated the legal regulation of

Legislation.	U.S.	Ala.	Alaska	Ariz.	Ark.	Cal.	Colo.	Conn.	Del.	D.C.	Fla.	Ga.	Hawaii	Idaho	Ill.	Ind.	Iowa	Kans.	Ky.	La.	Me.	Md.	Mass.	Mich.	Minn.	Miss.	Mo.	Mont.	Nebr.	Nev.	N.H.	N.J.	N.Mex.	N.Y.	N.C.	N.Dak.	Ohio	Okla.	Oreg.	Pa.	P.R.	R.I.	S.C.	S.Dak.	Tenn.	Tex.	Utah	Vt.	Va.	Wash.	W.Va.	Wis.	Wyo.
Defining a working day, in absence of contract, to be—																																																					
Eight hours																																																					
Ten hours																																																					
Defining a day's work on public highways to be—																																																					
Eight hours																																																					
Ten hours																																																					
Restricting the working day on public works to—																																																					
Eight hours																																																					
Nine hours																																																					
Restricting hours of labor of male adult employees of—																																																					
Steam railways																																																					
Street railways																																																					
Mines, smelting and refining works, etc																																																					
Cotton and woolen mills																																																					
Bakeries																																																					
Brickyards																																																					
Pharmacies																																																					
Restricting hours of labor of—																																																					
Women																																																					
Children																																																					
Recognizing, in some form, an eight-hour day																																																					

LEGISLATION RELATING TO RAILWAY LABOR

Legislation.	U.S.	Ala.	Alaska	Ariz.	Ark.	Cal.	Colo.	Conn.	Del.	D.C.	Fla.	Ga.	Hawaii	Idaho	Ill.	Ind.	Iowa	Kans.	Ky.	La.	Me.	Md.	Mass.	Mich.	Minn.	Miss.	Mo.	Mont.	Nebr.	Nev.	N.H.	N.J.	N.Mex.	N.Y.	N.C.	N.Dak.	Ohio	Okla.	Oreg.	Pa.	P.R.	R.I.	S.C.	S.Dak.	Tenn.	Tex.	Utah	Vt.	Va.	Wash.	W.Va.	Wis.	Wyo.
Employment of railway labor:																																																					
Examination of certain employees required	◇										◇											◇		◇											◇		◇													◇		◇	
No telegraphers under 18 years of age				◇	◇	◇								◇		◇			◇			◇		◇	◇		◇			◇				◇	◇		◇		◇						◇		◇			◇		
Hours of labor limited				◇							◇	◇				◇				◇			◇	◇	◇	◇	◇	◇	◇		◇			◇	◇	◇		◇		◇					◇		◇			◇		
No intoxicated persons to take charge of trains, etc.														◇							◇																◇																
Acts of railway employees:																																																					
Penalty for negligence provided	◇						◇				◇				◇		◇		◇			◇					◇		◇		◇		◇		◇		◇		◇	◇		◇			◇				◇		◇		
Abandonment of locomotives, etc., prohibited							◇				◇						◇									◇																												
Obstruction of trains, etc., prohibited							◇				◇				◇		◇																																				
Refusal to move cars of other companies prohibited							◇																														◇																
Rights of railway employees:																																																					
Companies liable for wage debts of contractors	-						◇										◇						◇																											◇			
False charges against employees prohibited				◇																																																	
Mechanical equipment for safety of employees:																																																					
Automatic couplers required	◆													◇				◇					◇		◇		◇							◇														◇		◇			
Power brakes required	◆						◇		◇								◇		◇								◇													◇			◇				◇		◇			
Frogs, switches, and guard rails to be blocked							◇					◇		◇		◇	◇		◇				◇		◇				◇																				◇		◇		
Telltales at bridges or tunnels required						◇																			◇		◇											◇					◇				◇					
Height of bridges or wires over tracks regulated							◇										◇							◇																													
Height of drawbars on cars regulated	◆																																																				
Grab irons on box cars required	◆															◇																																					
Inclosed platforms on street cars required						◇	◇									◇	◇	◇					◇	◇			◇		◇		◇	◇		◇						◇						◇	◇		◇		◇		
Equipment of safety appliances to be reported																																																					
Reporting and investigating accidents:																																																					
Railway companies to report accidents	◆	◇									◇												◇	◇													◇									◇			◇		◇		
Railway commissioners to investigate accidents																																			◇																		

◆Applies to all railways engaged in interstate commerce.

labor; and this really in spite of human opposition and in the face of extreme doctrines of non-interference. Industrial labor unregulated has everywhere developed the same symptoms. Competition between producers tends to encourage all possible reductions of cost, to reduce wages, to increase the use of cheap child labor, to perpetuate long hours of labor, etc., and to range the interests of the employing class against those of the operative class. In the struggle which results from this antagonism the employer has the advantage of position to force his own terms of contract upon the laborer, for he has in his hands an accumulated capital which is equivalent in power to effective organization. Such conditions left to work themselves out have invariably acted to degrade the social status of labor, the heaviest pressure falling upon those who could least resist it. This was the experience of England first, then felt on the continent and in this country in the New England states and other centers of manufacture, and to-day we are becoming aware of like tendencies in the cotton goods industry of the south.

It was almost universally the evils attending child labor that evoked the first acts of regulation. But although abuses were very serious, legal remedies were most timidly applied. Even with the example of the successful issue of the English laws the New England legislatures contented themselves with the passage of most inadequate measures, measures that could hardly have been looked upon as anything more than unenforcible threats. We realize how complete a change of attitude toward this intermeddling legislation has been brought about during the course of the past sixty years when we compare a few of these old laws with those to-day in force. Contrast, for example, the detailed and exacting requirements of the present law concerning child labor in Massachusetts with the older Vermont statute, which is quite typical of the earlier order and merely requires the selectmen of towns to inquire into the treatment of minors employed in manufacturing establishments; and if a minor's education, morals, etc., are unreasonably neglected, or he is treated with improper severity or compelled to labor unreasonable hours, they may, if he has no parent or guardian, discharge him from such employment and bind him out as apprentice with the minor's consent.

Early measures were certainly neither severe in the regulation imposed nor exact in defining the parties held to be responsible. They generally involved a question of volition, making willful transgression alone punishable, and thus unenforcible in the letter, were given into the hands of town officials who had neither the power nor the effective desire to investigate or to bring suit.

Such enactments stood for little more than a public recognition of abuses which they in no wise checked, but the increasing menace of the situation, the threat, not to be scorned, of a future sickly and illiterate labor population, forced the passage of more adequate measures and the resort to a better mechanism of enforcement than that of town officials and the general police. In such reforms Massachusetts took the lead, enacted and repealed several contradictory statutes, and finally by the slow process of continued amendment evolved the present really enforcible law.

We feel in studying the halting stages of this development not only that there was a pardonable ignorance of ways and means in attacking a new problem, but also the influence of a more or less skeptical public opinion concerning this policy of interference, which reflected itself in hedging clauses that weakened and sometimes vitiated what would otherwise have been good measures.

In spite of many drawbacks to advance, however, there was no retrograde motion, but a continued development of strictness and detail in exactions, of clearer definition and placement of responsibility and of more adequate provision for inspection. As these laws gradually demonstrated their practical usefulness and convinced the public of benefit instead of harm, the former attitude of timidity gave place to a decided peremptoriness, the former indiscriminate omnibus ad quos hae litteræ pervenerint, to placed responsibility.

Meantime the way was opened for more wide reaching regulations concerning hours of labor, workroom conditions, etc., and a broader conception of the province of such legislation and of that which might be considered proper subject of legal interference. Whereas the first attempts to protect even little children from conditions that imperiled their health and life were bitterly opposed in England upon grounds of national policy, to-day we find statutes that regulate not only child labor, hours of labor, factory constructions and the use of machinery, but also others that stipulate times and manner of wage payment, and forbid fines in dealings with adult male employees. And this has come to pass in America, where freedom of contract is the constitutional right of every individual citizen.

Our laws have indeed very steadily progressed from measures of simple protection to detailed regulation of conditions, and even to the securing of special benefits to labor.

This broader application of the legal remedy has been accompanied also by marked territorial extension, following the growth and spread of manufactures. Other states have felt the necessity of adopting a labor code and have naturally, in a general way, followed the forms of New England and New York. They range, however, through all stages of incompleteness. A curious phenomenon constantly appears in this imitative legislation. When a state legislature passes a new labor law, or revises an old one, it does not necessarily adopt the latest form nor that which has proved to work most satisfactorily in another state, nor yet a combination of choice clippings from several. A state legislature is generally perfectly content with a law that is about as poor as the average and looks forward most placidly to the inevitable train of amendments that must follow in its wake. By this I do not mean to criticise in the least the enactment of less strict regulations, as a lower age limit or longer hours of labor,which may be proper under given local conditions; but alone the continued repetition of blunders and faults of construction that have elsewhere proved their character and their power to nullify the intent of the law. Fortunately experience proves in the end an effective, if dear, teacher and one of the lessons that it ultimately drives home is that even a state legislature cannot legislate the laws of nature out of the world arena. As Jevons said, The state is the least of the powers that govern us. But as the physician through his knowl-

edge of medicine and physiology, and by his diagnosis of the
symptoms of disease, is able to pit law against law, and to
restore health where he found abnormal conditions; so the
statesman who understands the social order and the tendencies of economic forces is often able to control their action.
In either case, a knowledge of the active agencies is absolutely
necessary to the solution of the problem. The recent organization of bureaus of labor statistics is certainly significant in
this connection. To-day, when a question of labor legislation is presented, there is, in many states, such a qualified
advisory body to whom the whole matter may be referred for
investigation and study, and whose regular duty it is to inquire into and report upon labor and industrial conditions
within the state. This indicates a growing appreciation of
the necessity of accurate information and of the exercise of due
care in passing acts of regulation.

The problem of enforcement of these laws has proved
even more serious than that of their enactment. Labor laws,
however good, cannot enforce themselves. It may appear
to be for the laborer's own interest to report violations and
seek the legal remedy, but the indisputable fact is that he
does not do it. Moreover, not only is the individual laborer
often not in a position to do so safely, but even the labor
union shrinks from the task. The whole history of the movement for the regulation of labor shows the absolute necessity
of efficient inspection, a fact which has unfortunately been
most clearly demonstrated in the general lack of such inspection. In nothing do the states differ more widely than in
their provision for inspection. There are such specifically
differentiated departments as that of Massachusetts or New
York; there are such combinations as that of Connecticut,
where a single inspector with two or three assistants enforces
the factory, workshop and bakeshop acts, while the board
of education is charged with the child labor laws; and there
is dependence alone upon the general police force.

Inspection always lags too far behind legislation and has
given some ground of credit to the often repeated criticism
that this labor legislation is not in fact intended seriously,
but has been entered upon the statute books rather to still

the clamor of agitators for reform than to effect any real change in conditions. It is certain at least that the serious effectiveness of these laws develops in exact proportion with the inspecting power—with the organization, number and qualification of inspectors. If the charge of insincerity, however, had been true, we might expect to find that the better the laws became, the stronger the pressure that would be brought against the development of costly inspection. The legal remedy being given, is it not the privilege of the individual to avail himself of it, rather than the duty of the state to force it upon him? On the contrary, however, the history of inspection runs parallel and in the same direction with that of the legislation just reviewed. The same economic and social forces that were the raison d'être of these laws have quite as distinctly and steadily, though more slowly, created the supplementary machinery of enforcement. The unreliable and haphazard inspection of town officials has passed entirely, superseded by the inspector whose sole duty is inspection, in which duty he is aided by assistants immediately under his own command, or by members of other departments of government. The tendency towards the development of distinct inspection departments is quite unmistakable, though the exact form of their future organization is less easily predicted. There are two toward which present forms lean, one exemplified in Massachusetts, the other in New York.

In Massachusetts the inspectors are organized as a division of police, under the chief of police as chief inspector, exactly as the detective division, for instance. That of New York is a separate and distinct body under a chief appointed by the governor to hold that single office.

The question is therefore raised as to whether organic connection with the police department or separate and distinct autonomy is the more practical and advantageous form. It is conceded that Massachusetts has developed the most efficient corps of inspectors in this country, but this cannot at present be taken as conclusive proof of policy, because Massachusetts was earlier in the field, and because opposing obstacles were hardly so serious as those met in New York. Further, such connection with the police department in Massachusetts seems to have been largely due to local conditions and to have grown out of measures dictated by immediate convenience at the time of the passage of the early child labor laws, rather than a deliberately chosen system of administration. A clipping from the history of the department will make this clear.

"At first the unreliable mechanism of truant officers and local town or city officials was solely depended upon for inspection. Then, under new child labor statutes, a single deputy was in each case detailed by the police department to aid enforcement. The law of 1877, increasing the duties of factory inspection by regulations looking to the safety of employees, provided that members of the state detective department should act as inspectors of factories and public buildings, to report and prosecute violations of this act as well as of other measures relative to the employment of women and minors.

"In 1879, the governor was authorized to appoint two regular inspectors from the police department.

"Better administration was finally secured in 1888 by separating the detective and inspecting forces. . . . With the enactment of stringent steam boiler inspection laws, a new department of boiler inspectors . . . was created."

While in some ways this affiliation with the police has been helpful, there are also drawbacks in the combination under one head of work in fields that are so large and so distinctly marked off from one another not only in object, but most essentially in methods of work. It would seem that a due co-operation between district departments could be made to afford all of the advantages of the closer relationship, while it would insure the whole time and energy of the chief to a task that is quite enough to occupy his entire attention. Indeed, with the increasing number and detail of regulations, the many technicalities that arise in the application of labor laws and the rapid growth of the factory system of industry, another specialist will soon be demanded to fill such an office. The necessary increase in numbers alone must make the police connection awkward.

In framing many of these laws, for example the factory acts, much has necessarily been left to the discretion of inspectors in the decision of what is adequate provision. Especially where appliances not contemplated in the ordinary law are offered, very careful judgment is called for. Such powers cannot be entrusted to untrained and inexperienced persons, however well intentioned, nor is the training of police duty any sufficient preparation. It would not be considerd appropriate to appoint a policeman inspector of stationary steam boilers or examiner of engineers, yet under present factory laws, technical knowledge of industrial processes, machinery, etc., is sometimes equally demanded. In Massachusetts the original method of detailing police as inspectors when occasion demanded, or even permanently installing them in these positions, has been abandoned for the stricter and more adequate tests of civil service examinations open to all applicants. And again her example indicates a general trend.

The tendency in inspection already is, and in the future must be more markedly, toward the growth of a distinct and specialized department, in which the chief and his assistants are trained for their work. Such a department, while it would not stand in the relationship which some at present hold to the police, would come into closer touch with other departments, as the board of education and bureau of labor.

The influence of state boundary lines upon the course of legislation in this country is an interesting question, and one upon which entirely diverse opinions are held. Some go so far as to claim that there never can be really successful legislation so long as such boundaries hold; that if a good labor law is passed in one state and enforced there, the benefit that may result to the few operatives is balanced by the restriction which it puts upon the producer and the consequent discrimination against capital in that state as compared with its neighbors. Capital therefore seeks investment in those sister states instead of in the law trammeled one, thus reacting against the interests of the labor market there; while states that so profit in their freedom are the more loath to give over their advantage by enacting similar measures. Thus legislation in one state becomes at once detrimental to its own industrial interests, and a check upon legislation elsewhere. Loud protests of this tenor were heard, for example, in Massachusetts a few years ago, when at a time of business depression the cotton mills suffered from the competition of southern rivals. A somewhat extended study of the situation at that crisis, however, failed to show that these detrimental consequences had followed in actual life, or that the stress felt by the mills could have been removed by a suspension of the laws complained of.

On the other hand, when we begin to reckon with the difficulties that must be encountered in any attempt to legislate upon labor conditions in this country treated as a whole (even disregarding entirely the present constitutional impediment), we find arguments showing that local self government has probably furthered the development of labor legislation. In the first place, it is much more difficult to persuade a body with such wide jurisdiction to pass what must often be experimental measures and may endanger national interests. Suppose, however, that this legislation was undertaken, it would be well nigh impossible to frame a measure that would apply with justice throughout and in communities where industrial occupations differ entirely in kind, or, if of like order, range through many stages of development. It would mean that such legislation must conform to a very low margin of production in order to avoid injury to states where conditions are backward, and that would leave unregulated much that has clearly shown need of regulation in states where there is higher organization of industry. Would it not, in fact, be absolutely necessary to mark out territorial divisions that might not of course follow state boundaries, but would not in the end differ essentially from them in character? Again, such divisions mapped, what an impossible labor is put upon the central body if it would legislate wisely for the several sections! Would it not be necessary at least to appoint some advisory body to study the local needs of each section and to report recommending appropriate measures? In the end, what would we have in the least better than the present system?

LEGISLATION RELATING TO FACTORIES AND WORKSHOPS, MANUFACTURING ESTABLISHMENTS, ETC.

Legislation.	U.S.	Ala.	Alaska	Ariz.	Ark.	Cal.	Colo.	Conn.	Del.	D.C.	Fla.	Ga.	Hawaii	Idaho	Ill.	Ind.	Iowa	Kans.	Ky.	La.	Me.	Md.	Mass.	Mich.	Minn.	Miss.	Mo.	Mont.	Nebr.	Nev.	N.H.	N.J.	N.Mex.	N.Y.	N.C.	N.Dak.	Ohio	Okla.	Oreg.	Pa.	P.R.	R.I.	S.C.	S.Dak.	Tenn.	Tex.	Utah	Vt.	Va.	Wash.	W.Va.	Wis.	Wyo.
Regulation of labor in—																																																					
Factories and workshops																																																					
Mercantile establishments																																																					
Sweat shops																																																					
Bakeries																																																					
Laundries																																																					
Building construction work																																																					
Protection of health of employees:																																																					
Rooms to be properly ventilated																																																					
Rooms to be sufficiently lighted																																																					
Rooms to be sufficiently heated																																																					
Walls to be lime-washed or painted																																																					
Overcrowding prohibited																																																					
Exhaust fans, blowers, etc., required																																																					
Seats for females required																																																					
Separate toilet facilities for each sex required																																																					
Prevention of accidents:																																																					
Cleaning machinery by women or children prohibited																																																					
Guards to be placed on machinery																																																					
Mechanical belt and gearing shifters required																																																					
Means of communication with engine room required																																																					
Precautions required in handling explosives																																																					
Guards to be placed on elevators and hoistways																																																					
Stairs to have hand rails																																																					
Doors to swing outward and remain unlocked																																																					
Fire escapes to be provided																																																					
Working time of women:																																																					
Hours of labor limited																																																					
Night work prohibited or restricted																																																					
Working time of children:																																																					
Hours of labor limited																																																					
Night work prohibited or restricted																																																					
Inspection of establishments:																																																					
Inspection service provided for																																																					
Accidents to be reported																																																					

◆ Provision made for enforcement of laws by factory inspectors or health officers.

◆ No provision made for enforcement of laws by factory inspectors or health officers.

Within a single state the labor interest is united, the pros and cons of the situation can be more easily investigated, effects more easily watched and even more accurately predicted. Jevons might indeed have considered it a well fitted laboratory for his scientific experimentation in legislation. The success of a local experiment acts often as an incentive to labor elsewhere to demand like privileges, and as against the argument of an insignificant tax upon production, the political power of the labor party has very generally won the day. The second state feels itself at no greater disadvantage than that which took the initiative in the movement, and may easily take the precaution of passing restrictions that are a trifle under those of its neighbor.

This discussion, however, leaves us still face to face with a confusion of local regulations, among which there is total lack of any uniformity. The situation has for some time attracted public comment, and there is a growing desire for uniformity, especially in the protection of child labor and in the curtailment of the hours of labor, which are the regulations that particularly affect the interests of capitalists. Quixotic attempts to force an amendment of the constitution, and to secure the passage of a national eight hour day law, have been chronicled in the movement, which nevertheless, with more moderate aims, has steadily gathered strength. At last, under the industrial commission of 1898, the problem of uniform legislation has been clearly recognized and carefully studied, "in order," the act reads, "to harmonize conflicting interests and to be equitable to the laborer, the employer, the producer and the consumer." Empowered to report with recommendations either directly to congress or to the several state legislatures, the commission addressed itself in this matter of domestic law to the state legislatures. The report submitted is of such interest and importance that I quote in full its recommendations so far as they apply to factory labor:

"Perhaps the subject of greatest public interest to-day is that of the regulation of the hours of labor permitted in industrial occupations, and especially in factories. . . . Obviously, congress has no power, without a constitutional amendment, to legislate upon this subject. The commission

are of the opinion that a uniform law upon this subject may
wisely be recommended for adoption by all the states. We
believe that such legislation cannot, under the federal and
state constitutions, be recommended as to persons, male or
female, above the age of twenty one, except, of course, in
some special industries, where employment for too many
hours becomes positively a menace to the health, safety, or
well being of the community; but minors, not yet clothed with
all the rights of citizens, are peculiarly the subject of state
protection, and still more so, young children.

"The commission are of the opinion, therefore, that a
simple statute ought to be enacted by all the states, to regulate the length of the working day for young persons in factories (meaning by young persons, those between the age of
majority and fourteen); and in view of the entire absence of
protection now accorded by the laws of many states to children of tender years, we think that employment in any capacity or for any time, under the age of fourteen, should be prohibited. The question of shops and mercantile establishments generally appears even more subject to local conditions
than that of factories; therefore, the commission see no need
for even recommending to the states any uniform legislation
upon this subject. But child labor should be universally protected by educational restrictions, providing in substance
that no child may be employed in either factories, shops, or
in stores in large cities, who cannot read and write, and except
during vacation, unless he has attended school for at least
twelve weeks in each year."

These are certainly conservative recommendations and
illustrate again the difficulty of finding any common ground
of action even in the fundamental requirements of health and
education. The exception made with reference to shops and
mercantile establishments upon the ground of local differences
in conditions is interesting. So much evidence has been
brought of abuse of child labor in the mercantile houses of
many large cities, especially in respect to these two matters
of overwork through long hours and of interference with common school education (above recognized) that several states
have voluntarily extended provisions of the factory laws con-

cerning minors to cover such establishments. These conditions appear to reproduce themselves with remarkable similarity in various locations, and it is not altogether clear what local conditions could intervene to make the universal application of the measure proposed for factories undesirable.

Notwithstanding all moderation and the exceptions allowed, two of the commissioners still recorded themselves as considering it unjust and impracticable to attempt any uniform laws regulating labor in all the states, and a third concurring with these adds that the conditions to be dealt with will work themselves out better under local self government than under any ironclad rule adopted by or suggested from a central power.

The protesters are from the southern states and their protest seems peculiarly pertinent at this time, when the prevailing conditions of child labor in these states are attracting so much attention. Not to digress into a discussion that would lead us too far afield, let it suffice to sum up the evident facts of the situation in a single paragraph.

Whatever their previous condition of freedom, barbarism or poverty, there are to-day, in the cotton mills of the south, large numbers of little children, some under ten years of age, who can be and are employed sometimes eleven and more hours a day, sometimes eleven hours of the night. Indeed, conditions parallel the times of Shaftesbury in England! Attempts to pass bills that can hardly be deemed extravagant in the protection demanded, and even compulsory education measures, have been opposed and frustrated. The reasons given for such resistance of legal interference may be summarized about as follows, at least in Alabama, which has been the field of a recent encounter: That the bill presented by the Alabama Child Labor committee is outside interference and only the entering wedge; that Georgia (facing the more difficult task) in having double the number of spindles, should act first; that against the expressed desires of mill officers, parents insist upon the employment of their children or take their families to other mills where no objection is made (and this the law would make impossible); that the prodigiously early development of this particular class of southern children, together with the length and heat of the day, which are prime factors respecting the hours that may be appropriated to labor, make it inadvisable to limit the hours of labor of children to ten out of a possible twenty four, or to require that they should sleep and not work at night. We cannot say that the movement for uniform legislation or even for labor legislation under local self government is unopposed.

The recommendations of the commission also include the following:

"Further regulations, especially in the line of bringing states which now have no factory acts up to a higher standard, is earnestly recommended.

"In states which have many factories the well known factory act of Massachusetts or New York, based upon the English act which served as a model to all such, is recommended for adoption.

"The sweatshop law also, which is now practically identical in the important states of New York, Massachusetts, Pennsylvania and Ohio, is recommended for general adoption.

"A simple and liberal law regulating the payment of labor should be adopted in all the states, providing that laborers shall be paid for all labor performed in cash or cash orders, without discount, not in goods or due bills, and that no compulsion, direct or indirect, shall be used to make them purchase supplies at any particular store."

The report refers also to other statutes which reinforce certain common law doctrines, such as those concerning intimidation, strikes, boycotts and blacklisting, to those protecting the political rights and legal rights in suit of labor, and to the recognition accorded to trade unions in provisions for incorporation and protection of labels, making however no special recommendation concerning them to the states.

We see, therefore, that beyond the elementary regulation of child labor and hours of labor for minors, the commission would have the states establish a standard of good sanitation and of safe conditions in factories everywhere, and above this, especially suggests a scientific and well tested law for adoption in states having large manufactures. The restric-

LEGISLATION RELATING TO THE EXAMINATION AND LICENSING OF CERTAIN EMPLOYES

Legislation.	U.S.	Ala.	Alaska	Ariz.	Ark.	Cal.	Colo.	Conn.	Del.	D.C.	Fla.	Ga.	Hawaii	Idaho	Ill.	Ind.	Iowa	Kans.	Ky.	La.	Me.	Md.	Mass.	Mich.	Minn.	Miss.	Mo.	Mont.	Nebr.	Nev.	N.H.	N.J.	N.Mex.	N.Y.	N.C.	N.Dak.	Ohio	Okla.	Oreg.	Pa.	P.R.	R.I.	S.C.	S.Dak.	Tenn.	Tex.	Utah.	Vt.	Va.	Wash.	W.Va.	Wis.	Wyo.
Requiring examination and license for—																																																						
Barbers									◇										◇						◇									◇		◇			◇			◇								◇			◇
Horseshoers		◇																				◇			◇			◇												◇					◇		◇						◇
Mine managers and other mine employees						◇										◇	◇											◇									◇			◇										◇			
Operators of elevators																															◇																						
Plumbers							◇															◇			◇															◇							◇						
Railroad employees																◇	◇									◇																											
Stationary firemen		◇																							◇															◇													
Steam engineers		◇									◇						◇						◇					◇						◇		◇				◇													
Street railway employees											◇												◇		◇			◇						◇						◇													◇
Telegraph operators on railroads												◇																																									

LEGISLATION RELATING TO THE PAYMENT OF WAGES

Legislation.	U.S.	Ala.	Alaska	Ariz.	Ark.	Cal.	Colo.	Conn.	Del.	D.C.	Fla.	Ga.	Hawaii	Idaho.	Ill.	Ind.	Iowa.	Kans.	Ky.	La.	Me.	Md.	Mass.	Mich.	Minn.	Miss.	Mo.	Mont.	Nebr.	Nev.	N.H.	N.J.	N.Mex.	N.Y.	N.C.	N.Dak.	Ohio.	Okla.	Oreg.	Pa.	P.R.	R.I.	S.C.	S.Dak.	Tenn.	Tex.	Utah.	Vt.	Va.	Wash.	W.Va.	Wis.	Wyo.
Requiring wages to be paid in money	⊠	⊠		⊠			⊠							⊠		⊠	⊠	⊠	⊠	⊠		⊠	⊠	⊠	⊠		⊠	⊠			⊠			⊠		⊠	⊠		⊠	⊠		⊠	⊠		⊠		⊠		⊠	⊠	⊠	⊠	⊠
Prohibiting deduction from wages for fines, etc.		⊠					⊠									⊠		⊠		⊠			⊠	⊠	⊠			⊠			⊠			◇						⊠											⊠	⊠	
Requiring wages to be paid weekly or fortnightly								⊠									⊠		⊠			⊠	⊠	⊠			⊠				⊠	⊠		⊠						⊠		⊠									⊠	⊠	
Prohibiting payment of wages in barrooms																																																					
Prohibiting coercion to purchase at company stores		⊠																	⊠	⊠																														⊠	⊠	
Exempting wages from attachment, etc		⊠				◇																	⊠		⊠									◇								◇										⊠	
Preferring wages in assignments, executions, etc.		⊠		⊠			⊠							⊠		⊠	⊠	⊠	⊠	⊠		⊠	⊠	⊠	⊠			⊠						⊠		⊠				⊠			⊠							⊠	⊠	⊠	

tion of hours is always looked upon chiefly as a health measure, but it is certain that the general bodily vigor of the worker has been more markedly affected by modern improvements in ventilation, lighting, and sanitation than by any of the shorter day statutes. Factory acts assist materially in forcing this advance and have received a due recognition of their usefulness. In recommending the universal passage of a sweat shop act, the commission endorses the old saying, that an ounce of prevention is worth a pound of cure. As a matter of fact, such laws have been passed, and in an incredibly short time (since 1892, when New York passed the first of this series), in those states in which the evil is important. Attempts to extirpate the evil in these states threaten to drive it into neighboring sections. Connecticut, for example, lying between Massachusetts and New York, in both of which quarters the anti-sweatshop war is being vigorously pushed, has enacted a similar statute simply as a protective measure.

It is clear that the ultimate effect of uniform labor legislation will not be one law applying throughout the length and breadth of this great land, but rather a graded system. It will determine a minimum standard of regulations, a basal plane of competition for American industry. Above this it will still be necessary for the local government in many places to impose stricter requirements where there is complexity of organization, but in that which is fundamentally essential to the common well being of the community there will be one limit approved for all that may not be transgressed.

The suggestion made in the industrial commission's report as to how this standard may be determined is especially well considered:

"In conclusion the commission would recommend the establishment by all the states of labor bureaus or commissioners, who shall, besides their local duties as now defined, be charged with that of exchanging their statistics and reports, and of convening at least once in a year in national conference for general consultation, which national conference shall have power to submit directly to congress its recommendations for such federal legislation as a majority of the state commissioners may deem advisable, and shall also submit to all the states, through the commissioners of each separate state, their recommendations for such uniform state statutes upon labor subjects as may seem wise and desirable."

If we rightly interpreted the action of local governments in establishing these bureaus of labor, as a step towards more scientific legislation in those states, surely this plan of a national conference of state commissioners of labor stands for a still more important extension of the scientific method in questions of labor legislation. It also illustrates a tendency that is becoming more and more evident, namely, the fuller reliance that is being placed upon intelligence as a social regulator and publicity for controlling industry and commerce. Make known the actual conditions that prevail, point out the appropriate remedy, and the weight of an informed public opinion will go far to force reform whether through an act of legislation or through the influence which may be exerted by consumers upon producers. Indeed the battle cry of the day is, Give us but an enlightened public opinion and our fight is three quarters won.

The suggestion of regulating business relations through the pressure of public sentiment has been seized upon with almost too great avidity by some who would apply it as the immediate and sufficient solution of all labor difficulties and as an argument against the enactment of any statutory regulations whatever. Such a proposition appears, however, of doubtful value at present under the conditions of unenlightenment that unfortunately prevail, and it may be feared, does not proceed from the best friends of labor.

Recurring to this fact of opposition, already earlier noted, it has been questioned whether this counter movement does not offer a real menace to the future growth of the labor laws, and indeed to the continued existence of the present body of legislation. In a number of instances where labor laws have been brought to the test of a court decision they have been pronounced unconstitutional and annulled upon the ground that they contravene freedom of contract, are class legislation, and so forth. This has been the fate of statutes regulating the hours of labor for women over twenty one years of age in Nebraska, California, and Illinois; of weekly payment laws in Pennsylvania, Illinois, Missouri, West Virginia, and Indiana; of anti-truck acts in Pennsylvania, Ohio, Illinois, and West Virginia; and of those prohibiting company stores or coercion of purchase in Pennsylvania, Illinois, and Tennessee.

In Massachusetts, on the contrary, the regulation of hours was sustained as a health or police regulation. Also at the time when the bill for the extension of the act covering weekly payments was before the legislature the justices returned as their opinion to the house of representatives that such an act was within the constitutional power of the general court to pass. It is also worthy of notice, that in spite of the decision by the Supreme court of Nebraska in 1894, a new law defining hours of labor for women was passed in 1899, and to-day applies not only in factories, but in restaurants and hotels as well. Again, in the report just reviewed, the commissioners have recommended the general enactment of an anti-truck and freedom of purchase act in spite of the decisions of Pennsylvania, Illinois, and Tennessee courts.

Verdicts of unconstitutionality have therefore hardly affected more than the very border of the factory laws; the regulation of child labor, of workroom conditions, of hours of labor for minors, have never been questioned. It hardly seems likely that any of these laws will ever be put to the court test at all. Both in England and in this country, they have proven generally beneficial to public interest, they have been pretty cheerfully accepted and obeyed; they have gained public approval; they have the political support of a large labor party. Perhaps the apparently adverse action of the courts ought to be looked upon as a healthfully conservative influence against possible evil results of hasty and ill considered legislation or attempts to interpose legislation where the object could be better obtained by the effective organization of labor and should be left to the initiative of the unions.

Factory legislation has been inevitably necessitated by the action of economic and social forces, and may, in fact, be regarded as a natural phenomenon accompanying the growth of the factory system of manufacture. It has developed against the opposition of extreme doctrines of free contract, and having demonstrated itself in the facts of actual life has also created a new theory of the relation of the state to labor and industry.

The state may determine the plane of competition; it may equalize the conditions of contract as between employer and employee; it may intervene to protect the standard of living of the workers. The only limits that theory places upon these lines of interference are consideration of the general good.

In the historical development of factory laws, well marked tendencies are traceable. The early attitude of timidity has given place to that of peremptory command. Progress has been steadily toward increased severity in the regulations imposed, increased exactness in detail and definition, towards distinctly placed responsibility and towards more adequate inspection.

The expansion of industry in this country has of course been accompanied by a like territorial extension of the labor laws. Accomplished through the independent action of the several state legislatures, the result has been an unfortunate confusion of unrelated and nonuniform measures. One of the recent and most important tendencies of this legislation is the movement for greater uniformity, made especially prominent by the attention given to it as a part of the study of the industrial commission. It indeed seems probable that these efforts will eventually issue in the determination of a minimum standard of labor legislation for the country as a whole, above which common basis the states will rise in grade according to the development of industrial organization and consequent increase of regulation demanded. This is necessarily a matter of voluntary conformity on the part of the separate state legislatures and therefore a fulfillment to be awaited with all patience.

CO-OPERATION OF LABOR AND CAPITAL.

BY WILLIAM H. PFAHLER.

[William H. Pfahler, president of the National Association of Iron Founders; born Columbia, Pa.; educated in the public schools and at the Millersville state normal school; entered the iron manufacturing business; served four years as private and officer in the civil war; has always been active in economic movements, especially those for the improvement of the relations between employers and employees, and is a member of the executive committee of the National Civic Federation.]

There is no subject of greater general importance before the world to-day, none more simple in its character, and yet none so handicapped by fanaticism, as that of the relation of employer and employee.

Remove the curtain between the two real parties to the controversy, which is often held by men of selfish purpose on both sides, and you behold two simple factors, the wage payer and the wage earner, each dependent upon the other and both serving the same master, the great consuming public, of which they are also equal and very important parts.

The wage payer, being directly in contact with the purchasing consumer, claims that he must have a result in production equal in every way to the wages paid, while the wage earner contends that he must have a wage equivalent to his contribution in time, energy, and skill, to the article produced.

Every visible article of use, for food, clothing, or shelter, of necessity, luxury, or culture, represents three component parts, and the production of each such article depends upon the proper combining of these parts, which are: 1. Raw material. 2. Capital. 3. Labor.

Raw material, supplied by nature, is controlled only by the law of supply and demand, except when by legislation the natural law is for a time superseded, and it then becomes a matter of political action, in which the entire community, except the few who are directly interested in profit, join to abolish the corrupt legislation and restore the natural condition. Raw material, is, therefore, the basis of cost in determining the price of every product to the public.

Labor, whether skilled or unskilled, engaged in the reduction of the raw material to the finished product, is also dependent upon the law of supply and demand to fix its value or wage; and any effort to change this value brings the wage earner in direct conflict with the consumer, through his representative, the employer, whose duty it is to know, and who does know, what proportion of the entire cost of any article can be distributed in wage so as to retain the value of the article at a price not in excess of the ability of the consumer to purchase, and yet within limits which will prevent a more favored nation or district from furnishing the same article in competition, and thereby cause idleness for the wage earner and loss to the employer.

Capital represents plant, machinery, transportation, interest, and all the factors known as unproductive, and yet absolutely essential for the combination of material and labor. Capital is usually, though not always, the owner of material and the direct employer of labor, and therefore must stand for the silent partner in the combination. What is so frequently called a war between capital and labor is simply an effort on the part of the wage earner and wage payer to determine what part of the product of labor, as distinct from material, is represented in the price to the public, and after deducting the proper charge for plant, etc., how the balance, which is profit, shall be divided between the employer and the employee—or wage payer and wage earner.

The growth of prosperity in this country has always been in ratio to increased production, and until a recent period such increased production has been the direct result of the co-operation of the wage earner and the wage payer. In the beginning of our commercial history it was only necessary for one man to exchange the product of his own industry for that of other men to obtain the necessities of life, and then the results of labor were not measured by a unit of value or wage, but by the amount of energy expended in production.

When the rapid growth of the country required greater productiveness, and the enlargement of territory made necessary a change in the distribution of the products of labor, the factory system was introduced, whereby capital, or unproductive labor, was joined with productive labor to accomplish greater results than had heretofore been attained by individual labor.

This brought with it the employment of a number of wage earners under the direction of one or more employers, or wage payers, and made it necessary to determine the relation of one to the other, or rather the share each should have in the division of profits.

All conflicts which have ever arisen between men upon any subject, whether social, political, or religious, have been based, not upon difference in conditions really existing, but upon difference of opinion as to the relation which existed between the parties to the conflict; and strife, to a greater or less extent, has been brought into use to determine such position.

An excess of power on one side or the other succeeded in establishing for a time the opinion of the victor, but never removed the cause of dispute; and so the organization of wage earners into associations or unions enabled them to establish from time to time, by power which they never hesitated to exercise, such wages and conditions as in their opinion were fair to them, but not always in accord with the condition of supply and demand.

From their struggle arose the continual change of wages in ratio to the power of either party, the employer lowering wages when by reason of limited demand he could limit production, and the employee raising wages when his services were in sufficient demand to enable him to do so.

The union was able in many cases—I may say in all cases—to enforce its demands because of the combined power it could exercise against the individual employer, and, as is usual in such cases, soon began to exercise a power which was unnatural and unwarranted. The result of this was the necessity of forming an organized opposition to their force by creating an opposing force in the organization of the employer class, and this brings me to the history of two organizations of this character with which I have been closely identified during the past fifteen years, and which have been successful in establishing a new basis of relation between the employer and employee.

Fifteen years ago the industry in which I am engaged was in perpetual conflict, involving three or four strikes or lockouts every year, causing great loss in time and money to employer and employee. Unable longer to endure the strain, an association was formed of about fifty of the leading firms engaged in the business, for the sole purpose of defending the members against the unjust demands of their employees. It was decided to create a large fund for the purpose of carrying on a warfare against the union to which our men belonged. Within a year from the organization a strike occurred which resulted in every member of the defence association closing his shop, and the consequent defeat of the union. A second strike occurred in which, after many weeks of severe struggle, the union was again defeated by the united action of the defence association. In the third year of its existence, the defence association was invited by the officers of the union to appoint a committee to meet a similar committee from their organization for the purpose of discussing some plan by which strikes and lockouts could be avoided. Frequent meetings were held; many attempts at forming a plan were abandoned, until finally it was agreed that all questions of difference between any employer, member of our association, and his employee, member of the union, should be referred to a committee of three from each association for arbitration and that, pending such action, no strike or lockout should occur. As a result of this agreement, during the past ten years no strike has ocurred in this industry, and every point of difference has been amicably adjusted by conference. Each year a general conference is held, at which the wages are fixed for the ensuing year, and such other changes as may be of mutual advantage are adopted.

It is true that at first the members of local unions, led by some wild agitator, would make a demand upon their employer, and, failing to enforce the demand, would quit work; but the national officers of the union would require them to return to work at once and await the usual and proper means of adjustment.

The arbitration board is composed of an even number of men because then an agreement when reached becomes unanimous, and a failure to agree (although no such failure has ever occurred) will not result in the enforcing of the opinion of either side by the decision of a third party. We prefer rather to adjourn from time to time, under the agreement to have no strike or lockout, and let time and reason aid in finding some common ground upon which we can agree. These agreements made from time to time have been signed for the members of the union by their officers, and it gives me the highest pleasure, as a tribute to human nature, and in reply to those who deny the responsibility on the part of workingmen to a contract, to say that in the history of our organization no agreement has ever been violated in any manner.

The success of this organization led to the formation of a larger and more powerful one, known as the National Founders' association, of which I had the honor to be the first president. It required a long time to convince many of the larger employers of men that the formation of such an association was not dangerous, because in the negotiations it would be a virtual recognition of the union; but we at last succeeded in organizing with about fifty members.

Within six months the president of the union in which most of our men are employed addressed a letter to our body requesting a conference to devise a plan for conducting negotiations on lines similar to those of the stove defence association. This conference resulted in what has ever since been known as the New York agreement, which is as follows:

Whereas, The past experience of the members of the National Founders' association and the Iron Molders' union of North America justifies them in the opinion that any arrangement entered into that will conduce to greater harmony of their relations as employers and employees will be to their mutual advantage; therefore,

Resolved, That this committee of conference indorse the principle of arbitration in the settlement of trade disputes, and recommend the same for adoption by the members of the National Founders' association and the Iron Molders' union of North America on the following lines:

That, in the event of a dispute arising between members of the respective organizations, a reasonable effort shall be made by the parties directly at interest to effect a satisfactory adjustment of the difficulty, failing to do which either party shall have the right to ask its reference to a committee of arbitration, which shall consist of the presidents of the National Founders' association and the Iron Molders' union of North America or their representatives, and two other representatives from each association appointed by the respective presidents.

The finding of this committee of arbitration, by a majority vote, shall be considered final so far as the future action of the respective organizations is concerned.

Pending adjudication by this committee of arbitration there shall be no cessation of work at the instance of either party to the dispute.

The committee of arbitration shall meet within two weeks after reference of the dispute to them.

This agreement to go into effect Monday, March 4, 1901.

Occurring at the time when we were passing from extreme depression to a revival of business activity, when there was an enormous demand for good workmen, when wages were moving upward and when strikes were of almost daily occurrence in every industry, this agreement was observed in letter and in spirit, and, as a result, both employer and employee enjoyed industrial peace and prosperity.

Because of a failure to agree on certain demands made by the union, which would have resulted in reduction of production, a strike was commenced in the city of Cleveland by the union, which lasted over seven months and cost upward of a million dollars, but at the end resulted in a conference lasting some days, in which both parties to the conference agreed to prevent a recurrence of warfare and united in an agreement which marked greater progress in the labor situation than had ever been reached before.

The National Founders' association now numbers nearly 500 members, having a combined capital of over $400,000,000, and employing nearly 30,000 molders and more than 100,000 workingmen in other departments, and is daily adding to the number because the manufacturer has seen that it is the best— in fact, the only—method of dealing with organized labor.

On the other hand, the labor organization, recognizing the strength and fair dealing of the employers' association, is from time to time so modifying its plans and methods as to make it possible to work in harmony with the employer, and together secure results for both that have heretofore been impossible.

This brief history enables me to declare not only as a conviction, but as an axiom, that there is a common ground upon which the wage earner and the wage payer can safely unite to form a community of interest in the great industrial problem, and that negotiation for the adjustment of their several interests can be conducted without strife, to the mutual advantage of both.

The history of all associations of manufacturers formed for the purpose of establishing and maintaining just and fair business relations between their employees and themselves, proves beyond doubt that better results can be obtained in this way than in any other.

In England, several years ago, the great strike of engineers involving 75,000 men, and extending over a period of six months, was finally settled by conference between the representatives of the associated employers and representatives of the several unions, and resulted in an agreement which established harmonious relations between both parties, and has ever since prevented strikes or lockouts.

In Belgium, in 1899, a lockout, probably the greatest which has ever occurred, involving almost every industry, shutting out more than 50,000 men, and extending over a period of seven months, was only settled after the employers discovered to their own great advantage that matters can be arranged more satisfactorily when the representatives of organized capital confer with the representatives of organized labor. The result of their conference was the removal of all obnoxious demands and the adjustment of wages and conditions of labor upon an equitable basis, embodied in an agreement now in force and held equally binding on employer and employee, the result of which was, in England as in the examples cited in this country, the elimination of strikes and lockouts.

A review in detail of the results accomplished by the methods of conference and conciliation, in these cases referred to, would require more space than can be used in this paper, but warrants the following conclusions:

First. That labor organizations are the natural result of a great movement in the business world which is replacing costly competition with profitable co-operation, and are formed primarily for the protection of their members, upon the theory that collective bargaining for the sale of their labor is more profitable than individual contract.

Second. The accomplishment of their object requires labor organizations to secure the membership of the largest number of persons employed in any kindred trade, and (because voluntary advancement of wages rarely or never occurs) to demand a change in wages and betterment in conditions whenever it appears that the need for their labor is in excess of the supply, and therefore warrants such demand. Labor organizations are necessary also to resist collectively any movement on the part of the employer which would result in injury to the workingman.

Third. Whenever labor organizations by reason of false leaders have made unfair demands or established conditions which were unfair to the employer, it has been because of the use of collective force against the individual employer, and this has been defeated whenever the employers have organized similar associations for their own defence.

Fourth. That strikes for advance in wages and improvement of condition—occurring, as they do, during a period of prosperity—usually succeed, while strikes for recognition of the union, usurpation of the rights of the employer or against the reduction of wages almost invariably fail in their purpose.

Assuming that the employer is governed by honesty of purpose in dealing with labor, and that the employee is equally honest in his desire to give worth for wages, the organization of both parties must slowly but surely remove force as the means of securing results, and cause a resort to reason and conciliation as the best means to accomplish the greatest value for both.

There are two great obstacles which prevent the substitution of these means of settling the labor question at present, and which must be first removed before better conditions can be realized.

On the part of the employer there is the refusal (usually sentimental) to recognize the union, and the determination to destroy it. He forgets that his effort to destroy the union presupposes his recognition of it, else he would be fighting a nightmare, while the recognition in fact would enable him to learn its scope, purposes, and plans, and by co-operation secure a valuable ally instead of an unreasonable enemy.

In the use of the word union, I desire always to be understood to refer to such organizations of workingmen as are conducted along reasonable lines and are led by representatives worthy of the best element composing the membership, who formulate their demands in harmony with known business conditions and control their movements within the lines of law and order, because when they assume any other condition they are simply mobs, and deserve only the condemnation of every worthy citizen.

The obstacle on the part of labor is the effort to establish the idea that recognition of the union implies more than the agreement to make collective bargains between employer and employee at such times as a change in business conditions demands or permits, or to insist that it conveys the right to enforce rules and methods in the conduct of the business without the consent or co-operation of the employer.

To remove these obstacles and establish a condition of harmony and mutual prosperity, the employer must not forget that wage earners have formed powerful associations for the purpose of advancing and protecting their interests, and have delegated their individual power to, and placed their confidence in, the officers of their unions.

That these officers are in many cases far above the average of their craftsmen, and their highest ambition is to better the condition of their fellow workmen.

That the aggressive methods of labor unions are very frequently caused by the determination of the employer to destroy them, without giving them a chance to be heard in their own defence.

That in the conduct of business involving large investment for plant, and the employment of a large number of men, able management is required to secure the best results from machinery and power, but good government is necessary to secure the highest efficiency of men, and the best government is that which is founded on the consent of the governed.

That responsibility for the performance of such an agreement as should exist between employer and employee cannot be measured by legal or financial standard, but can be safely based on individual integrity, and in this I have found that a very large majority of the workingmen in this country hold an agreement which is made for them by the officers of their union as binding them in every sense of the word.

That the organization of associations of employers in kindred branches or industry tends to uniformity in method of regulating the employment of men, and at the same time affords protection against the demands which may be unfair or the strife which may be instigated by unwise leaders of organized labor.

The employee must not forget:

That the right to be a union man implies also the right to be a nonunion man.

That no honest employer can discriminate between the men in his employ, or recognize the right of any body of men to determine whom he shall employ.

That the effort to establish a minimum rate of wage, if based upon the lowest standard of efficiency, destroys the earning power of the more competent workman and lowers the standard of all.

That the effort to limit production is false in principle, and can only succeed, if at all, when the demand is in excess of the supply, and when it succeeds, it causes the creation of methods and machines which supplant the skill of the mechanic and brings into competition a lower grade of labor at a lower wage.

That the effort to create a monopoly by attempting to retard the privilege of the American boy to acquire a trade is destructive to the best interests of a progressive nation.

That the laws, rules and methods of labor unions must be changed to conform with present conditions, if the union hopes to be recognized as a factor in the adjustment of the labor problem.

That the right to strike, or refuse to work, under certain conditions, does not involve the right to prevent others from working, if the conditions are satisfactory to them, and involves responsibility for all the damage that may arise.

That the standard of wage cannot be measured by the standard of time employed, or energy expended, but by the results attained.

These, and many other differences which might be enumerated, are the causes which make for strife and dissent, and prevent the harmony which should exist for the mutual benefit of both classes. These differences can only be removed or harmonized by honest and intelligent conferences between the employer and employee, and to bring about such conferences is the purpose and aim of the national civic federation. The success of the effort promises, for the employer, the markets of the world; for the employee, continued and increasing profits; for the country, industrial peace and better citizens.

RESULTS ACCOMPLISHED BY THE INDUSTRIAL DEPARTMENT, NATIONAL CIVIC FEDERATION.

BY OSCAR S. STRAUS.

[Oscar Solomon Straus, merchant and diplomat; born Dec. 23, 1850; graduated from Columbia university 1871; Columbia Law school, 1873; practiced law, 1872–81; entered mercantile life as a member of the firm of L. Straus & Son, importers; United States minister to Turkey, 1887–89, 1897–1900. Appointed by President Roosevelt in 1902 to fill the vacancy caused by the death of ex-President Harrison as member of the permanent court of arbitration at The Hague; is president of the New York board of trade and transportation. Author: The Origin of Republican Form of Government in the United States; The Development of Religious Liberty in the United States; Roger Williams, the Pioneer of Religious Liberty.]

The contest between capital and labor is as old as the human race, and very likely will continue as long as there is employer and workman. Early in the history of our country, that rugged reformer, who stood for much of the liberty we enjoy to-day, Roger Williams, said: "What are all the wars and contentions about, except for larger bowls and dishes of porridge?" That is putting the question in a very graphic form. This struggle for the dishes of porridge is still going on, and unfortunately very often through clash and strikes the dish gets broken and neither side gets any of the porridge. We want to save the porridge; we want the dishes to be so large that labor will get its full share, we know that capital will take care of itself. In these industrial contests there are other interests at stake than labor and capital—the general public, greater in numbers than either of these. The civic federation believed that if it organized a machinery which contained within itself the representatives of both the laborers and the employers, and associated with these two the representatives of the general public, it would have the true basis for the solution of the labor question. The industrial department of the national civic federation is composed of twelve men representing the employers, twelve men representing labor, and twelve men representing the general public.

The civic federation feels there is a possibility of inaugurating a great work, of promoting a better feeling and better relations between the employers and the workmen, and thereby removing some of the chief obstacles militating against industrial peace. We have been criticised; peacemakers always are. The civic federation is not a board of arbitration. Its purpose is to mediate, to conciliate, and only in very exceptional cases, when requested by both sides, to arbitrate between capital and labor. It has been said that the existence of such a body would stimulate laborers to threaten to strike or to strike or to make demands which otherwise they would not make, with the hope that the subject might be brought before this body, and that they might thereby gain concessions which otherwise they could not hope to secure. It might as well be said that preventives and curatives stimulate disease. It has also been stated that we promote the organization of labor, and that organized labor stimulates strikes. The civic federation's platform or statement of objects distinctly provided that its province would embrace unorganized as well as organized labor. The scope of the federation is embodied in the by-laws.

The scope and province of this department shall be to do what may seem best to promote industrial peace and prosperity; to be helpful in establishing rightful relations between employers and workers; by its good offices to endeavor to obviate and prevent strikes and lockouts, to aid in renewing industrial relations where a rupture has occurred.

That at all times representatives of employers and workers, organized or unorganized, should confer for the adjustment of differences or disputes before an acute stage is reached, and thus avoid or minimize the number of strikes or lockouts.

That mutual agreements as to conditions under which labor shall be performed should be encouraged, and that when agreements are made, the terms thereof should be faithfully adhered to, both in letter and spirit, by both parties.

This department, either as a whole or a subcommittee by it appointed, shall, when requested by both parties to a dispute, act as a forum to adjust and decide upon questions at issue between workers and their employers, provided, in its opinion, the subject is one of sufficient importance.

This department will not consider abstract industrial problems.

This department assumes no powers of arbitration, unless such powers be conferred by both parties to a dispute.

The civic federation recognizes conditions and aims to improve them in the interest of the public welfare. Railroad accidents do not argue for the stage coach, but that the railroad should be better constructed so that accidents may be more and more eliminated. Education upon this great question of labor and capital is not entirely confined to the labor side. We have found in our short experience that education is needed upon the other side as well, and if the civic federation succeeds in bringing out a more conciliatory spirit on both sides it will be doing a very great public service.

It will perhaps surprise some of you, I confess, that before I became more familiar with this subject, I was agreeably surprised to hear, in the conferences recently held in the rooms of the national civic federation, one of the most important officers of organized labor state that he wished it to be understood that organized labor does not approve of sympathetic strikes, and that organized labor has come to the conclusion that restrictions of output should not be permitted, as all such efforts were uneconomical.

The chances for industrial peace in this country are greater than they are in any other country. The fact that this conflict and antagonism have existed and now exist in the countries of Europe, is no reason why the same conditions should obtain in the United States, and the reason is very evident. In the first place, we are not divided in this country into permanently distinct classes. There is no fixed gap between the laboring and capitalistic classes. The most successful capitalists in this country to-day are men who have themselves risen from the ranks of labor, men who have been the architects of their own fortune. The large fortunes of to-day are to a great extent held by the men who achieved them, and for that reason there is a natural and closer contact between capitalists and laborers in this country than in any other. In America, as a rule, the great fortunes are not as yet in the hands of the second, third and fourth generations and are never likely to be to any considerable extent.

The powers of the civic federation are entirely voluntary, and its effective force is public opinion. We can advise, endeavor to conciliate, remove misunderstandings, and invite both sides of the controversy to come together and confer. We cannot compel, except by the force of reason and public opinion. We may invite to arbitration; we may upon request of both sides arbitrate. Arbitration is a powerful weapon, and experience has shown that the side in the wrong is the first to object, upon the ground, there is nothing to arbitrate. That answer is itself a confession of wrong. It was Penn's famous maxim, "We must concede the liberties we demand." If both sides of this controversy will bear that maxim in mind, much trouble can be avoided. That maxim implies that organization on the one side justifies, if it does not compel, organization on the other side; and each side must concede the rights which it claims for itself, and any contest waged upon principles which conflict with such concessions the public will not justify.

The refusal to recognize conditions does not change those conditions, and often embitters the relations that exist between the respective sides. The mission of the civic federation is one of peace, and like all peacemakers will doubtless, as time runs on, come in for abuse and misinterpretation of its purposes. We are prepared for this reward, and so long as we remain true to our mission, and that we will so remain our membership is a guarantee, no amount of abuse will cause us to flinch from the duty that is before us.

THE LIMITATIONS OF CONCILIATION AND ARBITRATION.

BY SAMUEL GOMPERS.

[Samuel Gompers, president American Federation of Labor; born in England, Jan. 27, 1850; cigar maker by trade; has been connected with movements for organization of working people since his fifteenth year; editor of the American Federationist; with the exception of one year has been president of the American Federation of Labor, 1882–1903; author of many articles on labor topics.]

The subject under consideration involves the difference between the isolated bargain made by workmen acting as individuals and the joint or collective bargain made by an aggregation of workers. The individual bargain made by a workman with his employer is practically based upon the condition of the poorest situated among the applicants for the position, and the conditions of employment, accepted or imposed, are fixed by the immediate and dire necessities of the poorest conditioned worker who makes application for the job. The collective bargain is made upon the basis of about the average economic condition or situation of those who desire to fill the position.

The individual bargain is made at the entrance to the factory, the shop, the mill, or the mine; the collective bargain is made usually in the office of the employer.

When the period covered by the collective bargain has expired and the conditions under which labor has been carried on for a specific period become unsatisfactory to either or both, a conference is held and a new agreement endeavored to be reached under which industry and commerce may be continued. When there is a failure to agree, a strike occurs.

The effort at best in the joint bargaining or in the strike is the effort to secure the best possible conditions for the wage earners. Much as we deplore strikes and endeavor to avoid them, they are the highest civilized expression of discontent of the workers in any part of the world. China has no strikes. The people of India have no strikes, but in the

highest developed and most highly civilized countries strikes
do occur. In China, when discontent arises, we see it manifested in revolution against constituted authority, the venting
of prejudice against the foreigner; the stiletto, the bludgeon,
war brutality, are the manifestations of the discontent of the
poor and of the workers of those countries.

Our forefathers, when establishing our government,
wisely reserved to the popular branch of our federal government the right to control revenue and expenditure, a right
which had been struggled for and secured by the house of
commons of Great Britain. The strike of labor is in another
form the holding of the purse strings of the nation, to protest
against injustice and wrong being meted out to the laborers.
It is the determination of the workers that in the last analysis,
if there be no other means by which their rights may be accorded and their wrongs righted, they may say with Lincoln,
"Thank God, we live in a country where the people may
strike!" Nevertheless a strike ought to be avoided by every
means within the power of every man, capitalist, laborer, or
the neutral citizen, and he who would not give his best efforts
and thought to prevent a strike is scarcely doing justice to
his fellow men, nor is he loyal to the institutions under which
we live. But I reassert that there are some things which are
worse than strikes, and among them I include a degraded, a
debased, or a demoralized manhood.

Labor insists upon and will never surrender the right
to free locomotion, the right to move at will, the right to
go from Philadelphia to Camden or California, or vice versa,
at will. To achieve that right it has cost centuries of struggles
and sacrifices and burdens. Laborers, moreover, will insist
upon the right freely to change their employment, a right
they have secured through centuries of travail and sacrifices.
That right three fourths of the nation was up in arms a little
more than forty years ago to achieve for the black man, and
the white laborers of America will not surrender that prerogative. Laborers are aiming at freedom through organization and intelligence.

The industrial department of the national civic federation is erroneously thought by some to be an arbitration com-

mittee, whereas the first purpose is to endeavor to bring about a conference between employers and employees before any acute state of feeling shall occur relative to their diverse interests. If a rupture occurs, the committee endeavors to bring about a conference so that arbitration may be resorted to if both parties to the controversy shall so request.

As a rule, men do not care to refer matters in which they are particularly and financially interested to what are usually termed disinterested parties. They prefer to meet with those whose interests may be opposite to theirs, and, each conceding something in a conciliatory spirit, endeavor to come to an adjustment and agreement.

Unorganized workmen have a notion that they are absolutely impotent, that the employers are omnipotent, almighty. This is typified in the thought or expression, What can labor do against capital? Likewise the employers of unorganized workmen usually regard themselves as "monarchs of all they survey," and brook no interference. If any workman has the temerity to question the justice or sense of fairness of the employer or the wages paid, he is dismissed and a strike frequently results.

No strikes are conducted more bitterly than strikes of previously unorganized workmen. As soon as such men become desperate enough to strike, they are transformed; they no longer believe the employer all powerful, but attribute to themselves that function and faculty; the touching of shoulders brings a new found power to their minds, of which they never dreamed before, and they look upon their employers against whom they went on strike as absolutely at their mercy.

The employers, in these cases, usually regard the matter of request to be heard upon the question of wages, hours or other conditions of employment, as dictation by their workmen; but whether the strike is won or lost, if the workmen but maintain their organization, the initial step has been taken for a joint bargain and a conciliatory policy in the future. Both parties have learned a severe but a profitable lesson, that neither party is impotent, and neither all powerful. The organized labor movement in our day is an assertion of the principle that there is no hope that the workers can protect their interests or promote their welfare unless they organize; unless they advocate conciliation to adjust whatever controversies may arise between themselves and their employers upon any disputed points upon which they cannot agree. There are some who advocate compulsory arbitration. I concur with Senator Hanna, who did not believe in compulsory arbitration. Indeed, voluntary arbitration cannot be successfully carried out unless both parties are equally strong and powerful or nearly so. This is true between nations as well as between individuals. Russia never arbitrated the question of the nationality of Poland. England did not arbitrate the question with Afghanistan, but simply bombarded her. England in her dispute with Venezuela proposed to bombard her, and only when the United States said, "Hold on, this is of very serious consequence to us," did England consent to arbitrate. There has never yet been in the history of the world successful arbitration between those who were powerful and those who were absolutely at their mercy. There has never yet been arbitration between the man who lay prone upon his back and the man who had a heel upon his throat and a saber at his breast. Arbitration is possible, but only when capital and labor are well organized. Labor is beginning to organize, and when labor shall be better organized than it is to-day we shall have fewer disputes than we have now.

Of the agreements made between employers and employed, two thirds, if not more, of the violations, of the failures to abide by the awards of arbitrators, are on the part of employers. But if it were not so, if the awards were broken by either one or the other side or by both sides in equal proportion, it would be better, it would make for human progress and economic advantage, to have an award violated than to have the award forced by government upon either one side or the other. The employer if he choose could close his business, and that would mean his enforced idleness. On the other hand, if the state entered and forced workmen to accept an award and to work under conditions which were onerous to him or to them, you can imagine the result. Men

work with a will when they work of their own volition, then
they work to the greatest advantage of all. On the other
hand, if men were compelled to work by order of the state,
with the representatives of the state entering with whip in
hand or a commitment to the jail, it would create a nation
of sullen, unwilling and resentful workers; a condition that
we do not wish to encourage; a condition which would be
most hurtful to our industrial and commercial greatness and
success. It is strange how some men desire law to govern
all other men in all their actions and doings in life. The organized labor movement endeavors to give opportunities
to the workers so that their habits and customs shall change
by reason of new and better conditions.

We have our combinations of capital, our organizations
and federations of labor. These are now working on parallel lines and have evolved the national civic federation.
Through the efforts of men noted for their ability, for their
straightforwardness, noted for the interest they take in
public affairs, an effort is being made to bring about the
greatest possible success industrially and commercially for
our country with the least possible friction.

One of the greatest causes of the disturbance of industry,
the severance of friendly relations between employer and
employees, is the fact that the employers assume to themselves the absolute right to dictate and direct the terms
under which workers shall toil, the wages, hours and other
conditions of employment, without permitting the voice
of the workmen to be raised in their own behalf. The workers
insist upon the right of being heard; not heard alone at mass
meeting, but heard by counsel, heard by their committees,
heard through their business agent, or heard, if you please,
through the much abused walking delegate. They insist
upon the right to be heard by counsel; the constitution of
our country declares that the people of our country may be
heard through counsel. It is a saying in law, and I repeat
it, though not a lawyer, that he who is his own lawyer has
a fool for a client. The organized workmen have long realized
this truism and have preferred to be heard by counsel, and
we say that the political and civil right guaranteed to us by

the constitutions of our country and our states ought to be extended; the principle of it ought to be extended to protect and advance our industrial rights.

One of the representatives of the Illinois board of arbitration recently said to me that there were so many cases of employers who refused to recognize the committees of the organizations of their employees that the board was in doubt whether it ought to name each individual employer or simply group such employers together and give their number in round figures. No man in this world is absolutely right and no man absolutely wrong. If this be so, men ought, as organized labor has for half a century demanded, and as the national civic federation has emphasized, to meet in conference and be helpful in allowing common sense and fair dealing and justice and equity and the needs of the people to determine what shall be the conditions under which industry and commerce shall continue to advance until we shall be in truth producers for the whole world.

The movement for which we stand tends to foster education, not only among the workmen, but among the educated; for all those possessing class ignorance and prejudice regarding industrial matters, the educated man who takes his cue regarding the labor question from those who are always opposed to the labor movement, and who never takes the trouble to find out the laborer's side of the labor question, is in the most deplorable condition.

IS COMPULSORY ARBITRATION PRACTICABLE?

BY SETH LOW.

[Seth Low, former mayor of New York; born in Brooklyn, Jan. 18, 1850; graduated from Columbia, 1870; elected on the independent ticket as mayor of Brooklyn, 1881–85; defeated as candidate for mayor of greater New York, 1897; president Columbia university, 1890–1901; mayor of New York, 1902–03.]

When compulsory arbitration is spoken of in the interest of the community, it is apt to be challenged by both sides. The capitalist says: "Compulsory arbitration is unfair, because labor is not responsible;" and labor says: "Men are not slaves: they cannot be compelled to work against their will."

I venture to submit, however, that at one point capital and labor stand in precisely the same position before the law; and that, at this point, if it is desirable, compulsory arbitration may be insisted upon, and may be made practicable. Without the privileges given by statute, neither capital nor labor, as illustrated in corporations and trade unions, can lawfully combine. In the eye of the common law, such combinations as a corporation and a labor union are both conspiracies. In other words, in order to combine at all, in such forms, both capital and labor have to ask the same privilege at the hands of the state.

The state can certainly say if it will: Yes, you may combine, but only upon the condition that all disputes between you shall be arbitrated. And the state can as certainly secure the acceptance by both parties of the award of an arbitration, by providing that a failure to arbitrate, or to abide by the award of the arbitration, shall work a forfeiture of the privilege of combining. In the case of a corporation, it would, in that event, lose its charter; and in the case of a trade union, which is an association of individuals, each individual would become amenable to the criminal law against conspiracy. Such a provision would probably be equally effective as to both labor and capital; and it would be equally fair to both, because it would apply to both equally for the same cause; that is to say, because of a failure to observe the conditions upon which the statutory privilege of combining had been granted.

Of course, in this paper, I am not attempting to deal with the details of legislation. It would be altogether possible, I believe, instead of depriving a company of its charter, to deprive the responsible officers and directors for a term of months or of years, as the statute might provide, of the privilege of being officers or directors in any corporation within the state; and, similarly, if a trade union were at fault, only the officers or the men responsible for the fault need be deprived, as in the other case, for a term of months or of years, as the statutes might provide, of the privilege of belonging to any trade unions within the state.

The community, then, is not helpless. The question rather is, why should it not insist upon such legislation, limited, if you please, in the first instance, to public service corporations, where the evils felt by the community are greatest.

It may throw some light upon the problem to try to show the philosophy of the present situation. For many centuries the best men of the race, the world over, have been struggling to secure for the individual man equality before the law and freedom of opportunity. In this country, and at this time, these results have been achieved more generally than ever before. On the other hand, as we observe what is going on about us in the field of industry and commerce, it seems as if the individual capitalist was disappearing in the corporation, and the corporation itself in the trust; while the individual laborer is disappearing in the trade union, and the trade union itself in the brotherhood of federation. What does all this signify? Does it mean that, in this large field of human activity, the loss of individuality is threatened by the force of combination? I think not. It means, on the contrary, as I conceive, that we have reached, in human society, the era of combination simply because we have first succeeded in individualizing each man as to his legal rights and as to his social privileges. In other words, what has happened in society may be illustrated by the art of printing. Until each type had come to represent a single letter only, the era of limitless combinations of types did not appear, and there could be no art of printing. When every type had been individualized, then, and then only, the era of limitless combination was attained and the art of printing was born. This, I think, is what has happened in our day in human society. Men combine at will, because they are free to combine, and because they perceive that in combination they can accomplish what before was impossible. Combination does not threaten individuality: it is rather founded upon it. This proposition, I submit, goes to the very root of so-called labor troubles.

One sometimes hears it said, for instance, that labor combines because capital combines, as if combination on the part of labor was simply an act of self defence. I think that a very partial and inadequate explanation of the combination either of capital or labor. Men combine, in our day, because they are free to do so, and because they perceive the advantage of doing so, and they do it in obedience to a social law as irresistible as the force of gravity. If capital and labor seem often to be in conflict, through their different forms of organization, it is, as I conceive, because this universal social law affects the two precisely as the law of gravity affects us and our antipodes. The same force is felt by both, and if, in affecting both in precisely the same way, it seems to draw them into conflict with each other, that is because they start from opposite positions. If, then, this is a true philosophy of our times, the inference from it is important. Nobody thinks of antagonizing the force of gravity. Everybody simply takes it for granted, and adjusts his actions to it. Just as soon as, in a free community, the movement towards combination on the part of both labor and capital is recognized as a movement in response to a law as universal as the law of gravity, the bitterness of antagonism between capital and labor will tend to moderate. Each will take for granted the position of the other, and each will strive, as wise men always strive, so to adjust themselves to universal law as to get from it the greatest possible advantage. Then the effort to destroy the trade union, on the one hand, and the trust on the other, will give place to the wiser effort to regulate both so as to do away with the abuses of which each is capable.

This power of combination in industry and business, while of slow growth, in its recent manifestations is almost like the discovery of a new force. It has taken more than a century since the steam engine was invented for men to learn how to make the use of steam as effective and as safe as it is now; and yet, even now, from time to time, boilers explode and loss of life takes place. No one should be surprised, therefore, and no one need lose heart, if progress in learning the limits of safety in the use of the power of combination, on the part of both capital and labor, is slow, and if, in the process of learning, much injury is done. It is only through experimentation that men learn what can be done and what cannot, when they are put into possession of a new power. Especially must this be the case when the same power is put at once into the hands of men who occupy competing relations as to its use. The first impulse of human nature, when given control of a new power, is to use it to its utmost; and it is only as experience shows what are the limitations of its usefulness, that such limitations are accepted. Capital, in combination, has sometimes imagined that it could do anything that it wished. Labor, in combination, has often yielded to the same idea. Both have found, when they have carried their ideas to the extreme, that forces exist in society with which they are obliged to reckon, and which put a limit upon what they are able to do. In the first stages of the struggle growing out of the efforts of both capital and labor, each to secure for himself, by combination, a larger proportion of the joint products of both, resort was almost uniformly had to main strength. The appeal to justice and the appeal to the community's sense of right seemed to be unnecessary when one side or the other apparently had power enough to have its own way, no matter what people thought. I think it may fairly be said, speaking broadly, that this stage of the matter has been passed in the so-called conflict between capital and labor nowadays. At the beginning of every such controversy, both sides now put forth a statement of their positions, in the endeavor to secure the favor and help of public sentiment. This they do because both have discovered that seldom, if ever, can either side win, in such a dispute, unless it has public opinion with it. From this I infer that the time is ripe to urge that no breach of relations between employer and employee should ever be allowed to take place without a resort to arbitration.

When arbitration is urged in any controversy, one side or the other is pretty certain to say there is nothing to arbitrate. This phrase always has one of two meanings. First, it often means, on the part of the employer, that he does not admit the right of his employees to any voice in the decision of the points under discussion; or, second, it may mean, either on the part of the employer or on the part of the employee, that he feels himself so strong that he does not want to arbitrate. Men often say, with a great deal of force, that the finding in almost every arbitration is a compromise. The weaker side is always ready to arbitrate, because it feels that, while it may not get everything that it wants, it is pretty sure to get something. The stronger side, for the same reason, is unwilling to arbitrate, because it feels that, while it may not have to give everything that is asked, it will have to grant something, and it does not want to grant anything.

These two attitudes deserve consideration. And first, that of the employer who thinks that his employees have no right to a voice as to any of the questions under dispute. Abundant experience has shown that, in these days, this attitude concerns not only the employer and his employee, but also it often exposes the community to breaches of the peace, and always, to very many serious and direct evils. This claim, when made, is sought to be justified by saying that it is one of the rights of private property. Can such an attitude toward organized labor be, in fact, so justified? In all ages the rights of private property have been modified in the public interest. Witness the abolition of mortmain and the use of real estate as affected by municipal ordinances. It appears that, as to all lines of business that depend upon public franchises, no such claim can be admitted; because, for such purposes, the private corporation is only the agent of the state; and it may properly be said that no agent of the public has a right so to conduct his business as to involve the community in disaster. As to all business carried on by corporations, the soundness of this position may again be questioned; because every corporation receives from the state two very vital privileges—first, that of limited liability, and, second, that of indefinite life. The state may well demand of people who receive such privileges at its hand, that they also shall conduct their business in ways that are consistent with the public interest. Were it worth while, it might be shown that the argument in favor of arbitration, even as between the business firm, or individuals and their employees, is only less strong; but the amount of business likely to lead to labor disturbances, carried on under these forms in these days, is so small as practically to be negligible. It may be said, therefore, that it is very seldom indeed, if ever, in our day that the capitalist is justified in saying that there is nothing to arbitrate, because he is unwilling to admit that his employees are entitled to a voice as to the conditions upon which they will work for him.

Turn now to the second sense in which that phrase is frequently used, there is nothing to arbitrate; that arbitration after all, is merely a form of unwelcome compromise. Is it certain that this is an argument against it? I perceive that the round world is kept in place by an opposition of forces, and it may easily be that the best possible arrangement, as between employer and employee, is the arrangement, if they fail to agree, upon which a fair minded arbitrator would decide. That is to say, the equilibrium between the demands of the opposing forces, so established, may be, upon the whole, the best possible adjustment for the time being. Such a practice would certainly tend to adjust the relations between employer and employee upon the basis of reason and good will, instead of by force and compulsion. Relations established with good will are not only likely to be more permanent, but also more mutually advantageous, for my business experience convinces me that no business relations are enduring that do not involve advantage to both sides.

There are certain lessons vital to this argument to be drawn from the late strike in New York city upon the subway and elevated roads. From the moment that the breach occurred, and the public had read the statement of the two sides on the issues involved, there was never a moment's doubt that public opinion would be against the men, and that public sympathy would go to the railroad. For these two things were evident to the most casual reader: First, that there was no issue at stake that justified such immense injury to the public as was done by the strike; no issue, indeed, that could not have been easily adjusted by arbitration; and, second, that one section of the men, at any rate—the motormen—had gone out in flat violation of their agreement. Every friend of industrial progress through industrial peace, when he became aware of the facts of the situation, must have felt a sinking of heart, because it is perfectly evident that organized society cannot prosper when men will not keep their faith. Most happily, the day was saved by the good sense and the courage of the national labor officials, by promptly and publicly repudiating the locals who had broken faith. It is, therefore, now more clear than ever, that the more responsible labor leaders and the more responsible labor unions are to be trusted when they have once given their word.

As long ago as when the Book of Psalms was written, the writer said that the just man was he who kept his faith, although he had sworn to his own hurt. It is only because the laws of nature are uniform that men can live in the world subject to those laws; and it is only because the great mass of men, in their individual relations, do keep faith that human society is possible. It is idle to consider the establishment of trade agreements, or arbitration, or anything else, with men who will not abide by their contracts. Therefore, if it was discouraging that so intelligent a body of men as the motormen involved in the recent strike should absolutely disregard their agreement, it was, on the other hand, highly encouraging that this action should be so promptly and vigorously repudiated by the officials of the national orders. I venture the opinion that no one thing is more unfriendly to the success of the cause of arbitration, and also to the cause of trade agreements, than the claim on the part of the employers that the men do not live up to their bargains. The civic federation, therefore, can do no better work than to exert its great influence in bringing home to the business community the highly encouraging significance of this unhappy episode. Let it be once made clear that the men will abide by agreements entered into in their name by the unions to which they belong, and the movement toward arbitration and the movement toward trade agreements will both have received an immense impulse; and the day may yet come when this force that makes for combination in human society, as it affects both labor and capital, will show itself as consistent with the peaceful and orderly development of industry, as the same principle, applied to the art of printing, has shown itself to be friendly to the unimaginable development of that art, which men fondly call the art preservative.

OBJECTIONS TO COMPULSORY ARBITRATION.

BY JAMES P. ARCHIBALD.

[James P. Archibald, labor leader; born in Dublin, Ireland; educated at St. Mary's Christian Brothers college; learned the trade of a decorator; has been active in trade unions and is the most prominent member of his union in New York city and represents it in the Building Trades council of that city; has written much on labor topics.]

The general objections to compulsory arbitration, based upon political, social and economic grounds, apply to the specific phase of the question here under consideration, which would limit the application of compulsory arbitration to differences betweeen employees and employing corporations chartered to perform service, essential or important, to the public convenience, comfort and welfare. Despite that limitation, it will be found that nearly all, if not every one, of the broad reasons that can be adduced against legislation to make industrial arbitration compulsory will hold good as against the proposition to employ compulsory arbitration only in differences between employers and employed engaged in quasi-public service. Furthermore, this is true even if we admit at the outset that the corporation engaged, for instance, in transportation, owes to the state a duty, more or less defined and restricted, in requital for its charter, and that the employees of such a corporation are in a sense public servants who, in accepting employment, have incurred on their side the duty of exerting every effort to secure the safe and prompt conveyance of goods and passengers. Even to place thus in a category by themselves such a corporation and such employees, does not exempt them from the operation of universal principles.

The first of these broad objections to compulsory arbitration, to my mind, is that it must tend, in its practical operation, toward control of industry by the state; that is, toward socialism. The very definition of arbitration, whether compulsory or voluntary, implies a surrender of control of any

118

industry to which it is applied by either of the two parties whose co-operation is essential to its success and to their share in its prosperity. Arbitration is defined by the industrial commission as the authorized decision of an issue, as to which both parties concerned have failed to agree, by some person or persons other than those parties. That is, the decision thus reached may be unsatisfactory to either or to both of the parties. If each has agreed in advance to abide by the decision, whatever it may be, that agreement involves only a voluntary and temporary self sacrifice by one or the other or by both. But if the state is empowered to compel obedience to the award, to which each party is enforced to submit, the outcome would be, in case the parties should refuse either to carry on the business or to work, that the state would assume the conduct of the industry; that is, if its continuance were essential or conducive to the public welfare. It is not necessary here to enter into a discussion of socialism further than to say that opposition to socialism thus implies opposition to compulsory arbitration, whose ultimate tendency toward socialism is clear enough in theory and not to be measured by any experience

The next broad objection to compulsory arbitration is that it is unnecessary. It is a general principle that legislation should be framed only to meet requirements. Needless laws cumber the statute books and are a burden to society. The maxim that the best government is that which governs least may be carried to an extreme, but it is certainly true that no one would seriously contemplate a large extension of our judicial machinery without a clear demonstration of its necessity. Now, in the regulation of industry there has been no such demonstration of the necessity of the creation of a court of arbitration, to which either party to a dispute could cite the other at will or caprice, and from whose decision reached without reference to a jury, there could be no appeal. The advocates of compulsory arbitration are keenly aware of this vital objection. They usually preface their argument by statements designed to picture the United States as in an incessant ferment of industrial war, and at least one of them has gone so far as to apply the famous definition of war to the relations of capital and labor as a whole. But a calmer view will show that the normal and usual condition of industry is one of peace, and that war is the exception. So distinguished and experienced an observer as Andrew Carnegie recently remarked that "peace reigns in six sevenths of the industrial world." Mr. Carnegie reached this conclusion by pointing out that out of 22,000,000 engaged in gainful pursuits only seven millions are in mechanical and manufacturing occupations. Outside of these, in agriculture and domestic service, peace reigns. Out of the seven millions engaged in mechanical and manufacturing pursuits, he estimates that not more than three millions, or those having relations with large employers, are often disturbed by industrial war.

The strikes, then, that do occur, nearly all involve directly less than one seventh of the total wage earners of the country, and only a fraction of them at one time.

Official figures show that of the 22,783 strikes in the twenty years from 1880 to 1900, the industries most affected, in the order named, were the building trades with 4,440 strikes; the coal and coke industry, with 2,512; the metal and metallic goods industry, with 2, 079; the clothing industry, with 1,536; the tobacco industry, with 1,509, and, least of the six, transportation, with 1,262. Of the total 22,783 strikes, 58.09 per cent were in these six industries. In the number of establishments involved, transportation also takes lowest rank, few more than 5,000 establishments being involved in the twenty years, as against 41,910 in the building trades; 19,695 in the clothing industry and 14,473 in the coal and coke industry.

In this connection, it is to be noted that this lack of necessity for compulsory arbitration is progressively decreasing. The methods of conciliation, conference and voluntary arbitration are largely responsible for this decrease of industrial war. No one can fail to be impressed with the fact, of common knowledge, that there has been no strike of serious consequence upon any of the great railway systems since 1893, or for more than a decade. This, it has been pointed out, is due to the increase of organization among railway employees. Strikes upon such public service systems as gas or waterworks are so rare that they must be left out of account. There remain, then, only the strikes upon street railways in centers of population to be considered in relation to the necessity for compulsory arbitration, and as to them the necessity is yet to be demonstrated. In their case, it is not the capital or the number of employees involved that becomes important. It is the inconvenience of the public and the dislocation or the business of a community that cause the outcry for a drastic remedy or an effective prevention. The gravity and the reality of these public grievances cannot be minimized or obscured. Yet it is none the less true that their occurrence is local, though intense; their endurance temporary, though acute; their effect limited in time, though accompanied by an appreciable increase in danger of operation. These are not adequate causes for introducing an innovation into our judicial machinery.

The organization of employees, accompanied by the organization of employers, is a constantly increasing cause of industrial peace, and a constantly increasing argument against the necessity of compulsory arbitration. If, then, we accept the organization of labor as socially and economically desirable, as tending to elevate the mass and increase its power of consumption, we must oppose compulsory arbitration as inimical to the development of unionism. A primary object of unionism is the negotiation of trade agreements, otherwise collective bargaining with employers, organized as corporations or associations. Nearly every labor organization in the country is opposed to compulsory arbitration because of the conviction, that is shared by many professional economists, that its adoption must, in the words of Carroll D. Wright, "inevitably result in the destruction of trade unions." A decision in a contest adverse to a union would render that union liable to whatever penalty would be contingent upon disobedience. A violation of the decree of the arbitration court by the union would probably be followed by the imposition of a money fine or the loss of its charter and its dissolution. The only alternative, obedience to the decree, if the decree were against the sense of justice and therefore against the sense of self respect of the employees, would amount to working for specified wage under compulsion, or, in other words, to involuntary servitude, forbidden by the thirteenth amendment to the constitution of the United States.

The ready answer to this is that the operation of compulsory arbitration in New Zealand has not there destroyed the trade unions, but has strengthened them, just as it has promoted unions of employers. That may be in part because the New Zealand system is accompanied by the preferential employment of union labor under the terms of an award, accompanied by the requirement that the unions admit all competent workers, without ballot and upon the payment of a nominal fee. But, aside from that explanation, which implies a national closed shop in all industries, as well as making dependents of workers incompetent to earn the minimum wage and yet able to earn their living if permitted, the conditions of life and labor in New Zealand are so radically different to those in the United States as to make inapplicable to this country the lessons of the experiment in New Zealand. That experiment, moreover, has not reached conclusive results even in its own territory and under its peculiar conditions. Its strongest adherents have confessed their inability to transfer it to this country. The report of the anthracite strike commission said: "Apart from the apparent lack of constitutional power to enact laws providing for compulsory arbitration, our industries are too vast and too complicated for the practical application of such a system."

It is precisely the belief that the awards, or the bulk of awards, of a court of compulsory arbitration would be adverse to wage earners that impugns in advance the efficiency of this device. It is an essential precedent to voluntary arbitration that each disputant shall feel confident that his interests will receive the same consideration as those of his opponent. Each must have faith that the award will be guided by a spirit of perfect fairness. But when the element of compulsion is introduced, this essential element of confidence disappears. It is impossible, as men are constituted, to guarantee the fairness of a tribunal of arbitration clothed with power to compel the hearing of disputes and to enforce its conclusions. It is a condition that must be taken into account that the belief largely obtains among wage earners that state created courts or boards are generally, if unconsciously, on the side of capital or invested interests as against the more indefinite influence of labor.

Another general objection to compulsory arbitration is that it involves a surrender of the right to strike and of the corresponding right to lock out. These are weapons that neither self respecting capital nor self respecting labor can afford to surrender. The abandonment of the power to fight would make for the peace of subjection, for the craven submission of one side or the other. The possession of the weapons of war makes for peace in industry as surely as it does in international affairs. The arguments for an effective military force as an insurance of national security against foreign offence and of foreign respect for the rights of a nation abroad are quite parallel to the arguments for retaining an inalienable right to refuse to work or to refuse to employ, reinforced by thorough organization. The mutual respect of employer and employed is essential to harmony. The abandonment of liberty to fight for conviction of right would impair and ultimately destroy that mutual respect. It would be a confession of inability to reconcile mutual respect with a manly compact of peace.

I have enumerated all these general objections to compulsory arbitration as applicable to the specific class of public service corporations and their employees. It is for the advocates of compulsory arbitration to prove that they are not so applicable. It is for them to show that the injury to the public convenience and safety or to the conduct of business is so frequent, so serious, so important as to warrant an innovation that is repugnant to republican conceptions of liberty.

But, it is said, it may be possible to create a method of compulsory arbitration that will stop short of compelling either employers to continue a business or employees to continue to work. Let us see how any conceivable plan of non-compelling compulsory arbitration would work in practical application to a system of rapid transit in a great city.

The chief purpose of such a plan would be to prevent under any and all circumstances, the interruption of service. The first essential, then, would be to forbid by law either strike or lockout on the railroad, pending the submission of a dispute to the court of arbitration. Assume that the corporation on the one side and the employees on the other have been deprived by law of this weapon. The decision of the court follows. It is regarded, we will say, as unjust by the employees, who then enter upon their deferred strike. Pending the decision of the court, would the corporation be in contempt if it gathered an army of strike breakers? The strike breaking remedy is not immediately effective in preventing delay and interruption to traffic, and it involves danger to the traffic. The only alternative would be for the state or municipality to operate the road with police or military. If there were to be no interruption nor danger to traffic, the members of these forces would have to be trained to render instant and efficient service as motormen, trainmen, signal men and in all other capacities necessary to the continuous and safe operation of the road. Is the public prepared to include these accomplishments in the list of requirements for service in the police or army.

It has been suggested also that, as the final court of appeal in all industrial disputes is public opinion, a court might be created with power to compel the production of all testimony, persons and papers, and to render its decision. It is argued that under present conditions public opinion cannot learn the truth in industrial controversies; that it is bombarded with contradictory, ex parte statements and confusing and ill informed reports in the press, and that the creation of a court empowered to ascertain and publish the truth would make conclusive and morally compulsory, because necessarily right, the verdict of that highest court of arbitration—public opinion. Strictly speaking, this proposition is not compulsory arbitration, but compulsory investigation, with submission of the finding to the verdict of the community.

This proposition is based upon the assumption that public opinion, if correctly informed as to facts, is infallible. But what basis is there for this assumption? As to the ascertainment of facts, the historic conundrum, "What is truth?" is persistently pertinent. Especially does it apply to an industrial inquiry as to which only experts, not laymen, would be qualified to arrive at a just decision, and even experts might disagree. A task difficult for such a select body would assuredly be confusing to the judgment of that vast indeterminate jury known as the general public. Even in cases of litigation, carried to the highest courts of appeal, in the states and in the federal government, judicial decisions now divide the bench and fail to command by far the unanimous approval of public opinion. Yet those decisions are reached in accordance with procedure elaborated through centuries and with principles evolved through the teaching of all history. But judicial inquiry into industrial questions would explore unknown fields, would meet novel questions, involving both expediency and principle, would evolve new principles and in the absence of any body of industrial jurisprudence, would make of such a court in practice a legislative as well as a judicial agency.

Be it noted, the element of compulsion is still present. If there is to be a candid inquiry into the existing facts of an industry, the status quo must be preserved. If the industry be that of transportation, the employees must keep the trains running and the corporation must discharge none of its discontented employees, pending the inquiry. Each antagonist must appear in the judicial arena with hands tied. The contest must be reduced to statement and argument. It must be a battle of witnesses and counsel.

The objection to this procedure is that it is against the normal processes of human progress. The race does not emerge from barbarism by argument, but by deeds. Valor, not eloquence, wins battles. In the long run, right, truth, justice must win, and they must be demonstrated. But they cannot stand unsupported against the ever powerful forces of wrong, untruth, injustice. It is only by fighting, or by power to fight, that the weal of society is advanced through the adjustment of relations between its component parts. Remove this ability to fight by compelling peace while the issue is submitted to a tribunal, and that tribunal will inevitably and unconsciously be swayed by adherence to the old away from digression into the new. It must ever be kept in mind that the struggle of labor for betterment is not merely a question of here and now. It is eternally a question of the future, and not to be a combatant, at least potentially, would be for labor to turn its face backward.

There is a conspicuous illustration of these facts, which are facts of human nature, in the outcome of the anthracite coal strike. That was a struggle that in time came to affect the public convenience, comfort and health as vitally as could the paralysis of any public service corporation. That struggle was brought to an end through adjudication by a tribunal of inquiry. Very well, but be it observed that the battle preceded the inquiry. Had there been in existence a tribunal empowered to pronounce a verdict upon the issues between the mine workers and the operators, it never would have made an award so favorable to the advance of civilization among the mass of inhabitants of the anthracite region as was made by the anthracite strike commission, for the reason that there never would have been made the demonstration by the workers that they were so terribly in earnest in their conviction that their demands were just, that they were willing to go hungry and even to see their wives and children suffer, rather than work upon oppressive terms. There has existed for generations in Russia an office holding class whose function was that of an industrial judiciary. Against industrial adjustment by this bureaucracy, it was a crime for workers to organize for appeal. The result was the evolution of industrial conditions so shocking as to be incredible to Occidental minds and to cause a revolt in demand of rights that our civilization has grown to treat as axiomatic and to take for granted. Establish in the midst of our civilization such an industrial tribunal as proposed and retrogression would ensue, perhaps slowly, but surely, toward the suppression of the toilers whose hands are tied.

MONOPOLY AND THE STRUGGLE OF CLASSES.

BY JOHN BATES CLARK.

[John Bates Clark; born Providence, R. I., Jan. 26, 1847; educated in public schools; spent two years at Brown university, and graduated from Amherst college in 1872; took special studies in economics and history for two years at the University of Heidelberg, and a half year at University of Zurich; has been professor political economy at Carleton college, Smith college, Amherst college, and lecturer at Johns Hopkins; professor of political economy at Columbia since July, 1895. Author: The Philosophy of Wealth; The Distribution of Wealth; The Control of Trusts, etc.]

A certain clerical socialist used to preface his public addresses with the statement, "Society is under conviction of sin." It certainly is under an indictment, and is inclined to plead guilty on some of the counts. It is not perfect, and it owns the fact. The socialist's theological term, however, implies that society is conscious of being in a state of total depravity, and confesses by implication that it needs to be destroyed and made over. Its very principle of action is, in this view, so bad that nothing can save the organism but a new creation.

In this sense the accusation does not seem to many people to be true, and the revolutionary change that the socialist calls for does not seem to be impending. What we must admit, however, is that the principle of monopoly is a bad one, and that in the business world it is becoming too nearly dominant. Trusts are seeking to create monopolies of products, and trade unions are trying to establish monopolies of labor. Does this movement really tend towards the absorption of all industry by the state? Appearances favor the side of those who believe in the permanence of private business.

Many are ready to say offhand that we have already given ourselves over to private monopoly, which stands for oppression and all evil, and that the only possible escape from impending disaster is socialism. Business is anything but free, when, in many a department, a single corporation has the field so nearly to itself that its few surviving competitors are at its mercy. The multimillionaire who controls such a corporation is the modern counterpart of the great baron of feudal times. The field of his operation is industry, and the trust furnishes his particular domain. One of the most effective criticisms of society as it now is, bears the title, Our Benevolent Feudalism, and it makes much of the analogy between Europe under barons and America under industrial magnates.

With this seeming disappearance of competition, there has come a willingness on all sides to admit that while it lasted it was a power for good. When the enemies of the present order gleefully remark the departure of competition, they in reality pay to it a posthumous tribute. Now that it has gone, they say, the social state is becoming too bad to be endured. Ergo socialism. There is now little disposition to deny that the neck and neck rivalry of producers who are striving to undersell each other has cheapened production, which is the same thing as making labor fruitful. It has brought about a dazzling series of mechanical inventions whereby, in many a department, the product of a day's work has been multiplied by ten, and again by ten. It has worked, moreover, with a certain rude honesty—though not every one will admit this—since it has tended to give to each laborer what he is personally worth; and where it has not actually given it, the reason has been that the natural tendency has been thwarted by adverse influences. A good system may always be made to give an imperfect result, if the natural movement of it is here and there disturbed and obstructed. Competition has never worked in a perfectly free and unhindered way; but so far as it has worked, it has tended towards wealth, progress, and a rude approach to honesty in the sharing of the fruits of progress.

For monopoly there is no such thing to be said. He would be a bold attorney who would take a brief for it at all, and an infatuated one who would expect to defend it successfully before the great jury, the people. At the bar of public opinion it is condemned and outlawed, but unfortunately it is not actually banished. In spite of a universal protest, it is grimly asserting its power, and the issue of to-day, in which all others merge, is whether we shall rule it, or whether it shall rule us. For if we cannot rule it except by taking monopolized industries into the hands of the government, we shall in the end do even that. The logic of socialism is unimpeachable, if you grant its minor premise; for its major premise is one in which we are all agreed—the statement, namely, that a system of business founded on private monopoly is intolerable. Add, now, the proposition that the present system is thus founded, and you prove that this system is one which must, at all costs, be swept away; and if there is only one way to do this— through governmental absorption of our industries and their management in the name of the people—that way must be accepted. On the face the situation makes a strong plea for such a change, and wins thousands of converts. When we look a little deeper, we shall see that the action of monopoly in another sphere creates a practical barrier against a radical change of this kind. The trade union may seem friendly to socialism, but in principle it is opposed to it.

Are we, or are we not, given over to a régime of private monopolies in business? There is another syllogism which is here applicable, though in this case there is not a general agreement as to the truth of the minor premise, which is that a complete system of industries conducted by a democratic state would have results that would be intolerable. The major premise here is that the American people will never accept an intolerable situation, and the conclusion is that they must and will avoid the necessity for such a great public monopoly by curbing the power of private ones. Critics will declare that the people cannot do this, and the question whether they can and will do it is the one that is superseding all others in marshaling parties and giving shape to the struggles of classes. As between submitting to what is intolerable and doing what is impossible, an energetic people will do the impossible. They will make a way to do to-morrow what they cannot do to-day; and this probably means that they will fight it out on the line of regulation though it take many summers.

The whole attitude of classes towards each other has been transformed by the advent of the great monopolies. Socialism has gained supporters for the moderate parts of its program. It has itself learned to become evolutionary and Fabian, and to try to gain one point at a time. Whatever may be its ulterior views, the battles in which it can hope to have practical success are fought with the aid of men who have little sympathy with its ultimate aims. There is rapidly coming into the field a big auxiliary force which will fight effectively for a few things and then stop, leaving the pronounced socialist to continue his fight unaided.

Socialism began its career by hitching its wagon to a star, —by holding before the eyes of its followers the vision of a transformed and perfected universe in which wrongs should be done away with and equality and fraternity should rule. The early philosophers of the school included in the picture a transformed man as well as a renovated society, since they perceived that evil must be taken out of human nature itself if the full results of the new system were to be realized; and there are those at present who will accept nothing less than this. They dread and repudiate the tendency to make small gains, and wait for the great ones. They denounce whatever is Fabian and opportunist, and insist upon everything or nothing. A few of them, the more consistent and less practical ones, decry trade unionism itself, since it involves making terms with employers and sharing gains with them—a policy which gives to the wages system a license to continue. Logically these men are the truest socialists, and yet it is clear that without the help of the trade unionists they can accomplish nothing. If the great mass of those who favor bringing the state into the industrial field were reduced to this radical and consistent nucleus, it would become what has been called a nice little, tight little party, much too small to count in a political election.

Now the action of different classes and the character of their struggles with each other will be governed, in the near future, by their attitude towards the immediate issues created by monopoly. The main effort of a powerful body will be expended in trying to realize the preliminary part of a socialistic program, and here will be seen that mingling of regulars and auxiliaries which makes this army formidable. It contains many who never think of abolishing private capital, and who will surely draw back when the line of contention moves forward and the changes demanded become radical. There are in the force two distinct classes whose interests will impel them to drop out of the ranks when the march goes beyond a fairly well defined boundary. Is, then, the socialistic army getting large and dangerous? It is getting large, and therefore less dangerous than it might be; for it is gathering into its ranks elements that will disrupt when it attempts to do the more perilous things.

Who are the classes who thus mean present help and future trouble for the socialist party? Are there laborers among them? Radical socialism has been defined by one of its leaders as the political economy of the suffering classes, but that does not necessarily mean the political economy of the working classes. In a way all workmen are united, both in feeling and interest, against capital, since all of them want to make wages as high as they can at the cost of employers; yet it is very clear that they are not all in such a state of suffering that they can afford to throw away the advantages that they have. There have always been workmen whose skill has kept them well above the line of privation; there are now workmen whose organization keeps them there. Skill counts for less than it once did, but organization supplemented it as a means of creating an aristocracy of labor. The important question is, whether this favored body will, to the end, make common cause with the more democratic one? If organization causes some workingmen to thrive partly at the expense of others, there are limits to the extent of the co-operation of the two classes. Whether the gains of some are thus partly at the cost of others depends upon whether the different trade organizations are or are not monopolies. It is commonly said that most of them are so; and, if the statement is true, there must be something about the working of them that is contrary not only to the public interest, but to the interest of the remainder of the working class itself.

The whole relation of trade organizations to monopolies ought to be better understood than it has been. If there is such a taint upon them as current descriptions imply, it is not altogether their own fault; for with monopolies on the capitalistic side forming all about them, the temptation to get some of the benefits which they insure is irresistible, and inevitably one of the foremost objects of the trade union will be to force employers to give them a share of the grab which they are getting for themselves. The trust thrives by a price raising policy. It keeps down the output of its goods in order that it may raise the market rate for them, and, in doing this, is shuts up some of its mills, and turns off some of its men. This naturally has the effect of depressing wages in the general field. The trust, whatever it may profess, aims to be a monopoly, and cannot be so without reducing the real wages of men outside of its own employment. It is perfectly natural, then, that the men in the trust's employment should wish to fare better, and to do so by getting a share of what the public is made to pay. This involves, indeed, participating in tainted gains; but the taint does not, in the first instance, adhere to the laborers. There are few persons who will say that, where a monopoly has already cut down its output of goods and has begun to realize its extortionate returns, its employees should hold their hands and refrain from getting as large a part of these gains as they can. In doing merely this, they do not make the burden on the public any heavier. Naturally they organize, and bring pressure to bear upon the trust; and this body, having a hostile public to face, is willing to avert any further attack. It wants no fire in the rear; and, if moderate concessions will keep its men quiet, it will probably make them.

It is possible for a strong organization of workmen, of their own motion, to make a trust pay something that does not thus come out of its own gains. Give us an advance in wages, and charge it to the public, is often the demand tacitly or openly expressed; and, in this case, the men are not merely asking for a part of what the trust is already charging to the public, but are proposing that the corporation should keep all that, and make a further charge for the men's benefit. And at this point, therefore, wages begin to show a monopolistic color of their own. This creates an issue between these particular men and the public, and it is of importance to discover what classes really compose this tax bearing public. Very largely it consists of workmen who are not getting monopolistic profits of any kind. Whenever we say the public in this connection, what we necessarily mean is a body of people the majority of whom are laborers; and the demand for a concession at the cost of this public raises a sharp issue between labor that is strongly organized and the great mass of independent labor. Inherent in the situation is the motive impelling trade unions and trusts to form tacit alliances with each other to assure the gains that come by raising prices, and every such alliance makes one body of workmen help in oppressing another body.

Now a trade union may go even farther than this, and in a purely selfish way it may gain something by doing so. It may create a monopoly that is wholly its own. If a union in a building trade gets secure possession of a local field, and completely excludes outside labor from this territory, it is able to establish its own schedule of pay, and make employers concede it. So long as contractors are not in a combination, they have no means of securing for themselves any monopolistic profits. They are forced to make their estimates of the cost of buildings larger whenever the scale of wages is raised; and the greater part of what the public pays in the way of enhanced cost of building goes, in this case, to labor rather than to capital. The competition of the contractors with each other, so long as it lasts, prevents them from getting much of it.

The claim that organization can greatly benefit workers is no myth, if it means that it can keep the pay of men in the unions above the level of the pay of men outside of them. So long as the men on the outside are a part of that vaguely defined public which, patiently or impatiently, pays the bills of every kind of monopoly, they clearly have a certain tax to pay to the workmen who are in the monopolistic circle. This opposition of interest between labor in a unionized trade and other labor is irrepressible, and does not by any means confine itself to cases in which free laborers take strikers' places. In the struggle between the union man and the scab, antagonism is, indeed, carried to the final length, and creates the greatest conceivable bitterness of feeling. The scab, however, is to be distinguished from the nonunion laborer of the ordinary sort. He never appears while the tacit alliance between a trust and a trade union is in working order, but comes only when such an alliance is temporarily broken. He comes then as a boss's man to help fight the union, while the ordinary nonunion worker has no open issue with it. Quietly and indirectly, however, he pays his share of the tax which the union and the trust impose for their joint benefit. The worker in an unorganized trade has nothing to do with the monopolistic boss, and he does nothing to make the trade unionist dislike him. He is a submissive payer of tribute, and yet this very fact makes him, when he sees where his interest lies, the natural opponent of all monopolies, whether of labor or of capital. In proportion as the grabs become larger and the public feels the burden of them, the laborers who are in the rank and file of that public will more and more clearly see the rift that divides them from the men who profit by the tax they have to pay.

Would trade unionists, then, consent to the plan of sweeping away the whole system of private industry, and putting everybody into the employment of the state, which will have to treat them all alike. Not so long as they are governed by the interests of their own particular classes. Favored trades would lose by such a democratic leveling, and in the long run it will be found that they are poor material for socialistic propaganda.

The attitude of different trades toward socialism is interesting, and the grounds for their attitude in different cases may seem puzzling; but at bottom the dominant motives are simple enough. The union which stands by socialism through thick and thin will be the one that fails to hold its own in the struggle for mutual taxation. Stronger unions will make monopolistic gains at the cost of the public, and the union which favors collective industry and a general leveling will be the one that is a part of that public. It tries to recoup itself by taxing still others; but if it fails, and is remanded to the tribute paying rather than the tribute collecting half of society, it will vote for the leveling measure. The union which collects an ample tribute will not do this when the leveling is really imminent.

While socialism is only in the air, this line of demarcation is not clearly drawn. Many a strong union is willing to join in the demand for the nationalizing of all industries so long as that measure seems remote, and it is willing to demand the nationalizing of some industries in any case. Such unions consider all workers in a general way as brothers, and all capitalists, in the relations of the market at least, as enemies. They are carried along by a general trend of feeling which often thrusts interests into the background; and when they act on the basis of interest, they may be misled by an exaggerated idea of what the government could do in the way of raising wages, if it took charge of every kind of business. Most workmen think that employers, as a class, are getting far more than they actually get. The important question is, how far will such motives make them go if the state yields to pressure and takes one industry after another into its hands? In the long run real interests rather than imaginary ones will make them part company with the less fortunate masses, to whom socialism makes a really cogent appeal.

The interests of successfully organized labor and those of other labor permit them to work together in certain preliminary steps in the socialistic movement. Laborers might all rejoice together in seeing municipalities operate street railways and lighting plants, and in seeing the general government take possession of railroads and mines. Many of the employees of such monopolies could afford to take their chance in public employment rather than in private, for they would expect short hours and high pay under the government. But would trade unionists who are employed by manufacturing trusts favor giving them all over to the state? Not unless they could be sure that the government would treat them as well as they can force the trusts to treat them. They should have misgivings on this point, for the more kinds of business the state has to carry, the more difficult it will be to keep up in them a high rate of pay and short hours of labor. In a few cases the government could do this since, if the industries in its hands were run at a loss, it could collect the deficit by imposing new taxes, or by putting still higher prices on the goods it has to sell. It could give short hours and high pay to men on railroads and to those in mines, if there were not too many of them; but the more there were of them, the bigger would be the sum it would have to exact from the rest of society, and the smaller would be that remainder of society which would have to pay the tax. This is the essential point, and it shows that, if trade unions are at all successful in their present policy, they can never afford to abandon it for complete socialism. A government can always pay high wages in a few occupations, since it can take something out of the pockets of many men and put it into those of a few; but it cannot, by such a process, fill everybody's pocket. When a trade unionist finds himself urged to join in putting everything into the hands of the state, he will see that, if he thrives at all under the present system, destroying it would mean exchanging two birds in the hand for one in the bush. Only by making industries phenomenally productive could the state give large pay to everybody; and with the go easy plan of labor which a government would be forced to adopt, he would be a sanguine man indeed who would expect such an increase of productivity.

Socialism is nothing if not ultrademocratic; and if it is ever realized in practice, it will mean the obliteration of every such distinction as that which strong unions maintain between themselves and unorganized laborers. That distinction, as we have seen, is due partly to a tax, since high prices for goods which the unions make are one of the means of maintaining it, and every such tax is hostile to the democratic spirit. Taking railroads into the control of the government would enable the state to pay laborers on them well; but the public would have to stand the cost of this, either in the way of costly traveling or in that of heavy taxes. Taking all industries into public control, and raising everyone's pay to a satisfactory point, would take a larger income than the state could get from any source.

Of course there is always the resource which a confiscation of all capital would give. A government that should resort to this measure might add to wages the gross profits of the capitalist class; and a point that any body of workmen must consider, is how much would this add to their own wages? Even such statistics as are now available show conclusively that it would not give to workers generally as high pay as successful ones now get. Monopoly is more profitable than democracy for the strong trade union. Even a successful union might be willing to have the state take possession of its own industry, if it could be assured that its present preeminence over other labor would continue; but under general nationalization the very opposite would be the actual result. A leveling of wages would certainly be demanded; and the question that a union laborer must answer, whenever a project for complete socialism is before him, is, Will you share your gains with the mass of more needy men? Will you make common cause with the cheap labor which immigration has given us in abundance? It will require a heroic altruism to say yes.

Could a government possibly give high pay to everybody? If it were to strip capitalists of everything that they have, could it get a grand dividend large enough to make every worker happy? This is a vital point, and statistics need to be more complete than they are in order to answer the question accurately and conclusively; but such figures as are available show that pulling down the rich would lift the poor far less than most of them imagine. The trouble lies in the fact that workers are terribly numerous; and when they all have a claim on a sum of money, it takes a vast one to go around and give each one something. The income from the biggest private capital might possibly give to every American a fifth of a cent a day, and the income from all the capital in the land might possibly, on a very liberal calculation, suffice to raise wages sixty per cent above their present average. The resulting rate would be far less than the more fortunate workers now get; and these men, like the capitalists, would be pulled down by a general leveling of incomes. It is this hard fact which may be trusted to prevent them from favoring such a measure, if it were ever practically before them. A class consciousness, and a broadly fraternal feeling which includes everybody who labors, all workers may have; but the highly paid ones will halt when, under the influence of this feeling, the army is marching straight to the goal of complete equality. Monopoly, first on the side of capital and then on that of labor, has given to these men something that they will not knowingly sacrifice, and while they keep it they have a large stake in the present order.

If some laborers who favor socialism in theory will shrink from having too much of it in practice, capitalists will certainly do so. Many of them are in despair over the problem of regulating trusts, and are saying that the state will have to take them and have done with it. Many a man who owns industrial shares would gladly exchange them for bonds of the government bearing a smaller rate of interest. Farmers might like to see the state take over the railroads, the mines, and the banks, but they would expect it to pay for them. These seeming auxiliaries of socialism are merely anti-monopolists; and there is no communism in their creed. They want no abolition of private property; and for every industry that the government takes into its hands it must honestly pay, if it is to have their support. Clearly, they will not go far along the route that leads to the socialistic goal.

The fact about the powerful drift toward socialism is that three different classes are for the moment carried along in it. There are the socialists proper—men who will not shrink from the abolition of all private capital. There are some organized laborers who are united with the more radical party by sympathy, but separated from it by interest. There are honest holders of property who see that monopolies must be controlled, and think that nationalizing them is the only way to do it. Both of these latter classes will part company with the first when the dream of a community of goods begins to look like a reality. The three classes, in fact, are pursuing different paths, which happen at one point to intersect. Each of the parties wants public ownership of a few monopolies, but when that has been secured they will go their separate ways. Their unions give to socialism a temporary strength.

If the government should do the common carrying and some mining, it would not thereby abolish or weaken the wages system. In the general field, employers and employed would have their issues to settle, and both would have issues pending with the public. The bit of nationalizing which we may conceivably do will leave the greater problems of industry where they are, and we shall have to solve them as we should do if no socialism had ever taken practical form. The struggle over wages is fundamental and permanent, though monopoly has given it a new shape by drawing a sharp line between different classes of laborers. It is possible here only to state seriatim a few leading facts concerning the new form of the old contest between industrial classes.

(1) Collective bargaining is now the rule, and monopoly has made it possible to carry it out on the plan of paying and charging to the public. A single competing employer cannot raise his prices without letting his business go to his rivals, but a trust that has no rivals to fear can do this with impunity. Contracting with such an employer for higher pay either makes him divide what he now gets from the public, or compels him to get more and make it over to his men.

(2) The strike is the means of forcing the employer to do one of these things; and while monopoly makes the strike a promising expedient for the men, and even an endurable one for the employing corporation, it makes it a disastrous one for the public. The strike may shut up nearly all the mills in one line of business, and this disrupts the whole producing organism. There is no measuring the cost of that paralysis of business which this can occasion.

(3) The injury suffered by the parties in the strike is the chief motive that is acting to induce them to adopt expedients for maintaining the peace; but the terms of peace so secured are likely to be costly for the public. Joint agreements for adjusting the scale of wages, and plans for conciliation and for voluntary arbitration, furnish the more hopeful side of the situation, from the point of view of the parties engaged in the strife. For the public they are preferable to a state of constant warfare.

(4) Joint agreements and sliding scales mean, under a régime of monopoly, something radically different from what they formerly meant. Before employers were united in trusts, a sliding scale signified that, if the market price of a product should naturally go up, the men who made it would get a share of the gains that the rise would bring. Now it is

likely to mean that employers shall put the price up and share proceeds with the men. Employers and men become jointly interested in the price raising policy, and it is a curious fact that the men, by their strikes, are clubbing their employers into such an alliance with themselves. The party that pays the charges is the helpless though not patient public, and this fact gives a sinister quality to the peace which is so secured.

(5) There is opposition to every scheme for arbitration which has a trace of authority behind it. Why is this? Because there is a fear that an authoritative tribunal might give to strong unions less pay than they can get without it. It might take the interests of the public into account, and make it harder to carry out the pay and charge plan. Conciliation keeps quarrels in the family, and does not allow outsiders to have anything to say about the wages; while the fear is that a court established by the state might scale down the special wages that strong unions are able to get. Whether this would be done or not would, of course, depend on the rules which might be established for governing the court's action, and it would be entirely practicable to make rules which would prevent a court from acting in this way. Where a monopoly profit already exists, the court might even help the men to get some of it, and it might thus make it possible for the men to get an advance in wages without taking it out of the pockets of the people.

(6) The sustaining of unnatural prices involves force on the employers' side. It is necessary to club competing producers off from the field, and the mode of doing it is as hostile to the spirit of law as it would be if the thing were done with literal cudgels. Inefficient producers are driven out of the field even by fair competition, but the trust is driving off efficient producers, and is doing it by unfair competition. It has its own predatory methods, and its ill-omened power comes from the use of them. Stop predatory competition, and you simplify the whole situation, and make possible a reign of justice. Toward this consummation it is to be expected that with halts, blunders and retrograde movements we shall make our way.

(7) The sustaining of exceptional rates of pay, not by skill, but solely by organization on the workers' side, also involves force. The persuasion that is used to keep men out of a trade union's field is of a kind that has force in the background even when it does not come openly into the foreground. So long as unions vacate places of employment which other men are glad to take, it will require something positive to keep the other men from doing it. The unions claim a right of ownership of their positions even when they are out of them and when the community is suffering because of that fact. The thing to do is to enable the unions to get all they are entitled to in an orderly way, and without stopping production, or fighting off men who want to carry it on; and this can be done only by some kind of arbitration. If voluntary tribunals will do the work, well; if not, we shall be forced to look farther and find some which will do it.

(8) A proletariat we shall have in any case. No courts that will be established will level out the differences between the pay of organized labor and that of unorganized. While common laborers earn in foreign countries less than they do in America, notwithstanding the restrictions that are here put on their field of work, they will continue to come here. The immigrant will get more than he gets at home, and less than other men get in America. The system which holds him in this position is undemocratic in so far as its effect in America is concerned. Free immigration makes it impossible to have equality between classes of laborers. It is not to be desired that the highly paid men should be forced downward to the immigrant's level; and yet it is not to be permitted that they should hold themselves up and keep him down through a reign of club law. This one fact causes the word arbitration to be written large over the whole system which monopolies of capital and of labor have created. This does not mean compulsory arbitration, as that is commonly understood, but it does mean some effective appeal to justice. This will not do everything, but it ought to insure civil order, continuous production, a large wage paying power and some approach to a true democracy.

(9) What kind of tribunal is needed, and, in particular, what principles it shall follow in making its awards, are the vital questions which remain to be decided. Though there is no room in the present paper for the discussion of these questions, it is safe to assert that the coming system is revealing its general outlines. Joint agreements, sliding scales, conciliation and voluntary arbitration will be allowed to do their full part; but there will be means of insuring peace with justice in the cases where they fail.

(10) The new condition will not put an end to socialistic agitation, but it will reconcile so many classes to the present order that the agitation will have no radical effects.

THE GROWTH OF THE AMERICAN FEDERATION OF LABOR.

BY SAMUEL GOMPERS.

[Samuel Gompers, president American Federation of Labor; born in England, Jan. 27, 1850; cigar maker by trade; has been connected with movements for organization of working people since his fifteenth year; editor of the American Federationist; with the exception of one year has been president of the American Federation of Labor, 1882–1903; author of many articles on labor topics.]

Of the two million eight hundred thousand workmen who form the great army of trades unionism in America more than two million are affiliated with the American Federation of Labor.

The American Federation of Labor had its beginning in Pittsburg in 1881. John Jarrett, president of the Amalgamated Association of Iron and Steel workers, presided over a convention held in Turner hall November 15th of that year, at which ninety six delegates were assembled, representing union workingmen to the number of 262,000. An organization was effected, the object of which was the encouragement and formation of local, city, national and international trades unions and to secure legislation to the interests of the industrial classes. Resolutions favoring certain reforms were adopted at this initial session that were shortly made into the law of the land. One of these called for the establishment of a national bureau of labor statistics, and another protested against the importation of contract laborers.

The American Federation of Labor did not spring into existence over night. Neither was it a sudden discovery. It evolved in the natural course so that when the delegates from ninety five separate and distinct labor organizations came together to form its first convention they had a knowledge gathered out of long experience just what they wanted to do. That their knowledge was sound and that they built well out of it is now apparent. Trade unions had long existed. The New York society of journeymen shipwrights was incorpo-

rated in 1803—the first regularly constituted in the United
States. Unions of tailors trades unions, of which there is
record and carpenters, were organized in 1806 and hatters in
1819. In those days the workday extended from sunrise to
sunset and the members of those unions knew why they needed
to organize. Agitation began for a ten hour day, and Martin
Van Buren, president of the United States by proclamation
in 1840, fixed it so for all public works. Not until 1844, however, was the day shortened to the average workman, a long
series of strikes leading up to it. To commemorate the victory the shipwrights had a bell cast and erected on the river
front at Fourth street, New York, which for years rang out
the hour of beginning and quitting work. Unions were formed
now in every manufacturing center, but until the abolition
of slavery they did not pass beyond the stage of the isolated
unions except in unimportant instances. In 1863 the first
step in this direction was made by the organization of the
brotherhood of locomotive engineers in Detroit. The National Cigarmakers' union quickly followed with headquarters
in New York. The Bricklayers' and Masons' International
union was formed in 1864 and a number of national unions
came into being between that and 1872.

The good beginning thus made was checked by the panic
of 1873 and for lack of reserve funds many of these unions
died out during the long period of depression. Various secret
societies took their places and held attention for some time,
but soon lost their influence. The year 1872 saw the total
disruption of what was the first attempt at a general trade
union federation. It was known as the National Labor union
and its field was politics. It was going to work its reforms
by first electing a president of the United States. It began
in 1866 and its life, therefore, was six years. Many other like
movements were started, but ran their course quickly. The
Knights of Labor was born in 1869 in Philadelphia, having its
inception in a local union of clothing cutters. It was a secret
organization and spread with great rapidity over the entire
country and was for a long time a most powerful factor in
the affairs of the workaday world. It was at all times, however, out of sympathy with the ideals of the open trade union

MEMBERSHIP, AMERICAN FEDERATION OF LABOR

1881 TO 1904.

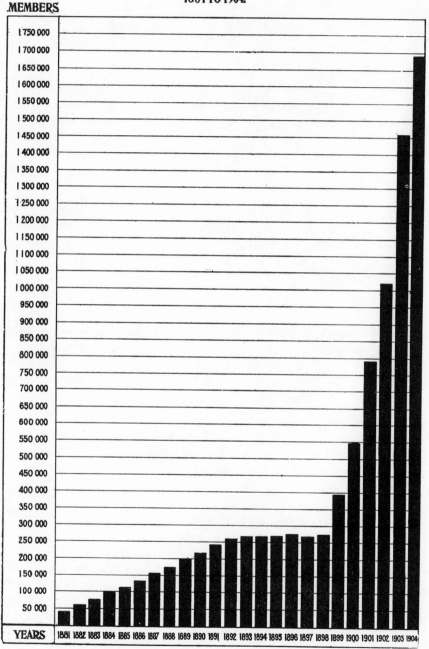

and its decline had long set in when in 1881 the trade unions, now revived and rehabilitated through a period of prosperity, called the convention of Pittsburg that resulted in the formation of the American Federation of Labor.

Samuel Gompers was chosen permanent president at the general session of the federation held at Cleveland, Ohio. This session was marked by the indorsement of a communication from P. J. McGuire of the brotherhood of carpenters, which declared the supremacy of industrial over political questions and at the same time defined more precisely the scope of the federation. It said:

"We favor this federation because it is the most natural assimilative form of bringing the trade and labor unions together. It preserves the industrial autonomy and distinctive character of each trade and labor union, and, without doing violence to their faith or traditions, blends them all in one harmonious whole—a federation of trade and labor unions. Such a body looks to the organization of the working classes as workers, and not as politicians. It makes the qualities of a man as a worker the only test of fitness and sets up no political or religious test of membership. It strives for the unification of all labor, not by straining at an enforced union of diverse thought and widely separate methods; not by prescribing a uniform plan of organization, regardless of their experience or interests; not by antagonizing or destroying existing organizations, but by preserving all that is integral or good in them and by widening their scope so that each, without destroying their individual character, may act together in all that concerns them."

At the third session held at New York city reports were made showing the ill success attending efforts made by the federation to establish a modus vivendi with the Knights of Labor

At Chicago, the fourth session, a resolution to inaugurate a general agitation for an eight hour workday was adopted.

The fifth session was held in Washington, where the methods of the Knights of Labor in organizing rejected, suspended and expelled members and their imitation of trade marks and labels of the trade unions were the principal subjects of discussion.

At the sixth session, held at Columbus, Ohio, the title of the American Federation of Labor was adopted, and from which point the organization dates the beginning of an aggressive, firm, onward march that has not ceased since. At this session the iron molders, printers, granite cutters, furniture workers, miners, tailors, bakers, barbers, metal workers, carpenters and cigarmakers joined the federation, and together with several local and city central unions swelled the ranks to a membership of 316,469.

During the last few years the growth of the organization has gone forward by long bounds owing to the energetic methods adopted for prosecuting its propaganda, the general recognition of its merits and the momentum acquired by its long and steady progress.

The American Federation of Labor is composed of constituent and representative bodies. Of the first are federal labor unions, independent local unions and international unions. The second are central labor unions and state branches. Federal labor unions are societies formed by wage earners working at different trades and are only established where there are not enough workers at the several trades to form separate unions.

Local unions having no international unions of their crafts are composed of members working at the same trade. These are recognized and allowed to affiliate only while there are as yet too few unions of the trade to permit the formation of a national union.

The supreme power of the American Federation of Labor is vested in its convention. This is composed of delegates, one or more according to its strength, from each national or general union, the delegates having one vote for each 100 members they represent. Independent local unions and federal unions are entitled to one delegate regardless of the number of their members. City central and state bodies are also entitled to one delegate, having but one vote.

The American Federation of Labor had affiliated to it May 1, 1904, 118 international unions. These international unions have complete jurisdiction over their own trades and have 23,500 subordinate or local unions with an aggregate membership exceeding 2,000,000. Besides the international unions there were affiliated to the American Federation of Labor 1501 local trade unions and federal labor unions, 604 city central unions and thirty two state federations.

The revenue of the American Federation of Labor is derived mainly from a tax levied on each union. at the rate of one half of one per cent per month from each member of international unions, of 10 cents per month from each member of local and federal unions having no internationals, and of a fixed tax of $2.50 per quarter from each city and state body. Of this, 5 cents of the 10 cents levied on members of federal unions is applied to a defence fund. The executive council has also the power to levy assessments on all affiliated unions to sustain unions engaged in industrial conflicts, the levies not to exceed 1 cent per member per week and for not more than ten weeks in each year.

The reports for the first six months of the fiscal year, October, 1903, to March, 1904, show total receipts for per capita tax of the federation were $72,810 as against $51,188 for the same months the previous year—showing the increase in membership.

TWENTY YEARS OF STRIKES AND LOCKOUTS.

BY FRANK J. SULLIVAN.

[Frank J Sullivan, author; born Oshkosh, Wis., June 7, 1870; educated in the public schools, and after serving apprenticeship became a printing pressman; has been president of the Chicago branch of the International Printing Pressman's union; swimming instructor at the Y. M. C. A. of Chicago, and writer of newspaper and magazine articles chiefly on topics of interest dealing with the life work and ambitions of the worker.]

Whether the strike and the lockout be causes or consequences is a question yet to be decided by the sociologist; whether the strike shall be one or the other is decided largely by the trades union individual, who may question after all whether the measure pays; but at all times the general public looks upon the strike condition with a first interest, while to everybody concerned in any way the sum total of the strike and lockout measures of the country carries stupendous figures and facts for assimilation.

For the twenty years period ending with the census year, the United States labor bureau has attempted to tabulate the totals of the strikes and lockouts of the country. In that period the strikes of the country cost the employee in loss of wages $257,863,478; they cost the unions in contributions to their fellows, $16,174,793; and they cost the employers a total of $122,731,120. Each of the 6,105,693 employees affected in these strikes lost $42 in wages, irrespective of the contributions of the sympathizing unions.

In the lockout instituted by the employers in these years a still greater per capita loss came to the employees to the number of 504,307. The individual cost of these lockouts to the employee was $97, with $4,915 cost to each establishment imposing the lockout. The strike loss to each establishment under strike duress was only $2,194 in the twenty years. The greatest single year of loss to employees and employers was in 1894 when the sum totals were respectively $37,145,532 and $18,982,129 for the year.

It is admitted that these loss figures are to a degree specu-
lative and necessarily arbitrary, for the one great reason that
the working year is not the possible 313 days, but rather from
200 to 250 days as the practical extremes.   In many of these
strikes a certain holiday and laying off period merely has been
anticipated by the workingmen, while on the side of the employers, time has been given for the overhauling of a plant
for improvements and repairs.   Not infrequently the employer
under such circumstances may profit by a short strike which
ends favorably to him and his cause.

Considering the strike and the lockout as the force measures of the two sides to labor troubles, it is a toss up as to which
is the more successfully carried to a finish.   Recognizing that
the strike involving only a handful of men in a single establishment is much more likely to be settled, the lockout under
similar conditions is much harder of adjustment agreeable to
the employees, and in this manner the general figures, irrespective of numbers involved in the labor troubles, may not
mean all that is on their face.   But for the strike and lockout lists of twenty years in the United States, the percentage of success and failure is shown in the following tabula-
tions:

	Successful	Partly successful.	Failed.
Strikes	50.77	13.04	36.19
Lockouts	50.79	6.28	42.93

Statistics of strikes and lockouts show some interesting
comparisons through twenty years.   The lockout lasts more
than four times as long as the strike, while involving scarcely
one twentieth of the establishments that are strike affected.
The average term of the lockout in 1900, for instance, was 265
days, as against a strike average of only 23.1 days for that
year—an average for the year below the average for the
twenty year period.

Tabulated for the twenty years under consideration one
may read at a glance a good deal of the history of the strike
and the lockout in that time:

	STRIKES.			LOCKOUTS.	
	Establishments involved.	Days duration.		Establishments involved.	Days duration.
1881.......	2,928	12.8	1881........	9	32.2
1882.......	2,105	21.9	1882........	42	105.0
1883.......	2,759	20.6	1883........	117	57.5
1884.......	2,367	30.5	1884........	354	41.4
1885.......	2,284	30.1	1885........	188	27.1
1886.......	10,057	23.4	1886........	1,509	89.1
1887.......	6,589	20.9	1887........	1,281	49 8
1888.......	3,506	20.3	1888........	180	74.9
1889.......	3,786	26.2	1889........	132	57.5
1890.......	9,424	24.2	1890........	324	73.9
1891.......	8,116	34.9	1891........	546	37.8
1892.......	5,540	23.4	1892........	716	72.0
1893.......	4,555	20.6	1893........	305	34.7
1894.......	8,196	32.4	1894........	875	39.7
1895.......	6,973	20.5	1895........	370	32.3
1896.......	5,462	22.0	1896........	51	65.1
1897.......	8,492	27 4	1897........	171	38.6
1898.......	3,809	22.5	1898........	164	48.8
1899.......	11,317	15.2	1899........	323	37.5
1900...	9,248	23.1	1900........	2,281	265.1
Totals....	117,509	23.8	Totals....	9,993	97.1

Considered by states, New York naturally leads in number and importance of these labor disturbances, while Illinois takes an unexpected third place, Pennsylvania being second. Massachusetts and Connecticut show evidences of a New England puritanism in their exaggerated proportion of lockouts as compared with their strikes. With 1,135 less strikes than Illinois has had in twenty years, Massachusetts has had two lockouts more than Illinois has had. With only one fifth of the strikes experienced in Illinois, more than half as many lockouts are credited to the state of Connecticut. The order of importance in the six states leading in strikes is:

	Strikes.	Lockouts.
New York......................	6,460	216
Pennsylvania...................	2,846	117
Illinois........................	2,840	95
Massachusetts..................	1,705	97
Ohio..........................	1,571	80
Connecticut....................	586	59

Notoriously the building trades have been involved in more strike troubles than have any other organization, though lockouts against them have been comparatively few.

RESULT OF STRIKES TO EMPLOYEES THROWN OUT OF WORK

1881 TO 1900, BY YEARS

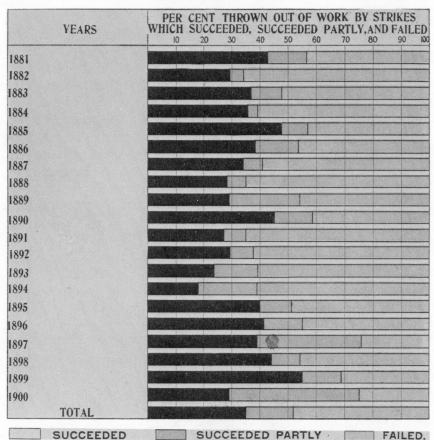

YEARS	PER CENT THROWN OUT OF WORK BY STRIKES WHICH SUCCEEDED, SUCCEEDED PARTLY, AND FAILED
1881	
1882	
1883	
1884	
1885	
1886	
1887	
1888	
1889	
1890	
1891	
1892	
1893	
1894	
1895	
1896	
1897	
1898	
1899	
1900	
TOTAL	

SUCCEEDED   SUCCEEDED PARTLY   FAILED.

RESULTS OF STRIKES UNDERTAKEN FOR FIVE LEADING CAUSES
1881-1900

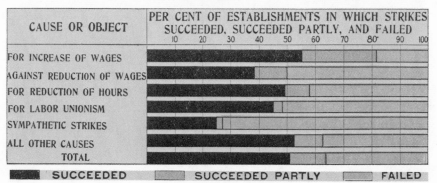

CAUSE OR OBJECT	PER CENT OF ESTABLISHMENTS IN WHICH STRIKES SUCCEEDED, SUCCEEDED PARTLY, AND FAILED
FOR INCREASE OF WAGES	
AGAINST REDUCTION OF WAGES	
FOR REDUCTION OF HOURS	
FOR LABOR UNIONISM	
SYMPATHETIC STRIKES	
ALL OTHER CAUSES	
TOTAL	

SUCCEEDED   SUCCEEDED PARTLY   FAILED

These trades and industries involved in greatest numbers are
as follows:

	Strikes.	Lockouts.
Building trades	4,440	95
Coal and coke workers	2,515	45
Metals and metal goods	2,080	130
Clothing	1,638	100
Tobacco	1,509	124
Transportation	1,265	23
Stone quarrying and cutting	856	43
Boots and shoes	862	59
Printing and publishing	765	88
Machines and machinery	453	25

There are 1,402 causes for strikes listed in the twenty
years prior to 1900. Perhaps one of the least of these was a
strike because a foreman swore at a workman; another because a man who had been discharged for drunkenness would
not be reinstated by the manager of the establishment. But
among the chief causes for these disturbances, that of the simple salary or wage question is first, while it is also mixed up
with a number of other qualified demands.

A tabulation of the causes for strikes in the order of their
number is:

Increase of wages	33,731
Increased wages and reduced hours	13,201
Reduced hours	13,116
Against wage reduction	8,423
Sympathetic strikes	4,078
Against employment of nonunion men	2,751
New rules and scales	2,742
Recognition of union	1,649
Increased wages and recognition of unions	1,111
Enforcing union rules	1,068
For reinstatement of discharged employees	868
Adoption of union scale	928
Against task system	917
Against reduction of wages and overtime	750
Increase of wages and Saturday half holiday	729

From these carefully prepared figures of the country the
individual union man may draw some conclusions of his own.
As a twenty year record of strike and lockout measures they
are full of possibilities.

STRIKES AND THE PHILOSOPHY OF THE STRIKERS.

BY FRANK K. FOSTER.

[Frank Keyes Foster, editor; born Palmer, Mass., December 19, 1854; received an academic education; is a well known writer on labor topics, and has been trustee of the Franklin fund and a member of the investigating committee of the Boston public library. Author: Evolution of a Trade Unionist, and many articles in maga zines and periodicals.]

A notable phase of the industrial history of the United States during the past decade is the number of strikes occurring in this period. Not alone have these conflicts between employers and employees increased in frequency, but they have also grown in scope and intensity. The sympathetic strike, where men belonging to crafts not directly affected by the original cause of disagreement have left their work for the purpose of assisting those first involved in the difficulty, is almost entirely a modern development, and suggests a future contingency in industrial warfare whose possible gravity it is hard to estimate with any degree of accuracy.

Both the pessimist and the optimist have had their deliverances as to the significance of the strike phenomena. The former apprehends in them a grievous menace to industry, the expression of a spirit hostile to American institutions and of vital danger to the public welfare. The incidents of disorder which occasionally accompany strikes are held to be the logical outcome of the purposes of the strikers, and to be of such a nature as to warrant the exercise of repressive agencies against the labor organizations themselves.

The optimist, on the other hand, while he may take issue with some of the methods used by strikers, and even hold that the strike itself is a costly and clumsy way of attempting to bring an industrial dispute to a conclusion, is, nevertheless, sensible that it is a most fortunate thing for wage earners that they have the legal right, and possess the power, to refuse, individually and collectively, to sell their labor under what they, at least, esteem to be unfair conditions. In a broader sense,

moreover, he recognizes that this power of resistance possessed
by the wage earner in an era of gigantic combinations of capitalists assists in maintaining that equilibrium between con-
tending interests, whose destruction would be the severest of
blows against industrial freedom. "So long," wrote Herbert
Spencer, "as men are constituted to act on one another, either
by physical force or force of character, the struggle for supremacy must finally be decided in favor of some one; and the
difference once commenced must become ever more marked.
It must be evident, therefore, that believers in democracy
who are of cheerful vision must find cause for felicitation
that the industrial masses possess the capacity to enter into
this struggle for supremacy."

But, to begin at the beginning, what is the economic object of the strike?

Labor is reckoned by the economists as a commodity to be
bought and sold in the market as other commodities are bought
and sold, and with its price regulated by the law of supply and
demand. A surplus of a commodity, under the natural operation of this law, creates a tendency toward a falling market; a
scarcity of a commodity creates a tendency toward a rising
market.

Even under the orthodox definition of labor, it becomes
apparent that within certain limits, there are two classes of
interests in the industrial world; the interest of the labor buyer
to purchase the commodity at a low price and the interest of
the labor seller to dispose of the commodity at a high price.

The lines marking this limit are roughly determined by
the margin of profit in production. It is evident that if the
margin of profit becomes absorbed by the abnormal forcing up
of the wage rate, the labor seller destroys the market for his
commodity. Conversely, if the wage rate be depressed below
the living wage, the labor buyer not only decreases the value of
the commodity he buys, but cripples the market for the joint
product of labor and capital, which is dependent in no small
degree upon the purchasing power of the wage earner.

It is useless to assert that, within these limits, the interests of the labor seller and the labor buyer are identical. In
the apt phrase of Col. Carroll D. Wright, chief of the national

bureau of labor statistics, they may be, and often are, reciprocal, but they are never identical.

But in the economic philosophy of the wage earner there is taken into account an element which the orthodox economist too often entirely ignores. The wage earner grants that labor is a commodity but a commodity plus the laborer. Labor thus differs from an inanimate commodity by all that marks the distinction between a man and a bale of cotton. The latter commodity has no volition as to the conditions under which it is disposed of. The cotton seller has to deal with merely the commercial element in the transaction of sale. He may ship his commodity to the other side of the world, receive therefor his bill of exchange, and the business is completed. There is a certain visible supply of cotton in the market, and excepting for the influence of tariffs and trusts and their like, the law of supply and demand works inexorably and decisively.

But the laborer and the commodity he has to dispose of are one. In selling his labor, the labor seller must to that degree, sell himself. He must go into the market where his labor goes; he must endure the conditions under which it is disposed of. But—mark the point—by virtue of his volition he may increase or diminish the amount of his commodity on the market. He may, individually or collectively, modify the normal operation of the law of supply and demand by willing to withhold his labor from an unfavorable market. It is as though a million cases of shoes should refuse to be sold, except under conditions approved of by them.

It is in this differentiation between the commodity of labor and inanimate commodities that the impossibility inheres of instituting a fixed science of political economy. A science demands absolute quantities. The laborer is not an absolute quantity, but is subject to continual change through the agencies of environment, education, and aspiration. The serf of to-day becomes the sovereign citizen of to-morrow. The Hungarian miner, content with a crust of black bread for food, wooden shoes, and the coarsest of fabrics for clothing, a miserable shanty for a dwelling, evolves into a member of the Miners' National Union of America, whose stimulated intelligence and awakened wants lead him to demand wages which will procure for him a far larger share of the comforts of life than he formerly required.

The modern trade union is as distinctively the product of an advancing civilization as is the town meeting, the daily newspaper, the university, or any other agency which has developed the faculties of men and led them towards higher levels of thought and action. The trade union is the historic and agreed upon agency selected by the judgment of the labor sellers to protect and advance their interests as such. It has evolved from the experience of centuries of back bending toil and travail as the most available means of securing an equality of bargaining power for the labor seller in his relations with the labor buyer. Its potential possibilities are limited by naught save the capacity of cohesion and wise action among the workers of the civilized world.

The trade union recognizes the strike as a legitimate weapon of offence and defence. It is grossly unfair to style the trade union, as some ungracious critics are in the habit of doing, a striking machine. It has countless other functions besides that of precipitating industrial war. In fact, the strike plays but a subordinate part in the history of the great craft organizations of America, and represents but a small part of their expenditure of funds and energy. But the power to strike is of great importance in the consideration of the status of these organizations, upon the same principle that the fighting power of a people, even though it is rarely resorted to, is largely instrumental in determining its status in the family of nations.

"Thank God we have a system of labor where there can be a strike," said Abraham Lincoln in a speech delivered in 1860. Whatever the pressure, there is a point where the workingman may stop.

But as the purpose of this article is to examine more particularly into the nature and causes of strikes, the benevolent, educational, and fraternal aspects of the trade union movement may not properly be entered into in detail. It may be said, however, that a form of organization which has enlisted the active support of over five millions of English speaking people constitutes a working force worthy the most respectful consideration of all students of sociology. In Carlyle's words, "The shadow on the dial advances without pausing. This that they call the organizing of labor, if well understood, is the problem of the whole future for all who will in the future govern mankind."

As has been stated, the trade union holds the strike to be a legitimate weapon for use in certain contingencies. It is a sound, general principle in law—subject to exceptions— that what one man may lawfully do a thousand other individuals may do. If one labor seller may refuse to sell his labor, except under certain conditions, a thousand labor sellers may lawfully do likewise. The business wisdom of the captains of industry and controllers of trade and commerce has sought to eliminate ruinous competition among those of their class and kind having like interests. The pool, trust, and combine among capitalists is an object lesson writ large in view of the laborer who slowly reads the lesson, and then says, It shall go hard but I will better the instruction.

The trade union does in a measure, dependent upon its completeness of organization in a craft, lessen the ruinous competition among laborers. Through its agency, A agrees that if B cannot secure the desired price and conditions for the disposal of B's labor, A will not enter as a rival to bear the labor market. As a purely business principle, this protects the interests of both A and B as the labor sellers, as against the interests of C, the labor buyer. It gives to B a greater equality of bargaining power than he would otherwise possess, while, if the compact of agreement in the trade union embraces D, E, F, and their fellows, it becomes the more effective. If, however, they withhold their co-operation, and stand ready to place B at a disadvantage in his dealings with C, the argument rests not against the strike method, but against its use on the specific occasion. But, moreover, it is not usually necessary for the trade union agreement to embrace all labor sellers in order that the object of the strike may be accomplished, but only that it may control a sufficient percentage of them to render it unprofitable for the

STRIKES, ESTABLISHMENTS INVOLVED AND EMPLOYEES THROWN OUT OF WORK
1881 TO 1900
BY INDUSTRIES

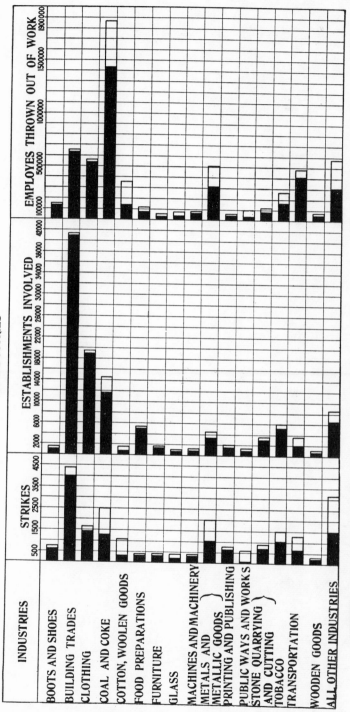

■ STRIKES ORDERED BY LABOR UNIONS. □ STRIKES NOT SO ORDERED.

labor buyer to continue his disagreement with the labor seller to the point of open conflict.

The virtue of the strike lies in its application. Of and by itself the strike is neither moral nor immoral. It is an instrument, a weapon, a piece of economic machinery. The surgeon's knife may be used to commit murder, the patriot's sword figure in a highway robbery, yet this detracts nothing from their utility when exercised in their proper functions.

The same logic holds good as to the strike. It has been truly said that the strike is industrial war. But if a war be righteous, if it makes for greater human freedom and the betterment of the race, then is that war justifiable. The lesser evil of the destruction of life and property is rightly held to be subordinate to the greater good of the advancement of the race. Society confers its highest meed of praise upon those who risk their lives in defence of home and country. History places the names of its Washingtons, Hampdens, and Lincolns upon the loftiest pinnacle of fame. In industrial war, then, the question becomes not as to whether the strike in general is moral, but as to whether the particular strike is moral; whether it is warranted by circumstances; whether it is entered upon in a judicial spirit, and as a last resort, and whether it is conducted with judgment and with due respect for the rights of noncombatants. In the words of John Stuart Mill: "A strike is wrong when it is foolish."

In the mythology of our Norse ancestors the legendary tree Ydrasgil sent its roots to the innermost recesses of the under world, while its topmost branches pierced the illimitable heavens. The myth fitly typifies the sphere of trade union activity. The underlying cause of strikes extends along the entire range of human passions. The strike may result from the most selfish of human desires, or it may be the expression of the consummate blossom of the highest aspirations of the wage earners' world.

From the official tabulation of 283 strikes entered into by the Cigar Makers' International union during five years, we find forty seven were for increase of wages, ninety four against reduction of wages, fifty eight victimization of members, twenty eight lockouts, fourteen against violation of apprentice laws, one against violation of eight hour law, and forty one for other causes, such as against nonunion cigar makers, retention of weekly pay, for strict union shop, retention of label shop rules, etc.

There are, broadly speaking, four distinct interests involved in nearly all strikes of any magnitude; first, the interest of the strikers; second, the interest of the nonunion men; third, the interest of the employers; fourth, the interest of the noncombatants, or general public.

Primarily, the objective point of the striker is to control the market in which his labor is to be sold. If his craft be thoroughly organized, the problem is to that degree simplified, and the question becomes one of a test of strength between the passionless endurance of the almighty dollar and the amount of will power and resistance the striker can put forth to gain his end. As a part of this method of resistance, every well regulated trade union aims to build up its treasury so that its strike fund may be of sufficient proportions to defray the actual living expenses of its members upon the contingency of their being called upon to withhold their labor in strike periods. To this end, modern trade unionism insists upon high dues from its membership—that is, high dues as compared with the system of low dues which obtained in the early period of unionism—but even the largest amount of dues paid by unionists is relatively insignificant in view of the objects sought to be attained by them. Average trade union dues run from twenty five cents a month per capita in the so-called cheap unions, which do little more financially than defray their routine expenses of hall rent, etc., to as much as fifty cents, or even more, a week.

It must be borne in mind, however, that the high dues unions use their funds for many other purposes than for strikes. The Cigar Makers' International union, for instance, which is one of the best examples of modern trade unionism, has not only accumulated a strike fund of over $300,000, with a reserve fund of as much more, which may be drawn upon in case of necessity, but it also pays sick, death, traveling, and out of work benefits, contributes liberally to other unions in need, and spends tens of thousands of dollars every year in advertising its label, which is placed upon the product of union factories. In fact, the amount expended for strikes by this union is but a small fraction of its entire expense account. The knowledge, however, that this organization possesses the power of resistance represented by its disciplined membership and strong treasury acts as a decided deterrent upon the buyer of the labor of cigar makers, who would otherwise feel inclined to enter into a controversy with the organization. It is worthy of notice, in this connection, that during the recent period of industrial depression when daily announcements of cut downs were being made by the press, that in no instance did the union cigar makers suffer a reduction of wages.

President Perkins, of the Cigar Makers' union, in submitting a report, adds: The tables furnish the gratifying information that trade disputes or strikes are growing less in number each year, despite the fact that the membership is increasing, and that the statistics show that we have made substantial gains in wages. This bears out the often repeated assertion that better organization means better trade conditions, and better wages with less strikes.

Among the other organizations with the system of high dues may be mentioned the glass workers, hatters, web weavers, boot and shoe workers, and many others, while there is a general tendency in all the older low dues unions to raise the amount of monthly payments and to increase the amount of benefits rendered in return.

Paradoxical as it may seem, there is nothing in the history of trade unionism to warrant the assumption that the possession of a large strike fund promotes a disposition to enter upon strikes. Responsibility breeds conservatism, and it is notable that the financially strong unions are the most cautious about appealing to the arbitrament of the industrial battlefield, while the more newly organized and less stable unions are apt to precipitate themselves into conflicts for which they are comparatively unprepared.

But the question of finances, or munitions of war, is but one of the problems which confront men who go on strike. There are but comparatively few of the crafts sufficiently organized upon trade union lines to enable them to control the labor market through control of their own membership. The nonunionist is to be reckoned with, and he is usually the prime source of strategic weakness in the position of organized labor.

There is possibly no one point as to which the methods of trade unions have been so severely criticised as in their attitude towards the men who take the striker's places when they quit work. The law itself has found it a knotty problem to decide the exact status of the striker toward his supplanter. The question has developed a fertile field for new decisions limiting the unionists' scope of action, and an ever growing barrier of injunctions hedges him about.

Waiving for a moment the legal question involved, it may be proper to state concisely the attitude of the unionist towards the man who fills his place when he goes on strike.

The trade union movement is a class movement. The unionist, if he be sincere, has arrived at the deliberate conviction that his duty towards his class demands his association with his fellow craftsmen for the protection and advancement of his class interest. In the labor decalogue the eighth commandment reads, Thou shall not steal thy neighbor's job. The unionist holds, rightly, or wrongly, that the workman has an equity in his job; that if he relinquishes his position to obtain a betterment of the conditions surrounding it, he by no means surrenders that equity, and that a third party has no more moral right to appropriate the job than to take any other property which may be left temporarily unguarded.

The unionist is often confronted with the proposition that freedom to labor where he will is the inalienable right of every American citizen. The unionist does not dispute the legal right of the man who takes his temporarily vacated situation to do so, but he does emphatically deny his moral right to do so, upon the same ground that he would challenge the moral right of any citizen to engage in an enterprise which would work harm to a considerable portion of the community. The unionist points out that the law may possibly give to him protection in his property rights against the act of another

RESULT OF STRIKES, BY STATES, 1881 TO 1900

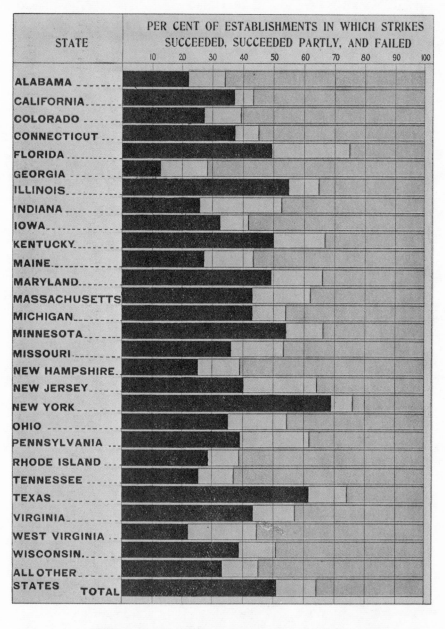

in, for instance, erecting and maintaining a nuisance in close proximity to his dwelling; but the law takes no cognition of the act of a third party in interfering with the means whereby the unionist gains a livelihood. He holds, therefore, that the man who takes his place when he is on strike is not only recreant to the interest of the class to which he belongs, but that he is also sinning against the general principle of liberty embodied in the proposition that one has freedom to do that which does not interfere with the equal freedom of another to do the same thing.

In the case of a strike, the majority judgment of the wage earners has decided that work shall not be performed under conditions which are assumed by them to be unfair. The job purloiner ignores the judgment of his fellow craftsmen, and sets up his minority judgment in its place. He has, therefore, according to trade union logic fairly forfeited his claim to the moral respect of his fellow craftsmen by his gratuitous interference with the original parties in interest.

But no trade union overlooks for a moment the fact that the nonunionist is within his legal rights in taking a striker's job. Its method of dealing with him must, therefore, be a legal method. The trade union does not countenance physical coercion or intimidation. It is unfortunately true that over zealous individuals may fail to grasp the distinction between moral and legal rights, and may attempt to visit their personal displeasure upon the man who, as they believe, has done them an injury. But these ebullitions of unbalanced proselytizers are common to all militant movements, and may not properly be charged against the real purpose of the organization. It is the absolute and unqualified truth that the trade union policy is to live within the law and to respect the legal rights of even its bitterest foe, the industrial deserter.

The two channels through which the trade unions endeavor to influence nonunionists from taking the places vacated by strikers, are persuasion and social pressure. In smaller communities, where there is a direct personal acquaintanceship among members of a craft, the social stigma which attaches to the man who takes a striker's place is a weighty deterrent against the act. Among the workers of the civilized world, social ostracism is the universal penalty paid by him who commits this offence against the traditions of his station. Sentimentalists have exploited exceptional cases where this ostracism has worked hardship to individuals, novelists have found here a fruitful mine for pathetic situations, and unfriendly censors have used the harshest terms in condemnation thereof.

But, as in most phases of the social problem, the point of view is all important in determining the justice of the attitude of men towards one another. If a thousand men honestly believe that ten other men have committed the most grievous of industrial offences toward the larger number, it is quite along the usual lines of human action that they should decline social intercourse with them. The trade unionist is willing to grant that there are certain contingencies—such as the absolute want of the necessities of life on the part of helpless dependents—under which such an offence may be condoned; but no well regulated trade union expects men to accomplish the impossible, and it does not ask men to stay on strike when the starvation period is reached. Industrial war entails privation, but the trade union doctrine holds that it is sometimes well to suffer privation for a time in order that greater future good may ensue.

Professor Bascom, in his Social Theory, puts the case fairly as follows: "When a strike is in progress, attended with much suffering, and nonunion workmen accept the rejected service, they are taking labor they have not themselves secured, and by so doing are aiding to bring about a reduction. The case is one in which the plea of industrial liberty is brought in a deceptive way against social progress. . . . The individual in a general movement for the public welfare must concede something of his personal liberty. A compulsory organic force gets hold of him and he must respond."

But the main reliance of the trade unionist on strike in dealing with one who may possibly supersede him is through persuasion, by appealing to the sense of justice of the nonunionist, to his fealty to his craft interest, by every legitimate argument and protest. In order to argue effectively with the nonunionist, it becomes necessary to interview him person-ally, and out of this necessity has arisen the universal cus-tom of picketing, or patrolling with union committees, the locality where a strike is in progress, in order that men who are brought to take the places of strikers may not do so in ignorance of the fact that trouble exists in the particular establishment concerned.

This practice has engendered much legal controversy, and has been the subject of widely varying decisions by the courts. The trend of these decisions has been decidedly hostile to this practice of organized labor, and many of the injunctions recently granted against union pickets have been dangerously near, even in the opinion of competent attor-neys, the verge of interfering with the constitutional right of free speech.

To mark the progress made in this direction, it is only necessary to compare the earlier and later rulings of the judges upon this issue. In the case of Vegelahn vs. Guntner, et al., in the Supreme court of Massachusetts, in 1893, Judge Holmes says: "I ruled that the patrol, so far as it confined itself to persuasion and giving notice of the strike, was not unlawful, and limited the injunction accordingly." Compare this with the language used by Judge Clark of Cincinnati, eight years later, when issuing an order against the striking machinists of that city: "I have arrived at the conclusion, beyond all shadow of a doubt, that picketing is unlawful; that it is immoral and wrong. Counsel for the defence must understand plainly that I am opposed to picketing in any form, and that I will promptly make the power of this court felt against it." In the order of Judge Wing of Cleveland, restraining union workmen from talking to the men who had taken their places, he says, "Persuasion itself, long continued, may become a nuisance and unlawful." Judge White of Buffalo enjoined striking machinists from attempting by argument to influence the men who had supplanted them. Judge Gager of New Haven enjoined one hundred and fifty strikers "from in any manner interfering with any person who may desire to enter the employ of the plaintiff, by way of threats, persuasion, personal violence, intimidation, or other means"; and more than two score of like decisions, recently, mark the evident temper of the judiciary towards the custom of picketing as exercised by the trade unions.

By some of these orders, no union man may speak to a nonunionist, at any time or place, no matter how far removed from the locality of the strike, without incurring the penalty of violating the injunction, even though he use the mildest language, and seeks an interview for no other purpose than to give the information that a strike is in progress.

The broader aspects of this question are not now under discussion, but it is nevertheless true that not trade unionists alone find matter for grave apprehension in this impingement of the judiciary upon the legislative branch of government, as well as in the serious limitation of the constitutional right of free speech which such decisions carry with them. The two following quotations from lawyers of high standing are but representative of the opinions held by many eminent members of the bar.

The Hon. Wm. H. Moody, one of the foremost members of the legal profession in New England, and since attorney general of the United States, said: "I believe in recent years the courts of the United States, as well as the courts of our own commonwealth, have gone to the very verge of danger in applying the writ of injunction in disputes between labor and capital."

Col. J. H. Benton, Jr., an attorney for one of the largest corporations in the country, in an address delivered before a bar association said: "The courts have, in the judgment of many of the most intelligent and thoughtful citizens, and of congress, exceeded their just powers; they have by the so-called exercise of equity power practically assumed to create and punish offences upon trial by themselves without a jury, and with penalties at their discretion."

The mass of the trade union membership is made up of industrious and peaceful citizens, men who earn their daily bread by arduous manual labor. These men are not law-breakers, either by nature or by the teaching of their class organization. They may fairly claim, however, that they should not be unduly hampered in the use of the power of their associated effort by judge made laws, enacted, as it naturally appears to them, in order to force them into the false position of lawbreakers, even when they are proceeding along the lines of moral suasion and legitimate argument.

In direct results, according to data compiled by the national and state bureaus of labor statistics, strikers are successful in rather more than fifty per cent of the controversies into which they enter. But this by no means, in the view of the trade union, represents even the economic value of the strike. Not alone is the direct gain in wages, hours, and conditions to be considered, but also the check on the tendency to reduce wages inherent in even the strike which results in temporary defeat.

In regard to the assertion that a day's labor once lost cannot be regained, the trade unionist points out that while there is idle labor in the country—a condition which universally exists—and while the productive capacity of shops and factories so far exceeds the normal demand for the product, the enforced idleness of the strike does not materially diminish the aggregate of the year's labor which will be performed. There is, moreover, the moral effect of the strike to be taken into account, and this, in the judgment of the wage earner, warrants the conclusion arrived at by John Stuart Mill, when he says: "Strikes, therefore, and the trade society which makes strikes possible, are for these various reasons, not a mischievous, but on the contrary a valuable part of the existing machinery of society."

Civilized warfare is governed by certain established canons which apply to belligerents on both sides of the conflict. In industrial warfare, trade unions grant the legal right of employers to obtain control of the labor market and to receive full protection for their property and the conduct of their business. In the earlier days of trade unions, there was ground for just accusation that organized labor did not respect these rights as it should have done, but these conditions no longer exist, especially among American trade unions.

In the case of labor disputes of magnitude the noncombatant general public frequently suffers seriously, and may

rightly exclaim, "A plague on both your houses!" This
is the inevitable consequence of war, for which there seems
to be no remedy except through the force of public opinion
and the exercise of greater consideration for the public welfare by both parties most directly concerned.

The delegates to the national conventions of the American Federation of Labor have repeatedly pronounced against
the endorsement by that body of the principle of compulsory arbitration, holding that the phrase itself is a misnomer.
This attitude is mainly due to two reasons: first, the un-
desirability, if not the impossibility, of erecting a tribunal
of appeal endowed with such arbitrary powers over the acts
of employees; and, second, a well grounded distrust of the
probable personnel of such a body. The trade union policy
places little faith in the ministrations of holders of political
appointments, and prefers to rely in the struggle for the
victory of the best, upon its own organized instrumentalities.

These objections do not hold, however, as to the principles of conciliation and voluntary arbitration, which are
quite generally endorsed by associations of wage earners.
By far the majority of trade unions, when signing an agreement with employers, are ready to incorporate in the contract
a stipulation that any differences arising in the interpretation thereof shall be decided upon by a mutually appointed
board of adjudication.

With the increasing growth and strength of organized
labor will assuredly result a greater willingness on the part
of both factors in industry to adopt conciliatory methods of
treating with each other. As Abram S. Hewett, himself a
large employer of labor, well said, in speaking of the resisting
power possessed by the trade union: "The great result is
that capital is ready to discuss. It is not to be denied that
until labor presented itself in such an attitude as to compel
a hearing, capital was not ready to listen."

The power to strike and the resultant greater equality
of bargaining power procures for workmen that consideration which is a most essential preliminary to conciliation
and arbitration. So long as the employer talks dogmatically
of "My business," conciliatory methods are barred. When

the truth dawns upon him that the workman who expends life and vitality in his employ has a claim in equity upon that employment, a saner ground of mutual relationship is established. "We consider," said James Mundella, the great apostle of arbitration and conciliation in Great Britain, "in buying labor we should treat the labor seller just as courteously as the seller of coal or cotton." When this stage of progress is reached by labor sellers, the strenuousness of the industrial relationship will be materially modified and the strike epidemic be abated.

"In dealing with the question of wages," said the gentle and gracious Arnold Toynbee, "I do not hesitate to say that you cannot separate it from the whole question of human life."

What then, is the final word to be uttered by the optimist after surveying the economic waste and social bitterness generated by the clash of antagonistic human interests on the industrial battlefield? Has the future no greater promise than in the continuance of the rule of material strength; no remedy save in the appeal to the gage of battle; no peace save in armed neutrality?

The spirit of forbearance and mutual toleration has steadily developed along theological and political lines, and now, though possibly in a lesser degree, is percolating through the strata of the industrial world. Those same qualities which make for righteousness in society at large must be depended upon to work out industrial regeneration.

HOW A STRIKE IS MANAGED.

BY HOLLIS W. FIELD.

[Hollis W. Field, author and editor; born Williamsburg, Mo., April 10, 1865; educated in the public schools of Missouri; began his career as a writer on the Kansas City Times, and afterwards became city editor of the San Antonio Express; removing to Chicago, he became connected with the Chicago Record, of which paper he became editorial writer and literary editor; writer of many articles for magazines and periodicals, chiefly on scientific and business topics.]

To the citizen of the average metropolitan city in America the news that some particular union is on strike is commonplace, save as it may promise to involve a whole community. Some union or some unions have struck. Why they did it is a matter of some interest. How they did it is for the most part an unknown procedure.

In the main it seems to be a growing impression that union labor for the least of excuses and at an instant's decision is likely to break out into the most intricate of strike involvements, something after the manner of whooping cough in a kindergarten.

As a matter of fact, the strike that is of magnitude sufficient to be felt in the streets of New York, Chicago, Philadelphia, or Boston is the creation of growing conditions and sentiments that are, perhaps, weeks and months brewing. The primary cause may have been that a single nonunion workman adjusting plumbing in a $2,000 house was retained for a week against the protests of a local union's business agent. But the disrupting strike that follows will have had just as much and no more sober consideration and preparation than the strike that may involve the most sacredly guarded rights of unionism.

Most of the great strikes of the great cities come about at the end of a certain definite agreement period, usually one year. In such agreements it is customary to insert clauses requiring sixty or ninety days' notice of dissatisfaction with the agreements before action for strike or lockout shall be taken. For instance, if the typographical union shall go on strike in January, 1906, it will be after the national body's expressions for an eight hour day talked in the convention of August, 1904, and after its second discussion in the session of August of the present year. Thus the employing bodies will have had sixteen months at least for consideration of some of the aspects of the situation.

Striking the average of all strikes all over the United States it requires twice as much time to prepare for a general strike as that general strike will last. A strike lasts 23.8 days; preparation for the strike of any magnitude will require sixty days before it is in effect, even after the first strike move has been undertaken.

The typical union of any great city involves as integers the locals which are related to that union's district or joint council, as the spokes of the wheel are related to the hub. In ten years in the United States more than 1,400 separate causes for strikes have been taken from the disaffection that arises within the territory of a local union.

Within the territory of this local, some infractions of an agreement occurs sufficient to cause disaffection. The disaffected members of the particular union in some particular establishment bring the matter before the local body at one of its meetings. A business agent is asked to come to the disaffected plant and consider the two sides of the matter. This agent ordinarily is an old tried member of the union, chosen for his knowledge of the organization and its business relations with employers. He has no written credentials. He has no arbitrary powers. He has been recognized individually by the employers as a man recognized by the union to treat as amicably as possible between the two forces of capital and labor. Among the employees of the establishment is the steward—an officer of the local union—with whom the business agent comes in direct touch on the one hand, and on the other side of the controversy is the employer.

The matters in controversy, however, cannot be settled through the business agent's diplomacy. Perhaps neither employer nor employee will recede a hair's breadth from the first position of estrangement. The next recourse is for the local union to carry the matter to the central district council.

In this body the representation is on a senate basis, each local having its fixed number of representatives regardless of the number of its members. Before this central body the differences between the single house and the group of union employees in that house are brought up and canvassed. If the central body is impressed sufficiently, the question of strike or not to strike is submitted to a vote there. This may be a secret ballot of the membership, or it may be a yea and nay vote, put by a calling of the roll.

The result is the calling of a strike against that certain house. The business agent is instructed to visit the plant at a certain time and call the strike. He goes, appearing before the steward in the establishment, and through this official the union members are ordered to walk out of the place, reporting at headquarters of the union. There enough of the members of the local on strike are selected for picket duty around the plant. Squads of pickets are told off under captains selected, and these are posted around the struck establishments to use influence against the places of the strikers being filled with nonunion workers. Perhaps some of the members of the firm are engaged in other lines of industry. Having become unfair, disaffection arises in these places of business and the strike spreads through sympathy. At a meeting of the district council it becomes evident that to make the strike effective, all members of all local unions must be ordered out. This is voted and by the same general procedure the working members of all local unions are called out of all establishments employing that particular class of men.

But in the meantime, in all this preparatory work for the interests of unionism, the national executive board of the union has been kept in touch with the merits and possible demerits of the controversy. Before the final order has gone out for a general strike of the union in Chicago, for instance, the national board has been appealed to for ratification of the strike, and this executive board has passed favorably upon the move. Only when this national body has given assent does a strike become of distinct significance and bearing, but after this ratification such a strike becomes active, promising, perhaps, to involve every district council in the United States unless somewhere on one side or another the necessary concessions shall be made.

Occasionally within the territory of a single local union there may be a gross violation of all agreements made by some particular employer, at which the union men employed in the establishment may drop their tools or work of whatever kind and walk out without the sanction of even the district council, But these are sporadic examples of strike measures, usually quickly settled.

Necessarily the question of money for carrying on the general strike is of first importance. In many ways this necessity is anticipated in times of prosperity in a union where the benefit insurance system, forms of membership dues, and the like are resorted to; while in the emergency of a strike assessments upon the working memberships of the union and even measures for raising money by entertainments, by solicitations at lectures and such become matter of fact necessities.

In the small territory of a local union appeal may be made to the district council asking for aid from the other locals for the local strike. Under such circumstances the district council investigates and makes its levy as the situation seems to demand.

But in the modern strike, as in the modern war, the question of success has become in great measure a question of money. War is becoming more terrible to the civilized nations, not because it is killing too many thousands of men, but because it is costing too many millions of money. A great strike costs its millions now and then, but whether it is to become obsolete because of that fact, as is predicted for war, is still a proposition subject to a wide difference in opinions.

HOW LABOR UNIONS BENEFIT THE WORKING=
MAN.

BY FREDERICK F. INGRAM.

[Frederick F. Ingram, born Barry Co., Mich., 1856; educated at high school at Hastings, Michigan, and Olivet college; learned the telegraph business, and later became a clerk in a drug store; in 1877 bought a drug store for himself, borrowing the capital, and a few years later established in Detroit a small wholesale drug business which has developed into one of the leading proprietary manufacturing concerns in the country; in his few spare moments has made himself an authority on municipal and labor questions and has contributed several articles on this subject to periodicals.]

What has society or civilization gained by the organization of labor? That is a question that must be answered according to each individual point of view. If we say that it has improved social conditions we must look for the proofs in a better relation of man to man. If we say that it has advanced civilization we must take note of the successive stages of progress.

Wherein has organized labor benefited society? In the elevation of morals and the exaltation of the home. The pillars of true society are anchored to the brain and brawn of the workers of the age. Upon men who earn their bread in the sweat of their brow must society depend in all ages for its preservation. Privilege, the breeder of idle leeches, is the cankerworm that has destroyed past nations and civilizations.

A society that is built upon the uncorrupted homes of unpurchasable producers is the society that we must depend upon to preserve our liberties, make our country truly great, and protect us from the greed of those who are able to live without working and at the expense of others who, as a consequence, must work without living. Organized labor has been a benefaction upon the humble homes of the toiling masses, enlarging their comforts, widening their intelligence, strengthening their morals, and upbuilding their sacred ties.

Organized labor has advanced wages and shortened the workday not only for its supporters, but for the nonsupporters, its competitors in the labor market. It has striven that all workers may have respite from toil to improve their minds and cultivate the graces of social intercourse. The almanac and household receipt book that formerly comprised the home library have been succeeded or superseded by well chosen and well bound volumes of poetry, history, economics, and fiction.

Organized labor has broadened the great doctrine of universal brotherhood that an injury to one is an injury to all. It has succored the oppressed, girded the loins of the weak, and helped right to overthrow might in contests for simple justice. It has brightened the homes of millions by its self invited contributions to relieve the sick and feed the hungry. It has erected homes for its weak and superannuated members. It has endowed hospitals, built churches, contributed to charitable institutions, and scattered with prodigal hands those seeds of kindness which afford shelter and rest to the weary and heavy laden. Its principles are grounded in sympathy; its aims are benevolent; its ideals are illumined by the overshadowing nimbus of eternal justice. If it sometimes errs in choice of agencies or weapons to carry forward its campaign for the amelioration of its oppressed, that charity which thinketh no evil should shield it from carping criticism and vindictive denunciation.

As did its ancient prototype in past centuries, organized labor has made its impress upon the political progress of the century just closed. The ancient guilds demanded and forced from the reluctant hands of their rulers rights and concessions that redounded to the good of all the common people. They secured and preserved their liberty by appeals to the reason and conscience of the masses. Similar forces in 1610 wrung from a reluctant king the declaration that private monopolies were against the laws of the realm and commanded his courtiers not to presume to ask him for any more, followed 13 years later by parliament resolving that all monopolies are altogether contrary to the laws of this realm, and so are and shall be utterly void and of no effect, and nowise to be put into use or execution.

Now, after the lapse of centuries, private monopoly, new in form, but even more sinister in purpose, has again re-established itself.

Organized labor has again sounded the alarm and assumed leadership in a demand that monopoly rule must be dethroned and majority rule re-established.

We are not infrequently admonished by philosophers and economists that there is going on betwixt capital and labor a war for existence; an irrepressible conflict; a something fierce and dreadful that aligns labor in uncompromising hostility to capital; a clash of interests that has been and will be perpetual—an endless battle for the supremacy of the arena of production.

The picture of these embattled hosts, as painted by the average academician, alternately sways us from emotions of pity for the principles to despair of the future. We discern in the perspective forbidding shadows of an impending bloody revolution in which established institutions will be wrecked, government will be overthrown, society disrupted, and our homes shattered. In short, an uprising of the toiling masses in which anarchy is finally to triumph and all law to be overthrown.

With such a horoscope of the future I have small patience. It is narrow, mean, and wicked. It assumes that the Almighty is responsible for present conditions, which are, therefore, unchangeable. On the contrary all laws and all conditions that oppress labor, all laws that are unjust and unnatural, are man made. Repeal them, change them, and the bloody revolution will become a peaceful emancipation. I have naught but pity for the cynical prophets of an irresponsible conflict; nothing but compassion for the lachrymose croakers who predict industrial discord and discontent as the heritage of our children. Like barnacles to the ship, these nightmare dreamers impede progress toward industrial equality.

The composite conscience of the great common people whom Lincoln said, "God loved so well because he made so many of them," is the final arbitrator of labor-capital disputes, and it will prove neither dishonest nor biased. Under informed leadership of experience and training, the industrial inequalities of the future will be gradually resolved into fair play and fair pay.

The rise of labor unionism in this country may be briefly noted in order to understand the present situation. It is of comparatively recent origin, and we must go back to colonial times if we would learn why it was retarded. In 1607 a party of British adventurers, looking for land, debarked from their ship where now is Jamestown. With them were craftsmen and professional men, but very few laborers. There was nothing much for professionals and craftsmen to do. The soil was the raw material upon which they must work. To cultivate tobacco, laborers must be had. To recruit the feeble force of laborers word was sent back to England to ship them. Magistrates and jailors of English cities and ports undertook to supply the demand by secretly selling to press gangs such criminals as had been sentenced to death or imprisonment, and by kidnapping boys on the streets, to be hurried aboard ship for emigration to America. Thus was introduced the first involuntary servitude, and it will be noticed that the slaves were white men. Nine years later a Dutch war ship, having on board 20 negroes captured from Spaniards, put into port for supplies, and the negroes were exchanged for tobacco and provisions. That was the beginning of black servitude in this country—a servitude that endured for three centuries, only to be uprooted and destroyed by a war that cost more blood and treasure than any other of modern times.

We know that it adhered to the body politic of this country until Lincoln emancipated the slaves as a retaliatory war measure. He who said, "Capital is the fruit of labor, and could not exist if labor had not first existed. Labor therefore deserves the first consideration;" gave the slave labor consideration at the opportune time. Five months after the slaves were freed there was organized the brotherhood of locomotive engineers. The cigar makers, bricklayers, and printers subsequently organized unions, and they quickly took on the character of national bodies. In the northern states there had been unions long before.

The panic of 1873 came just as many newly formed unions were building up. A long period of idleness and industrial inertia ensued. The pendulum of activity which had swung so far toward prosperity in the years following the war swung back again, and remained suspended at a standstill. Union members, on account of hard times produced by speculation, could not meet their dues, and as a result most of the infant organizations were obliged to disband. In the year 1873 an attempt to federate the young unions had collapsed. Then secret societies sprung up, the most conspicuous of them being the Knights of Labor, a vestige of which organization yet remains; but it was badly counseled, and disintegrated from inherent weaknesses.

Eight years later, at Pittsburg, was made a successful attempt to federate the existing unions. There were in the convention 96 credentialed delegates, representing a quarter of a million of wage earners. After free and open discussion the constitution of the American Federation of Labor was formulated. The new organization did not include all labor unions, but it has since affiliated most of them. It is the towering master of all, and the most potential labor organization in the world. Its jurisdiction now extends to over 114 national unions, and to more than 2,000 subordinate unions, with a total membership of 2,000,000 breadwinners.

It is the representative labor organization of this country, if not of the world, and without doubt wields greater influence upon legislative and economic conditions than any other. Its president is Samuel Gompers, a man of great executive ability, shrewd and wise, and the members of the federation look upon him as a tower of strength to the cause of unionism.

Labor can do without capital. If all capital were destroyed in a night, labor, nevertheless, if free, would soon be better off than before, for then labor, having unrestrained contact with all the God given and natural resources of the earth, would soon reproduce capital, and each, unshackled from the exaction of idle, luxurious drones, now possessing a monopoly of natural resources and exchange, would receive its just reward.

It is not more room at the top of the ladder, where we are told there is plenty of area, but more room on the bottom rungs that justice and equality demands. Not one in a thousand, or in ten thousand, ever gets to the top, while those there often injure the rank from which they rise by depriving it of its most energetic workers. If there were more area on the lower rungs of the ladder there would be smaller concentration of wealth in the hands of the few at the top, and a larger diffusion of wealth at the bottom.

Comfort would be universal, long hours of ceaseless toil would be no longer necessary in any occupation, and the wide gap that now separates the worker and his employer would be closed.

While the changes in the methods of production have made new adjustments necessary in industry, yet present conditions are far from the desired golden age.

Organized labor at all times has been the one kopje that withstood the assaults of greed, cunning, bribery, and cajolery in its constant warfare for economic justice and industrial liberty, and though it has made many mistakes, has often met with defeat, in my judgment it has greatly advanced the cause of civilization, has been and is a potent factor in preserving our liberties and increasing the comforts, diminishing the worries, and broadening the intelligence of the common people.

TRADE UNIONS AN INFLUENCE FOR INDUSTRIAL PEACE.

BY JAMES DUNCAN.

[James Duncan, first vice-president of the American Federation of Labor; born Kincardine county, Scotland, May 5, 1857; educated in the public schools of that country and at Aberdeen college; his trade is that of granite cutter, and he has been secretary of the International Granite Cutters association since 1895, and for the same period editor of the Granite Cutters' journal; since December, 1904, has been first vice-president of the American Federation of Labor.]

The time is fast approaching when the great majority of corporations, as quite a number have already done, will realize that the proper and business like way is to meet the representatives of organized labor to discuss and agree upon properly defined working rules and carefully prepared wage scales. Distrust and misunderstanding are the two greatest disorganizers of modern industry, and as long as the two great factors, capital and labor, stand aloof and fire at long range, that long will indiscriminate and unfriendly acts be perpetrated by each toward the other. Trade unionism stands for peace and prosperity. In crafts where it is strongest and best administered, conditions for the worker are the most desirable and the greatest amount of industrial tranquillity is obtained. Capital is there found to be in its soundest realm. Great financial bonanzas may not be visible, but neither do we find the misery and despair of the poorly organized worker or of the nonunionist.

No contract should be more sacred than the trade agreement of organized labor. It is a matter of honor between the contracting parties, that is circumscribed neither by surety companies' bonds nor by compulsory edicts which enslave the body or dwarf the mind. It is regrettable that in too many instances these principles are violated both by the unscrupulous employer and by ignorant or unadvised workmen; but such mistakes should not be viewed as failure of the labor movement any more than the collapse of a business venture should be considered a slap to civilization. The bar has members with a peculiar itching in the palm of their hands, which only unearned greenbacks will soothe; the church has within its fold men who fall by the wayside or hear the voice of God calling them to a larger salary, and the labor movement has its bribe takers. The more is the pity that such should exist, but those who expect the trade union to be perfect, while to that extent complimenting it, are expecting too much for the time in which we live.

Again, asserting that the economic movement is one of honor, words fail to express sufficient contempt for the official who barters the confidence of his fellow workmen, either for lucre or for other personal preference. Such a man may revel in notoriety for a brief time, but honest and practical procedure will assert itself and, distrusted both by bribe giver and by his old constituents, the dishonored official will be relegated to the rear and will be remembered only as one recalls a disease. So much for the individual. No organization can long maintain the respect necessary to success, a majority of the members of which permit an agreement to be openly violated or even casually disrespected, and in the trade union movement the young organizations, which have not yet learned to follow the lead of older unions in that particular, cannot do better than pattern after such of them as have by experience proved that a fair and square observance of craft settlements is an essential and fundamental principle of the labor movement.

That such violations sometimes occur is true, but it is also true that in every such instance a great mistake has been made. Sometimes the cause is found in hasty action by the oppressed or overzealous workman, but often employers in a mad desire to outdo some competitor, inflict unbearable conditions on workers which arouse their antagonism and retaliation, and thereby violate the spirit of the agreement as fully as the other case, and both causes are equally reprehensible. This feeling will be in evidence on both sides as long as either retains the idea that the other has no rights to be respected— but if the up-to-date method fostered by trade unionism and advocated by the civic federation, of each conceding that the other has inherent rights and that both should meet and adjust their differences in conference if possible, and if not by arbitration, is followed, ninety per cent of the labor disputes causing suspension of production and inconvenience to the public would be prevented. Along this line of thought the moral effect of such a body as the industrial department of the civic federation, standing as preceptor for the logical, rational, and pacific adjustment of commercial affairs, will go a long way toward bringing otherwise discordant elements in unison. It is not only essential to provide or suggest a way to adjust affairs of this kind after trouble has ensued, but they will be statesmen indeed, of the highest rank, who can formulate and put into use either customs or rules which will bring employers and representatives of labor together to formulate new arrangements a month or more before the expiration of the old ones. Men's minds are then cool and calculated to reason well, but when the excitement of a change is at its height, ill digested advantage takes the place of better judgment and less satisfactory settlements are obtained.

Unless in a few instances where physical endurance is at stake, organized workers do not limit production. In their collective bargain they declare for a minimum wage rate and leave the individual to produce what he can. Too often, however, the minimum rate in the bargain is considered a maximum rate by the employer, and the public is thereby led into a misconception of conditions, and trade unionism is again required to bear a burden which should be on the other fellow's shoulders. If law will continue to tolerate the sweating system, for instance, sapping the vitality of men, women, and children in their effort to earn a mere pittance, it becomes a question of practical consideration if trade unionism should not supply the deficiency, as it does others, by seeing to it that human beings shall not be treated as mere machines, and be ground to death at the behest of a false commercialism.

RESULT OF STRIKES ORDERED BY LABOR ORGANIZATIONS AND NOT SO ORDERED, 1881 TO 1900

BY INDUSTRIES

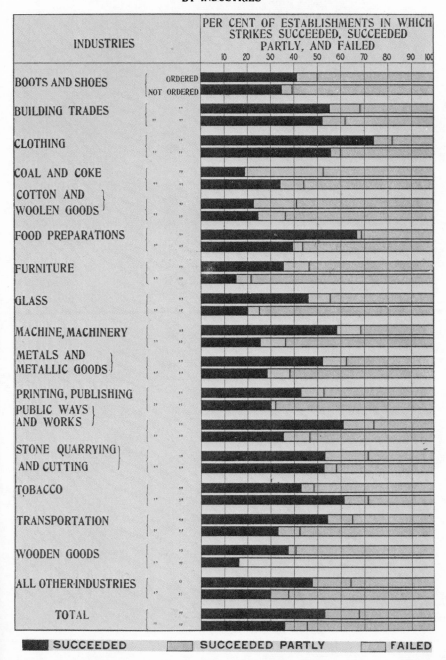

THE TRADE UNION LABEL.

BY JOHN GRAHAM BROOKS.

[John Graham Brooks, head of the Chicago Commons; born Ackworth, N. H., July 19, 1846; graduated from Harvard division school, 1875; studied three years abroad and became lecturer on economic subjects; for two years was instructor at Harvard university; was for several years lecturer in the extension department of the University of Chicago; two years expert United States department of labor at Washington, making report of 1893 upon the Workingmen's Insurance company in Germany. Author: The Social Unrest.]

No sign of a trade union label has been found by the writer earlier than 1874. It appears to be wholly of American origin, nor is any evidence at hand that unions elsewhere, except in Canada, show special interest in it. The chief reason for its adoption here is doubtless in the intenser and more embarrassing forms of competition under which labor unions suffer. Many devices, both good and bad, to which the American trade union has been driven, find their origin in the exigencies of this severer competition. If the distinctively race element is included, no single factor in this competition is so powerful as that of immigration. It is not merely a question of numbers. It is not merely a question of multitudinous unskilled labor. It is also a question of race. All a priori theories of liberty and brotherhood yield quickly before the actual competition of different standards of living in a common market.

The Australian trade unions were powerful enough practically to exclude the yellow race. The unions there, as in England, are overwhelmingly of the same race. This fact makes the competitive struggle relatively a simple one. The attempt to understand the American trade union is incomparably more perplexing because of the racial effects. The constant pressure, through immigration, of a great multitude of half skilled laborers, representing far lower standards of life and at the same time introducing race antagonisms, has driven the trade union in this country to catch at every weapon of defense. The label is one of these weapons. Its first appearance was in California during the sand lot agitation against the Chinese. The Burlingame treaty with China was concluded July 28, 1868. In article 5 both countries cordially recognize the inherent and inalienable right of man to change his home and allegiance, and also the mutual advantage of the free migration and emigration of their citizens and subjects respectively from one country to the other for the purposes of curiosity, of trade, or as permanent residents. This hospitable mood was of short duration. In this same year (1868) 11,085 Chinese landed on the Pacific coast. In 1872 a San Francisco firm of cigar makers took on a number of Chinese. The number which came into direct competition with the work of any trade union must have been slight, except perhaps with the cigar makers, yet, as with the insignificant product of prison labor, it aroused instant hostility.

Much of the more recent state legislation concerning the label throws light upon its origin, as in Illinois, where it is held that a label upon cigars showing them to have been made by a first class workman, a member of an organization opposed to inferior, rat shop, coolie, prison, or filthy tenement house workmanship is legal, etc. Against the rat shop, coolie made cigars the California cigar makers first struck. But how should a sympathizing public know which were rat shop and coolie made cigars, and which the product of American labor with its superior standard? To meet this practical difficulty a label was adopted, not the blue label in present use, but a white one, to show the buyer that he was patronizing white labor. It was thus against the competition of a low class unorganized labor that this weapon of the label was first directed. Its appeal was to the smoker: Buy no cigars except from the box marked with the trade union label, thus you help maintain the white as against the coolie standard of life and work.

In 1875 another label appeared in St. Louis during a strike of the cigar makers against a reduction of wages. The color was changed from white to red. The fight was, however, strictly over the issue of organized and unorganized labor. Both were putting cigars upon the market. The trade union wished in this instance to win the support of the consumer for a product made under union conditions. To show this a red label was used. There was at least success enough in this attempt to cause the counterfeiting of this label, upon which the trade union placed on the label its own seal. At that time there was no thought of legal protection against counterfeiting. At the convention held in Chicago, 1880, a dispute arose between delegates from the Pacific slope and those from St. Louis as to the color of the label. Let us, said an eastern delegate, take the other color on the flag, upon which the present blue label was adopted.

At this convention great stress was laid upon the fact that the unions were suffering not only from Chinese labor, but from the competition of the prisons and the tenement house. A further and more systematic use of the label was urged in order to strengthen the cause of the union against such competition.

The apparent success of the label among the cigar makers raised the question of its adoption with other unions in 1883 and 1884. The powerful organization of the hatters introduced it in 1885. The label is attached under the lining or sweatband of the hat. Its use has become so common in stiff hats that a visit to 12 New York stores (not the more fashionable ones) showed that 9 of them regularly kept the labeled hats. It is admitted by manufacturers that the influence of the label is increasing.

The label appeared in the ready made clothing trade in 1886 at a time when the Knights of Labor were in control of organized labor. It took the form of a small card tied to the garment by a thread. The present form of the label was adopted by the National union in 1891. It is of cloth attached to the inside of the garment, and costs the seller of the garment one third of a cent, the purpose being merely to cover its cost. The inscription on the label shows that it is issued by the authority of the general executive board of the United Garment Workers of America, and the garment is guaranteed union made.

From 1891 the label has been taken up by printers, bakers, wood workers, harness makers, iron molders, broom makers, coopers, photographers, shoemakers, custom tailors, mattress makers, horseshoers, brewers, egg inspectors, and barbers (who display their label in the window). Labels are found even upon coal carts, indicating that union men only are employed in distributing coal.

Among the cigar makers, hatters, and printers the label is an influence of very considerable importance. The label of the printers, for example (adopted November, 1891), is in use in more than 200 cities in the United States and Canada. Several cities have gone so far as to pass ordinances requiring all city printing to bear the union label. The state of Nevada requires all state printing to be done in union offices and to bear the trade mark of the union. This recognition of the trade union by the municipality is the boldest step yet taken. The city thus becomes the model employer, accepting frankly the principle of the trade union wage, and endeavoring, to the extent of its patronage, to uphold the standard of hours and wages, conditions for which the union stands. The action taken by Josiah Quincy, when mayor of Boston, is so significant that the paragraphs from an address to the city council are given in full:

"For a number of years the typographical union has been endeavoring to secure the recognition by the city of the organization of the printing craft through the appointment of some member of the union as superintendent of printing. I stated a year ago that in some foreign countries organizations of wage earners take a constant, active, and intelligent interest in municipal questions, and some of their members occupy important positions and render useful service in connection with city governments, and that similar co-operation might well be encouraged to a greater extent than in the past in American cities. After mature consideration I concluded that it would be advisable, in pursuance of the policy thus indicated, to place in charge of the city printing some member of the typographical union thoroughly qualified to fill such a position, and that this step would be in the public interest; I am now entirely satisfied that this has proved to be the case. It seems to me highly desirable to make organized bodies of intelligent wage earners feel that they are directly represented in the management of public business, particularly such as pertains to their several trades.

"The city printing has been done for the last twenty years under a contract made in 1876, and allowed to run on without change since that time. About $70,000 a year is now paid out for composition and press work alone. When the present superintendent of printing took office I instructed him to examine carefully into the expenditures for printing, and to report to me whether the city could not with advantage establish a plant for itself, to do a part or the whole of its own printing. After careful investigation, both the superintendent and myself have become satisfied that the city should take steps in this direction. The continuance of the contract referred to stood in the way of adopting this policy, as it gave the contractor all of the printing of the city. As it was originally made through the joint committee on printing of the city council, at a time when it exercised powers since vested in the executive, it seemed necessary that action for its abrogation should be taken by this committee, as well as by the superintendent of printing, and this has just been effected.

"Typographical unions have for many years urged the establishment of public printing plants for the execution of public printing, and the printers of this city have warmly favored the proposed establishment of a municipal plant. The new policy will be inaugurated in a careful and conservative manner. Probably only a portion of the city printing will be undertaken at first, and the work of the municipal plant only gradually extended. In the meantime the present contractors will continue to do such portion of the city printing as the municipal plant is not ready to take. It should be stated, in justice to them, that both the quality of their work and the manner in which it has been executed have been found satisfactory."

It is hardly open to doubt that such action on the part of municipalities would greatly strengthen the use of the label, at least until such time as the experiment was found to fail. Upon its theoretic side the label stands, primarily, for better pay and for improved conditions of labor. As will appear later, this is thus far but slightly realized in practice. Its practical and immediate purpose is, of course, to strengthen the union   The label is the chosen symbol of work done under union conditions.   Any open and distinct recognition of the union and its principles of collective bargaining must so far help their trade mark.   Some of the local and college settlements take the same step, not merely of dealing with unions as distinct from individuals, but expressly recognizing the label.   The Prospect Union, carried on in Cambridge, Mass., as a kind of college settlement, expressly recognizes the label of the typographical union, which does work on the co-operative plan with good measure of success. The aim is, moreover, to make the label in this instance stand for excellence of workmanship, restoring something of the ideal of the craft guilds in their better days.   That this has not been done more generally with the label is clearly a weakness, especially if appeal is to be made to a larger purchasing public.   It has been usual to claim for the label that it represented merely that the work was done under strictly union conditions.   So far as these conditions—wages, hours, sanitation, etc.—stand for higher excellence (as in many cases they do) it may be claimed that the label also represents a better quality of work.

Further than this very indefinite claim, the label can not be said to stand for excellence of workmanship or of product.   The cigar makers usually admit this, although they have an organization of extraordinary completeness and efficiency.   A sort of minimum of quality is, however, set, as will be seen in the following extract from their constitution, sec. 154: "In no case shall the union label be used in any factory which pays less than $6 per thousand; nor shall it be allowed on any cigars sold for less than $20 per thousand."   This action of the international body does not, however, cover the procedure of local unions, which may allow a label on cheaper cigars.

In the case of the hatters, it is even more difficult to trace any relation whatever between the label and quality or improved conditions.   Many shops conspicuous for the high character of their product, wages, and entire circumstances under which the laborer works, have never used the label, nor is there any likelihood of their so doing.

Nowhere better than among the hatters can the matter of fact side of the label be seen. It is, like the strike or the boycott, an instrument of warfare. The published literature of the hatters' union is filled with evidences on this point. No printed matter on this subject is so wholly frank as to the primary objects to be sought through the label. It is of course assumed that the mere fact of labor organization implies of itself higher wages and better surroundings; otherwise there is singularly little pretense that quality of work, for example, or sanitation enters into their calculation.

A movement to strengthen the ideal character of the label, to help make it what many unions claim that it is, grew out of the activities of the Social Reform club in New York. The first announcement of the club, signed by its committee on organized labor, is as follows:

"The working people have an answer of their own to these perplexing questions. They advocate the use of the union label—the workingman's trade mark. Placed upon goods by the workers themselves, this mark assures the buying public that these goods were made for fair wages and under healthful conditions.

"This device, invented by American labor, is still new, but it promises a quiet adjustment, through business methods, of these ethical difficulties which are now troubling the minds of consumers. People who are anxious to help in mending matters can do so by asking for the union label on the goods they buy. The undersigned committee holds itself ready to give full information concerning the various labels, and what are the best methods of advancing the movement."

The club has begun the publication of a series of leaflets to make the idea, the history, and possible use of the label known, not only among members of trade unions, but also among the general public who may wish to know effective ways in which the unions may be strengthened.

The first leaflet issued said:

"To promote the use of the union label means, then, to unite with the workers in their struggle to make the conditions under which work is done more sanitary, the conditions of the worker safer, and the products of better quality.

"The union label, therefore, appears to be the only means of helping the workers in the factories to help themselves. For this reason, and because of the benefits to the public as well as to the workers for which it is guaranteed, the support of the union label is strongly urged by the committee on organized labor of the Social Reform club.

"The committee regards the label as the only sign which indicates that the work has been done under suitable conditions and with any consideration of the rights of the employees, and therefore urges the conscientious public in making purchases to ask for articles bearing the union label."

In the second leaflet issued, the point is fairly made that the general public has had its attention called chiefly and inevitably to the dramatic side of trade union life and effort. It has heard constantly of the violence and strife. It has known far less, or not at all, of the educational and peacemaking tendencies in the unions.

"The label brings us to the union when it is in another mood, and we find it a peace loving association bent upon improving society through improving the conditions of work among its own members. It is an enthusiastic reformer. Here is no contradiction; none ever fight with so much fervor as those who fight for ideals.

"The label has resulted from that steady constructive effort toward improvement which is carried on by wage earners through the many months or years when they are not at war. It has great interest for every one who loves fair play, self help, and equal chances for all. Its capacity for affecting trade seems likely to produce rapid changes, and consequently the principal labels, how they are applied, just what they signify, and whether they may be misused, are matters that really concern our whole community."

Certain weaknesses of the label are frankly recognized:

"Plainly the scheme is not without its dangers and drawbacks, such as are inherent in all man's dealings. The danger of counterfeiting is the same as with any other trade mark. The label is copyrighted and a strong union protects its own label; the label of a weak union scarcely attracts counterfeiters. Treachery among the men is more difficult to meet. The label sometimes is sold out. But a fraudulent label is so injurious to the union that the evil is soon detected and likely to be quickly corrected. These are misfortunes incident to all trade."

The leaflet concludes:

"This, then, is the union label, a mere business device of the American workingman, invented to protect himself from broken promises and crooked dealing in the business world of bargains and competition. It originated without sentiment and without consciousness of having anything more than the most sordidly practical of uses. But like all sound business methods, it is notably well fitted to help along the progress of humanity. Considerably to its own surprise, it proves to be an object for enthusiasm. To any one who realizes the underlying significance of the trade union this is no surprise, however, and the practical good sense of the device becomes its strongest claim to confidence. Though the trade union does not always handle it well or wisely, and there are plenty of unavoidable inconveniences and imperfections in its actual use, nevertheless the label has great possibilities, and closely concerns others as well as the men who planned it. To these men it means stable advantages in wages, hours, surroundings, honesty, and fair competition. Its right to receive these things is sometimes questioned, but this leads into the whole economic argument about trades unionism, which has no place here. Its actual value to the craftsman in securing him the sort of life he needs is clear enough.

"As for the buyer, on whose demand the success of the label's work depends, its value to him, though less evident, is quite as great. He, as well as the employer and the worker, may find positive advantage in using the union label. The evidence and proof of this are matter for another discussion."

The occasional selling out of the label and other abuses here referred to are true and constitute a real weakness in the history of the label. A perfectly fair criticism, however, admits some extenuation. The abuses will be found at those points (as among garment and cigar makers) where the struggle of organized labor is very intense. Here, as in any fight

190 JOHN GRAHAM BROOKS

which waxes hot, principles suffer. The high phrases in political platforms do not deceive us. We allow for a very wide and sharp difference between the printed ideals and the compromises which mark the actual work of party warfare.

It would not be fair to hold cigar or garment workers to stricter responsibility. The awful struggle which goes on in the clothing industry is marked by broken faiths, in the case of the manufacturer, contractor, and laborer alike. It is too much to expect under these circumstances that the label should come off unscathed. It has undoubtedly been often used and allowed under conditions which violate every principle for which the label stands.

The conditions against which the cigar makers (and even more the garment workers) have had to contend are not overstated by Helen Campbell in her Prisoners of Poverty:

"A block or two beyond, the house entered proved to be given over chiefly to cigar making. It is to this trade that women and girls turn during the dull season, and one finds in it representatives from every trade in which women are engaged. The sewing women employed in suit and clothing manufactories during the busy season have no resource save this, and thus prices are kept down and the regular cigar makers constantly reinforced by the irregular. In the present case it was chiefly with regular makers that the house was filled, one room a little less than 12 by 14 holding a family of seven persons, three of them children under ten, all girls. Tobacco lay in piles on the floor and under the long table at one end where the cigars were rolled, its rank smell dominating that from the sinks and from the general filth, not only of this room but of the house as a whole.

"Two of the children sat on the floor stripping the leaves, and another on a small stool. A girl of twenty sat near them, and all alike had sores on lips and cheeks and on the hands. Children from five or six years up can be taught to strip and thus add to the week's income, which is far less for the tenement house manufacture than for regular factory work, the latter averaging from $8 to $12 a week. But the work if done at home can be made to include the entire family, and some four thousand women are engaged in it, an almost equal but unregistered number of young children sharing in with them. As in sewing, a number of women often club together, using one room, and in such cases their babies crawl about in the filth on the wet floors, playing with the damp tobacco and breathing the poison with which the room is saturated."

In the case both of cigar makers and garment workers, it is incontestable that the additional strength which the unions have gained by the use of the label has made conditions like those described above somewhat more difficult in a few centers. Theodore Roosevelt is reported as saying at a public meeting, "I have visited these pest holes personally, and I can assure you if smokers could only see how these cigars are made we should not need any legislative action against this system."

This trade mark is first and last a weapon with which to defend the union. Sanitary and other improved conditions are of secondary consideration. If the pressure of competition is too great, there is naturally no thought of any end except to induce the employer to maintain a strictly union shop and thus insure the payment of members' dues. Even in the constitution of the International Cigar Makers, section 160, it is said: "In localities where the open shop system is in existence it shall be optional with local unions to refuse labels to manufacturers (who employ no hands) until they have been members one year." Section 154 says: Where the manufacturer deals in Chinese, tenement house, or scab cigars, it shall be optional with local unions to withhold the union label from such firms."

It is recognized that much elasticity is necessary in applying principles. Where competition is too strong or the union too weak, abuses have shown themselves, or no attempt has been made to enforce rigidly the broader principles of the label.

Even at present, in an organization as powerful as the cigar makers, there has been great license in granting the label. It is distinctly maintained that the label is a guaranty against tenement made goods and against goods made under insanitary conditions. This is clearly the aim of the unions;

but a careful examination showed plenty of cases—in Chicago, for example—in which the label was used with dangerous laxity. It is certain that in many of these instances the label was counterfeited, the proof being that prosecutions were very common. In other cases the label had been given out carelessly, on the one condition that all dues were paid and no charges pending.

It also appeared that an extremely liberal definition of a tenement was in use. It is but fair, however, to say that as the union strengthens the abuses are less and less frequent. The testimony from several firms who have had experience with the label, as well as many contractors, confirm this view.

The head of a large firm in New York said to the writer: "I did everything that I could to get hold of the label on my own conditions, but it was refused until my shop became strictly a union shop, and I have been held rigidly to the contract. They have been straight and fair with me." This is also the testimony of a large firm in Boston.

Wholesale firms are often led to adopt the label because of the form of propaganda in use among the unions. In hundreds of country towns where trade unionism is strong an agitation is organized among the various unions, lecturers sent out, and literature distributed to induce the local traders to keep labeled goods in stock. This demand leads the trader to ask in the large cities from the wholesale departments that the label shall be put upon hats, garments, shoes, cigars, etc. If this demand becomes serious enough the firm, if a manufacturer, must unionize his shop and sign a contract to adhere strictly to union conditions.

The contract between manufacturer and union often contains a promise on the part of the union to do all within its power as a labor organization to advertise the labeled goods and otherwise benefit the manufacturer. The United Garment Workers of America has a contract with a large firm of clothing manufacturers in the west. This contract contains an admirable form of arbitration, which has proved entirely satisfactory. The head of the firm assured the writer that the label had subjected him to no trouble, and that he had found the officials perfectly fair as to the conditions of the contract, which is as follows:

"Know all men by these presents: Agreement entered into between the firm of ———, party of the first part, and the United Garment Workers of America, party of the second part.

"In consideration of the use of the union trade label of the party of the second part, party of the first part agrees to abide by the following rules and regulations governing the uses of the same:

"First. All employees engaged in the manufacture of garments for the party of the first part shall be good standing members of the party of the second part.

"Second. All proper sanitary conditions shall be observed in all shops manufacturing garments for the party of the first part.

"Third. The said label shall be controlled by Local Union No. ——, who shall attend to the proper issuance of the same.

"Fourth. The said label shall be in the sole charge of a responsible member of the party of the second part in the shop of said firm, and who shall report weekly to the respective unions, giving an account of the quantity of labels used.

"Fifth. Party of the second part agrees to do all within its power as a labor organization to advertise the labeled goods and otherwise benefit the business of the party of the first part.

"Sixth. The party of the first part agrees to pay for the printing of the labels used.

"Seventh. Should any difference arise between the party of the first part and the employees as to conditions of labor, it shall be adjusted by a committee of three selected by the firm and a committee of three from local union No. ——. Should these committees fail to agree, then both committees shall select a seventh party, who shall decide any said question in dispute.

"This agreement to go into effect —— and to terminate two years from date."

This contract gives the officials of the union much help in doing their own work, as it becomes the interest of the manufacturer to see to it that his workmen fulfill the conditions (paying dues, etc.), which the unions set. This is indeed the real influence which the advocates of the label seek to advance.

F. J. Stimson, in his Handbook to the Labor Law of the United States, says:

"To meet these cases the statute has very generally been passed allowing members of trade unions, or labor unions, or associated laborers in any shop or class, to adopt labels or trade marks to be used solely to designate the products of their own labor, or of the labor of members of their own trade unions or labor unions in alliance with them; and provision is usually made for the registration of such label or trade mark in the office of the secretary of state, and a penalty imposed for counterfeiting it; and in most of the above mentioned states remedies by injunction or equity process are expressly given the laborers or the labor union against the infringement of their trade mark or label, or unauthorized use of such trade mark by other persons. In fact, the Kentucky statute provides that such union label shall not be assignable at all.

"Such statutes are constitutional, and are not class legislation. (a) And it has further been held in Illinois, and denied in Pennsylvania, that a label declaring union made cigars to have been made by a first class workman, a member of . . . an organization opposed to inferior, rat shop, coolie, prison, or filthy tenement house workmanship, is not illegal as being immoral or against public policy within the meaning of the law of trade marks."

It will thus be seen that such praise or blame as the label may receive will be determined largely by general views upon the trade union itself. If it is conceded that labor organization is a necessity of the time, that it is especially necessary at the points where competition is most intense, it will not be denied that the label is an effective weapon to fortify the union in its struggle for a higher standard of living.

If the label is to win a larger and more strictly public sympathy, it is obvious that far greater effort must be made to have it stand—as it stoutly claims to stand—for improved sanitation and other better conditions.

In trades like that of the garment makers, a label that should be confidently known to stand for definite improvement in the life of the worker, would attract a powerful public sympathy. There are many indications at hand that a growing public interest will soon demand from some source—from manufacturers, storekeepers, voluntary associations like the consumers' league, or from trade unions—a label that shall be an absolute guarantee that the goods upon which it is placed are not made in sweat shops. Every increased effort of the unions to have their label a sure symbol of higher standards of life and work among the wage earners is certain to command more cordial and more helpful recognition from the general purchaser.

The Illinois act of July 1, 1891, as amended by the act of July 1, 1895, and the Massachusetts act of 1893, are good illustrations of legislation regarding labels.

The Illinois act is as follows:

"Section 1. Whenever any person, or any association or union of workingmen, has heretofore adopted or used, or shall hereafter adopt or use, any label, trade mark, term, design, device or form of advertisement for the purpose of designating, making known or distinguishing any goods, wares, merchandise or other product of labor as having been made, manufactured, produced, prepared, packed or put on sale by such person or association or union of workingmen, or by a member or members of such association or union, it shall be unlawful to counterfeit or imitate such label, trade mark, term, design, device or form of advertisement, or to use, sell, offer for sale, or in any way utter or circulate any counterfeit or imitation of any such labels, trade mark, term, design, device or form of advertisement.

"Sec. 2. Whoever counterfeits or imitates any such label, trade mark, term, design, device or form of advertisement, or sells, offers for sale or in any way utters or circulates any counterfeit or imitation of any such label, trade mark, term, design, device or form of advertisement, or knowingly uses any such counterfeit or imitation, or knowingly sells or disposes of or keeps or has in his possession, with intent that the same shall be sold or disposed of, any goods, wares, merchandise or other product of labor to which any such counterfeit or imitation is attached or affixed, or on which any such counterfeit or imitation is printed, painted, stamped or impressed, or knowingly sells or disposes of any goods, wares, merchandise or other product of labor contained in any box, case, can or package to which or on which any such counterfeit or imitation is attached, affixed, printed, painted, stamped or impressed, or keeps or has in his possession, with intent that the same shall be sold or disposed of, any goods, wares, merchandise or other product of labor, in any box, case, can or package to which or on which any such counterfeit or imitation is attached, affixed, printed, painted, stamped or impressed, shall be punished by a fine of not less than one hundred (100) dollars, nor more than two hundred (200) dollars, or by imprisonment for not less than three (3) months nor more than one (1) year, or by both such fine and imprisonment.

"Sec. 3. Every such person, association or union that has heretofore adopted or used, or shall hereafter adopt or use, a label, trade mark, term, design, device or form of advertisement, as provided in section one (1) of this act shall file the same for record in the office of the secretary of state, by leaving two (2) copies, counterparts or facsimiles thereof with said secretary, and by filing therewith a sworn statement specifying the name or names of the person, association or union on whose behalf such label, trade mark, term, design, device or form of advertisement shall be filed, the class of merchandise and a particular description of the goods to which it has been or is intended to be appropriated, that the party so filing, or on whose behalf such label, trade mark, term, design, device or form of advertisement shall be filed, has the right to the use of the same, and that no other person, firm, association, union or corporation has the right to such use either in the identical form or in any such near resemblance thereto as may be calculated to deceive, and that the facsimile copies or counterparts filed therewith are true and correct. There shall be paid for such filing and recording a fee of one (1) dollar. Any person who shall for himself, or on behalf of any other person, association or union, procure the filing of any label, trade mark, term, design, device or form of advertisement in the office of the secretary of state, under the provisions of this act, by making any false or fraudulent representations or declarations, verbally or in writing, or by any fraudulent means, shall be liable to pay any damages sustained in consequence of any such filing, to be recovered by or on behalf of the party injured thereby in any court having jurisdiction, and shall be punished by a fine not exceeding two hundred (200) dollars or by imprisonment not exceeding one year, or both such fine and imprisonment. The secretary of state shall deliver to such person, association or union so filing or causing to be filed any such label, trade mark, term, design, device or form of advertisement so many duly attested certificates of the recording of the same as such person, association or union may apply for, for each of which certificates said secretary shall receive a fee of one (1) dollar. Any such certificate of record shall in all suits and prosecutions under this act be sufficient proof of the adoption of such label, trade mark, term, design, device or form of advertisement. Said secretary of the state shall not record for any person, union or association any label, trade mark, term, design, device or form of advertisement that would reasonably be mistaken for any label, trade mark, term, design, device or form of advertisement theretofore filed by or on behalf of any other person, union or association.

"Sec. 4. Every such person, association, or union adopting a label, trade mark, or form of advertisement, as aforesaid, may proceed by suit to enjoin the manufacture, use, display or sale of any such counterfeits or imitations; and all courts having jurisdiction thereof shall grant injunctions to restrain such manufacture, use, display or sale, and shall award the complainant in such suit, such damages, resulting from such wrongful manufacture, use, display or sale, as may by said court be deemed just and reasonable, and shall require the defendants to pay to such person, association or union the profits derived from such wrongful manufacture, use, display or sale; and said court shall also order that all such counterfeits or imitations in the possession or under the control of any defendant in such case be delivered to an officer of the court, or to the complainant to be destroyed.

"Sec. 5. Every person who shall use or display the genuine label, trade mark, or form of advertisement of any such person, association or union, in any manner not authorized by such person, union or association, shall be deemed guilty of a misdemeanor, and shall be punished by imprisonment in the county jail not less than three months nor more than one year, or by a fine of not less than one hundred dollars nor more than two hundred dollars, or both. In all cases where such association or union is not incorporated, suits under this act may be commenced and prosecuted by any officer or member of such association or union on behalf of and for the use of such association or union.

"Sec. 6. Any person or persons who shall in any way use the name or seal of any such person, association or union, or officer thereof, in and about the sale of goods or otherwise, not being authorized to so use the same, shall be guilty of a misdemeanor, punishable by imprisonment in the county jail of not less than three months nor more than one year, or by fine of not less than one hundred dollars nor more than two hundred dollars, or both.

"Sec. 7. The fines provided for in this act may be enforced before a justice of the peace in all cases where the party complaining shall so elect, and in case of conviction before such justice of the peace the offender shall stand committed to the county jail until the fine and costs are fully paid, under the provisions of section 8, article IX of an act to revise the law in regard to criminal jurisprudence, in force July 1, 1874, or otherwise."

CAUSES OF THE OPEN SHOP POLICY.

BY JOHN R. COMMONS.

[John Rogers Commons, economist; born Darke county, O., October 13, 1862; graduated from Oberlin, 1888; A. M., 1890; student Johns Hopkins, 1888–90; professor
sociology Oberlin college, 1892; Indiana university, 1893–95; Syracuse university,
1895–99; expert agent industrial commission, 1902; assistant secretary National
Civic Federation, 1903; professor of sociology, University of Wisconsin. Author:
The Distribution of Wealth; Social Reform and the Church; Proportional Representation, etc.]

The open shop controversy, in its extreme form, is
peculiar to America. The British labor delegates, in 1902,
were surprised to see the bitterness of the American unionist
toward the scab. This feeling has its roots in conditions and
history peculiar to this country. For three generations the
American workingman has been taught that the nation was
deeply concerned in maintaining for him a high standard of
living. Free traders objected that manufacturers would not
pay higher wages, even if protected. Horace Greeley, who,
as much as any other man, commended the American system
to wage earners, admitted the force of the objection, but he
held that socialism, or, as he called it, association, would share
the benefits of the tariff with them. But this must come
through the workmen themselves. Some of them tried it.
The communistic experiments failed. They tried co-operation,
education, politics. Neither did these seem to reach the high
aims of protection. Meanwhile they were discovering the
power of the strike. By this kind of association those who
could hold together found themselves actually sharing the
benefits of protection which Greeley mistakenly predicted for
his fantastic kind of association.

But the gains from strikes were temporary. The federal
laws which protected manufacturers against the products of
foreign labor, permitted them to import the foreigners themselves. In many cases strikes were defeated by the immigrants, and in many more cases the immigrants went into
the shops to share the gains won by the strikers, or gradually
to displace them with their lower standards of living. With

a unanimity never before shown the unions entered the political field and got the Chinese exclusion acts and the alien contract labor laws. These theoretically rounded out the tariff system, and they somewhat lessened the pressure on the skilled trades. But the amount of immigration itself was not lessened. Rather have the laws been evaded and the influx has swollen greater than before, while the sources have shifted to still lower standards of life. By a minute division of labor and nearly automatic machinery unknown in any other country, the skilled trades were split into simple operations and places created for the unskilled immigrants. The strike thus seemed likely to lose permanent results. The unions were unable in politics further to check immigration. Endorsing the tariff on products as a necessary first step they were left to enact their own tariff on labor. The sympathies of the American public were with them, but these sympathies, lacking the historical sense, have recently somewhat declined, when it is found that the union theory is that of protection and not that of free trade. The British unions are protected by long periods of apprenticeship. The nonunionist is only another Englishman who can be talked to, and whose class feelings are strong and identical with those of the unionist. The employers are not protected by a tariff, neither have they imported foreign workmen. Division of labor is not minute, and the skilled workman is not directly menaced by the unskilled. But the American unions have very little industrial or racial protection. Apprenticeship is gone, except as enforced by them against the protests of employers. In order to enforce this and other measures needed to keep wages above the market rate, the unions found themselves compelled to enforce the rule that no one should enter the shop except through the union. Without this rule their efforts were nullified.

It naturally is objected that, in comparing the closed shop with the tariff, a corollary cannot be drawn from the laws enacted by government to the rules imposed by a union. The presumption is in favor of free trade, and only the sovereign power has the right to interfere, and that in the general interest. Where private associations restrict competition the act becomes conspiracy. But here the unions found that public sympathy and judicial decision have made an exception in their favor. While a combination to put up prices is illegal, a combination to put up wages was gradually relieved of legal penalty. It was felt that the laborer was the weaker party to the bargain; that the same public policy which would keep down prices to the level of domestic competition, would encourage the laborer to keep wages above the level of immigrant competition. Capital could take care of itself, and the capitalist who failed in competition would only drop into the ranks of wage earners, but the laborer who failed had no place lower to drop. Consequently, while, on the one hand, the doctrine of protection to manufactures was gaining hold, on the other hand its corollary, the exemption of labor from the conspiracy laws, was being established.

Some decisions went even further. Granting that it is not criminal conspiracy to quit work in a body in order to benefit their own members, it is not easy to draw the line at quitting work in a body to secure the discharge of a foreman or a nonunionist whose acts are injurious to the members. Though the decisions here are conflicting, yet there were early decisions sustaining this right, and so essential is it to their existence and so persistently have the unions asserted it, that, amidst conflicting decisions, many have established the union shop. Here the logic of politics has been with them, and the politicians have been more consistent than the manufacturers, for the high wages to which protection campaigners point, are usually wages kept high by a closed shop policy. Even the wages in unprotected industries like the building trades, which depend mainly on the closed shop, are offered as evidence of protection's benefits, while in the protected industries it is the closed shop wages of tin plate workers, molders, blacksmiths, etc., and not the open shop wage of woolen and cotton textiles, to which attention is directed.

A curious flank movement has taken place in the use of the terms closed and open shop. As the unions originally employed the terms, a closed shop was one which was boycotted or on strike, and in which consequently the union forbade its members to work. An open shop was one where union men were permitted by the union to get employment if they could. To declare a shop open was equivalent to calling off a strike and boycott. The terms as now defined are different. The closed shop, instead of being nonunion, is the union shop. And the open shop is declared open by the employer to admit nonunionists, and not by the union to unionists.

Yet, even from this new standpoint, the terms are not clearly distinguished. Many employers have what they call open shops, and yet they employ only union men. The union would say that these are union shops, whereas the public generally would call them closed.

The confusion arises from different points of view. The employer has in mind the contract or trade agreement with the union. He looks at it from the legal or contractual side. The union has in mind the actual situation in the shop. They look at it from the side of practical results. The agreements made in the stove industry, in bituminous coal mining, in three fourths of the team driving agreements, in railway machine shops, and many others, are plainly open shop agreements, where it is often even stipulated that the employer has the right to employ and discharge whomsoever he sees fit, only reserving that he shall not discriminate on account of union membership or union activity. Many agreements are silent on the question of employment and discharge, and in such cases the presumption is in favor of the employer's freedom in selecting his men.

It is evident that with these different points of view it is difficult to reach an understanding. Clearness would be promoted by adopting a use of terms which would bring out the above distinctions as they are found in practice. In doing so, the closed shop would be viewed from the side of the contract, and would be designated as one which is closed against the nonunionist by a formal agreement with the union; the open shop as one, where, as far as the agreement is concerned, the employer is free to hire union or nonunion men; the union shop as one where, irrespective of the agreement, the employer, as a matter of fact, has only union men. Thus an open shop, according to agreement, might in practice be a union shop, a mixed shop, or even a nonunion shop. The closed shop would, of course, be a union shop, but the union shop might be either closed or open.

The contention of some union defenders that the term closed shop is a misnomer, I do not agree with, if its use is limited as here proposed. They say it is not closed, because any competent man can get into it by joining the union. What they really mean is that the union is an open union, but this is another question, and an important one. Much can be said for a closed shop if the union is open, but a closed shop with a closed union cannot be defended. The use of terms above proposed makes it possible to draw these essential distinctions and to discuss each separate question of fact by itself and on its merits.

The historical steps were somewhat as follows: First, the union got the union shop by quitting work, or threatening to quit, in a body. Next they got the closed shop by a contract with the employer. If the employer would not make a closed shop agreement, they either retained their original right to quit if he hired a nonunionist, or their open shop agreement provided for negotiation whenever a nonunionist became obnoxious. In this way the open shop agreement might mean, in individual cases, the union shop in practice.

Now the significant fact respecting the agreements just mentioned in the coal, stove foundry, railway shops and other industries, is that, while they are open shop agreements, they are, on the whole, satisfactory to unions which in other branches of their work are most uncompromising for the closed shop. In all cases their satisfaction is based on three or four considerations. In the first place, the agreement is made, not with each shop, but with an association of employers, including the strongest competitors in the industry. It is to the interest of such an association to require all of its members faithfully to observe the agreement, because it places them all on the same competitive level as far as wages are concerned. The employer who would violate the agreement would get an advantage over the others in the largest item of his expenses. This the others, in self interest, cannot permit, and consequently as long as he is a member of the employers' association, the union is relieved of the burden of enforcing the agreement, and the employers themselves, as a body, assume the responsibility of doing what the union could do only by means of the closed shop or the strike. If the employer persists in violating the agreement, after his association has exhausted its powers of discipline, he is expelled, and then, being no longer protected by his fellow employers, he is left to the tactics of the union.

In the second place, the agreement is made, not only for members of the union, but for all positions of the same grade, whether filled by union or by nonunion men. No employer, therefore, can get an advantage, in lower wages or longer hours, by hiring a nonunionist. No amount of protest or solemnity of promise, and, especially, no appeal to the Declaration of Independence from those protected by a tariff that violates the Declaration, can persuade the unions that the employer wants the open shop except to get his labor below the union rate. Some employers and some associations of employers, as in the machinery line and in iron and steel, have been frank enough to admit this, when they insist that their agreement with the union covers only union men, and that they are free to make a lower scale of wages for nonunion men. But, as a rule, an agreement cannot stand for long on such an understanding, and very soon it goes to pieces in a strike for the closed shop or the dissolution of the union. There have been isolated exceptions where the union is strong, and thinks that the nonunionist, in order to get the higher rate of pay, will join the union. But, in general, only when the agreement covers the nonunionist as well as the unionist, and when the employers show that they have the power and the will to enforce it, can the union consent to the open shop. Even this takes time, for power and good will are shown only through experience, and the workmen have undergone many bitter experiences of dishonesty, and many more experiences of inability, through the pressure of competition or changes in management, to live up to agreements honestly made. The stove founders, the soft coal operators, and others, after several years of associated action, seem to have won confidence in their ability and honesty of purpose in enforcing their open shop agreements, and for this reason, the unions, though not entirely satisfied, are not driven by their more radical members to demand the closed shop.

In the third place, that clause of the agreement which provides for the so-called arbitration of grievances covers all matters of discrimination as well as all matters of wages, hours and rules of work. By discrimination is meant all questions of hiring, discharging and disciplining both union and nonunion men. In this respect it seems to me a mistake was made by the anthracite coal strike commission in its award as interpreted by the umpire, Colonel Wright. The commission had awarded that no person should be discriminated against on account of membership or nonmembership in any labor organization, and had provided a board of conciliation and an umpire to decide any disagreement that should not be settled by the parties concerned. Under this clause the umpire stated the principle involved as follows: A man has the right to quit the service of his employer whenever he sees fit, with or without giving a cause and the employer has a perfect right to employ and discharge men in accordance with the condition of his industry; he is not obliged to give a cause for his discharge.

The mistake in applying this principle of reciprocal rights lies in the fact that the union, under the agreement, had given up its right to strike. Having done so, it gives up its right to protect a member against discrimination or unjust discharge. In lieu of settling such a grievance by a strike the agreement sets up a tribunal to investigate and decide according to the facts. Of course, individuals retain their right to quit, and the employer retains his right to discharge, yet since the union has abandoned its right to strike, in view of the tribunal, the employer must be held to have abandoned his right to discharge a union man whenever the union alleges a grievance and appeals to the board. The employer always claims that discrimination was not intended, but this is a question of fact to be determined by the tribunal. Otherwise the most vital injury, one that concerns the very life of the union, is taken out of the hands of the board of concilia-

tion and falls back upon the original remedy of the union—
the strike. This is well understood in all trade agreements
except the peculiar one in the anthracite coal industry. Every
grievance or alleged grievance in the hiring or discharging of
union or nonunion men is taken up by the officers of the two
associations and settled on its merits, under the terms of the
agreement. Under no other condition could the union be
assured against discrimination or unjust discharge; which is
but another way of saying, under no other condition could
it trust itself to an open shop agreement. With this protection, the case of each nonunion man can be taken up in conference by the officers of the two associations, and he can be
disciplined the same as a union man for any acts injurious to
the members of the union or menacing to the agreement.

These three conditions, I think, have been found essential in most open shop agreements that have lasted for any
length of time: namely, a strong and well disposed association on each side; the same scale of work and wages for unionist and nonunionist; and the reference of all unsettled com-
plaints against either unionist or nonunionist to a joint conference of the officers of the union and the association.

In describing these conditions I have indicated, conversely, certain conditions under which the union is forced
in self protection to stand for the closed shop. Such cases are
those where there is no employers' association, or where the
employers' association cannot control all of its members or
all of the industry, or where the association is hostile or has
a menacing, hostile element within it; as, for example, when
it does not insist that its nonunion or open shop members
shall pay the union scale. In these cases the maintenance
of the scale and the life of the union depend on maintaining
the union shop. Whether it shall be a closed shop or not, i.e.,
whether it shall be unionized by a contract in which the employer binds himself to employ only union men, and becomes,
as it were, a union organizer, or whether, as far as the trade
agreement is concerned, it shall be an open shop, depends on
circumstances, and the same union will be found practicing
both methods, according to the locality or shop.

The closed shop contract has recently been attacked in the courts, and in some cases overthrown, on the ground of illegality. Without branching into that side of the question, it should be noted in passing that such a contract usually carries a consideration. If the union has a label protected by law, this is a valuable consideration which the employer cannot be expected to enjoy unless he agrees to employ only union men, and consequently all label agreements of the garment workers, brewery workers, boot and shoe workers, and others, are closed shop agreements. However, the main consideration to the employer is the enlistment of a responsible national authority on the part of the union to compel the local union or shop to fulfill its side of the agreement. The local union is moved by personal feelings, but the national officers have wider responsibilities and a more permanent interest in living close to the letter and the spirit of the agreements. This is the consideration distinctly stated in the agreements of the typographical union with the newspaper publishers' association, several of whose members have non-union or open shops, it being agreed that the national union will underwrite every closed shop agreement made by a publisher with a local union. The same consideration is found in the longshoremen's agreements, in all label agreements, and though not always expressly stipulated, it is understood to exist, more or less, in all agreements whether actually underwritten by the national officers or not. If the employer wishes the national union to be responsible for its local members he logically will agree to employ only members of the union. The open shop, by the very terms of the contract, leaves it to the employer to enforce the agreement by hiring nonunion men, but the closed shop makes the national union responsible by requiring it to discipline the local union or even to furnish other union men. It is this consideration, more than anything else, that has led the stove founders and other employers' associations, under open shop agreements, to watch without protest the gradual unionizing of nine tenths of their shops.

There is no doubt that the object which all unions aim to reach is the complete unionizing of the trade. In support of this there are two kinds of arguments, one of which I should call sentimental, the other economic or essential. Certain of the economic arguments I have just indicated. But there are some places where these do not apply; and a union which relies solely on a sentimental argument cannot win the support of the public, which eventually makes the laws and guides the decisions. This sentimental argument holds that he who is benefited should bear his share of the expenses of the benefactor. The union which raises wages and shortens hours should be supported by all whose wages and hours are bettered, and the nonunionist, because he refuses support, should be shut out from employment.

An argument like this, if not backed by an evident necessity, falls under attack. Such is the case in government and municipal employment. The government fixes a scale of wages. In the United States this scale is considerably above the scale in similar private employment. Trade unions have doubtless taken the lead in establishing these favorable conditions, but they really depend, not on the unions, but on politics. They are the natural outcome of universal suffrage, and are not found to the same extent in countries or localities where the labor vote is weak or labor is newly enfranchised. Formerly the political party filled such positions with its partisans. The situation is no worse when the union fills them with its members. But competitive civil service, or civil service reform, is an advance on both partisanship and unionism. Government pays the scale to all alike. There is no competition of outsiders to force it down. The state can be a model employer because its products do not compete on the market. The nonunionist or the aggressive employer is not a menace to the wages of government employees. If the government should let out its work to the lowest bidder the union then could maintain a scale only by the union shop. But when the government hires its own workmen the union shop is not needed. A strike would be absurd, and the appeal for fair wages must be made to the people at large, through their representatives. The appeal is ethical and political, and not to the judgment of a strike, and such an appeal is stronger when free from the onus of an exclusive privilege.

This is not saying that government employees should not be organized. In fact, the highest form of civil service in a nation committed to representative democracy is that where the public employees are organized in a union, so that all grievances can be taken up by their agents and arbitrated with the head of the department. This was demonstrated by Colonel Waring in the street cleaning department of New York, and he showed that only by requiring his employees to join in a union could partisan politics be wholly shut out and the highest efficiency secured. But this sort of unionizing depends on a favorable administration and an enlightened public opinion, and not on the strike or the closed shop.

There is a class of private employment similar to that of government employment in the conditions which make the closed shop unnecessary. This is railway transportation. A railway company establishes a scale of wages for its higher classes of employees. This scale is uniform over its system, is paid to all alike, and is not nibbled down by dickers with individuals. When the railway brotherhoods accept such a scale, they know that it will be paid to nonunionist as well as unionist. Therefore they do not even ask that it be kept in the form of an agreement, but are content that it simply be issued as a general order from the manager. They probably would take a different view if the company let out the hiring of employees to the lowest bidder among competing contractors, or even if they themselves tried to maintain a scale for section hands who are not protected by a long line of promotion. They certainly would refuse to work with a nonmember to whom the company insisted on paying lower wages than the scale. The closed shop policy on the railroads could be supported only by the sentimental argument, and the railway brotherhoods have recognized its futility when not backed by the economic argument. It is most significant that the agreements of the machinists' union for railway shops are likewise open shop agreements, similar to the brotherhood agreements, issued as a scale of wages by general order for the entire system and making no mention of the union. This is also true of the machinists in government navy yards and arsenals, where the union has won several advantages for members and nonmembers alike. This is the union which, in general manufacturing, outside railway and government work, has been most bitterly assailed for its 'closed shop principles, but it is evident, from the contrast, that these principles have been forced upon the union by the different character of the industry and the different attitude of employers.

The situation is different with street railways. Some of these companies are conducted on a large scale like interstate roads, and the unions are safe with an open shop agreement. Others are conducted like shops, and the street railway union seeks closed agreements, and has been known in a few cases to go on strike against nonunion men. This union is entirely different from the brotherhoods in that it admits to membership every employee of the company, including even the car cleaners, excepting only those who already belong to an old line trade union. Its motormen and conductors are not protected by a long period of apprenticeship or slow line of promotion, like the locomotive engineers and railway conductors, and consequently their places can be filled by men fresh from the farm or from any other occupation or profession. In fact the union contains ex-lawyers, ex-ministers, college graduates, and a variety of ex-talent that is unique. To them, therefore, the closed shop is often essential, and to the companies also it is an advantage, for the international union then guarantees the local contract.

The sentimental argument, of which I spoke as applied to government work, sometimes becomes more than sentimental when applied to private employment, even where the nonunionist gets the same pay as the unionist. There are always selfish and shortsighted members in a union. If they see a nonunionist enjoying the same privileges with themselves without the expense of union dues, and especially if the foreman shows a preference for the nonunionist, they too demand exemption from union burdens. Thus the union disintegrates, and a cut in wages or stretch in hours cannot be warded off. Experience is a hard teacher and has taught this lesson thoroughly. It is not a mistake that the persistent nonunionist in private employment should be looked upon generally as a menace.

Another fact regarding this sentiment is often overlooked. Being compelled to work together and help one another in the same shop, men's feelings toward each other are personal and intense. The employer in his office need never see the competitor whom he is trying to crush, and only their products meet on the market. He scarcely can understand that his workmen in the shop are also competitors, but, in addition, are under enforced personal contact, and their sentiments cannot be kept down. What to him is business seems malice in them. Yet these feelings are really a factor in his cost of production, as much as the coal under the boiler or the oil on the bearings. It is not surprising that the open shop, even from the employers' standpoint, is not permanently practicable, and tends to become either union or nonunion.

It would be possible to run down the entire list of unions, and to show in each case the industrial circumstances which make the union, or closed shop necessary or unnecessary from the standpoint of maintaining wages. Wherever there is a large number of small contractors, as in the building trades or the clothing industry, an open shop union cannot survive. The building trades in London though less effective on wages than American unions, are nevertheless safe with their open shop agreements, because, in addition to the fact that the unions are not compelled to protect the common labor working with them, the master builder does not sublet his work, but has his own large establishment and permanent force, and hires all the trades directly. He takes up all grievances when they arise, including the grievance of the nonunionist. But in the United States the master builder has usually only an office force. He sublets all but the mason work to ten or thirty different contractors. These contractors often require little or no capital, and a mechanic to-day may be a contractor to-morrow. A nonunion contractor, with his lower wages and imported labor, would soon drive the union contractor out of business. The building trades are there-

fore compelled to put their closed shop policy foremost, and
where they have been defeated in this policy, as in Chicago
in 1900, they soon have regained all they lost of the union
shop, even though working under explicit open shop agreements.

In the clothing trades, the sweatshop is simply the open
shop; for the sweatshop is the small contractor with fresh
immigrants, long hours and minute division of labor, crowding into the market and underselling the shops where wages,
hours and conditions are better. Such would unquestionably
have been the outcome in the building trades had the unions
not been able to enforce the closed shop. No amount of good
will on the part of clothing manufacturers or master builders
could stand a market menaced with the product of open shops.
It was through the open shop that the American born tailor
was displaced by the Irish and German tailor; that the Irish
and German were displaced by the Jew and by Polish women;
and that the Jew is now being displaced by the Italian. In
the building trades the Irish, German and American have
stopped this displacement by means of the closed shop. The
Jew is vainly trying to stop it, and the Scandinavian in Chicago
until recently had stopped it in one branch of the clothing
trade. Each displacement has substituted a race with a
lower standard of living. As soon as a race begins to be
Americanized and to demand a higher standard, another still
lower standard comes in through the open shop. This is the
history of many American industries. Whether the conditions in the clothing trade are preferable, for the American
nation, than conditions in the building trades, is a question
open for differences of opinion. The difference, however, is
not apparent among the workmen in those trades. The immigrant, the manufacturer, the consumer, may hold a different
view, but if so, it should be understood that the question in
dispute is that of the wages of those workmen. As things are,
the union shop or closed shop is the wage earners' necessary
means to that end.

It is sometimes asserted that American unions, like the
British unions, should place more reliance on reserve funds,
benefit and insurance features, and that, with these attrac-

tions they would not have been compelled to put forward so strongly the closed shop policy. The British workman joins the union at the close of his long period of apprenticeship, and his motive is not the coercion of the closed shop, but rather insurance against sickness, death, loss of tools and out of work. His union is like the American railway brotherhoods which also rely on insurance and previous promotion. But the American unions do not have this period of apprenticeship to work upon, except as they have established it by the union shop. They are confronted by foreigners in language, modes of thought and standards of living, pressed on by necessities in a strange country, and eligible without previous training on account of minute division of labor. Should American unions wait slowly to build up their organization on the open shop and insurance benefit policies, they would be displaced by foreigners before they could get a start. The foreigners again would have to set up the union shop as soon as they in turn began to demand better conditions and were confronted by a new race of immigrants. This is exactly what they have done, and the union or closed shop in America is necessary to support those very insurance and benefit features which are proposed as a substitute for it.

That there are many serious problems springing from labor unions is evident. But they would properly be discussed under other headings. The present discussion is not merely of their good or bad methods—it is of their existence and their power to raise wages. Under a different order of industry or a socialistic policy of government unions might be superfluous. Their existence and their methods arise from the nature of the industry and the attitude of employers. A method necessary in the building trades or coal mines may be superfluous on the railroads. Their methods also arise from the universal human struggle for power. No institution or individual can be trusted with absolute power. Constitutional government is a device of checks and balances. Employers' associations are just as necessary to restrain labor unions, and labor unions to restrain employers' associations, as two houses of congress, a Supreme court, a president and political parties, to restrain social classes. Progress does not come when one association destroys the other, but when one association destroys the excesses of the other. This kind of progress is going on in the several industries mentioned above. There the open shop question has never been even considered or mentioned, or else in course of time it has become only an academic question, because the employers' association takes up and remedies every real grievance or disproves every fictitious grievance that provoked the union into existence, and does not permit any of its members to smash or undermine the union. The bad methods of the union are gradually reduced by discussion backed by the power of organization, and its good methods are encouraged. Education improves both parties; mutual respect succeeds suspicion. In those industries it is accepted that protection to capital carries with it protection to labor; that fair profits imply fair wages; that well disposed associations on each side shall together discipline the nonunionist the same as the unionist; that the employers, having lost despotic control of their labor, regain a nobler control through co-operation with the union; that the opposition to nonunionists is not based alone on sentiment or malice, but on economic necessity; and that a question, which only stirs up class hatred in the field of pronunciamentoes and abstract rights, works out a peaceable solution when men acknowledge mutual rights.

THE LAW AND THE CLOSED SHOP CONTRACT.

BY WALTER DREW.

[Walter Drew, lawyer; born Williamstown, Mich., September 13, 1873; graduate of literary and law departments of University of Michigan; instrumental in organization of employers and business men in Citizens' Alliances first of Grand Rapids and later of Bay City, Saginaw and Muskegon; as manager of employers' campaigns during strikes he has had prominent part in labor troubles in Michigan.]

A closed shop may be defined as a shop in which none but members of a certain union or unions can secure employment. Shop is a general term for any business requiring the employment of labor. A closed shop in itself is a mere condition, and cannot properly be spoken of as lawful or unlawful. The law, however, will look to the active forces by which the condition known as the closed shop is brought about or maintained and will determine if those forces in their purposes or workings be lawful or unlawful.

A closed shop contract is a contract the immediate purpose of which is to secure or maintain the condition known as a closed shop.

Such contracts are susceptible of division into several classes according to the parties to them.

(1) Contracts among the several members of a union in which they agree not to work in a shop where nonunion men are employed. These contracts are usually in the form of by-laws.

(2) Contracts between a union and an employer by which none but members of the union are to be employed in the employer's shop.

(3) Contracts between a proprietor and a contractor by which the contractor is to employ none but union labor upon work to be done for the proprietor.

Such contracts may also be classified as public and private. A public closed shop contract is one which a public corporation, such as a city, county, or board of education is a

215

party. A private contract is one all of the parties to which are private persons or corporations.

The courts have unequivocally condemned public closed shop contracts as unlawful and void upon constitutional and other grounds, and with no diversity of opinion.

The legal history of trades unions, their conduct, incidents and agreements, is in large measure a history of the application to labor combinations of the common laws of conspiracy. It seems to have been true under early English common law that workingmen had no right to combine for any purpose connected with labor conditions and that their mere combination was a criminal conspiracy. The restrictions upon the right of workingmen to act in combination have been more and more removed, until, at the present time, there is no substantial difference from a legal standpoint between a labor combination and any other combination. The old common law restrictions upon combinations of workmen in general also applied to combinations of masters, the courts viewing with distrust any combined effort to influence or control trade conditions. This removal of restrictions or grant of greater freedom to act in combination may be called the development of the right to combine.

All the different legal questions connected with trades union activities are directly or indirectly connected with this so-called right to combine. The right to strike is the right of men to combine to quit work in a body. The right to boycott is the right of men to combine to refuse to deal with another. So too the closed shop contract is related to the right to combine, for it is the act of men in combination, and expresses the terms upon which they have combined. The right to make such a contract necessarily presumes the right to combine.

Besides the greater recognition by the courts of the workingmen's rights to act in combination, there are two other doctrines associated with recent judicial views upon labor questions. One is the comparatively recent doctrine that labor is a commodity to be bought and sold in the market in like manner as any other article of trade. The other is the right of individual contract, which, by the development of the view of labor as a commodity, has gained a new meaning or

application in labor matters.   The workingman like the merchant has something to sell, and has the right of individual
contract in regard to the terms of sale.   The fact that his
commodity is labor, and not goods, has ceased to make any
difference in the methods he may use in his bargaining.   Undoubtedly these views have influenced the attitude of the
courts toward labor combinations and have had much to do
with the judicial recognition of the workingmen's right to
combine.

The development of the right to combine, or rather, the
greater recognition by the courts of the right to combine, from
the time when a combination of workmen for any purpose
connected with labor matters was held to be a conspiracy, to
the present, is summed up and expressed in the modern definition of a conspiracy.   A conspiracy at common law has now
come to be generally defined as a combination to do an unlawful act, or to do any act by unlawful means.   In other
words, mere combining is no longer criminal.   It must be
further shown that the combination has an unlawful purpose
in view, or contemplates the employment of unlawful means.

With the former restrictions upon the right of workmen
to act in combination in mind it becomes clear that the question of the validity of a closed shop contract must be a comparatively recent one.   Under the early doctrines such a contract would have been not only void, but also evidence of a
criminal conspiracy.   Does the right to act in combination as
now recognized justify or legalize the closed shop contract?—
is the question to be answered.

In this country the right to combine on the part of workmen has been fully established and recognized by the courts
without the coercion of any statute.   This right to combine
was not recognized by the common law at the time our country was separated from England and English common law
became American common law.   The action of the American
courts, therefore, in recognizing this right on the part of workmen, though not so stated, has been in the nature of a departure from the early English common law and has amounted
to a grant or creation of a right not before enjoyed.   Of course
there are cases to be found where our American courts have

followed to a greater or less extent English precedents. These cases, however, have been more and more discredited until it may be considered as firmly established in this country that there are no restrictions whatever upon the laborer's right to combine, other than that the combination shall not be for an unlawful purpose or employ an unlawful means.

We come now to the discussion of the closed shop contract as affected by the recognition by the courts of the right to combine within the limits of the law of conspiracy.

Every contract starts with a presumption of validity. It may be said, therefore, that a closed shop contract is valid unless its purpose be unlawful or it be secured or enforced by unlawful means. But no closed shop contract which has ever come before the courts has stood this test. There is no case at law or in equity holding such a contract valid; there are many and some most recent holding such contracts void.

A closed shop contract, the purpose of which is to establish or foster a monopoly of the labor market, is contrary to public policy and void.

The rule that a contract, the purpose of which is to secure a monopoly, is void, is a familiar one. In its application to closed shop contracts two classes of cases arise: (1) Where the court holds that it is apparent on the face of such a contract that its manifest purpose and inevitable tendency is to establish a monopoly, and, therefore, that such a contract is per se void. (2) Where the courts do not hold such a contract void per se, but inquire whether under the facts of each case the purpose of the particular contract is to secure a monopoly. In the first class of cases no outside or extrinsic evidence is necessary. In the second, outside evidence is considered in order to make clear the purpose of the particular contract in question.

The purpose of compelling nonmembers to join the union against their will is unlawful. Closed shop contracts having such a purpose, are, therefore, unlawful, and the attempt to enforce such a contract to the injury of persons not parties to it, is an actionable wrong.

This is practically the same rule as the one preceding, except that it is stated from the standpoint of the nonunion man. Evidently the ultimate purpose of compelling non-union men to join the union is to create a monopoly of the labor market. From the standpoint of the public, as we have seen under the previous rule, this purpose is contrary to public policy. From the standpoint of the nonunion man sought to be coerced, this purpose is not only unlawful, but if attempted to be carried out to his injury, it gives him a right of action.

The agreements or conduct of combinations must have a legitimate and proper motive. The injury of third persons from mere malice, or without any justification, is an actionable wrong.

Under this head come chiefly cases involving attempts to enforce or perform closed shop contracts and the rights of third parties affected thereby.

Ordinarily, the act of an individual done with malice involves no greater legal liability than one done without malice. So long as the individual stays within his strict legal rights his motive is immaterial. Many judicial utterances may be found to the effect that the same rule applies to combinations, and the question has been much debated. It may be said, however, that the later authorities, and the present weight of authority, is to the effect that malice or other improper oppressive purpose on the part of a combination resulting in injury to a third party, confers a right of action upon the one injured. In other words, malicious conduct on the part of a combination is unlawful when it would not be so on the part of an individual.

A closed shop contract must be the voluntary act of all the parties to it, both in its inception and in its performance.

This is a most important limitation upon closed shop contracts. It means that closed shop by-laws or closed shop agreements with an employer, adopted by a majority vote of the union, do not bind the minority. It means that the vote of a majority ordering a strike or boycott to enforce a closed shop by-law or contract, does not bind the minority. It further means that if the assent or co-operation of the minority is secured by means of any coercive measures such as fines, forfeitures or other penalties, the contract becomes unlawful, and its enforcement to the injury of others becomes an actionable wrong.

If this article shall have made it clear that the closed shop in and of itself is not an unlawful thing, and has further clearly defined the limits set by the courts upon efforts to secure or maintain the closed shop, it has accomplished its purpose. The question of the closed shop contract, and the other labor questions now of such acute interest, are but different phases of an epoch in industrial history through which we are passing. The epoch started with the entry into the labor world of the spirit of combination. The epoch may be called the epoch of incomplete combination.

The very fact that combination on the part of labor is partial and incomplete, makes inevitable strife and war and legal questions. If there were 1,000 carvers in the United States, all of whom belonged to a union, it could not be said that such a union was trying to gain a monopoly or to injure nonunion men in any agreements it might make. Such a union could carry on its collective bargaining with the employer unhampered. It could name any wage or other conditions it saw fit, and the employer would have no option but to accede or go without the services of its members. Unreasonable demands would thwart their own purpose, for the public would arrange to do without services for which a wage not warranted by trade conditions was insisted upon. In other words, complete combination of labor secured and maintained would do away with the present epoch of strife, with its attendant bitterness and legal questions. It would bring an era of collective bargaining when the different questions at issue between labor and capital would be settled more than ever before by the laws of trade and not by the laws of the courts.

It is the belief of the writer that the courts are more and more recognizing the fact stated, that they look upon complete combination of labor as a good and not as an evil; and that within the limitations already set they will put no unnecessary obstacle in the way, but that their attitude toward labor in combination will be broad and liberal.

WRECKED LABOR ORGANIZATIONS.

BY ETHELBERT STEWART.

[Ethelbert Stewart, special agent, United States Bureau of Labor; born in Illinois, April 22, 1857; educated in the public schools of Illinois; commissioner of labor in Illinois for eight years, and special agent in the United States Department of Labor since September, 1889. Author, Fines and Fining Systems in Illinois, Early Organization Among Printers, Restriction of Output, etc.]

Talking with a man who believes trade unionism is about to be wiped out in the United States, he said: They come up and go down. The wrecks of labor organizations are strewn all along our path for forty five or fifty years. This is quite true; indeed, he might have said 3,000 years, for trade unionism, of a kind, was as strong in Rome at the birth of Jesus as it is in Chicago to-day. The shores of time are strewn with the wrecks of trade unions.

The shores of time also are strewn with the wrecks of kings, of empires, of governments. You find wrecks of religions, too, along that shore, and yet the real solid foundation of religion as a spiritual inspiration and ethics is stronger to-day than it ever was. You will find civilizations among the wrecks; and whole races have gone out—but man is still here, more numerous than ever before. The only sane purpose there can be in studying wrecks upon the sands of time is to know whether the wrecking of the vessel was due to mistakes of the crew; if so, avoid them; or to bad construction of the boat; if so, build a better one.

When a king went down another king or a better thing than kings came on to take the place. The wreckage of governments along the line has humanized and improved; remodelled, helped to perfect governments—it has not abolished them.

Government, in the sense of an organization of the people for a purpose, is, as an idea and as a fact, stronger among mankind to-day than it ever was. Its form and its purpose may be changed frequently, but it stays.

Out of every civilization wrecked by time has grown a better civilization. From the ashes of every trade union movement, the wreck of which is noted so triumphantly by esteemed contemporaries, has, Phœnix like, arisen a better trade unionism.

Take a few samples of wrecks of trade unions. In the machinists' trade, for instance, the international machinists and blacksmiths organized in the late '60's, busted in 1875, but at once reorganized as the mechanical engineers. This organization dwindled to a remnant and that remnant merged with the newly organized metal workers' union in the early '80's. The wreck of this organization formed a nucleus for an organization of machinists in the Knights of Labor as machinery constructors. With the passing of the Knights of Labor came the international machinists of America, formed in 1891 and which went down in 1895 to make way for the present international association of machinists, which, if not perfection, is the best organization the craft has ever had.

Small comfort for pessimism or Parryism in a survey of the wrecks along that shore. So, too, in the history of co-operative associations among the trades.

If the national labor congress, organized in 1866, went down in 1872; if the industrial congress of 1874 died a bornin', the amalgamated labor union came in 1878, and in 1881 issued a call for, and itself hied into the federation of organized trades and labor unions of the United States and Canada. This was a greater and better organization than any that had preceded it; and it voluntarily and in its own convention after a four days' debate began the life of and died into the present American Federation of Labor in 1886. Twenty years from the national labor congress of 1866 to the American Federation. Labor can stand that kind of wrecking fairly well, thank you.

I only wish I had space to go into a few more cases; the unions of bakers in colonial times whose wrecks have resulted in better and better unions, local, it is true, but now national and international, until boarding with the boss is a thing of the past, and the bakeshop and the brewery are no longer one.

The shoemakers' guilds of colonial New England forced the organization of journeymen shoemakers' unions just as it did in old England, and many of these came long before the revolutionary war. The road from colonial caulkers' clubs to the national union of shipwrights, joiners, and caulkers of America may have some wrecks along the way, if you wish to call them wrecks; we will treasure them ever as milestones on the path of progress.

Perhaps the necessity for differentiation has carried the movement to individualize trades too far, but that is correcting itself. In 1803 a glassblower must blow window glass, druggists' bottles, beer bottles, and make stoppered goods all in the same establishment. In short, he must do everything then done in glass. The differentiation of the window glass blower from the bottle blower was an imperative necessity from every point of view.

So, too, in scores of trades the extremes of differentiation are correcting themselves and unions are merging into unions. It may be just as well to note here for information of wreck hunters, that these mergers are not wrecks in labor matters any more than in railroad circles.

The man who reasons that, because a strike in a single factory in Podunk has failed, the downfall of trade unionism is sure, should have had better school books than he seems to have been provided with. No local defeat, no temporary rebuff, can stem the tide of organization. No student who has got away from the straw man of the old school of political economists doubts that industrial organization is as much an inherent function of the social organism as is government, religion, or the social control of sex relations.

Whether we are evolutionists from the Darwin standpoint of forced adaptation of structure to physical environment, or whether we believe with the bigger Lamarck and Hegel that perfection is a spiritual germ within and that evolution is that germ unfolding itself, the very idea of evolution necessitates a belief, an absolute faith, in the final perfection of the thing evolving.

There can be but one goal for evolution, and that is ultimate, absolute perfection. To any sociologist not absolutely stifled mentally by the political economy of the schools there is not the least doubt that labor organization is a differentiation in society of the central evolving force, as much inherent and as indestructible as any other of its functions, and not to be destroyed either by opposition or by its own mistakes.

The church was not destroyed because it burned witches; its destruction was not advocated even by the witches it tortured. On the other hand, the church has become a better and better organ of the religious instincts of the race with each mistake, with each intelligent opposition. But even suppose the church should be destroyed as an organization by some awful blunder of its leaders, or a masterly fight on the part of a united opposition. The religious instincts of the race, the spiritual intuitions and impulses of mankind would not be injured—would not, in fact, be touched by the destruction of this organization or agency.

You might as well say you destroy the power of steam when you disable a locomotive. This religious instinct would at once construct a new and better organized expression of itself. Those religious institutions which were the original cause of an organized church, would organize another, and as many others as the destroying forces made necessary.

This is but to say that function precedes and produces organism, and this is just as true in the social structure as it is in the physical structure of animals.

Sympathetic association of men who work together for each other's protection and benefit is just as much an inherent instinct in man as are any other of his religious or social faculties; and this inherent impulse always has asserted itself, and when its outward means of manifesting itself, its organization, was destroyed, it formed another. In other words, the sympathetic association of men along trade union lines is just as natural as the instinct to worship God, and you can no more destroy one than the other.

In some it is so strong that you hear men say, trade unionism is my religion.

All the blood spilled throughout the ages in religious wars has only strengthened religion—a lesson the czar has yet to learn. All the fight against labor organizations but crystallizes their producing instinct in the human soul—a lesson that may reach our Indianapolis and Dayton friends ultimately.

Like all other forces, this force moves along lines of least resistance, and the wrecks along the road are only wrecks because they had served their purpose of pointing to better methods.

There has never been a time when more responsibility rested upon leaders than to-day, nor a time when such serious postponement of further progress might result from a lack of conservative sense. But the final welfare of labor is not now, nor ever was, in the hands of any set of men; it is a part of the power that evolves, and a backward look at the wrecks of labor organizations inspires in me very much the same feeling toward those same wrecks as the religious awe and consequent worship the old Aztecs had for a woman who had given up her life in maternity.

INFLUENCE OF TRADE UNIONS ON IMMIGRANTS.

BY ETHELBERT STEWART.

[Ethelbert Stewart, special agent, United States Bureau of Labor; born in Illinois, April 22, 1857; educated in the public schools of Illinois; commissioner of labor in Illinois for eight years, and special agent in the United States Department of Labor since September, 1889. Author, Fines and Fining Systems in Illinois, Early Organization Among Printers, Restriction of Output, etc.]

The influence of the trade unions among the foreign element employed in the packing business in Chicago is exceedingly interesting and throws a valuable side light on the whole question involved. The immigrant is, in the first instance, a wage reducer, either directly or indirectly, although the extent of his influence upon wages can not well be stated; but as a prospective wage reducer he is met by the trade union in self defence, just as the trade union meets female and child labor, except in this, the union seeks to organize the immigrants, while it seeks by legislation to prohibit or limit the work of women and children—that is, the union seeks the aid of the state to prevent wage reductions by means of female and child labor, and it seeks by organizing the immigrants to prevent reduction of wages by immigration. It makes no claim of undertaking any charitable or primarily civic education among the immigrants, but the secondary effect of the union on the immigrant is distinctively civic in character. It is the first, and for a time the only, point at which he touches any influences outside his clan. Even the progressive forces inside the nationality lines consider the immigrant hopeless and seek only to reach his children—as, for instance, the officers of the Polish National Alliance direct their effort toward getting the Poles to send their children to American public schools and to have them mix up with and become a part of the whole people. The trade union, however, must deal with the immigrant himself, and the immigrant, when he learns that the union wants to raise his wages, decrease his hours of labor, etc., begins to see the necessity of learning the English language, of understanding the institutions he hears talked about in the union meetings, and other matters which interest him.

From 1880 to 1886 the nationalities employed in the Chicago stock yards, in the order of their numerical importance, were Irish, Americans, Germans, and a few Scotch. The great strike of 1886 disrupted the only organization of workmen in the yards—that of the Knights of Labor—and after the failure of the strike a notable exodus of Americans and the more active men among the Irish began. Whether this was entirely voluntary, or in part resulted from activity in the strike, is not germane to this subject. The Poles began to come into the yards in 1886, after the settlement of the strike, but not as strike breakers. This appears to have been a voluntary immigration, increasing in volume until by 1890 the most of the unskilled occupations were filled by Poles, who by 1894 had practical control of the common labor.

The Bohemians began to affect noticeably the situation in 1894, going first into the inferior positions, which they shared with the Poles. There were two minor strikes between 1890 and 1894, which in a measure aided in bringing about this result. There was some movement upward among the Poles—that is, from lower to higher occupations, but not so marked as among the Bohemians. The Bohemians, coming in later, began under the Poles—that is, took the lower positions as the Poles went up, and divided the entire unskilled labor possibilities with the Poles. The Bohemians, however, soon outstripped the Poles in the movement upward from unskilled to skilled occupations.

The strike of 1894 unsettled these movements temporarily. Negro labor was employed to break the strike and has been an element in the situation ever since. In 1880 but one negro was employed in the yards, and he worked in Armour's killing gang. While few of the strike breakers of 1894 were retained, yet that event marks the real beginning of the employment of negroes. At the beginning of the 1904 strike some 500 negroes worked in the yards, many of whom belonged to the union.

After the strike of 1894 was settled the Bohemians were introduced more rapidly, and this continued up to 1896. In 1895 the Lithuanians began coming in, followed by Slovaks in 1896, and this continued steadily until 1899, when the number began to increase rapidly. Two years ago an enormous influx of Lithuanians, Slovaks, and Russian Poles occurred, swamping the labor market in the yards. This was caused largely because of the threatening war between Russia and Japan, and the consequent rush of people to escape compulsory military duty. This has been appreciably checked within the last six or eight months.

The proportion of workmen of the various nationalities in the yards at the beginning of the 1904 strike was approximately: Irish, 25 per cent; American and Scotch, about 2 per cent; Germans, 15 per cent; Poles, 20 per cent; Bohemians, 20 per cent. The remainder were Lithuanians, Slovaks, a very few Krains, and, among the most recent arrivals, Finns and Greeks, the latter, however, not being appreciable in number. No attention has been paid in this investigation to immigrants having a representation fewer in number than the Lithuanians and Slavonians.

Of these nationalities, excluding the Irish and Germans, which are not here considered as immigrants, the Bohemians are the most progressive, and have the industrial advantage in this, that many of the foremen are Bohemians and give preference to their nationality when taking on new men. There is no apparent surplus of Irish, Germans, Americans, or Bohemians in the labor market of the district affected, the surplus being composed of Poles, Slovaks, and Lithuanians.

Among all the immigrants mentioned, except the Irish and Germans, the clan spirit is at first all powerful. The Bohemians, while Catholics, are Bohemian Catholics, and the Poles are Polish Catholics. This is even more true of the Lithuanians and the Slavonians, who are the most clannish of all. No doubt difference in language has much to do with this, but it is by no means the most serious feature. Each nationality has not only its own church, but its own school system, the Lithuanian schools making no pretence of teaching English, some of the teachers not being able

even to speak it. The Slavs and Galicians have not as yet
opened schools of their own. While the religion of these
different nationalities may be said to be one, the associations
are along exclusive nationality lines. They settle or rent
properties by districts, and in branching out to occupy more
territory one side of the street will first become Lithuanian
for a block or so, and then the other side of the street will
be occupied by the same nationality. The single men invariably board only in families of their own clan. Language
has something to do with this, but really less than might be
apparent on first consideration, and less than might seem
to be true. When organizing building and loan associations
it is done along strictly clan lines. The Bohemians have
four of this class of associations, the Poles three, and the
Lithuanians one. The Slavs as yet have none. There are
other clannish distinctions, as Lithuanian Republican clubs,
Lithuanian Democratic clubs, Bohemian Socialist clubs,
Bohemian Democratic clubs, everywhere and always along
the strictest lines of nationality.

It is currently reported that before the organization
of the union this condition occasionally threatened riots
along clan lines, owing to the fact that foremen showed such
preference for men of their own clan. The union was organized by trades and departments, and the officials refused to
permit nationality lines to be recognized. In the sheep butchers' union are to be found all the men connected with sheep
killing, regardless of nationalities. So severe was the fight
made upon this plan by the clan leaders—those who drew
emoluments or secured social prestige as leaders of the
various strictly clan societies—and so seemingly insurmountable was the objection raised by the Lithuanians to the union,
that in 1900, when the Lithuanians were first organized,
it was permitted in one case to organize a Lithuanian union.
The experiment, however, was a signal failure. No subse-
quent experiments have been permitted.

The unions in the stock yards are controlled by the Irish,
ably assisted by the Germans. As a Bohemian or a Pole
learns the language and develops, he is elected business
agent or other official. In the pork butchers' union, for

instance, there are about 1,800 members, 600 of whom are Irish, 600 Germans, 300 Poles, and 300 Lithuanians and Slavs. This union recently elected a Pole as president of the local. In their business meetings the motions made, resolutions read, and speeches delivered are usually interpreted in five languages, though in some locals in only three. All business, however, is transacted primarily in English, although any member may speak to any motion in the language he best understands, his words being rendered into English for the minutes of the meeting and into all the languages necessary for the information of members. It is here that the practical utility of learning English is first brought home forcibly to the immigrant. In all other of his associations not only does his own language suffice, but, for reasons that can be well understood, shrewd leaders minimize the importance of learning any other. The only notable exception to this is the National Polish alliance, and even here only the Polish language is used. There is no apparent influence exerted, however, to create the impression that the Polish is all sufficient.

In his trade union the Slav mixes with the Lithuanian, the German, and the Irish—and this is the only place they do mix—until, by virtue of this intercourse and this mixing, clannishness is to a degree destroyed, and a social mixing along other lines comes naturally into play. Not only is the Amalgamated Meat Cutters' union an Americanizing influence in the stock yards, but for the Poles, Lithuanians, and Slovaks it is the only Americanizing influence, so far as could be determined in this investigation. It is true this Americanizing is being done by the Irish and Germans, but it is Americanizing, nevertheless, and is being done as rapidly as the material to work on will permit, and very well indeed. Again, the reaction is good in its results. The feeling among the Irish against the Dutch and the Polack is rapidly dying out. As the Irish in Chicago express it, "association together and industrial necessity have shown us that however it may go against the grain, we must admit the common interests and brotherhood must include the Polack and the Jew." It is also admitted that when the speech of the Lithuanian is translated in the meeting of the trade union the Irish and the German see in it the workings of a fairly good mind. Some of the best suggestions come from Bohemians, and mutual respect takes the place of mutual hatred.

An investigation disclosed the influence of the union in teaching the immigrant the nature of the American form of government. The records, independent of this, show that during an investigation of building and loan associations a few years ago information from the Bohemian, Polish, and other clannish associations of that character could be obtained only through the services of an interpreter. It was found that as soon as a Bohemian or a Pole heard the word government, or government agent, he closed his mouth, and it was impossible to secure any information.

This has been true in other investigations, notably in collecting family budgets; but with an intelligent interpreter, using their own language, the nature of the work was explained, and no further difficulty experienced. The union is breaking down this trait of character in the foreigners of the nationalities mentioned. This it is doing not as a matter of philanthropy, but from a selfish necessity. The immigrant must be taught that he must stand straight up on his own feet; that the ward politician is dependent on him—on his vote, etc.—and not him on the ward politician. In this way he first learns that he is a part of the government, and while this is done by indirection, in a large sense, there is no other force that is doing it at all. The Pole, the Bohemian, the Lithuanian, the Slovak, and to a much lesser degree the Galician, have inherited the feeling that somehow government is a thing inimical to their natural development—a power forcing itself upon them from afar; an intrusive power for repression, taxation, punishment only; a thing which they must stand in awe of, obey, pay tribute to, and wish that it had not come among their people, even if they did not secretly hate it—a thing, in short, which ought not to be. Being weaker than it they must be silent in its presence, and if forced to speak, lie, as for them to tell the truth would mean imprisonment or death.

It is not necessary for these things to be true in order
that the illiterate peasants should have believed them for
generations. Seventy five per cent of the stock yards immigrants are of the peasant and agricultural laborer class
of Europe, and comparatively few of them can read or write
in their own language. To make such a people feel that the
government is their friend, that they are a part of it, that
development and education, not repression, are its objects
and its purposes with and for them, is an enormous task,
and one which a trade union single handed and alone can
not be expected to accomplish by indirection in a few years,
with the flood of new ignorance that has been brought in
by the high tide of immigration into the stock yards.

In every trade union, however conservative, there are
members who will occasionally get the floor and advise
their hearers to vote high wages and shorter hours at the
ballot box. As the groups of Slovaks gather around after
the business is over to have these things explained to them,
many get their first real idea of what the ballot and election
day means, and the relation of these to the government itself. In their own home countries the two essential, if not
only, elements of the peasant and agricultural laborer's
mind is to believe and obey, or follow. Advantage is taken
of this fact here by clan politicians, as well as the clan leader
in every department. Once the leader can make these people
believe in him, he thinks for the entire group, and insists
that their duty consists in following his lead implicitly. Necessarily, the trade union, in order to get them to break away
from the leader that opposed the union on industrial lines,
would be compelled to urge them to consider their own personal and group interests as wage workers; to think and
act for themselves along lines where they knew the real conditions better than anyone else, and certainly better than
their leader in a child insurance society, or something else
as remote. Here, too, are the first germs of what may be
called the departmental thinking implanted in their minds—
that is, that while a leader may be worthy of their confidence in one thing, it does not necessarily follow that he is
so in some other class of interests.

It is doubtful if any organization other than a trade union could accomplish these things, for only the bread and butter necessity would be potent enough as an influence to bring these people out of the fixed forms and crystallizations of life into which they have been compressed. Certain it is that no other organization is attempting to do this work, at least not by amalgamation, which is the only way assimilation can be secured among these various foreign elements. The drawing of these people away from their petty clique leaders and getting them to think for themselves upon one line of topics, namely, the industrial conditions and the importance of trade organization, result in a mental uplift. The only way they can pull a Slovak away from his leader is to pull him up until he is gotten above his leader along the lines of thought they are working on. The very essence of the trade argument on the immigrant is—unconsciously again— an uplifting and an Americanizing influence. The unionist begins to talk better wages, better working conditions, better opportunities, better homes, better clothes. Now, one can not eternally argue better in the ears of any man, no matter how restricted the particular better harped on, without producing something of a psychological atmosphere of better in all his thought and life activities. If better food, better wages, or even better beer, is the only kind of better one might get a Slovak or a Lithuanian to think about, then the only way to improve him is to inject the thought of better into the only crevice to be found in his stupidity.

Of course, many object to attempts to improve these people because the immigrants from Lithuania, Slavonia, and Russian Poland are better off here than they ever were or could be in their own countries; that, left to themselves, they would not only be perfectly satisfied, but delighted with their improved condition; that the union must first produce discontent and dissatisfaction with what would otherwise be entirely satisfactory before it can get these immigrants even to talk about joining the union. Again, it is urged that at home these people do not expect to eat as good food as other people, nor to dress as well, nor to live in as good houses;

that, as peasants, they never compare themselves with other people or classes of people.

In opposition to all these things, the union begins by teaching the immigrant that his wages are not so good as another man's, doing practically the same kind of work, while it neglects to tell him he is not doing it so well, so intelligently, nor so much of it perhaps; but the union gets him to compare himself not with what he was in Lithuania, but with some German or Irish family, and then stings him with the assertion that he has as much right to live that way as anybody. The union attempts to show the immigrant that he can live better only by getting more money, and that by joining the union he will get it. If left alone he would be entirely satisfied, perhaps, with what he was getting before. It is perfectly true, probably, that in most cases the union does not care for the Lithuanian in the first instance, the real purpose being to protect their own wages by getting the immigrants to demand high wages for their labor. So later on some degree of fellowship is engendered, but self defence is the real motive.

The union point of view is that for a Lithuanian peasant to be contented, satisfied and happy with the Lithuanian standard of living in America is a crime, a crime not only against himself but against America and everyone who wishes to make individual and social development possible in America, and that whatever the union's motives for creating discontent, the fact that it does create a discontent among the immigrants —which is the first step toward their improvement and ultimate Americanization—renders the union so far a public benefactor.

Many persons were interviewed in securing information along these lines—bankers, professional men, and all classes. One gentleman, in the banking business in the stock yards district for many years, said that the Slavonians and Galicians have been buying homes within the last eighteen months to a most remarkable and unprecedented extent, and that this is in a measure true of the Lithuanians, but not to such a marked degree. He testifies that the union has given these people a sense of security in their position. By mixing up the nationalties in the union meeting it has made them acquainted with each other and dispelled an undefined dread of pending race war or struggle between nationalities in the yards. Formerly most of the Slovak and Lithuanian immigrants were a floater class. About the only ones who return to their homes now are the Galicians, in whose country a more or less representative form of government prevails. Others testified in a similar way, although some thought the union had done little except to agitate for higher, higher, and higher wages, regardless of economic conditions.

On the police side of the problem, a sergeant of the twentieth precinct, in Chicago, that known as back of the yards, which is crowded with the Bohemian and Polish elements, said that there had been the greatest improvement since the union was formed, in 1900—less disorder, better living, more intelligence, and more understanding of American institutions and laws; that they employ fewer policemen in the district, and that less crime is committed than prior to 1900.

The studies of the various nationalities involved in the 1904 meat strike brings out some valuable points relative to the restriction of immigration. Among them there seems to be an unalterable opposition to laws excluding those who can not read and write in their own language, and their argument is that the peasant population of central and eastern Europe, from which they came, have more rugged morals, simpler lives, and fewer vices than the inhabitants of the cities and towns who can read and write, as a rule. They consider themselves not responsible morally or politically for the fact that Russia has fewer schools than Illinois and spends less money on education in a year than does that state. They assert that their ignorance is not of the kind that is synonymous with vice or with crime; that they are as innocent as ignorant, whereas a far worse town and city population would be admitted without question under such laws. They have some peculiar ideas about prohibiting absolutely any immigration for a specific term of years and then allowing only a certain percentage to come in each year thereafter; but the main point they make is as to the illiteracy of the peasant class, the most desirable we can secure, and the literacy of the criminal classes of the great cities, which could come in under such restrictive legislation.

IMMIGRATION AND LABOR PROBLEMS.

BY JOHN R. COMMONS.

[John Rogers Commons, economist; born Darke county, O., October 13, 1862; graduated from Oberlin, 1888; A. M., 1890; student Johns Hopkins, 1888–90; professor sociology Oberlin college, 1892; Indiana university, 1893–95; Syracuse university, 1895–99; expert agent Industrial commission, 1902; assistant secretary National Civic Federation, 1903; professor of sociology, University of Wisconsin. Author: The Distribution of Wealth; Social Reform and the Church; Proportional Representation, etc.]

Had it been left to the initiative of the emigrants the flow of immigration to America could scarcely ever have reached one half its actual dimensions. While various motives and inducements have always worked together and it would be rash to assert dogmatically the relative weight of each, yet to one who has carefully noted all the circumstances it is scarcely an exaggeration to say that even more important than the initiative of immigrants have been the efforts of Americans to bring and attract them. Throughout our history these efforts have been inspired by one grand, effective motive, that of making a profit upon the immigrants. The desire to get cheap labor, to take in passenger fares and to sell land have probably brought more immigrants than the hard conditions of Europe, Asia, and Africa have sent us. Induced immigration has been as potent as voluntary immigration. And it is to this pecuniary motive that we owe our manifold variety of races and especially our influx of backward races. One entire race, the negro, came solely for the profit of shipowners and landowners. Working people of the colonial period were hoodwinked and kidnapped by shippers and speculators who reimbursed themselves by indenturing them to planters and farmers. The beginners of other races have come through similar but less coercive inducements, initiated, however, by the demand of those who held American property for speculation or investment. William Penn and his lessees, John Law, the Dutch East India company, and many of the grantees of lands in the colonies, sent their agents through western Europe and the British Isles with glowing advertise-

ments, advanced transportation, and contracted for indentured service by way of reimbursement. In the nineteenth
century new forms of induced migration appeared. Victims
of the Irish famine were assisted to emigrate by local and
general governments and by philanthropic societies, and both
the Irish and the Germans, whose migration began towards
the middle of the century, were, in a measure, exceptions to
the general rule of induced immigration for profit. Several
western states created immigration bureaus which advertised
their own advantages for intending immigrants, and Wisconsin especially, in this way, settled her lands with a wide
variety of races. After the civil war, induced migration entered upon a vigorous revival. The system of indenturing
had long since disappeared, because legislatures and courts
declined to recognize and enforce contracts for service. Consequently, a new form of importation appeared under the
direction of middlemen of the same nativity as that of the
immigrant. Chinese coolies came under contract with the
Six Companies, who advanced their expenses and looked to
their own secret agents and tribunals to enforce repayment
with profit. Japanese coolies, much later, came under contract with twelve immigration companies chartered by the
Japanese government. Italians were recruited by the padroni,
and the bulk of the new Slav immigration from southeastern
Europe is in charge of their own countrymen acting as drum-
mers and middlemen.

These labor speculators have perfected a system of inducement and through billing as effective as that by which
horse and cattle buyers in Kentucky or Iowa collect and forward their living freight to the markets of Europe. A
Croatian of the earlier immigration, for example, sets up a
saloon in South Chicago and becomes an employment bureau
for his greener countrymen, and also ticket agent on commission for the steamship companies. His confederates are
stationed along the entire route at connecting points, from
the villages of Croatia to the saloon in Chicago. In Croatia
they go among the laborers and picture to them the high
wages and abundant work in America. They induce them
to sell their little belongings and they furnish them with

through tickets. They collect them in companies, give them
a countersign and send them on to their fellow agent at
Fiume, thence to Genoa, or other port whence the American
steerage vessel sails. In New York they are met by other
confederates whom they identify by their countersign, and
again they are safely transferred and shipped to their desti-
nation. Here they are met by their enterprising countryman, lodged and fed, and within a day or two handed over
to the foreman in a great steel plant or to the boss of a construction gang on a railway, or to a contractor on a large
public improvement. After they have earned and saved a
little money they send for their friends to whom the boss has
promised jobs. Again their lodging house countryman sells
them the steamship ticket and arranges for the safe delivery
of those for whom they have sent. In this way immigration
is stimulated and new races are induced to begin their American colonization. Eventually the pioneers send for their
families, and it is estimated that nearly two thirds of the immigrants in recent years have come on prepaid tickets or on
money sent to them from America.

The significance of this new and highly perfected form of
inducement will appear when we look back for a moment upon
the legislation governing immigration.

At the close of the civil war, with a vast territory newly
opened to the west by the railroads, congress enacted a law
throwing wide open our doors to the immigrants of all lands.
It gave new guaranties for the protection of naturalized citizens in renouncing allegiance to their native country, declaring
that expatriation is a natural and inherent right of all people,
indispensable to the enjoyment of the rights of life, liberty, and
the pursuit of happiness.

In the same year, 1869, the famous Burlingame treaty
was negotiated with China, by which Americans in China and
Chinese in America should enjoy all the privileges, immuni-
ties, and exemptions enjoyed by citizens of the most favored
nation. These steps favorable to immigration were in line
with the long continued policy of the country from the earliest
colonial times.

But a new force had come into American politics—the wage earner. From this time forth the old policies were violently challenged. High wages were to be pitted against high profits. The cheap labor which was eagerly sought by the corporations and large property owners was just as eagerly fought by the unpropertied wage earners. Of course, neither party conceded that it was selfishly seeking its own interest. Those who expected profits contended that cheap foreign labor was necessary for the development of the country; that American natural resources were unbounded, but American workmen could not be found for the rough work needed to turn these resources into wealth; that America should be in the future, as it had been in the past, a haven for the oppressed of all lands; and that in no better way could the principles of American democracy be spread to all peoples of the earth than by welcoming them and teaching them in our midst.

The wage earners have not been so fortunate in their protestations of disinterestedness. They were compelled to admit that though they themselves had been immigrants or the children of immigrants, they were now denying to others what had been a blessing to them. Yet they were able to set forward one supreme argument which our race problems are every day more and more showing to be sound. The future of American democracy is the future of the American wage earner. To have an enlightened and patriotic citizenship we must protect the wages and standard of living of those who constitute the bulk of the citizens. This argument had been offered by employers themselves when they were seeking a protective tariff against the importation of pauper made goods. What wonder that the wage earner should use the same argument to keep out the pauper himself, and especially that he should begin by applying the argument to those races which showed themselves unable rapidly to assimilate and thereby make a stand for high wages and high standards of living? Certain it is that had the white wage earners possessed the suffrage and political influence during colonial times the negro would not have been admitted in large numbers and we should have been spared that race problem which of all is the largest and most nearly insoluble.

The first outbreak of the new founded strength of the
American wage earner was directed against a race superior
even to the negro immigrants in industry, frugality, intelligence, and civilization—the Chinese. And this outbreak was
so powerful, that, in spite of all appeals to the traditions and
liberties of America, the national government felt driven to
repudiate the treaty so recently signed with the highest manifestations of faith, good will, and international comity.

Very early in the settlement of California the Chinaman
had encountered hostile legislation. The state election had
been carried by the know-nothings as early as 1854. Discriminating taxes, ordinances, and laws were adopted, and even
immigration was regulated. But the state and federal courts
declared such legislation invalid as violating treaties or interfering with international relations. Then the wage earning
element of California joined as one man in demanding action
by the federal government, and eventually, by the treaty of
1880 and the law of 1888, Chinese laborers were excluded.
Thus did the Caucasian wage earner score his first and signal
victory in reversing what his opponents proclaimed were
principles coeval with the foundation of our government.

The next step was the alien contract labor law of 1885
and 1888, placed on the statute books through the efforts of
the Knights of Labor. As early as 1875 congress had prohibited the immigration of paupers, criminal, and immoral
persons, but the law of 1885 went to the other extreme and
was designed to exclude industrial classes. The law is directed
against prepayment of transportation, assistance, or encouragement of foreigners to immigrate under contract to perform
labor in the United States, and provides for the prosecution
of the importer and deportation of the contract immigrant.
This law has been enforced against skilled labor, which comes
mainly from northwestern Europe, but, owing to the new
system of padroni and middlemen above described, it cannot
be enforced against the unskilled laborers of southern and
eastern Europe, since it cannot be shown that they have come
under contract to perform labor. By the amendment and
revised law adopted in 1903, after considerable discussion and
an effort on the part of the labor unions to strengthen the law,

it was extended so as to exclude not only those coming under contract but also those coming under offers and promises of employment.

From what precedes we see that there are two exactly opposite points of view from which the subject of immigration is approached. One is the production of wealth; the other is the distribution of wealth. He who takes the standpoint of production sees the enormous undeveloped resources of this country—the mines to be exploited, railroads and highways to be built and rebuilt, farms to be opened up or to be more intensively cultivated, manufactures to be multiplied and the markets of the world to be conquered by our exports, while there are not enough workmen, or not enough willing to do the hard and disagreeable work at the bottom.

He who takes the standpoint of distribution sees the huge fortunes, the low wages, the small share of the product going to labor, the sweatshop, the slums, all on account of the excessive competition of wage earner against wage earner.

Consider, first, the bearing of immigration on the production of wealth.

Over four fifths of the immigrants are in the prime of life—the ages between fourteen and forty five. In the year 1902 only 12 out of every 100 were under fifteen years of age, and only 6 out of every 100 over forty five years of age. The census of 1900 offers some interesting comparisons between the native born and the foreign born in this matter of age distribution. It shows quite plainly that a large proportion of the native born population is below the age of industrial production, fully 39 per cent, or two fifths, being under fifteen years of age, while only 5 per cent of the foreign born are of corresponding ages. On the other hand, the ages fifteen to forty four include 46 per cent of the native and 58 per cent of the foreign born. Thus, immigration brings to us a population of working ages unhampered by unproductive mouths to be fed, and, if we consider alone that which produces the wealth of this country and not that which consumes it, then the immigrants add more to the country than does the same number of natives of equal ability. Their home countries have borne the expense of rearing them up to the industrial period of their lives and then America, without that heavy expense, reaps the profits on the investment.

In another respect does immigration add to our industrial population more than would be done by an equal increase in native population, namely, by the large excess of men over women. In 1902, nearly three fourths (72 per cent) of the immigrants were males and slightly more than one fourth (28 per cent) were females. And the census shows that men predominate over women in the proportion of fifty four to forty six, although among the native born population the sexes are about equal, being in the proportion of 507 males to 493 females.

This small proportion of women and children shows, of course, that it is the workers, not the families, who seek America. Yet the proportions widely vary for different nationalities. Among the Jews 43 per cent are females and 27 per cent children. This persecuted race moves in a body, expecting to make America its home. At the other extreme, the Greeks send only 4 per cent females and 8 per cent children, the Croatians 11 per cent females and 3 per cent children, the south Italians 19 per cent females and 11 per cent children. These are races whose immigration has only recently begun, and, naturally enough, the women and children, except in the case of the Jews, do not accompany the workmen. A race of longer migration, like the Germans, has 37 per cent females and 19 per cent children. The Irish have a peculiar position. Alone of all the races do the women exceed the men, but only 4 per cent are children. Irish girls seeking domestic service explain this preponderance of women.

Such being the proportions of industrial energy furnished by immigration, what is the quality? Much the larger proportion of immigrants are classed as unskilled, including laborers and servants. Omitting those who have no occupation, including mainly women and children, who are 23 per cent of the total, only 17 per cent of the remainder who are working immigrants are skilled, and 83 per cent are unskilled. The proportions vary greatly among the different races. The largest element of skilled labor is among the Jews, a city people, more than half of whom are skilled workmen.

The proportion of skilled labor is probably larger than the foregoing figures would indicate, for it must be noted that they refer only to steerage passengers and that the reports of the commissioner of immigration do not classify cabin passengers as immigrants. Hence in 1902 there were 80,000 immigrants, visitors, and travelers of the more prosperous condition, of whom we have no record respecting their social and industrial qualities. These must have included many skilled workmen, and also many of the professional classes, of whom only 3,000 came by steerage.

The skilled labor which comes to America, especially from northern and western Europe, occupies a peculiar position in our industries. In the first place, the most capable workmen have permanent places at home and it is in general only those who cannot command situations who seek their fortunes abroad. The exceptions to this rule are in the beginnings of an industry like that of tin plate, when almost the entire industry moved bodily to America, and the highly skilled tin workers of Wales brought a kind of industrial ability that had not hitherto existed in this country. As for the bulk of skilled immigrants, they do not represent the highest skill of the countries whence they come.

On the other hand, the European skilled workman is usually better trained than the American, and in many branches of industry, especially machinery and shipbuilding, the English and Scotch immigrants command those superior positions where an all around training is required.

This peculiar situation is caused by the highly specialized character of American industry. In no country has division of labor and machinery been carried as far as here. By division of labor the skilled trades have been split up into simple operations, each of which in itself requires little or no skill, and the boy who starts in as a beginner is kept at one operation, so that he does not learn a trade. The old time journeyman tailor was a skilled mechanic who measured his customer, cut the cloth and trimmings, basted, sewed, and pressed the suit. Now we have factories which make only coats, others which make only vests, others trousers, and there are children's knee pants factories and even ladies' tailor establish-

ments where the former skilled seamstress sees her precious
skill dissipated among a score of unskilled workers. Thus
the journeyman tailor is displaced by the factory where the
coat passes through the hands of thirty to fifty different men
and women, each of whom can learn his peculiar operation in
a month or two. The same is true in greater or less degree
in all industries. Even in the building trades in the larger
cities there are as many kinds of bricklayers as there are kinds
of walls to be built, and as many kinds of carpenters as there
are varieties of woodwork.

So it is with machinery. The American employer does
not advertise for a machinist—he wants a lathe hand or a
drill press hand, and the majority of his hands are perhaps
only automatic machine tenders. The employer cannot
afford to transfer these hands from one job to another to
enable them to learn the trade. He must keep them at one
operation, for it is not so much skill that he wants as it is cheap
labor and speed. Consequently, American industry is not
producing all around mechanics, and the employers look to
Europe for their skilled artisans. In England the trade unions
have made it their special business to see that every apprentice learns every part of his trade, and they have prevented
employers from splitting up the trades and specializing machinery and thereby transforming the mechanic into the
hand. Were it not for immigration, American industries
would ere now have been compelled to give more attention
to apprenticeship and the training of competent mechanics.
The need of apprenticeship and trade schools is being more
seriously felt every year, for, notwithstanding the progress of
division of labor and machinery, the all around mechanic
continues to play an important part in the shop and factory.
American trade unions are gaining strength and one of their
most insistent demands is the protection of apprenticeship.
The bricklayers' union of Chicago even secures from its employers instruction for apprentices in a trade school. Not
much headway in this line, however, has yet been made, and
American industry has become abnormal, we might almost
say suicidal, or at any rate, non self supporting. By extreme
division of labor and marvelous application of machinery it

makes possible the wholesale employment in factories of the farm laborers of Europe and then depends on Europe for the better trained types of the skilled mechanic, who, on account of the farm laborer have not been able to learn their trade in America.

Not only does immigration bring to America the strongest, healthiest, and most energetic and adventurous of the work people of Europe and Asia, but those who come work much harder than they did at home. Migration tears a man away from the traditions, the routine, the social props, on which he has learned to rely, and throws him among strangers upon his own resources. He must swim or drown. At the same time he earns higher wages and eats more nourishing food than he had ever thought within reach of one in his station. His ambition is fired, he is stirred by the new tonic of feeling himself actually rising in the world. He pictures to himself a home of his own, he economizes and saves money to send to his friends and family or to return to his beloved land a person of importance. Watch a gang of Italians shoveling dirt under an Irish boss, or a sweatshop of Jewish tailors under a small contractor, and you shall see such feverish production of wealth as an American born citizen would scarcely endure. Partly fear, partly hope, make the fresh immigrant the hardest, if not the most intelligent, worker in our industries.

But, however hard one may work, he can only exercise the gifts with which nature has endowed him. Whether these gifts are contributed by race or by civilization, we shall inquire when we come to the problems of amalgamation and assimilation. At present we are concerned with the varying industrial gifts and capacities of the various races as they actually exist at the time when immigration, annexation, or conquest may take place.

The mental and moral qualities suited to make productive workers depend upon the character of the industry. It is not conceivable that the immigrants of the present day from southern Europe and from Asia could have succeeded as frontiersmen and pioneers in the settlement of the country. In all Europe, Asia, and Africa there was but one race in the seventeenth and eighteenth centuries that had the preliminary training necessary to plunge into the wilderness, and, in the face of the Indian, to establish homes and agriculture. This was the English and the Scotch-Irish. The Spaniards and the French were pioneers and adventurers, but they established only trading stations. Accustomed to a paternal government they had not, as a people, the self reliance and capacity for sustained exertion required to push forward as individuals, and cut themselves off from the support of a government across the ocean. They shrank from the herculean task of clearing the forests, planting crops among the stumps, and living miles away from their neighbors. True, the pioneers had among their number several of German, French, and Dutch descent, but these belonged to the second and third generations descended from the immigrants and thrown from the time of childhood among their English-Scotch neighbors. The English race established itself in America not because it was first to come, not because of its armies and navies, but because of its agriculture. Every farm newly carved out of the wilderness became a permanent foothold and soon again sent out a continuous colony of sons and daughters to occupy the fertile land. Based on this self reliant, democratic, industrial conquest of the new world the military conquest naturally, inevitably followed.

But at the present day the character of industry has entirely changed. The last quarter of the nineteenth century saw the vacant lands finally occupied and the tribe of frontiersmen coming to an end. Population now began to recoil upon the east and the cities. This afforded to manufactures and to the mining industries the surplus labor market so necessary for the continuance of large establishments which to-day need thousands of workmen and to-morrow hundreds. Moreover, among the American born workmen, as well as the English and Scotch, is not found that docility, obedience to orders and patient toil which employers desire where hundreds and thousands are brought, like an army, under the direction of foremen, superintendents, and managers. Employers now turn for their labor supply to those eastern and southern sections of Europe which have not hitherto contributed to immigration. The first to draw upon these sources in large numbers were the anthracite coal operators of Pennsylvania. In these fields the English, Scotch, Welsh, and Irish miners, during and following the period of the civil war, had effected an organization for the control of wages, and the outrages of a secret society known as the Molly Maguires gave occasion for the importation of new races unaccustomed to unison and incapable, on account of language, of co-operation with English speaking miners. Once introduced in the mining industry these races rapidly found their way into the unskilled parts of manufactures, into the service of railroads and large contractors. On the construction of the Erie canal in 1898, of 16,000 workmen, 15,000 were unnaturalized Italians.

On the Pacific slope the Chinese and Japanese immigrants have filled the place occupied by the southeast European in the east and the negro in the south. They are the workmen who built the Pacific railroads and without them it is said that these railroads could not have been constructed until several years after their actual completion.

The immigration of the Chinese reached its highest figures prior to the exclusion laws of 1882, and since that time has been but an insignificant contribution. In their place have come the Japanese, a race whose native land, in proportion to its cultivable area, is more densely populated than any other country in the world. The Chinese and Japanese are perhaps the most industrious of all races, while the Chinese are the most docile. The Japanese excel in imitativeness, but are not as reliable as the Chinese. Neither race possesses the originality and ingenuity which characterize the competent American and British mechanic. In the Hawaiian Islands, where they have enjoyed greater opportunities than elsewhere, they are found to be capable workmen in the skilled trades provided they are under the direction of white mechanics. But their largest field of work in Hawaii is in the unskilled cultivation of the great sugar plantations. Here they have been likened to a sort of agricultural automaton, and it becomes possible to place them in large numbers under skilled direction and thus to secure the best results from their docility and industry.

In the United States itself the plantation form of agriculture, as distinguished from the domestic form, has always been based on a supply of labor from backward or un-Americanized races. This fact has a bearing on the alleged tendency of agriculture toward large farms. Ten years ago it seemed that the great bonanza farms were destined to displace the small farms, just as the trust displaces the small manufacturer. But it is now recognized that the reverse movement is in progress, and that the small farmer can compete successfully with the great farmers. It has not, however, been pointed out that the question is not a merely economic one and that it depends upon the industrial character of the races engaged in agriculture. The thrifty, hard working and intelligent American or Teutonic farmer is able to economize and purchase his own small farm and compete successfully with the large undertaking. But the backward, thriftless and unintelligent races succeed best when employed in gangs on large estates. The cotton and sugar fields of the south, with their negro workers, have their counterpart in the plantations of Hawaii with their Chinese and Japanese, and in the newly developed beet sugar fields of Nebraska, Colorado and California, with their Russians, Bohemians, Japanese and Mexicans. In the domestic or small form of agriculture the bulk of immigrants from southern and eastern Europe are not greatly desired as wage earners, and they do not succeed as proprietors and tenants because they lack oversight and business ability. It is the immigrants from northwestern Europe, the Germans and Scandinavians, whose thrift, self reliance and intensive agriculture have made them the model farmers of America.

These are a few of the many illustrative facts which might be set forth to show that the changing character of immigration is made possible by the changing character of industry, and that races wholly incompetent as pioneers and independent proprietors are able to find a place when once manufactures, mines and railroads, with their captains of industry, have sprung into being to guide and supervise their semi-intelligent work.

We have seen that the character of the immigrants for whom a place can be found depends upon the character of the industry. It also depends upon the laws governing property in labor. Here the industrial problem widens out into the social problem.

There are four variations in the treatment of labor as property in the United States, each of which has had its peculiar effect on the character of immigration or has grown out of the relations between races. They are slavery, peonage, contract labor, and free labor. Under slavery the laborer and his children are compelled by law throughout their lifetime to work for an owner on terms dictated and enforced by him. Under peonage the laborer is compelled by law to pay off a debt by means of his labor, and under contract labor he is compelled by law to carry out a contract to labor. To enforce peonage and contract labor the offence of running away is made punishable by imprisonment at forced labor or by extension of the period of service. Under freedom the law refuses to enforce a contract to work, making this an exception to the sacredness of contracts, and refuses to enforce the payment of a debt by specific service. This leaves to the contractor or creditor the usually empty relief of suing for damages. The significance of these varying degrees of servile, semi-servile and free labor will be seen in the following discussion of the social relations of the superior and inferior races.

In the entire circuit of the globe those races which have developed under a tropical sun are found to be indolent and fickle. From the standpoint of survival of the fittest such vices are really virtues, for severe and continuous exertion under tropical conditions bring prostration and predisposition to disease. Therefore, if such races are to adopt that industrious life which is a second nature to races of the temperate zones, it is only through some form of compulsion. The negro could not possibly have found a place in American industry had he come as a free man, and at the present time contract labor and peonage with the crime of running away are recognized in varying degrees by the laws of southern states. These statutes have been held unconstitutional by a federal court in Alabama, but the condition of peonage which they contemplate is considered by many planters as essential to the continuance of the cotton industry. One of them, in southwestern Georgia, a graduate of Columbia college, with five years of business training in the northern states, is quoted in an interview as follows:

"We have two ways of handling our plantations. We rent small sections of forty acres each, and with these go a plow and the mule. In addition, I have about 450 hands who work on wages. These men are paid nine dollars a month, in addition to a fixed rate of food, which amounts to four pounds of meat a week, a certain percentage of vegetables, tobacco, sugar, flour and some other commodities.

"These negroes live on the plantation, are given a roof over their heads, have garden patches and several other more or less valuable privileges. They invariably come to me for small advances of money.

"These advances of money and rations and clothing, although there is not much of the latter, are frequently sufficient to put the negro in debt to us. The minute he finds he is in debt he naturally conceives it to be easier to go to work somewhere else and begin all over again, instead of paying his debts.

"Now, when a negro runs away and violates his contract, leaving us in the lurch, not only short of his labor, but short of the advances we have made to him in money and goods, what would happen if we depended simply and solely on our right to sue? In the first place, with 450 hands we would have 450 suits before the season is out, and if we won them all we would not be able to collect forty five cents.

"The result is, that in Georgia and Alabama, and, I believe in other states, the law recognizes the right of the planter to reclaim the laborer who has left in violation of his contract, whether he be actually in debt or not.

"Whether Judge Jones has declared this law unconstitutional or not, the planters in the black belt will have to maintain their right to claim their contract labor, or else they will have to go out of the business. Under any other system you would find it impossible to get in your cotton, because the negroes at the critical time would simply sit down and refuse to work. When they are well, we compel laborers to go to the field by force. This is the truth, and there is no use lying about it."

The Malay races, to which the Filipinos belong, are, like the negroes, careless, thriftless, and disinclined to continuous exertion. In order to induce the Javanese to work the Dutch government of Java sets aside a certain tract of government land for coffee planting, and compels each head of a household to set out and keep in order a certain number of coffee trees. On private estates in Java and in other Malay and Indian colonies, such as Burma, Ceylon and the Philippines, where the government does not compel the native to take a contract to work, it nevertheless enforces contracts voluntarily made. In certain provinces of the Philippines the tenants are usually in debt, and the old law which permits the creditor to imprison the debtor for nonpayment of debt is still in force. Landowners of a district frequently come together shortly before the crops are sold and agree among themselves how much interest to charge the tenants on their debts. This is for the purpose of charging the highest possible rate and at the same time retain tenants, who then could not leave, finding the same conditions prevailing throughout the district. In the densely populated countries like Java and southern India, where the native cannot set up for himself, he has no alternative except to work under these contracts, and this is also true in the more thickly populated districts of the Philippine islands. But the case is different in sparsely settled countries, like Burma, East Sumatra and the greater part of the Philippines, where wages are so high that natives are not compelled by necessity to work continuously. "Speaking generally," says Professor Jenks, "the unskilled Filipino laborer, while intelligent enough, is careless and thriftless. He in most cases wishes to take two or three days a week on the average to celebrate as feast days. In individual cases, where his wages have been increased, he has been known to lessen correspondingly the number of days per month which he would work. His income being sufficient to satisfy his modest needs, he could see no reason why he should toil longer than was necessary to earn his income."

Hence in these sparsely settled countries the Dutch and English governments have adopted, and Professor Jenks, in his report to the war department, has recommended, a limited use of the system of contract labor, not, however, for the native, but for imported Chinese. This system has existed in another of our newly acquired possessions, Hawaii, since 1852, where it applied to Chinese, Japanese, Portuguese and German immigrants, and whence it was abolished by the act of annexation in 1898.

Contract labor of this kind is quite different from the peonage and contract labor of the nonindustrial races. It is similar to the indentured service of colonial times, in that the term of each contract is limited to a few years, and the contract is made by way of compensation for advanced expenses of immigration. The object is not, as in the case of slavery and peonage, to compel a shiftless race to work, but it is to develop the country by the introduction of an industrious race. The Chinese, after the expiration of their contracts, often become skilled laborers and merchants, and in the latter position their frugality and wiliness make them dangerous neighbors for the native Malay and Filipino races. For this reason Professor Jenks recommends that employers be placed under bonds to return each contract Chinese coolie to China at the expiration of the period of the contract, not to exceed three years, unless the government gives special permission for renewal of the contract. Governor Taft, in his report for the year 1902, while advocating a limited employment of Chinese contract coolies, said, "The truth is that, from a political standpoint, the unlimited introduction of the Chinese into these islands would be a great mistake. I believe the objection on the part of the Filipinos to such a course to be entirely logical and justified. The development of the islands by Chinamen would be at the expense of the Filipino people, and they may very well resent such a suggestion."

Governor Taft's opinion is strongly supported by the special commissioner of the American federation of labor, who after inquiries in the district surrounding Manila, reports as follows:

"Their reluctance to work, continually harped upon by many employers, is simply the natural reluctance of a progressive people to work for low wages under bad treatment. When wages rise above the level of the barest and poorest necessaries of life, and where treatment is fair, there Filipinos are at work in any numbers required."

There is a statistical fallacy in the foregoing statement. It is true that when high wages are paid Filipinos can be found to work, but in order to secure 200 steady workers at these high wages it is necessary to hire and fire a thousand or more.

"Of course," continues Mr. Rosenberg in his report, "the Filipino worker cannot successfully compete—cheap as he can live—with the Chinese standard of living, hence the unceasing vilification of the Filipino workers by those employers and their following, who, seeing near by the unlimited supply of cheap Chinese labor, wish these islands to be thrown open to such labor, not only for the purpose of reducing the small wages of the Filipinos, but also to reduce that of the Chinese laborers now here. As one employer stated to me, "We want more Chinese to keep them here for one or two years, then ship them back and get another lot, for the Chinese I have here now are becoming too independent and want more pay."

The free laborer is not compelled by law to work. Then, why should he work? Why does he work? The answer is found within himself. He wants something that he cannot get without working. Though this may seem a trifling question and a self evident answer, the question and answer are the foundation of all questions of free institutions. For the nonworking races and classes or the spasmodic and unreliable workers are the savages, paupers, criminals, idiots, lunatics, drunkards and the great tribe of exploiters, grafters, despots and leisure classes, who live on the work of others. Nearly every question of social pathology may be resolved to this, Why does he not work? And nearly every social ill would be cured if the non workers could be brought to work.

There are just two grand motives which induce the freeman to work—necessity and ambition. Necessity is the desire for quantity, quality and variety of things to be used up. The term is elastic. It is psychological, not material. It includes, of course, the wants of mere animal existence—food, clothing, shelter. But this is a small part. The cost of the mere quantity needed to support life is less than the added cost needed to secure the quality and variety that satisfy the taste and habits. A pig enjoys raw corn, but a man requires corn cake at five times the cost. Tastes and habits depend on one's childhood, one's training, one's associations and kind of work. The necessities of a Chinese coolie, Italian immigrant, or negro plantation hand, are less, and cost less than those of a skilled mechanic or a college graduate, because his associations have been different, and his present work is different. But necessity goes farther. It includes the wants of the family considered as a unit and not merely the wants of the single man or woman, else the race would not continue to increase. Furthermore, social obligations impose added necessity. Compulsory education of children compels parents to support their children instead of living on their wages. Laws regulating sanitation and tenements compel the tenant to pay more rent. The necessities of a farm hand on the estates of Italy are less than those of the same hand in the cities of America.

Ambition is the desire for an improved position for one's self and family—for better quality and greater variety of material things. It demands a style of clothing and living suitable to the improved position aspired to. It demands an education for one's children superior to the minimum set by compulsory schooling. It demands thrift and economy for the sake of independence or the ability to hold out until one's demands are conceded. Ambition looks to the future— necessity is based on the past. The negro or the Malay works three days and loafs three because three days' wages procure his necessities. The Chinaman or Italian or Jewish immigrant works six days and saves the wages of three, because the future is vivid to his imagination. With similar necessities one is ambitious, the other is content.

But ambition has its penalty. It is equivalent to an increase in the supply of labor. Rather than lie idle the ambitious workman accepts a lower rate of pay. His fellows see the reduction and go still lower. The seesaw continues until wages reach the level of necessities and there is nothing left for ambition. The Jewish sweatshop is the tragic penalty paid by that ambitious race. In the Illinois coal mines the wages were reduced one third during twelve years of Italian and Slavic immigration. The ambitious races are the industrial races. But their ambition and their industry bring the momentous problem of destructive competition. There is but one immediate and practical remedy—the organization of labor to regulate competition. The method of organization is to do in concert through self sacrifice what the non industrial races do individually for self indulgence, namely, refuse to work. Where the one loafs the other strikes. While the necessities of the workers set the minimum below which wages cannot fall, the labor union, by means of the strike or the threat to strike, sets a higher minimum which leaves room for ambition. Eventually the higher minimum becomes habitual and becomes a higher level of necessities. Gifted individuals may, indeed, rise above the wage earning class by their own efforts, but labor organization alone can raise the class as a whole.

The organization of workmen in labor unions has been more difficult in this than in other countries, owing to the competition of races. Heretofore it has been the easiest possible matter for a manager, apprehensive of agitators in forming a union, to introduce a new race and a new language into his works. Indeed, almost the only device and symptom of originality displayed by great American corporations in disciplining their labor force has been that of playing one race against another. They have, as a rule, been weak in methods of conciliation and feelings of consideration for their employees, as well as in the means of safeguarding life and health, but they have been strong with the weapon of autocrats, divide and conquer. The number of races they have drawn upon is often amazing. The anthracite mine workers comprise nineteen languages and dialects. The employees of the Colorado Fuel and Iron company belong to thirty two nationalities and speak twenty seven languages. Such a medley of races

offers indeed a disheartening prospect to the union organizer.
And, therefore, when these races finally organize the change
in their moral character must be looked upon as the most
significant of the social and industrial revolutions of our time.
The United Mine Workers of America, with 300,000 members,
is very largely composed of recent immigrants from southern
and eastern Europe. So with the Longshoremen and the
United Garment Workers. These are among the strongest
and best disciplined of American labor unions. The newest
races of the past twenty years have been coming long enough
to have leaders who speak the English language and act as
interpreters and leaders, and this is essential where the
speeches at a union meeting must be translated often into four
or five languages before the subject can be voted upon.
Furthermore, the recruiting area for the new races has been
nearly exhausted, and the races now coming find their fellow
countrymen already in unions. In the anthracite coal field
I saw a dozen Slovaks just arrived from Hungary, but per-
suaded by their unionized precursors not to take the place of
strikers. Such a sight would have been unlikely a dozen
years ago.

The competition of races is the competition of standards
of living. The reason the Chinaman or the Italian can save
three days' wages is because wages have been previously fixed
by the greater necessities of more advanced races. But competition has no respect for superior races. The race with
lowest necessities displaces others. The cotton textile industry of New England was originally operated by the educated sons and daughters of American stock. The Irish displaced many of them, then the French-Canadians completed
the displacement; then, when the children of the French had
begun to acquire a higher standard, contingents of Portuguese, Greeks, Syrians, Poles, and Italians entered to prevent
a rise, and lastly the Scotch-Irish from the Appalachian
mountains came down to the valleys of the south, and with
their low wages, long hours, and child labor, set another brake
on the standard of living. Branches of the clothing industry
in New York began with English and Scotch tailors, were then
captured by Irish and Germans, then by Russian Jews, and

lastly by Italians, while in Boston the Portuguese took a share, and in Chicago the Poles, Bohemians, and Scandinavians. Almost every great manufacturing and mining industry has experienced a similar substitution of races. As rapidly as a race rises in the scale of living and, through organization, begins to demand higher wages and resist the pressure of long hours and overexertion, the employers substitute another race, and the process is repeated. Each race comes from a country lower in the scale than that of the preceding, until finally the ends of the earth have been ransacked in the search for low standards of living combined with patient industriousness. Europe has been exhausted, Asia has been drawn upon, and there remain but three regions of the temperate zones from which a still lower standard can be expected. These are China, Japan, and India. The Chinese have been excluded by law, the Japanese are coming in increasing numbers, and the Indian coolies remain to be experimented upon. That employers will make strenuous efforts to bring in these last remaining races in the progressive decline of standards, to repeal the Chinese prohibitive laws and to prevent additions to these laws, naturally follows from the progress toward higher standards and labor organization already made by the Italian and the Slav.

The trade union is often represented as an imported and un-American institution. It is true that in some unions the main strength is in the English workmen, but the English are little inclined to become American citizens. The majority of unionists are immigrants and children of immigrants from countries that know little of unionism. Ireland and Italy have nothing to compare with the trade union movement of England, but the Irish are the most effective organizers of the American unions, and the Italians are becoming the most ardent unionists. Most remarkable of all, the individualistic Jew from Russia, contrary to his race instinct, is joining the unions. The American unions, in fact, grow out of American conditions, and are an American product. Although wages are two or three times as high as in his European home, the immigrant is driven by competition and the pressure of employers into a physical exertion which com-

pels him to raise his standard of living in order to
have strength to keep at work. He finds also that the law
forbids his children to work, and compels him to send
them to school. To maintain a higher standard and to support his children he must earn more wages. This he can do
in no other way than by organizing a union. The movement
is, of course, aided by English speaking outsiders or agitators,
especially by the Irish, but it finds a prompt response in the
necessities of the recruits. Labor organization is essentially
the outcome of American freedom, both as a corrective to the
evils of free competition and as an exercise of the privilege of
free association.

When once moved by the spirit of unionism the immigrants from low standard countries are the most dangerous
of unionists, for they have no obligations, little property, and
but meager necessities that compel them to yield. The bituminous coal miners were on strike four months in 1897, and
the anthracite mine workers five months in 1902. Unionism
comes to them as a discovery and a revelation. Suddenly to
find that men of other races whom they have hated are really
brothers, and that their enmity has been encouraged for the
profit of a common oppressor, is the most profound awakening of which they are capable. Their resentment toward
employers who have kept them apart, their devotion to their
new found brothers, is terrible and pathetic. With their
emotional temperament, unionism becomes not merely a
fight for wages but for a religious crusade. It is in the nature
of retribution that, after bringing to this country all the industrial races of Europe and Asia in the effort to break down
labor organizations, these races should so soon have wiped out
race antagonism and, joining together in the most powerful
of labor unions, have wrenched from their employers the
greatest advances in wages.

There is but one thing that stands in the way of complete
unionization in many of the industries, namely, a flood of
immigration too great for assimilation by the unions. With
nearly a million immigrants a year, the pressure upon unions
seems almost resistless. A few of the unions which control
the trade, like the mine workers and longshoremen, with high

initiation fees and severe terms of admission, are able to protect themselves by virtue of strength already gained. But in the coast states and on miscellaneous labor this strategic advantage does not exist, and the standards are set by the newest immigrants.

We have now stated at some length the two standpoints from which the immigration of industrial races is viewed. One standpoint is that of the production of wealth, the other, the distribution of wealth. One is the development of our natural resources, the other is the elevation of our working population. If we inquire somewhat more critically and take into account all of the circumstances, we shall find that the motive of this difference in policy is not really the above distinction between production and distribution, but the distinction between two opposing interests in distribution, namely, profits and wages. Unfortunately, it is too readily assumed that whatever increases profits does so by increasing production. As a matter of fact it is only secondarily the production of wealth and development of resources that is sought by one of the interests concerned—it is primarily increase of profits at the expense of wages. Cheap labor, it is asserted, is needed to develop the less productive resources of the country—what the economists call the margin of production. It is needed to develop the less productive industries, like beet sugar, and the less productive branches of other industries, like the construction of railways in undeveloped regions or the reconstruction of railways in older regions, or the extension of a coal mine into the narrow veins, and so on. Without cheap labor these marginal resources, it is asserted, could not profitably be exploited, and would, therefore, not be developed.

This argument, within limits, is undoubtedly true, but it overlooks the part played by machinery and inventions where wages are high. The cigar making machine cannot profitably be introduced on the Pacific coast because Chinese cheap labor makes the same cigars at less cost than the machines. High wages stimulate the invention and use of machinery and scientific processes, and it is machinery and science, more than mere hand labor, on which reliance must be placed to develop the natural resources of a country.

But machinery and science cannot be as quickly introduced as cheap immigrant labor. Machinery requires accumulation of capital in advance of production, but labor requires only the payment of daily wages in the course of production. Consequently, in the haste to get profits the immigrant is more desired than machinery. But excessive profits secured in this way bring reaction and a period of business depression which check the production of wealth even more than the period of prosperity has stimulated production. Consider, for a moment, the extreme vacillations of prosperity and depression which characterize American industry. In a period of prosperity the prices of commodities rise rapidly, but the wages of labor, especially unorganized labor, follow slowly, and do not rise proportionately as high as prices. This means an enormous increase in profits and production of commodities. But commodities are produced to be sold, and if the market falls off, then production comes to a standstill with what is known as overproduction. Now, wage earners are the mass of consumers. If their wages do not rise in proportion to prices and profits, they cannot purchase as large a proportion of the country's products as they did before the period of prosperity began. Overproduction is mainly the under consumption of wage earners. Immigration intensifies this fatal cycle of booms and depressions. A natural increase in population by excess of births over deaths continues at practically the same rate year after year, in good times and bad times, but an artificial increase through immigration falls off in hard times and becomes excessive in good times.

The swell of immigration in periods of prosperity increases the supply of labor, but the protective tariff prevents a similar increase in the supply of products. Thus immigration and the tariff together prevent wages from rising with the rise in prices of commodities and cost of living. This permits profits to increase more than wages, to be followed by overproduction and stoppage of business.

Furthermore, when once the flow of immigrants is stimulated it continues for some time after the pinnacle of prosperity has been reached. In 1903 the boom met a check at the beginning of the year, but the number of immigrants continued to increase during the summer and fall at the rate of 20,000 per month in excess of the number during the high period of prosperity in 1902. This has made it possible for great corporations to continue their investments by means of cheap labor beyond the probable demands of the country, with the result of overproduction, loss of profits, inability to pay fixed charges and consequent panics. Thus it is that immigration, instead of increasing the production of wealth by a steady, healthful growth, joins with other causes to stimulate a feverish overproduction followed by a collapse. It helps to create fortunes during a short period of speculation and intensifies the reaction during a period of stagnation.

CAUSE OF HIGH WAGES IN THE UNITED STATES.

BY A. MAURICE LOW.

[A. Maurice Low, journalist; born London, Eng., 1860; educated at King's College, London and in Austria; since 1866 has been in charge of the Washington bureau of the Boston Globe; for several years was chief American correspondent of the London Chronicle; since 1896 has written for the National Review, of London, an article every month on American Affairs; contributor to leading English and American reviews and magazines, principally on international and political topics; investigated phases of English labor legislation, 1900. Author, The Supreme Surrender and Protection in the United States.]

According to the theory of protection, protection, in so far as wages are concerned, is both cause and effect. The effect of protection is to increase wages, and the increase of wages, that is, the higher scale of wages resulting as the effect of protection, increases the wealth of the country, puts into circulation a larger volume of money, and enables the wage worker to become a larger consumer, thus creating a larger demand for all commodities, and is one of the reasons (but not the only one) why the manufacturer is able to pay high wages. It is an endless chain, beginning in protection and ending in protection.

It seems unnecessary to waste time in the discussion of what no one disputes. It is a fact conceded by economists, statisticians, manufacturers and workingmen, by protectionists as well as free traders, that wages are higher in the United States than in any other country in the world; higher than in England, the country, next to the United States where labor is most liberally remunerated; in some trades in America wages are more than twice as large as those paid in England.

While it is no longer disputable that wages are higher in America than elsewhere, the assertion is frequently made that these earnings are more nominal than real, as the cost of living in the United States is so great as to absorb the difference between the European wage and the American. In other words, that the purchasing power of a shilling in America is no greater than sixpence in England, and while the American workman is paid a shilling for the same amount of work which brings only sixpence in England, after both men have paid for the necessaries of life, the money remaining in the hands

262

of both would balance. That phase of the subject will be considered later; for the present an attempt will be made to show what the effect of protection has been on wages, and the reason why wages are higher in America than elsewhere.

One of the definite and most important results protectionists hoped protection would accomplish was to raise the general scale, to bring about a higher standard—a higher standard of living, of wages, of intelligence, of initiative, of the physical strength of the nation. These things, protectionists frankly admit, cannot be had for nothing, they must be paid for, and though the cost of living in America as compared with the cost in free trade countries may be a trifle higher, the difference is more than met by the advantages derived. Moreover, the cost of living in America compared with that in England is not the difference between the wages paid in America and those paid for like labor in England.

Cost is only a relative term. The price of an article or a service may be high or low compared with a similar article or service elsewhere or at some other time; the price of an article is high or low as measured by the amount of labor that will purchase the desired commodity. If in one country a man must work, for the sake of illustration, twelve hours before his labor enables him to purchase a loaf of bread, the price of bread would be high and the price of labor would be low. If, on the other hand, a man need work only six hours to purchase a loaf of bread, even if the loaf of the same weight should sell in the market at twice the price of the loaf in the first country, the workman would still be twice as well off. It is true that simply comparing the prices of the two loaves one is higher than the other, but compared relatively to the earning capacity of the two men it is the first and not the second loaf that is the more expensive. In the one case the workman must give twelve hours of labor—which is his maximum capacity—to obtain a single loaf, and has therefore expended all of his resources for that one purpose. He has made a draft upon all his vital energies and has no further stock to be converted into labor and exchanged for some other commodity. In the other case the workman has expended for his loaf of bread only one half of his raw material or his capital (accord-

ing as one may choose to call the pent up energy of a laborer
before it has been transformed into service, the laborer's raw
material or his capital; the terms being interchangeable and,
in this case, synonymous) and has still remaining a stock of
energy which may be converted into other articles of diet,
clothing, means of amusement, anything, in fact, for which
he has a desire.

It must be obvious that the man whose day's labor yields
a loaf and a pound of meat is better off than the man whose
day's labor is the equivalent of only a loaf of bread. The
question of actual cost in England or America is of only minor
importance, and the comparative cost is of still less consequence. The only practical consideration is the ease with
which the article can be procured or, conversely, the labor
which must be expended to earn the required amount of
money to pay for the article in question.

It may be well to say that the use of the word labor must
not be taken to apply solely to manual labor. Every man
who does not derive his means of subsistence or his income
from rents or other forms of investment is a laborer, whether
he be a day laborer, a skilled artisan, a clerk, a writer, a doctor,
a lawyer or a preacher. Each has to contribute a certain portion of his own particular form of labor to obtain a return in
the shape of wages or salary or income, and his comfort and
happiness are measured by the value which his labor produces.
Protectionists constantly point out that free traders made
the mistake of believing that protection is in the interest of
a class and that it is not of equal benefit to the entire community. This, from the standpoint of protection, is a fundamental fallacy which free traders have long cherished. American experience has proved the contrary. A nation in which
a wide gulf exists between prosperity and poverty is not really
prosperous. The day laborer no less than the clerk and the
professional man profits by protection and a high return for
labor.

The American workman demands a higher standard of
living than the European workman. Various reasons for
this have been ascribed by various writers. Levasseur finds
that "the democratic spirit of the American people has as-

sisted materially in preserving the custom of high wages,"
and de Tocqueville wrote: "In proportion as social conditions
become more equal, wages rise; and as wages are higher social
conditions become more equal."

I shall not go too narrowly into the causes that make
the American workman insist upon certain diet and comforts
which the European workman does not deem necessary.
Every observer is aware of the fact, exactly as he admits that
wages are higher in America than elsewhere. The standard
which the American workman has set can be maintained only
by high wages. It may be open to discussion whether the
standard is the cause or the effect of high wages, and whether
it tends to increase wages or simply acts as a restraining influence in preventing their decrease, but I think it must be
accepted that the higher the standard the greater the demands
that will be made upon capital by labor, and the tendency
will be to increase wages. The more wants a man has the
greater his desire to satisfy them.

The standard of living in the United States being higher
than in any other country, employers are compelled to pay
higher wages. To make this highly paid labor remunerative
the employer might increase the hours of labor over those
prevailing in other countries and thereby obtain a larger output per man, or he might by more scientific methods make his
labor more productive. He could not put in force the first
method because labor in the United States will not allow itself
to be unduly exploited or sweated for the profit of capital.
Consequently, the alternative left to the manufacturer is to
devise a system whereby the laborer in America, frequently
paid double the wages of the laborer in England for the same
class of work, shall produce an output so much greater that
the actual cost per unit of production is lower in America.

The experience of the American manufacturer engaged
in every branch of productive industry has shown that the
cheapest labor is not the labor that commands the lowest
price in the labor market, but, on the contrary, that the cheapest labor is the labor that is the most productive irrespective
of first cost. Here the American manufacturer with his practical experience runs foul of the theories of Adam Smith,

Ricardo, Mill and other economists who believed that a day's labor in one country was the equivalent of a day's labor in any other country, if the work engaged in was the same in both places, and on this theory the so-called iron law of wages was founded, a law which was not a law, but merely an assumption, which the facts have routed. The American manufacturer has learned that low wages do not mean cheap production, and that the best instructed and best labor proves itself to be the most productive, so that the rate of wages and the cost of production are not alternative or equivalent expressions, although so frequently and ignorantly confused. The American manufacturer has made the further discovery that the highest paid labor is usually the quickest labor, and is capable of turning out work which commands the highest price in the market, and produces better workmanship than labor less highly paid. In fact, so thoroughly is this now recognized, that one of the best known American advocates of free trade was compelled to use this significant language:

"In almost every employment of an industrial nature a very great amount of training is requisite to make it effective or make it serviceable at all. Only in times of very great demand and scarcity of labor would any one employ crude labor in factories where skill is required. The first question at all times for an employer to put would be, What can you do? How skillful are you? What are your earnings? Never would he ask, How cheaply can you work? He would surely take the one offering his or her services first who had been in the habit of earning the highest wages, doing the greatest amount of work, etc. In times of depression or lesser demand, he would surely dismiss those of his hands who earn the lowest rate of wages, and keep those who are best paid per diem, etc. How, then, can it be that wages cannot rise beyond the point of mere subsistence of the worker, when the skill of the worker is so powerful a factor in determining the rate of wages?"

Another equally well known American writer, who has championed the cause of free trade, finds that wages must be determined in the long run by what the product will bring, and not by what the capitalist may promise or be willing to pay for a given time. Low wages are not essential to a low cost of production, but on the contrary they usually indicate a high cost of production.

"Even at piece work," says an English author, "the rapid working man is cheaper than the slow one in industries in which costly machinery is required. The cost of production is less with fast working men because the cost on capital per unit of production is less."

Many other equally eminent authorities might be cited, but cumulative evidence is unnecessary. It may be accepted as an economic axiom that the cost of labor is not the determining cost of the product of labor, and that the highest paid labor, which is always the most expert labor, produces the cheapest product.

While Ameircan labor commands the highest price in the world, the product of that labor is able successfully to compete with labor paid at a much lower rate. What is the explanation of this seeming paradox? Intelligent British workingmen find the answer in the enterprise of the American manufacturer, his readiness to adopt more improved machine processes, and the substitution of machine for hand labor; and the British workingman also believes that the American workingman is compelled to work longer hours and under a greater strain, the Englishman being satisfied with lower wages and an easier life. Scientific observers and writers are content to ascribe it to the greater productive power of the American workingman, without explaining the secret of the productivity of the American workingman. Thus one writer says, "American higher earnings are only in other words an expression of a higher working capacity," which is doubtless true, but it teaches nothing. "The whole product of a nation," says another writer, "depends upon two factors, its natural advantages and the efficiency of its laborers," but the causes which produce efficiency are not revealed.

The belief entertained by British workingmen that the increased productivity of the American workingman is due in part to the more extensive use of machinery, and especially the latest and most improved type of machinery, is true; but the general substitution of machine for hand labor is possible only because labor is expensive. It is only where a high rate of wages prevails that machinery can be profitably employed. It has been pointed out that in railroad building and canal work in India it is found that the low day rate at which laborers can be hired for carrying the dirt away from the banks makes the employment of machinery unprofitable and unnecessary.

In America, on the contrary, railroad building, canal digging, and other like work can be more profitably done by the use of steam shovels, excavators, and similar machinery, than by an army of workingmen. The relation which the use of machinery bears to the cost of labor is concisely expressed by a distinguished French author. A manufacturer considering the purchase of a machine, he says, which will cost $10,000 and displace four laborers, but which must pay for itself in ten years, will not hesitate to make the purchase in a country where wages are $500 per annum. The machine will affect a saving of $1,000 per annum. A manufacturer in a country where wages are $200 cannot use the machine, however, because it would cause an annual loss of $200.

This explains in very few words why the American manufacturer so quickly disregards an obsolete machine, and is always willing to substitute for it a machine that will do its work better and cheaper. A machine costing $5,000, which in five years has saved $6,000 in wages, can be sacrificed at the end of that time without the manufacturer feeling that he is losing money. He is not losing money. He has made money by the use of the machine, and if he can obtain something better, something that in the next five years will have paid for itself, and saved $7,500 in the cost of production, he will feel that he has made a good investment. But it must be understood that it would be impossible for him to make these changes, unless the money he invested in machinery effected a saving in the difference between machine and hand labor, and this is only possible in a country where high wages prevail.

The economy of machine over hand labor is now recognized by all writers on economics. One of the strongest American advocates of free trade, who denounced protection and the injury which the McKinley bill would do to the country, is forced to recognize the advantages possessed by the American manufacturer over his European competitors. Our labor, he says, being machine labor, is generally cheaper than European labor, which is to a large extent hand labor, or inferior machine labor, or unproductive, under fed labor, as compared with higher productive American labor.

The doctrine of high prices is always preached by the protectionist; and high prices for labor, he believes, is a nation's salvation. Let no one, he says, manufacturer or workman, be deluded by the belief that cheapness means prosperity, or that because things are cheap a man can have them in abundance. Nothing is cheap to a man without money; nothing is expensive if a man can afford to pay for it.

But it will undoubtedly be asserted, and believed, that while conditions in America result to the advantage of the workingman, in that he obtains higher wages, they entail an additional and unnecessary expense upon the manufacturer, and that in the last analysis this cost is paid by the consumer; and the workingman, being a consumer as well as a producer, bears his burden of the cost, and is no better off than the workingman in foreign countries. The history of American industry affords, however, convincing proof that the use of the most improved types of machinery and the most highly specialized and best paid labor results not in increasing the cost, but, on the contrary, in decreasing it. A machine can better do that which was formerly done by hand, and the greater the skill of the hand which controls the machine the greater the production, and consequently the lower its cost. It follows, therefore, that the use of machinery in charge of intelligent and highly trained men is of advantage to the employer, because his profits are increased; to the advantage of the consumer, because cost is decreased; to the advantage of the laborer, because the employer can afford to pay higher wages in proportion as the cost of manufacture decreases and its profits are increased.

American experience has demonstrated that the manufacturer who would keep control of his market and not be crowded out by more enterprising rivals must keep pace with the march of scientific or mechanical improvement or yield to a competitor with more brains or more capital. Writers frequently deplore the fierceness of competition by which a manufacturer who has a large amount of capital invested in plant is compelled to send expensive machinery to the scrap heap because it has become obsolete, although it is still in good condition. No one who studies economics philosophically and in their broader relations to the welfare and progress of nations need waste a single tear over this tragedy. It is immaterial to the world whether a manufacturer, after having spent $500,000 to equip his plant, must spend still another $500,000 or else go out of business. If he is forced by improvement to replace the first set of machinery by other machines, it means simply that inventive genius has succeeded in producing a machine that will make certain articles at a lower cost than was possible by the employment of the machinery then in use. It is pathetically true that the individual manufacturer may be compelled to increase his capital by $500,000 or be forced into bankruptcy, but that is more than counterbalanced by the advantage derived by the entire world being able to obtain a better article at a lower price, and by its increased consumption, for increased consumption always accompanies the reduction of the price of an article of daily use; greater profits also accrue to the manufacturer, who is able to pay larger wages to the laborer.

A manufacturer, describing a new loom before the United States industrial commission, said:

"The cost of the machines per spindle is about $4, making $60,000,000 invested in spinning frames; and these $60,000,-000 are doing to-day what $120,000,000 would be required to do under the old method."

In a report of the chief of the bureau of labor of the state of New York there is testimony as to the use of machinery in the two principal manufacturing countries of the world:

"The United States and Great Britain are the greatest owners and users of machinery. Compare the general condition of the workers of those two nations with that of any other country on the face of the globe where machinery is unknown except in its most primitive form. Where lies the superiority? It seems almost a paradox, but it is true, that machinery conduces to employment and to betterment; not only increasing production, but multiplying the chances of employment and incidentally the consumption of products."

The use of machinery, therefore, in its largest and most varied forms is a thing that every protectionist believes that every laborer as well as every consumer should heartily welcome. The man who has only one thing to sell, that is, his labor, can obtain for it more when he is required intelligently to direct the operations of a machine than he can when his labor is to be expended in the cruder forms of manufacture. The greater the use of machinery the higher the general rate of wages, and to repeat what has already been said of cost, because too much emphasis cannot be laid upon a fact which some economists ignore, the laborer, while a consumer, is also a producer, and the laborer as well as every other person is vitally concerned in maintaining a high standard of wages and securing a low labor cost of production. The more extensively machinery enters into manufacturing processes the lower the cost to the consumer. Therefore, machinery increases wages and cheapens production, so that the laborer obtains a double benefit by receiving a greater reward for his labor and having to spend less for the necessaries of life, which means a surplus to keep him from the border line of starvation. Furthermore, the physical and mental condition of the laborer is immeasurably improved by the substitution of machine for manual processes. It is claimed that the effect on a man placed in charge of a machine is to degrade him, because his work is so monotonous that it blunts his faculties and in a short time he becomes practically an adjunct to the iron and steel of which he is in charge. But no unprejudiced person who is familiar with conditions existing in industries before the use of machinery became general, and who knows present conditions, will deny that the general level of intelligence and the general condition of the workingman are higher now than ever before. It must be obvious that the strain on a weaver who has to watch a few automatic looms is a much less drain on his vital energies and less dehumanizing than the task imposed upon his grandfather who worked a hand loom. The automatic loom tender works about nine hours a

day with less physical discomfort than his grandfather, when
fourteen hours counted as a day, and the wages of the modern
weaver are as much larger than those of his predecessor as
his hours of toil are fewer.

To the credit side of the use of machinery must also be
added all the other things that have followed in consequence
of its introduction. Compare the well kept, well ventilated
shop of to-day with the miserable cottage at the time when
cottage industries flourished in England, and before the factory system became universal. In countries where machinery
is extensively employed the condition of labor is better than
in countries where machinery is only sparsely used, and it
will be found that the more general machine processes enter
into all branches of manufacture the higher the social condition of the laborer.

One explanation of the greater productivity of the American workingman, I think it will now be conceded, is the
greater use of machinery, and it has been shown that only in
a country where the rate of wages is high is it economical to
use machinery. But it is the belief of British workingmen, a
belief shared in by many British manufacturers as well as
British and foreign writers, that the American manufacturer
is a hard taskmaster who, figuratively, stands over his workingmen with lash in hand and compels them to excessive
labor, which they can only accomplish at the expense of their
physical well being. Never was there a more mistaken idea.
The greater productivity of the American workingman is not
due to the fact that, like the slave condemned to the galley,
he is pushed to the extreme limit of exhaustion, but because
the American workingman is the best fed, the best housed,
and the best clothed workingman in the world, which enables
him to do better and more work than any other workingman.
That is the secret of his efficiency.

The American workman is the best clothed, best housed,
and best fed workman in the world. He lives in more comfort than men of the same class in Europe; he has more money
to spend on luxuries and pleasures; as a child he is not half
starved or insufficiently clad; his mental and physical development is not stunted; he is not compelled to work at an age

when nature requires that the growing child shall have much time for sleep and play, and when good food is essential to make bone and muscle and brain.

All these things make up the sum total of the efficiency of the American workingman. The American who comes to the starting line of the race of life, who must spend all his days at the forge, the loom, or the lathe, is by reason of the higher environment into which he has been born, the better and more abundant food which he eats, the greater comforts generally with which he is surrounded, and the higher standard of living, more competent to perform work requiring skill and energy than the workman of a lower vitality or an inferior physical and mental equipment.

Can anybody question the cause of the American workman's efficiency or the effect which that efficiency must have upon the national welfare and the productivity of its workers? Apply the same test to an animal and it would not be disputable. Will a well fed horse, kept in a properly ventilated stable, do better work with less exertion than a horse insufficiently fed, whose stable is dark and rank, whose coat has never known the currycomb? Where shall we look for the better stock to perpetuate the strain, and would any sensible man in purchasing a colt hesitate in his choice between the colt of the former and that of the latter; and would it not be certain that if the colt was put to work when still immature it would break down at an earlier age than the colt which had been allowed to run wild until the time came when nature intended that it should cancel its debt by labor?

"In England," says Schoenhof, "I frequently heard it said that laborers brought from Ireland usually break down after the first week's trial; had then, living with friends, to first get used to the English standard of life, and feed up in order to do work at the English rate. Gradually, in keeping with their better feeding and living, they became as good and strong workmen as the English. Now, in American mills the very same holds good."

And the same author also says:

"They don't eat and don't work, said a shoe manufacturer of Vienna, when we compared notes on the productiveness of

Austrian and German labor and of American labor. Bread and beer swilling, and an occasional bit of sausage cannot give strength sufficient to compete with you."

The late Mr. Schoenhof, it may be remembered, was for many years one of the foremost American free traders.

To sum up: The American workingman has a productive energy greater than that of any other workingman, and this higher capacity is due to his being able to obtain more and a greater variety of food that is suited to his wants; to his being better housed and better clothed and having better surroundings than the workingman in other countries. Because he is a superior workingman it is profitable to make a more extensive use of machinery in America than in other countries, and this more general use of machinery has made it profitable to pay high wages, while at the same time it has reduced the price of commodities.

COMPENSATION OF SKILLED LABOR.

BY J. RICHARDS.

[John Richards, engineer; has been president of the Technical Society of the Pacific coast; he has spent more than twenty five years of his life in organized works, is himself a practical workman in various branches of mechanical art, and for twenty years was foreman, manager and owner of works during which he made a special study of wage systems.]

The subject of skilled labor and wages is by no means a simple one. Its complexity arises from the rapidly changing conditions and relations of skilled industry during the last sixty years. It is a branch of social economics that has but little useful literature, and, indeed, none at all that deals with the equities of the subject, unless it be in the current serial matter of the day, and that is almost never impartial.

Even the word wages lacks logical definition. Does it mean the money compensation for workmen's time, or does it mean compensation for work accomplished? These things are essentially different and require terms to define them. The first is a rate of wages, while the second is the amount of wages. I beg that you will keep these terms in mind, because out of them and the relation between them must arise much that will be said of compensation.

The amount of wages, or compensation for work accomplished, is the labor cost that enters into commodities, and constitutes the real economic problem, the one that directly affects our industries and determines their success.

The rate of wages, or compensation for workmen's time, is a social rather than an economic problem, dealing with the intellect and skill of workmen, their ingenuity and power of producing; consequently it affects directly the workmen themselves.

The amount of wages is very uniform the world over when measured by product—indeed, must be so, as will appear —but the rate varies with the productive power of workmen.

It does not much matter to an employer whether it requires one, two, or three workmen to produce a given result in a given time. He can as well pay the amount of wages to three men as to one man or two men. The amount of the wages, measured by production, is the matter he is directly interested in; but to the workmen the rate is a serious matter, directly affecting their social and other conditions, because it is a measure of their personal compensation.

Thirteen or more states have bureaus of labor statistics, which every year publish voluminous reports, amounting collectively to between four and five thousand pages. We have also a national bureau of labor statistics, equipped with all required means of ascertaining facts respecting the rate and amount of wages, with all that concerns or belongs to the subject of labor. Voluminous statistics have been printed. One document of more than 850 pages, called Young's Labor Statistics, was issued in 1876, and many editions of this have since appeared. In one place more than 50 pages were devoted to slave labor among the Egyptians and the Romans, and during the feudal ages in Europe—almost an insult to modern skilled industry—but in no case, so far as I know, can anything be found bearing upon the relative productiveness of labor, or upon the relation between the rate of wages and the amount of wages.

The first attempt in this country to distinguish between the rate and the amount of wages was made about 1887, when Mr. Schoenhof, of Paterson, N. J., was sent abroad, under a commission from the department of state to investigate into the amount of wages or the labor cost of commodities in Europe. The facts gathered by him can be found in the consular reports of 1888; but the inquiry was suddenly abandoned for political reasons, and since that time it has not received much attention in a public way in this country; but it is safe to say that until the relation between the rate and amount of wages is understood and appreciated by both employers and workmen, no solution of the present condition will be reached.

I myself had something to do with this matter. In 1886 the late Thomas G. Shearman, of New York, came to the works in England to ascertain something concerning wages, and was amazed when I told him the wages could not be ascer-

tained by the usual means, at least by the pay roll, because
the work was contracted.   He was a man of celebrity and of
wide experience, and, at the time, a federal officer, and had
always considered the subject of wages as one of rate only.
At my suggestion he visited several works in England, and,
on his return home, induced the president to send out a special agent to investigate in Europe the amount of wages or the
cost of the labor component in various commodities.   His investigations covered steel rails, boots and shoes, woolen cloth,
and perhaps other commodities, as can be seen in the consular
reports before named, also in writings of Mr. Schoenhof that
I am not able to cite at this time.

To arrive at the first stage of a practical application of
this theory of wages, the following postulates will be assumed:

First.   The cost of manufactured articles of every kind
is made up of four elements or components; namely,—material, wages, expense and profit.

Second.   All staple articles of manufacture, such as enter
into the world's trade, must have a nearly uniform or international value.

Third.   The amount of wages, entering into the cost of
manufactured commodities, is also nearly uniform, and must
be so, irrespective of the rate of wages paid for their production.

Fourth.   The rate of wages depends upon what workmen
produce, or upon efficiency of their labor, and to some extent
on artificial values.

Fifth.   Fluctuations in the rate of wages are commonly
a result of demand and supply.

Sixth.   The amount of wages that can be paid to produce a commodity is not an accident, but is the result of
fixed commercial laws of general operation, and upon the
relation to other components.

Briefly expanding some of these postulates, the first one,
relating to components, is merely an axiom, capable of proof
by simple accounts.   Profit, as a component, is just as essential as material, labor or expense.   Without profit, no industry can be carried on, and when the amount of profit is
declared **or** known and is reasonable, it never leads to dis-

content or labor disturbances. A man so obtuse as not to know that profit is an essential component cannot be an intelligent mechanic.

The second postulate is also an axiom. Machinery, cotton cloth or any other commodity cannot have a difference of price in different markets except as affected by local taxes. For staple products of all kinds there is a world's price, which can vary within narrow limits only, and the range between these is constantly becoming narrower, as the price of commodities becomes more fixed in the neutral markets of the world; so obviously must the sum or value of the components be fixed. The aggregate must come out the same. If the cost of one component is raised, that of the other components must be lowered accordingly; and as material, expense and profit are approximately uniform, or should be, so also must the amount of wages be, but not the rate of wages. This may vary in any degree without disturbing the balance of components. The amount of wages in a watch must be the same in Waltham as it is in Geneva, although the rate of wages paid to workmen be as four to one, as was the case twenty years ago. The watches made in these places met and were sold in London and had to conform to a general price.

When the balance of these several components—material, labor, expense and profit—is lost, and their aggregate exceeds what we may call the general or world's value of the product, then the industry affected must either die or be moved to a new environment. Industry follows the line of least resistance, especially in these times when powerful combinations are indifferent to localities and when local or empirical skill has nearly disappeared in our industries.

I mentioned a general or world's value of products. We are all the time coming nearer to such a standard for common commodities, and the fallacy of the demand and, in the same degree, the supply theory is becoming apparent. All commodities, including wages, have a natural value, measured by the cost of their production, and it seems strange that anyone should think so important a matter as the general rate of wages could be governed by so transient a cause as demand and supply. It is, in fact, assuming that the rate of wages is an accident and not the result of a fixed law of exchanges, as has been pointed out.

The fluctuations of the labor rate are undoubtedly affected, if not produced, by demand and supply; but to contend that the general rate of wages in any country is thus produced, or governed, shows scant acquaintance with the subject. There is nothing to hinder skilled labor from flowing to any point where it is scarce, and, therefore, better paid. There is no duty or legal restriction on labor. It enters free into nearly all countries. In one week it can be transferred from New York to San Francisco, and in eight days from Manchester to Philadelphia.

Wages may rise for a time when there is a sudden demand for some product and a want of labor at some particular place; but this lasts only until workmen can move to that place and wages soon settle down to the normal rate.

No one would think of investing in a manufacturing or other business if he believed the important component of labor was to be the result of an accident or of demand and supply, which is the same thing; but this is not the principal evil produced by such a doctrine. It is one of the main causes, perhaps the principal cause, of strikes and many other circumstances that attend on skilled industry. Under such an assumption workmen naturally conclude there is no limit to wages and the more they can exact the better.

Mr. Jay Gould, during the great strike on the Missouri Pacific railway system, in 1887, said: "Labor is like any other commodity. Its value depends on demand and supply." If this is true, why should not his workmen cut off the supply and increase the rate? Like Shylock, the workmen on the Missouri Pacific lines were only practicing the iniquity which their employer taught.

Jay Gould was a worthy representative of the school to which he belonged—one that incites men to commit blunders and crimes by taunting them with their dependent position, and telling them their earnings and the conditions of their employment are an accident and not amenable to economic laws, which both employer and employed must alike respect;

also, that labor and capital, instead of being joint agencies mutually dependent on each other, are antagonistic elements or components in useful industry.

I will now revert to the circumstances of employment, or the conditions under which personal service is rendered, and in doing so I will take the privilege of using a few extracts from a lecture delivered before the engineering classes at the Stanford university, in 1898, on Works Administration.

First. In the scale of personal service is slavery, where workmen are not responsible.

Second. Time service, in which workmen are partially responsible.

Third. Piecework, where a workman is responsible for his own work alone.

Fourth. Contract work, where a whole working force is collectively responsible.

Now these four methods or systems of service have the several degrees of responsibility named; that is, from all to nothing. Responsibility is the key to efficient skilled service. It forms the distinction between free and slave labor and the incentive of effort. This proposition may seem strange, but it is certainly true. Whether it be a cause or a sequence, or both, we need not stop to inquire, so long as we find it a constant characteristic of contented and efficient effort on the part of those employed.

In respect to slavery, that no longer exists in any country where skilled industry is extensively carried on, and we need to refer to it only in illustration. A slave is not responsible for the product of his labor. That may vary more or less in proportion to what a master gives in return; but personally a slave is not responsible, because he is not a free agent. Emulation, respect and a sense of duty may in a limited degree enter into his incentives; but the subordination of his will and the fear of punishment are the main causes that enforce his service.

Time work, wherein the workman is paid for a term of service, is yet the most common form of employment. It stands next to slavery—not very near to it, perhaps, but next in the scale towards responsibility—and is practicable only because of the sense of personal honor and of justice due to the degree of self respect existing among skilled workmen.

Under this system workmen are responsible so far as their sense of manhood and emulative pride produce responsibility, but no farther. A man is hired by the hour, day, week or month; but the terms are indeterminate. His wages are merely a rate. If he spoils his work or fails to render such service as common custom demands, he can be discharged and nothing more. The conditions of his engagement do not make him responsible. If he spoils work or fails by incompetence to earn his wages and a profit for his employer, it makes no difference; the law will give him his wages irrespective of everything but willful negligence and the malicious destruction of his employer's property.

The results attained by a time system in this country are certainly a compliment to the integrity and good faith of the skilled workmen of our time. Contrast it, for example, with the usages of common trading. If exchanges were to the same extent based solely on good faith and manly honor, would a like result follow? I am not claiming that faithful service is always rendered from honorable and unselfish motives. The penalty of discharge is always present, and the sentiments engendered by unions or trade organizations are often independent of an employer's interests, so that we can only wonder that the circumstances are not worse, when the time rate manner of compensating skilled service is considered.

The extent to which time work is used in skilled industries may be cited as an argument for its necessity; but it is not universal, and is constantly becoming less. Greater progress would long ago have been made toward a better system had it not been for efforts that have been made toward paternal systems, such as profit sharing. These efforts, made, in most cases, by earnest and philanthropic men, have nevertheless failed to meet the real causes that lie at the bottom of labor dissension.

Such a statement as this needs some defence, but one may ask, what have workmen to do with profits not earned directly by their efforts and skill? Only a part of the profits in an establishment are thus earned. The profits depend on many things beside faithful and efficient labor, and, if profits not earned by labor are divided with workmen, it is a gift or bribe that destroys their independence and responsibility. The better class of skilled workmen of our day do not want such favors. This sort of patronage, especially when it takes the form of free gifts, is especially provocative of discontent and dissension indicating, as it does, class distinction and an unfair distribution of profits. What workmen want and need is justice, fair dealing and responsibility for what they themselves perform and produce, and above all to learn what part this is. They have no right to more. They have as much reason to risk their labor as an employer has to risk his capital, service, management and implements, and what is wanted is to segregate the labor component and let it rest upon its own responsibility, do away with premiums, and, so far as possible, with a time system of service. It is degrading in the skilled industries of our time, and, while it cannot be at once removed, a beginning can be made, and above all we can study its nature and effects in the labor problems now convulsing the industrial interests of the country.

To illustrate this matter I will mention that, when in Switzerland, I visited the works of Messrs. Sulzer Brothers, at Winterthur, where 3,500 men are employed in machine making. There was a large building called a Casino, containing a library, dining hall, bath rooms for hot, cold and Russian baths, a fully equipped surgery, etc. The cost of this building could not have been less than $100,000, and I said to Mr. Henry Sulzer, senior member of the firm, "This Casino is a great concession to your workmen, for which they are no doubt very grateful." His answer was, "We did not give the Casino to the men. It is an essential part of the works, built out of earnings, and belongs to the workmen as much as to the firm. They manage it. It is a community property." "But," said I, "the profits to build the Casino were deducted from those of the firm." "Not at all," said he, "we had our share."

The piecework system, by which is meant personal contracts with particular workmen—a mixed system, in which a part of the working force is made responsible and the rest are employed on the time method, is a bad system in many ways, for many reasons. In the first place, it is discriminating and unequal; and secondly, there is no impartial standard from which prices can be be determined. The price is a matter of chance, depending on the choice or conscience of the employer. It is a provincial idea, so to speak, and is a crude effort toward a contract system. It increases the responsibility of workmen without adding much to their independence. It does not succeed unless very carefully adjusted.

We are well aware of the extent to which it has been carried out in various shops, especially in New England; but if one will look into the matter carefully, it will be found that, wherever successful, there have been a very high class of workmen and some features of a contract system involved that modified discrimination among the men, and that rates were not fixed by accident or independently in each shop, but by rules that have been generally established by custom in a district. Individual piecework is an undemocratic idea, not consistent with the spirit of our times, and will, no doubt, pass away for something better in the future.

The next system of service, if that term applies, is what has been called the contract system, or, as we may call it, the responsible system, in which labor is set off as an independent element in production.

To make clear what is meant by a contract system of labor, the best way will be to illustrate by an assumed example; and, as one class of manufactures is as good as another, a joiner works will answer the purpose.

In a factory of this kind are prepared all kinds of timber, house furnishing material, such as flooring, ceiling, doors, sash frames, moldings and so on. All these things have regular prices, because made very uniform for average houses, and there are price lists published that apply over wide districts. For some things, like doors, sash moldings and flooring, the lists apply to the whole country within reasonable distances of transportation. The work, when not included in the price lists, is made to estimates in which the labor is always made up as a separate item, and the labor in listed articles is either known or ascertainable in all establishments; is better known, indeed, than other elements, such as material and expense, that must be included in estimates.

Suppose, then, that a joiner works is to be established, and that the owners, instead of hiring men by time to do the work, establish a contract system for the labor. The men are employed as in any other case, and are permitted to draw, in proportion to their rank and skill, a certain amount of money each week in proportion to the usual wages paid in such establishments; but the work, as a whole, is all contracted to the men, or to the shop, as we would say, and whatever money is advanced for wages is deducted pro rata from the labor estimates due at the end of the week or month for work turned out. The men being apprised of, or already knowing, the rate for making standard work, no difficulty would arise from this, and all irregular or special work would have to be estimated and include the element of labor. That amount could be posted in the works, or entered in a book kept by the foreman and accessible to the workmen. Each man would, as is the present custom, enter, each day, on his time card, the number of hours engaged on different jobs, which would, as is also the custom in most places, have a catalogue or order number that would be entered on the tickets, with the time given to each number or order.

The whole shop would now be working on a contract system; every man, boy and apprentice included, and at the end of a month, week or any other time convenient, the completed work could be made up and compared with the amount paid out in advances to the men. If there is a balance due them, it is divided pro rata among all, in proportion to their pay rate, as indicated by the weekly or daily wages on which the advances are made. If there is a deficit, the men must make it good by a corresponding reduction.

All losses, by accident, carelessness or inefficiency of the men, should be made good to the firm or company, and all losses chargeable to the owners by detention, want of material or implements, or accidents due the plant, would have to be made good to the men. If a man seeking work represents himself falsely as to his skill or rank, the owners need not concern themselves about that. The men in the works will attend to that matter; because if rated above his capacity he would be imposing on all the rest and lowering their wages.

The establishment would be co-operative, divided into two departments or interests closely allied and interdependent. The workmen would have nothing to do with material, expense, profits, risks, or capital, except in sustaining these as a foundation for their own part. The labor and their compensation would depend on their own efforts and skill. No foreman to watch the men would be required. They would do the watching themselves, and do it in an effective manner. Drones would be weeded out, or, what is more likely, they would be reformed, or not exist at all under such a system. The working force would be independent, interested, and responsible. If a man needed assistance or favor, the whole force could extend it by giving him easy work, or in other ways. It is an ideal system, but is not an idea. On the contrary, it is a demonstrated fact.

The main ground of objection to a contract system of labor is the matter of estimates; but does anyone undertake work without an estimate? and do not such estimates include a labor component? There may be a few exceptions, but not many.

This objection arises mainly from a desire to conceal the components of an estimate, and out of a system that has no fixed rate of profits. If employers have a rule of get all you can, they should not complain if their workmen adopt a like rule. And if employers cannot provide and maintain a reasonable expense account, to be charged to product, and can not estimate the components, including labor, they must not expect co-operative effort in their works. There are difficulties to overcome, all must admit, but how many we do not know until efforts are made to establish a contract system.

In the Manchester district, and I believe over England generally, this system prevails in the machine works of the country, and the accounts for wages are nearly double as much as on the continent of Europe. In the Cornwall Iron works, at Birmingham, there are about 6,000 workmen, and, from information given me by one of the owners and the manager some years ago, I doubt whether, among all this number, there is any mechanic paid on the time system. I once brought out from England example accounts to show how the divisions are made in the Geesley Iron works, at Manchester, and published the matter here.

Some such system is used in the Baldwin Locomotive works, Philadelphia, where, for 25 years, and after a great strike at that time, not a word has been heard of labor dissension. The same result will, no doubt, occur in any works where the skilled work is made free and responsible.

The policy of the skilled labor organizations in this country is at this time directly arrayed against the individuality and responsibility of their members, demanding that they do only time work, determine the working hours, limit the amount performed, avoid responsibility, destroy all distinctions of skill and become a homogeneous class like common unskilled laborers. One can understand how routine and unskilled labor might resort to a policy that must, to some extent, eliminate individuality, responsibility, and manhood, in order to defend itself against the aggressions of organized employers; but skilled labor of our time is another matter and requires a different system.

I fear that by adopting the tactics of unskilled labor, the mechanics of our time have missed an opportunity of becoming a co-operating factor in our skilled industries, assuming the responsibility of their part of the work and basing the wages demanded upon the product of the wages, looking at the rate instead of the amount, and, as remarked, have lowered their calling to the rank of common labor, thereby provoking an opposition that is as serious as it is extensive.

In demanding a time rate for wages, irrespective of skill, and limiting the work produced, skilled workmen have assumed the Jay Gould theory of wages, adopting the demand and supply theory, which leads to cutting off the supply to raise the rate.

The employers are obliged to act on the same theory, while most of them well know that the labor component in their cost account could be reduced, and the rate of wages raised 25 per cent by a contract system in which the workmen would be free, responsible and co-operative in their efforts. I am not arguing in favor of the employers' position; I am only showing that they accept the workmen's demand and supply theory at its own valuation.

It may seem a selfish proposition to set off skilled labor as a peculiar calling. It must become so or disappear. The intellectual standard required is all the time increasing. Implements supplant empirical skill. The colleges are each year furnishing a greater share of the apprentices. In some recent visits to works in the eastern states I was amazed to find how many of the apprentices had come from the colleges, and how rapidly such young men advanced. The natural sciences are taking the chief place in our institutions of learning, and if the skilled workman cannot conquer a place above the rank of common labor, it will be his mistake and misfortune.

The skilled labor component in industrial production presents at this time a greater problem than ever before. It is surrounded by new circumstances, by vast combinations of capital and interests that naturally tend to separate employers from workmen and to promote what the unions seem to be aiming at—the elimination of the individual and substituting a catalogue number in his place.

The aims being the same on both sides, the issue is thus narrowed down to how wages can be exacted or withheld. Animosities are growing stronger, and what the end will be no one can foresee. Secret profits, secret organizations, elimination of the personal element and of humanity, point to an increase of labor disturbance, which, as our European friends predict, will have its center in this country and its focal center on the Pacific coast.

I think that anyone who has carefully observed the matter, must conclude that the first and only logical remedy is to make skilled labor responsible, so that its earnings shall arise directly out of its product by some method such as has been indicated.

Suppose, as another example of a contract system, the owner of a foundry were to assume an estimate for iron, fuel, sand expense, losses by accident, profits, and so on—data which his own books will furnish—and then contract with the workmen to produce the castings by the ton, paying a weekly wage, charging it to the labor estimate and dividing the surplus if any, pro rata among all the workmen—not dividing it between the workmen and the firm, as the profit sharers propose to do, but giving it to the men who earn it. Castings could be put into classes, according to weight, green or dry molds, and so on.

I can imagine no impediment to such an arrangement, except a want of confidence between employers and workmen; and, if confidence is wanting, we are in a bad condition indeed. I have acted as arbitrator in settling disputed points in such a system, and have found no trouble whatever. If tackle broke, or if losses occurred, by accident partly the fault of owners and partly of workmen, or if faulty castings were made, such things were adjusted without difficulty; and I must add that in no case were there any unreasonable demands on the part of the workmen, who became, in effect, copartners in the business, and relieved the owners of many details of management and of expenses attendant on time work.

The basis on which contract work must rest is an inflexible honesty in accounts and in all other matters; and, unless this component is present, there is distrust, and the co-operative idea cannot be put in practice. Under a contract system I have no doubt that the product of a certain amount of wages would, in most cases, be increased 25 to 50 per cent over what time wages would produce, and there would be no grounds for strikes and contention, when custom had established prices, and this would soon follow.

Even our Asiatic friends are moving in this direction. The Chinese take contracts for building dykes in the Sacramento valley at a certain price per cubic yard.

The title and scope of this paper do not include any remarks upon the immediate causes that have led to recent strikes of skilled workmen; but, as these causes are the results of conditions that have been discussed, some brief remarks will be in place here. Principal among these immediate causes is the fluctuation of prices in products and commodities, especially in the necessaries of life, such as fuel, food, and clothing. During several years past these have appreciated in price from 30 to 40 per cent, according to different authorities. This is a tremendous change, even at the lowest figures. The increment in the price of commodities has been distributed among the components of production. One portion, I do not think more than 10 per cent of it, has gone to wages, and the rest is distributed among the other three components—material, expense, and profit. A good deal is consumed in rebates to foreign buyers of products.

We need a campaign of education, not only in determining the labor component in commodities, but also in the relation of wages to prices; and, above all, we need education in the policy and circumstances that can so suddenly affect the balance between the various components of cost. One would naturally expect a redundant literature on this subject from the unions; but, so far as I know, they do not discuss even the elementary laws that govern wages. The amount and rate are never separately considered, and, until this is done, no solution of the labor problem is possible on logical grounds, or need be looked for.

When skilled labor demands greater compensation, let such demand be put upon logical and equitable grounds, and it will find support in both public opinion and in legislation. A strike is war, and war is a relic of barbarism. The Swedes have a saying, Killing people proves nothing. This might be translated into, Destroying wealth, time, and business proves nothing.

If the labor component in production falls below its proper place, let skilled men show and prove this thing, and if strikes are then unavoidable workmen will have public sympathy. If a manufacturer sells his product abroad for a third less than he does at home, and taxes his workmen and his countrymen to make up the difference, let this be shown. If the expense account and profit are overestimated, and if the labor element is cut down accordingly, let this be shown; but force without reason is war, and war is barbarism.

The boards of conciliation and arbitration in New Zealand offer at this time the most advanced solution of labor disturbance in so far as treatment is concerned. It dispenses with the barbarism of labor war, is logical and deserves attention in all countries. The limits of this paper do not permit its discussion here, further than a suggestion that it be examined carefully by everyone interested in the subject.

THE PREMIUM SYSTEM OF WAGE PAYMENT.

BY ALEXANDER E. OUTERBRIDGE, JR.

[A. E. Outerbridge, Jr., of Philadelphia, is a careful student of and most acceptable writer upon the sociological and industrial influences of modern machinery. He has written many notable articles on these subjects for the Engineering Magazine and the Annals of the American Academy of Political and Social Science which have attracted wide attention of economists.]

If an observer should notice a gang of ten men in any large establishment standing idle all the day long he would naturally be amazed at the apparent lack of discipline; yet it may be confidently asserted that there is no establishment employing a thousand men in which the actual loss of time every day, through idling and gossiping, does not exceed in the aggregate the entire time of ten men for ten hours each day. A loss of but six minutes a day in this way by one thousand men equals 6,000 minutes or 100 hours, or the equivalent of the full time of ten men for ten hours. Thorough supervision of each one in order to prevent this evil of loitering—which in factory phraseology is designated soldiering—is a physical impossibility. Unlike the slave of olden time, whose sole aim was to accomplish as little as possible, even under the stimulus of the lash, the operative of to-day turns out the largest product when he is a willing worker, not needing constant overseeing. The true way, therefore, to influence the individual to accomplish the best results for his employer is to convince him that in so doing he is accomplishing the best results for himself. Few operatives succeed in obtaining regularly day by day the maximum output from any machine; some have not the requisite skill, others fail through lack of attention to small details, such as forethought and method in grouping or assembling the work, others through laziness or disinclination to turn out more than a certain amount of finished material in a day. An operative may also, perhaps, through lack of constant attention to the work, unconsciously limit the output of a costly machine and thus cause loss to his employer far exceeding the entire amount of his wages.

If no system of espionage can prevent this loss of time, how can it be minimized? Profit sharing has been advocated as one method by which the employee could be induced to take a personal interest in the management of the business. The writer is skeptical about the permanent success of any system that has yet been devised of so-called profit sharing in any kind of manufacturing business with which I am familiar. There are so many conditions affecting profit and loss in manufacture of raw material into finished products with which the operative has no connection that it would be manifestly unfair to charge him with a share of such loss, and, on the other hand, profit may be due to outside causes to which the operative contributes nothing. He would, therefore, not be entitled to share in such profits. But apart from ethical considerations, it would be manifestly impossible to open the books of a manufacturing concern for the inspection of all of the operatives, and they would not understand the methods of accounting, even if it were practicable to do so. For these, and other reasons, profit sharing is, in my judgment, doomed to failure. Other schemes for giving the operatives an interest in the management come under the general head of business and philanthropy. This is a delicate subject and needs to be handled carefully. As a general proposition the two do not, as a rule, work together successfully. Some of the reasons therefor are not hard to find. The American workman is self respecting, independent, and generally well to do; he resents any approach to paternalism on the part of an employer. He does not desire, and will not accept, anything savoring of charity; he is suspicious of philanthropic schemes devised for his apparent welfare, especially if they curtail in any way his cherished liberty and freedom of conduct.

One of the most interesting and, for a time, promising schemes for the mutual benefit of the employer and the workmen was that of Mr. Alfred Dolge, of Dolgeville, N. Y. Here was a town created by one man; everybody was employed in one industry, and there were no clashing interests. The proprietor of the great establishment of Dolgeville graduated from the ranks of labor, and, having begun as a poor workman, he was familiar with the hardships of the laboring class.   As soon as he became an employer of labor he began to formulate his long cherished co-operative schemes; but, unfortunately, his ideas were doomed to failure in the end, although apparently based on sound principles.   This lamentable failure— whatever the cause may have been—has given a sad blow to all such semi-philanthropic undertakings.   In Europe many similar plans have been tried, and failures have generally resulted.   In Germany a large glass works was started a few years ago by wealthy philanthropists.   The entire plant was a gift to the workmen, and the necessary capital was furnished.   Each employee was given an interest in the concern, and work was commenced under extraordinarily favorable circumstances.   Before long internal dissensions arose; each man considered himself a boss, and within a year the working capital was sunk, the workmen scattered and the plant sold at a sacrifice.   It rarely happens that business and philanthropy can unite to form a working partnership.

In my judgment, the best way to solve the problem is to make every man the treasurer of his own time, and the only practical way to do this is to pay the largest premium in addition to the standard wage rate for the largest individual output.   The piecework system was devised with this in mind, but in its original form it is open to one serious objection, which always will exist, and that is that the workman fears that if he does more than a certain amount in a day, sooner or later the piecework price will be cut and the result will be that he will have to work harder than before to acquire the same amount of money.   This is gradually being improved upon and the premium piecework system is the chief improvement.   It has added an entirely new feature in the relation of employer and employee, and in several concerns, it has increased the rate of wages, while at the same time it has decreased the cost of the product.

While there are different methods in vogue, adapted to different circumstances, the premium system consists essentially of the addition of a premium to the base price agreed upon for any job, the amount of the premium depending upon the reduction of time in performing the work. The method of remuneration differs radically from the ordinary piecework system of payment, for it makes each workman's interest the same as that of his employer; it pays a premium for high efficiency, and soon convinces each man that it is for his permanent advantage to turn out each day the best quality and maximum quantity of work. Briefly stated then, the premium system consists in paying a higher rate per piece for a greater amount of work done without imperfection in a given time. Several years ago Mr. Fred W. Taylor devised and put into practical operation at the Midvale Steel works a premium piecework plan which he called the differential system. This may, perhaps, be regarded as the pioneer of all the premium systems in use to-day, and it proved immediately successful. The following illustration, representing actual results obtained in daily work, will show the economy of high wages under Mr. Taylor's differential system as applied to turning certain steel forgings, of which many thousands were made.

Cost of Production Per Lathe Per Day.

ORDINARY PIECE-WORK SYSTEM.	DIFFERENTIAL RATE SYSTEM.
Man's wages.................... $2 50	Man's wages.................... $3 50
Machine cost.................... 3 37	Machine cost.................... 3 37
Total cost per day............ $5 87	Total cost per day............ $6 87
Five pieces produced; cost per piece...................... 1 17	Ten pieces produced; cost per piece...................... 69

To further explain the difference between the simple piecework system and the premium system, reference may be made to a case where new work was introduced into an establishment undertaking an entirely new kind of manufacture. The concern had never done the work before, so did not know at all what it was going to cost. Parts of the machines were given out to the different departments to be made by day's work, because nobody knew what the cost was liable to be. The people selected to work by the day were the men who were considered the quickest and best workmen in the establishment, who would be likely to make those parts under the system of day's work as cheaply as they could be made, so that the actual cost of making them in this way might be made the basis for a piecework price.   Quite a large number of the parts were made by day's work.   I saw some of the work being done myself, and did not observe anything that led me to believe that there was any loafing on the part of the men. A piece price was finally fixed based upon the average cost by day's work.   After the men got more skilled in their jobs they did a little better, but the average was taken for the piecework price.   It so happened that some precisely similar things were made in another establishment, and through an accident it was ascertained that an article which cost about twenty four dollars to make under this system of piecework cost about thirteen dollars to make in the other establishment where a premium system was in vogue.   An investigation showed that the actual amount of labor required to make the pieces was the same in each foundry, but in one the simple piecework system of pay obtained; in the other a premium system.   Then an entire change of personnel in the department, including the foreman, was made; new men were engaged to do the work on a premium system and the result was surprising.   In a very short time the new men were making nearly double the wages of the former operatives and the cost per piece was reduced nearly one half.

This system, of course, does not spare the tools, which are run at a high rate, and, since its introduction, the views of progressive manufacturers regarding the economical use of machine tools have materially changed.   Formerly, old tools were venerated and carefully preserved as long as they could be used.   Now, the aim is to obtain the full life service in the shortest possible time, and then to consign the tool to the scrap heap.   In this way tools are worn out long before they have become obsolete in design.   Soldiering on the part of the operatives is effectually eliminated, wages are raised, the output increased and cost of production is decreased in an amazing ratio.   All this is accomplished without exhausting toil on the part of the operative, for the machine has relieved him of most of the hard work; especially is this noticeable in handling heavy materials.   In former days rupture was very common indeed among moulders in foundries, caused by frequent severe straining in lifting flasks and moulds; now it is a rare thing to find rupture among the younger moulders, owing to the fact that in all modern foundries traveling cranes and other hoisting appliances are provided for lifting heavy materials and carrying them from one place to another.

Within my own experience there has been a great improvement in this respect. I can recollect at least six moulders in one foundry who were badly ruptured from lifting their moulds, while to-day I never hear of this trouble, for the main cause has been removed. The mechanic of to-day, who is engaged in riveting a boiler or a bridge structure, no longer spends ten hours a day in striking blows with monotonous regularity upon the rivet heads, but he is employed to control the steam or hydraulic riveting machine, a sort of giant hand, which presses the red hot rivet into place with a simple, silent squeeze of its powerful finger far more effectually than can be done by two strong men striking one hundred blows each with a riveter's hammer. This has been proved by official tests.

Certain conditions are necessary for success of any system. There are laws regarding the relation between employers and employees which are immutable, and the most fundamental of these laws is that mutual confidence and respect are necessary precedents to the inauguration of any marked change in the methods of management or the conditions of payment. Such confidence is especially important when changes are made from time wages to some form of piece wages intended to increase the output by increasing the inducement to labor. Workmen are invariably suspicious of such changes. They fear that the piece rate will be cut as soon as the capacity of the worker has been shown. Without the fullest confidence in the good intentions of the employer, therefore, so radical a reform as the one suggested can with great difficulty be introduced. Employers can acquire and retain this confidence by courtesy, by fair dealing, by providing healthful and pleasant surroundings for their employees and by protecting them and their families against the consequences of sickness or accident.

A personal incident that happened in my own case and among workmen with whom I was brought into contact illustrates the advantage which comes from cultivating the good will of employees. About fourteen years ago I began a series of metallurgical investigations in the establishment with which I am still connected that resulted in a considerable change, an absolute change in fact, in the character of the metal operated upon by some of the machinists. These men were, at that time, inclined to be suspicious of any change, and there was a theory ever since the days of the machining of iron that it was impracticable to do what we were attempting; it met with great incredulity, and when several very large castings thus treated were sent to the machine shop to be planed and drilled to make finished machines, opposition began immediately to come from the mechanics, who were not interested in any-thing that might go on in the foundry department. It was necessary for me, therefore, to walk around through the machine shops every day to examine these castings so as to find out whether the new treatment had interfered in any way with the work of the machinists; and, as I have naturally a genial feeling for my fellowman, I would always say good morning to the mechanics tending the machines. I found that this salutation was a surprise to these men, for they were not accustomed to it; some of them had been there for forty years or more and had rarely heard good morning said to them by any one in authority. It was not the custom, but I was not aware of that. One man replied to me: "What did you say?" and I said again, "good morning." Well! in the course of time these workmen began to realize that the new metallur-gical method was not interfering in any way with their wages; that it did not take any longer to finish up the work and that was what they were interested in, as they were paid by the piece. So, after a while, I began to notice a change in the faces of these operatives when I said good morning, and a good many said good morning to me; but one man had told me in the beginning that I was going to take the bread out of the mouths of his wife and children, and having once said that, he was not a man to take back his word as long as he could help it. Time went by, and never did I get any answer from this man to my morning salutation although all the others had forgotten their original objections and had become most friendly, until one day when I came along he muttered some oaths, and then, to my surprise, I noticed a smile stealing over his countenance and he said: "It isn't any use trying to make you mad, here's my hand." That was very amusing to me, but it was a conquest after years of patient waiting, and to this day we are good friends. This shows that little things count, and that social amenities in business life are not to be despised.

Another important consideration making for the successful establishment of such innovations as the premium system is a care for the well being of the employees. In my discussion of business and philanthropy I do not wish to be misunderstood, or to seem to underrate the advantages which may accrue to employees, as well as to employers, of philanthropic plans devised for the aid of sick, injured or infirm operatives. In one of the largest and most successful manufacturing establishments in the world an admirable system is in vogue, whereby unfortunate men are helped in time of need, but so judiciously and secretly is this done that the world knows nothing about it, and if I should name the establishment it would violate confidences that I have received, not from the managers of the works, but from men who have been thus aided in a way which has not awakened any other feeling than that of gratitude. You cannot find any illusion to these matters in the rules posted up in the works, and, in fact, I believe there are no rules on that subject. There is no contract in existence; there is no guarantee that if a man is injured, or if he is sick, or in trouble, that the helping hand will be extended to him, yet I doubt not that every one of the thousands of men employed in those shops goes to his daily work with a contented feeling that should an accident befall him while on duty, his family would be cared for while he might be incapacitated for work. It thus appears evident from whatever point of view the question may be studied that the value of the personal equation in management of large industrial works is a most important factor in the successful conduct of affairs.

Moreover, my views are pronouncedly toward recognizing the responsibility which rests upon the employer to the fullest extent practicable, not, however, based upon philanthropic grounds, but because observation has taught me that one of the most profitable investments of money that can be made in a manufacturing plant is to give the largest possible advantages, in the way of conveniences and sanitary arrangements, etc., to the operatives. I remember years ago finding it a difficult matter to impress upon the superintendent of a foundry the importance of having the windows washed. They had not been washed for years, and on dark winter days the dimness in the foundry necessitated artificial light; indeed at all times the conditions were bad for the eyes of the moulders. I had a great deal of trouble to get those windows washed, and yet I am quite sure that the cost was repaid in a very few days in the saving of bad work. The introduction of steam heat into another foundry that I am familiar with was a source of expense that the managers were loath to incur, but that was also a profitable improvement; it avoided irritating and blinding smoke in the foundry on cold mornings caused by lighting woodshavings on the dirt floor; not only did it contribute to the comfort of the men, but the steam heat kept the sand warm, and the moulds did not crumble as formerly by reason of freezing of the moisture in the sand on cold nights. The introduction of shower baths, dressing rooms, water closets, and other similar comforts and conveniences, improves the character of the work and conserves the health of the workmen. I maintain that every operative who gets sick in the employ of a concern, causes more or less loss, even though he may receive no wages during the time he is incapacitated for work; another and presumably an inferior or less experienced man must be put in his place and the interests of the firm must therefore suffer. For this reason I believe that every kind of legitimate comfort and convenience that may be provided for the operatives is a source of profit to the employer although apart from the moral obligation to care for the health and comfort of the employee.

There is one impending menace to the continued success of the premium system, that is the arbitrary and shortsighted policy of some of the labor unions, which are continually striving to curtail the activities of labor by limiting the work of the more competent members of the union to the capacity of the

less competent or more indolent members. This is certainly
detrimental to progress. The immediate result of such methods is to antagonize the employer, who does not object to
labor unions when they confine their activities to legitimate
fields of usefulness. It was just such dictatorial methods of the
labor unions in Great Britain that precipitated the great and
disastrous strikes of mechanics a few years ago. The loss in
wages alone, though amounting to millions of dollars, was
small as compared with the permanent loss sustained by the
manufacturing industries in that country, caused directly by
the preposterous acts of the labor unions. The ostensible
ground on which this policy of the labor leaders is defended
is that there is only so much work to be done and that if a
machine is introduced in place of a man, or if machines are
run at higher speed, the aggregate earnings of labor will be
reduced. The absurdity of this opinion is by this time sufficiently apparent.

If it were not for the assistance of costly mechanical aids,
so freely furnished to operatives, enabling them in many cases
to quadruple the effect of their efforts, the American mechanic
would be to-day making less wages, while having harder work;
the output from the workshops would be smaller, and the
general prosperity of the country would be less marked. If
it were not for these mechanical aids the premium system
would not have been developed and the true policy of the labor
unions should be to foster this system in every way.

It may seem anomalous to say that the higher the class
of labor in manufacturing establishments the cheaper the product, yet this has been proved time and again, and it has come
to pass through the aid of machinery. The skilled workman
of to-day in almost any trade is a man who can so deftly and
judiciously operate a machine, or a number of machines
(representing often an investment of many thousands of
dollars), that the output is largely increased thereby, without
necessarily increasing unduly his own physical or mental
labor; the employer can well afford, therefore, to offer large
pecuniary inducements in the shape of premiums to the most
productive operators.

An impression has prevailed in the minds of many intelligent people, especially those not engaged in mechanical pursuits, that the substitution of so-called automatic machinery for hand labor is detrimental to the intellectual development of the wage earner, tending to make him a mere automaton, like the machine which he tends; that the skilled handicraftsman of former generations is fast disappearing, and that his successor is becoming a mere marionette, to whom the gift of brains is almost a superfluity.   Daily observation in large industrial works extending over a score of years, has led me to form a different conclusion.   I believe it is now generally admitted that the educational influence, upon the mind of the operative, of daily contact with machinery is a potent one, enlarging his mental horizon, giving him more accurate perceptions of the true relation of parts and fitness of things, and elevating him intellectually above the place of the old time handicraftsman.   The machine once regarded as the robber of the wage earner is destined to become, indeed, has already become the missionary for his enlightenment; and when its advantages are fully appreciated in the labor world the conflicts which have marked the transition period will become a mere memory of a past era.   Just as every new invention in scientific mechanism of warfare is a step toward the ultimate settlement of international disputes by arbitration, so the general diffusion of knowledge among the wage earning class through the aid of machinery and its products, is a step toward the settlement by peaceful processes of the complex questions which will, without doubt, continue to arise in the future regarding the mutual relations of capital and labor.

PROFIT SHARING AND CO=OPERATION.

BY NICHOLAS PAINE GILMAN.

[Nicholas Paine Gilman, professor sociology and ethics, Meadville Theological school since 1895; born Quincy, Ill., December 21, 1849; graduated from Harvard divinity school, 1871; Unitarian clergyman in Massachusetts, 1872–84; professor in Antioch college (Ohio), 1878–81; editor Literary World, Boston, 1888–95; The New World, 1892–1900. Author: Laws of Daily Conduct; Socialism and the American Spirit; Profit Sharing between Employer and Employee; A Dividend to Labor.]

It is one of the commonplaces of current socialism that the wages system is a later form of slavery; but it has been well pointed out there are essential differences between a system entitled to be called slavery and that under which the laborer lives at the present day. Under real slavery the worker himself is a commodity, owned by his master. He receives payment in kind sufficient for a bare maintenance. The amount of this is determined by the sole will of the master, and the slave can never become a capitalist. He has no choice of masters, and no freedom to forsake one occupation for another. The wage earner is the political equal, at the polls in this country, of his employer. He is paid in money according to regular rates determined largely by associations of his fellow workmen. He can leave one employment and take up another; he can move with comparative freedom from one place to another; in fact, were he not informed by over ingenious people that he is a slave, the fact would probably never have occurred to his mind, in most instances. Thinking people recognize that, in a rhetorical sense, all men are slaves to circumstance; that we are too often the serfs and not the lords of our condition, things being in the saddle and riding mankind. Every man who has to work for his living is, in a degree, the slave of his work; the problem for him is to alleviate the rigor of the conditions under which he works and increase his leisure.

The labor problem is one part, perhaps the most important part, of what is roughly known as the social problem. The social problem includes a great variety of difficult questions relating to modern man under civilization. To be precise, however, there is in fact no such thing as the social problem. As Gambetta once said, "there are social problems." There are a great many of them, and they are likely to continue long, if not to multiply greatly as the years go by. What we less loosely denote as the labor problem is a more restricted and more manageable question. I take it to include, as its main matter, the problem of the best relation of employer and employed in this great, complex, and marvelous world of modern work and modern machinery. Certainly, whatever minor issues may be connected with this chief issue, they would, in all probability, be adjusted with comparative ease could we once have and maintain a friendly union of master and man.

That there will always be, at least for many centuries, two such parties to labor contracts as master and man, or employer and employee, is altogether probable. We need to observe but a few specimens of our common humanity to learn that this distinction has its roots in great natural facts. Differences of mental ability, differences in strength of character, as well as differences in fortune, are the causes of the persistence of this distinction. The need of labor is perpetual. This world of ours is a world in which he that worketh not shall not eat. To be sure, his work may have been done for him, in a few cases, by his fathers, and he may come into large leisure by inheritance, not having earned it through his own personal exertion. But the rule is that work is the condition of food as well as of leisure; we find no one eating whose food has not been paid for by himself or by others who have given it to him. We find no one enjoying leisure who has not himself earned it by hard work, or to whom the hard work of others has not given it.

The first of labor problems, then, for man, who must work to live, is to find some work to do. Happily, the stimulus to exertion through the complexity of human needs is very great, and the world is crowded with work needing to be done. As fast as one want is satisfied, it creates a dozen others. If one piece of work is well done, it points the way for a hundred times as much to be done in the same line or elsewhere. Nothing is more irrational in the conduct of modern labor unions than their attempts to diminish the hours or the tasks of laboring men, under the impression that there is a fixed quantity of work to be done so that, if ten men can do it all while there are twenty needing food, the only way out of the difficulty is for the first ten to do half as much as they can do, and leave the rest of the work to the other ten. It is a pure assumption that the second ten could or would do this half of the work if it were surrendered to them. Probably it would be found by trial that they were neither competent nor willing to equal the performance of the first ten, selected by a long sifting as the most capable and successful workers. The lump of labor fallacy, as Mr. Schloss calls it, will not stand examination. As a matter of fact, however, there is plenty of work for the first ten and plenty of work for the second ten also, if they are able and willing to work and will go where the work is to be had. The theoretical competition supposed by the orthodox school of political economists under which the workman is always perfectly free to seek work in any quarter, is not indeed an actual condition, and there is much room for exertion in bringing the work and the worker together.

If a man is working for himself, he will turn out the largest product, under existing human nature. There is no means for extracting industry, thrift, skill, and all the virtues of work, from the most unpromising character, to be compared for a moment with the magic of private property, as all the economists have noted. The peasant proprietor in Italy, France, or Germany, for instance, or the independent farmer of New England or Dakota, sets the highest standard of achievement. Self interest, whatever we may say of its excesses, is the most potent motive to exertion with the ordinary man. Working his own few acres, the small farmer will rise early and go to bed late. He will economize time, tools, and materials. He will perform prodigies of work in the hard contest with the powers of nature if he is sure from the beginning that the whole result of his labor will be his own. We are not speaking of pure selfishness; his own includes that larger self, that most natural and persistent of all associations, the family of which he is the head. Not all men, of course, take the sturdy and heroic view of work on their own property; but when a man has thus before him every reason for exertion, and prefers idleness and dissipation, the labor problem is purely a moral and personal question of the individual.

Let us suppose that our small farmer has so far prospered that he has outgrown his few acres and can not even superintend satisfactorily the numerous workers whom he is obliged to hire for his several farms.

He has not had to look far before finding other men who are not independent proprietors, and who, for this reason, are seeking work from such as he, which will give them daily bread. As long as his hired men were few in number and he could work with them, the result was fairly satisfactory. But suppose that he inquires how he shall derive the most income from one of the farms which he is no longer able to superintend in person. He need know but little of human nature to be sure that if he leaves this farm to be worked by hired men without superintendence the product will be small. The complaint of all employers of labor is perpetual, and to a considerable degree well founded, that the laborer is not worthy of his hire, if to be worthy of the hire means to display as much zeal and interest as the proprietor himself. This expectation, however, is irrational. The owner of the farm can not in reason expect that his hired workers shall manifest that extreme zeal and that persistent interest in making a large product which he himself displays, if energetic and capable. They are not working for their own interest in any such degree as himself; although if they work side by side with him his example will be to some degree contagious. The hired worker has, of course, the stimulus of need to keep him up to an average standard of work, but this standard is much lower than that of the independent proprietor. One need not dilate before people who have ever had occasion to hire another person to do work which they themselves understand and are capable of doing, upon the shortcomings, the neglects, the waste of time and material of the hired worker, as compared with the employer.

For our farmer there is an alternative. He may agree with one of those workers, whom he has found to be the most industrious and competent, to take a farm on shares and pay not a fixed money rent, but half of the net product as rent. The system of product sharing, which has had a wide prevalence in numerous countries, practically assures the owner as large a rent as the renter can earn. Though the worker has not before him the force of the motives to industry and economy which would be his were he the full owner of the place, his half share of the product will augment with his own zeal and skill. With his eyes fixed, perhaps, on the ownership before long of this very place, he will not be slow to make this half share as large as possible, and may even rival, under the spur of this ambition, the energy of the actual proprietor.

The system of product sharing is naturally restricted to such vocations as agriculture, the fisheries, and mining. It is not easily applied to the great variety of manufacturers. But that which can be said of the excellence of the system in the fields where it has been so largely practiced can also be said, in considerable degree, of the system which is logically its successor. I refer to that modification of the wages system known as profit sharing, in which the employer adds to fixed wages a bonus to labor, varying according to the prosperity of the business. No one will pretend that the employee in a large manufactory, working on the ordinary wages system, has every possible motive to exertion held out to him. As a matter of course, his usual exertion will be far below the standard of the man who carries on a small business at which he works by himself or side by side with his few workmen. As manufactories increase in size they become more and more unwieldly, and there is even more need than in the earlier days of the factory system for improvements in the labor contract practiced in them. There is much more demand in a large concern where no one person can effectively superintend the whole business, than in a small one under the view of a single eye, for enlisting every motive of self interest on the part of the employee. The same tendencies which have built up the great manufacturing concerns of our day will probably long continue. They illustrate very forcibly the aristocratic principle which calls to the front the natural leaders of industries and commerce, and they forcibly exemplify the well known scriptural doctrine that "to him that hath it shall be given." Great changes may take place through the application of electricity to industry, rendering possible some return to small factories, and even to house production. For the present we must make up our minds to the continuance of such methods as we see practiced so extensively. We have bidden a long farewell to the familiar association of the employer with a small body of workmen; we must accept as inevitable the massing of workers in great buildings, often far removed from the commercial department of the industry. The practical problem is, first, how to counteract the natural tendency of the wages system to an inferior grade of accomplishment. The system which gives the largest product to be divided is the best.

We must accept just as much the natural and inevitable organization of workers among themselves for the purpose of raising wages and otherwise improving their condition. However much we may lament the loss of personal touch, and however much we may deplore the almost warlike array of workmen drawn up on one side against the smaller but more compact body of employers on the other, we must accept the situation as it is, and consider every method of feasible evolution before we, for a moment even, talk of revolution. The violent introduction of socialism as a fully developed scheme of collective capital and state production is quite out of the question; nor is the more peaceful revolution of pure co-operative production near at hand. The tendencies of modern industry are almost as hostile to pure co-operative production as they are to numerous small concerns.

The deficiencies and disadvantages of the wages system are obvious to clear sighted observers. One plain reason for this is that it is the system under which the work of civilization is actually being conducted. In this respect the system has, of course, great inferiority to fanciful schemes which have never been tried. Putting aside these imaginary constructions, we may say that the choice in the solution of the specific labor problem lies between the continuance of the unmodified wages system, the system of co-operative production, and such an intermediate measure as profit sharing, shading off into forms of co-operative production. It is necessary to draw some lines of distinction here which do not everywhere exist in the same clearness, for there are various modifications of the wages system—such as piecework, premiums, and progressive wages—which tend toward profit sharing and answer some of the objections made to the method of simple day wages. Thus the wages system runs into some method of profit sharing, and profit sharing naturally tends to some form of co-operative production. Mr. David F. Schloss, in his work on Methods of Industrial Remuneration, has well described the different modifications of pure wages in vogue in England. He has done a special service in this work, as the information which he gives could not be found anywhere else in such convenient form.

The advocates of co-operative production usually contrast with this plan the unmodified wages system, under which no special inducement is held out to the workman to do his best. The prevailing tendencies are to make him satisfied with an average amount of work, corresponding to the ability of the mediocre, unsatisfied, uninterested worker. The objection which the advocate of co-operative production and the socialist also makes against the wages system, that it is entirely unjust, I prefer to pass over, for the present at least, for the reason that the application of abstract ideas of justice to complicated questions like this is generally very unfruitful. The employer has one idea of justice and the workman has another idea. A more fruitful method asks which system, the wages system or co-operative production, succeeds best in actual experience. The success of the co-operative productive enterprise is to be determined by the amount of product and its quality, actually realized, and the resulting income to the workman, year in and year out.

Everyone who desires the progressive elevation of mankind must heartily sympathize with the system of co-operative production as laid down so admirably by such writers as Judge Thomas Hughes and the late Mr. Vansittart Neale. The system is evidently near to the ideal, since it promises to all the workers a just division of the entire profits of the business. But it cannot be said that the actual record is very inspiring. There are, to be sure, in England at the present time some eighty productive societies more or less connected with the co-operative movement. Although some few of these are important and well established, the great majority are small, or yet in the trial stage. In America the imitation of societies like these has been almost as slight and intermittent as the reproduction of the English co-operative stores here, of which we have so few. The difficulties in the way of co-operative production are very great. The financial obstacle increases rather than decreases with time. Manufacturing in these days is carried on in such large establishments, demanding such elaborate machinery, that the capital needed to compete successfully with existing enterprises is almost entirely lacking to ordinary workingmen.

If the necessary capital for a comparatively modest undertaking in co-operative production is at hand, if a considerable number of workingmen of unusual character and ability put together their hard earned savings, the moral difficulties are still before them. One of the first of these is an entire willingness on the part of these workmen to submit to the orders of one of their own number, placed at the head of the business of manufacturing and buying and selling, with that readiness which is indispensable for competition with other establishments. A man may very well be a workman in one cotton factory, as in Oldham, England, and a stockholder in another; but when he is at once a worker in a mill and a part owner of it, he will not obey orders from a superintendent whom his own vote has helped to put in office, and whom his vote can also help to depose, as readily as he will conform to the discipline of a mill in which he has no financial stake. The ordinary corporation, which is, in one sense, a plain instance of co-operation, seems to be the nearest approach to co-operative production now feasible under most circumstances. In large corporations the great majority of the stockholders own so few shares that the conduct of the enterprise is practically in the hands of a few persons, whose financial interests teach them to combine, rather than to fight each other. When one considers how difficult it is to get a number of people usually regarded as above the average in intelligence and character to co-operate in schemes demanding but a limited amount of money from each, and but a small part of his time, it will be seen how severe a demand the developed scheme of co-operative production makes upon the workman, for he is expected to put in all his available capital, to give all of his working time to the enterprise, and to surrender the management to one of his associates. This associate must be a man of great ability and high character to carry on the business successfully. He must be willing to receive, for the most part, a much smaller compensation for his uncommon business talent than he would receive under the wages system as foreman or superintendent. The opportunities for suspicion and distrust are very many, and the first financial reverse may be sufficient to bring down a very promising attempt at co-operative production.

But, however discouraging the record of the system may be thus far, there is an undeniable fascination in the idea itself that the capital requisite for carrying on a business should be furnished by those who are to do the work, and that they should divide equitably among themselves the entire profits of the enterprise. This surely would seem to be the application to industry of obvious notions of justice, right and equity. But the workmen must furnish from their own body not only the manual labor but the faculty for superintendence and commercial management; besides this, they have to reach a higher level of character, leading to a much greater mutual confidence, than we find in the ordinary world. The place of that constraint and discipline which the present wages system enforces, and which sentimentalists call a system of slavery, must be taken under co-operative production by a high moral development, which shall justify complete confidence by the workmen in each other. This confidence they must have not only in those who work with them at the bench or the loom, but most of all in the men of unusual ability, belonging to their own condition in life, whom they select as responsible managers of the enterprise.

Such considerations as these of the tendencies of the existing wages system on the one hand, and of the immeasurable discontent which workingmen penetrated by the democratic spirit naturally feel; of the actual weakness of the system of co-operative production, owing to the large demands, intellectually and morally, it makes upon working people—lead one to inquire if there may not be methods which may lead up by easy transition from the pure wages system to the more ideal system of co-operative production. The system of industrial partnership, for which term profit sharing is an inadequate designation, has at least this much to recommend it: It has, in several very important instances, bridged over the gap between the wages system and a system of co-operative production entitled to that name by its actual results, although not corresponding in every respect to the usual ideal of the workingman. Such houses as the Maison Leclaire and the Bon Marché of Paris, and the Co-operative Paper mills of Angouleme, France, for instance, show how profit sharing may be induced upon the wages system and developed into a substantial system of co-operative production. The process in these three instances has been long and slow, but such is the nature of all sound and durable education. The numerous years occupied by the transition sufficed to educate the employer and the employed alike; they justified the employer in gradually divesting himself of his powers and responsibilities; they taught the workmen very gradually the virtues and the faculties demanded by the employer's position, and they rendered easy the gradual supersession of the original proprietor by men from the ranks of his own establishment. In these cases regulations have been made for the continuous application of a system of promotion, so that a body like the Mutual Benefit society of the Maison Leclaire can furnish out of its membership at any time of need the partner or partners, as they are called, to direct the working of the entire business. These partners, or managers, however, when they assume their new position, find a moral condition about them such as no co-operative productive enterprise starting out de novo could furnish. The new manager, fresh from the ranks of the workers, finds the whole body of his former fellows ready and accustomed to obey orders from the heads of the establishment, and to give them as full powers as partners enjoy in establishments conducted on the ordinary wage system. The new partners have been chosen by a sensible body of workingmen because of their approved character and their tested ability. They have been shown by time to belong to the natural aristocracy of ability and character, and their fellow workmen take pleasure in promoting them, and a rational pride in co-operating with them, not henceforth as complete equals, but as members, each in his own place, of an establishment proud of its history and determined to maintain its high standard in the years to come.

Such instances as the Maison Leclaire and others of a similar nature lead me to believe that we shall obtain in time, in a large number of cases at least, the substantial benefits of co-operative production through the process of education by means of profit sharing. The details of the systems thus worked out may not be in all respects those laid down even by the wisest heads for a scheme of co-operative production ideally just. Deference to the democratic principle may easily lead even such thinkers astray, while the experience of such firms as I have mentioned supplies the needed corrective, in paying the due tribute to the aristocratic principle, just as natural as the democratic.

I am decidedly of the opinion that the labor problem, considered as substantially the problem of the best kind of contract relations between the employer and the employed, is to be solved in the gradual development of the existing wages system, through profit sharing, into some system of co-operative production. I do not wish to undertake the office of prophet, and I quite decline to predict even how soon there will be so modest a number as one hundred such co-operative establishments as the Maison Leclaire in the whole civilized world. With confidence, however, I declare my conviction that such a development itself does more justice to all the factors in production than any other measure which I know. Profit sharing is thoroughly entitled to the full credit of being an evolutionary method. The one great and crying defect of the wages system is that under it an immense amount of work is not done which could be done, to the great benefit of mankind, if the whole body of workers were thoroughly interested in producing just as much and just as good work as possible. This being so, we should be quick to make modest attempts toward a system which brings into play a great reserve force. Under the wages system this reserve of unusual power lies largely among the workingmen; but one need only stop and think a moment to realize how the extreme friction of the existing system diminishes the actual working power of the employers. Under a system which secured to them the hearty co-operation of their men, their own force would undoubtedly be largely increased. We want to increase it.

Looking at the system of co-operative production, as usually practiced to-day, in comparison with such an evolutionary system as I speak of, it is a striking fact that its advocates virtually leave out of sight the immense working power of the present captains of industry. It is not to be supposed that we can immediately convert any considerable number of the great manufacturers and masters of transportation, for instance, so that they will be willing to put all their ability at the service of the workmen for modest salaries. Imagine, then, if you can, the effect if to-morrow morning the skill and ability of all business men above the grade of common hand labor were withdrawn. Imagine the city of Brooklyn, for instance, left to-morrow to be run, so far as private business is concerned, by the workingmen alone, with nearly all the brain capital of the present system reduced to temporary idleness. It would require but a few hours of such a régime to convince even the most determined advocate of the democratic principle in industry of the fallacy of his theories of manual labor as the source of all value and of the equality of all heads in business. Any system which, like most plans of co-operative production, makes little account of the men who are really leading the business of modern civilization and furnishing employment and bread for the great army of hand workers, neglects one of the vital factors in the situation. In point of fact, we need every particle of ability and of working force in head and hand to do even the larger part of the work that must be done. The captains of industry of whom I speak are not yet sufficiently moralized to be willing to accept the very modest position which the system of co-operative production would assign to them. This is no reproach to them; the level of morality among them is at least as high as that among workingmen or any other large class of people. They need, however, education into some larger ideal and up to some nobler standard, like all the rest of us, and it is to some gradual process of taking their workmen into partnership in the profits of industry, managed on substantially the present lines, that we are to look for the educating agency needed. Both the employer and the employed under present conditions need to evolve new capacities and new virtues to give co-operative production a fair field in which to develop.

The question just how large a share of the profits the employed shall receive is not important at the outset. The fact that a regular dividend paid to labor out of the profits of the year has been shown to be good business policy in a large number of cases, resulting in at least as large net profits to the employer himself as before and in the general improvement of the industrial situation in the establishment— recognition of this fact is the main matter at the beginning. If the workman is guaranteed by his employer a modest dividend of five or ten per cent on his wages, varying according to the returns of the year, he is taken into a kind of partnership such as he did not before know. He will in time, if he belongs to ordinary humanity, begin to have the feelings and the ambitions of the partner. The increase in the amount of product and the improvement in its quality, and other gains from economy of material and care of machinery, and from the absence of labor difficulties, which have usually resulted, are arguments of great weight for such a limited partnership. Into the details of the very considerable body of experience furnished in the last fifty years by the numerous firms which have tried the system, beginning with the Maison Leclaire in 1842 and coming down to the more than three hundred firms which now practice profit sharing in Europe and America, I can not here enter. My chief claim for profit sharing, as compared with the wages system now in force and with that system of co-operative production which is desired by so many, is that it does more complete justice to all the factors in the situation than either of these two systems—that which is now a fact and that which is now largely a hope. The objection commonly made to profit sharing—that it does not include the sharing of losses by the employed—rests upon a gross misconception of the scheme. It is a limited method to be distinguished carefully from the more developed system of co-operative production under which loss sharing is plainly inevitable.

The progress which has been made in the last few years by the system of industrial partnership is encouraging to all believers who have never allowed themselves to put it forward as the one solution of the labor problem or as a panacea for social difficulties. If I may speak for the great body of advocates of the system, we see in it one excellent method of improving the relations between the workman and his employer, which it is highly desirable should be applied and tested in a great many directions in order to ascertain the fields in which it will prove itself to be a better system than any yet practiced. If in one direction a system of premiums for economy in the use of material, or in another direction a system of increasing the wages according to the amount of good production, is found to bring a larger return to the workman and a better result for the employer than profit sharing, we are entirely ready to acknowledge the fact. There are directions in which profit sharing is likely to justify itself at once, as in trades where a large amount of skilled labor is employed; in others, owing to the great use of machinery, there is less room for wise economy on the part of the employee. A large part of the business of the world, of course, is done on a no profit basis. There are numerous fields, from such matters as common domestic service to the work of the teacher in the public school and the professor in the college, from which the whole notion of profits is absent, and to which consequently such a system as profit sharing has no application. In these fields, if service is defective and unsatisfactory, means of improving it must be sought in other ways than by resort to such a system.

If we look forward in a general way to consider the parts which the three systems—of wages, profit sharing, and co-operative production—are likely to play in the comparatively near future, it is only rational to suppose that they will for a long time continue side by side. As the world grows older, wiser, and more humane, and as the democratic principle asserts itself more and more vigorously, the wages system, which is now virtually monopolizing the field, will gradually suffer modifications. Profit sharing or industrial partnership, under the various forms which as a guiding principle it readily admits, will steadily make converts, encroaching upon the wages system to an indefinite extent. The wages system, however, will persist in some quarters because no other system is so well adapted to the demands of the situation; and in other quarters it will yield place but very slowly to more democratic methods. The wages system, however, will probably be much more influenced by the advance of profit sharing for a considerable time to come than profit sharing will be by the spread of co-operative production growing out of it.

A steady and permanent increase in the number of true co-operative productive establishments, in the light of all the experience which profit sharing can give, we must all heartily desire. No industrial future, however, is likely to be less complex than that which we behold in wonderful variety round about us to-day, and he would be a rash prophet who should predict the day when any one system of the three under consideration will have driven out the other two. He would be much less wise who should protest that no system which the human mind is capable of imagining will ever supersede co-operative production. In all these matters we do well to keep ourselves free from the conceit of inerrancy and infallibility. We have no call to legislate for an indefinite future or to lay down an industrial or economic creed for all our descendants. It is our one imperative duty to consider the existing situation, not as capitalists, not as employers, not as workingmen, not as members of a particular profession, but scientifically and philosophically. It is our business to see facts as they are and to consider them calmly, with a view to that improvement which a progressive civilization demands. We cannot escape the application of the notion of evolution to these matters, and such an application at once forbids our declaiming against the wages system as a·system of slavery, or exalting co-operative production as the sacred ideal to which the future must conform, or preaching profit sharing as the one panacea for all our industrial woes.

The labor problem, I began by saying, is a problem of finding work and finding the just reward for it. More specifically, it is the problem of the best relation between the man who has more work than he can do himself and the man who must find work. The interests of these two parties are not directly and obviously identical; but society includes both the employer and the employed, and a good many other persons not to be ranked under either of these heads. The interest of entire society unmistakably is that as much work and as good work as possible shall be done without overworking any human being; that every worker shall receive a fair return for his toil; that the whole product of all the workers shall be so increased by such material agents as improved machinery, and such moral agents as greater interest in the work on the part of all, and a closer union and harmony, that the share of every worker may be augmented.

The labor question grows out of the advance of civilization and the development of humanity. While we isolate it for the purpose of clearness of thought and to facilitate the adoption of practical measures of improvement, we have to remember that it is not the only problem, perhaps not the chief problem, of mankind from age to age. The present absorption of so many earnest and able minds in labor problems and social questions does not mean that these are to be perpetually so absorbing. The present deep interest is a sign of progress; it is a sign of the elevation of mankind; a sign of hope, not of despair; it is a token of the increasing spread of sound morals and rational religion. It is, we may firmly trust, the sure omen of a gradual and incessant improvement in the condition of civilized mankind.

THE SOCIAL ENGINEER.

BY WILLIAM H. TOLMAN.

[William Howe Tolman, economist; born Pawtucket, R. I., June 2, 1861; graduated from Brown university in 1882; post graduate in department of history and politics, Johns Hopkins; Ph.D., 1891; officer and member of several public charitable societies, both national and foreign. Author: History of Higher Education in Rhode Island; Municipal Reform Movements in the United States, etc.]

In the changed industrial and economic conditions of to-day the great concentration of capital and the massing of thousands of the employed have brought about new problems. In the old times, master and man lived and worked together—there was a daily point of contact, a continuous personal touch. To-day all is changed. The employer, in many cases, is as much of an absentee as were the nobles in France in the latter part of the eighteenth century and the landlords of some of the worst tenements in slumdom. With the growing intelligence on the part of the workers, evidencing itself in a dissatisfaction with their social and economic surroundings, they are slowly learning how to crystallize their incoherent wants and their smothered discontents into definite propositions for an improvement of their conditions.

The personal touch between employer and employed has largely been lost, and it is not desirable, even if it were possible, to return to the earlier days. But for the successful conduct of the business of the twentieth century a point of contact must be sought for and established, though in a different way. This need has created a new profession, that of the social engineer, a man who can tell the employer how he may establish such a point of contact between himself, his immediate staff, and the rank and file of his industrial army. Thus the writer was summoned in this capacity some time ago to advise a firm employing 2,000 men and boys on the subject of a building to serve as a social center for their employees and also for the community where the factory was located.

On another occasion an employer of 5,000 men asked me what form of industrial betterment he could begin. This led to a few questions on my part. First, were the men allowed to drink beer on the premises, especially at the noon hour. "Oh, no," was the answer; "we are very strict about that." Secondly, I inquired whether any rooms were provided in the factory where the men could eat their lunch, or any kind of a shelter outside to protect them from the hot sun of the summer. I found that nothing was provided. In summer they were obliged to eat their luncheon in the shadow of the buildings; frequently their heads were shaded while their bodies were exposed to the hot sun. Under these conditions it was not surprising that the men went to saloons where they could have their beer and the privileges of the free lunch counter in comparatively cool and comfortable rooms.

To change these conditions I advised the fitting up of a room with plenty of windows and fresh air, and a temporary shelter in some part of the yard for summer use. I reinforced my suggestion by the instance of a certain factory where one large room is furnished with tables and benches. A kitchen is provided where plain, substantial food is furnished at cost price. The men are divided into sections and are given cards on which they write down their orders for the following day. One of their own number serves as waiter, going to the kitchen five minutes before the whistle blows to get the tray with the food which has already been placed there, corresponding to the written orders given on the cards. As soon as the men are seated at the tables, the food, smoking hot, is placed before them, so that there is not a moment's loss of time. The average price of a meal is 15 cents.

After dinner they may adjourn to one end of the room where are tables filled with reading matter, trade papers, technical journals, magazines—in fact, just the kind of reading matter that will appeal to the man at the bench who has a few minutes' leisure after eating. The men are also allowed to smoke for half an hour after they return to their work. The manufactured product is such as to permit this privilege in nearly all the rooms. There are very few factories where smoking could be allowed, but the fact that it is allowed here shows that the employer is willing to do all in his power for the comfort of his men. My visit to this factory happened on a Friday, when a religious talk of seven minutes is given to the men after luncheon. The speaker gave the men a straight from the shoulder gospel talk on the Prodigal Son. I watched carefully to see how many would stay for the talk. With the exception of about 20 men, who were reading, the remainder, 180, stayed for the address. When you consider that the men took their own time to listen to the religious talk, it is very significant. Since the establishment of this factory lunch room three saloons in the neighborhood have gone out of business, and the fourth is having a hard time. In this particular factory the men appreciate the co-operation of their employer, and show it; however, in the majority of cases appreciation is not expressed, even if it be felt, but that fact does not lessen the obligation of doing one's duty. Noblesse oblige was never truer than to-day.

One of the first steps, in the writer's opinion, towards improving the condition of the employed is the provision of clean and comfortable rooms where men or women may eat their midday meal away from the noise, dirt, and routine of the workbench or machine. The most farsighted employers have been quick to see that taking care of their employees is good business, and have fitted up kitchens where a warm meal of plain, substantial food may be served at cost. The captains of industry are slowly learning a lesson from the captains of war, who lay great store on the physical equipment of their army, fully recognizing that the best fed and the best nourished soldier is the most efficient one.

In a large paint factory it was found that a great deal of illness was caused by poor drinking water. This was a loss to the men, who could not work while disabled, and also to the firm, who lost the continuous service of good workmen. On making a study of the local conditions, it was ascertained that a service of filtration would overcome these evils, and accordingly a complete filtering installation was added to the factory equipment at considerable expense, with the result that now typhoid cases are unknown there.

In the dry color room in this same factory the workmen are provided with two sets of jumpers, which they wear daily. At night the outer one is laundered. In the morning a clean one is put on next to the underclothing, while the inner jumper of the day before becomes the outer one of the next day. The lavatory is fitted up with spray baths, and each worker is obliged to use them, being given time of the company for this purpose. Those who wish may have their underclothing washed at the factory laundry. By the baths the pores of the skin are kept open, so that all impurities are worked out of the system. Formerly in this department a man lasted only five or six months; now lead poisoning is a thing of the past. The employee gains in having good health, and the firm do not lose time and experience in breaking in new workmen.

For the purpose of stimulating the employee to do his best, an increasing number of employers are offering cash awards for the best suggestions from their staff. In one large company a wagon driver called the proprietor's attention to the poorly paved streets about the freight stations, stating that he was never able to haul a full load of merchandise, to say nothing of the needless wear and tear on the horses and wagons. The attention of the city authorities was called to the poor paving, with the result that the streets are now in a proper condition. Thus the whole city gained by the suggestion made by one driver to an employer who had drawn him out by the offer of an award for suggestions.

These are some typical conditions, and their betterment, which confront the social engineer. He must inform himself of all the various phenomena, while referring each manifestation to the underlying principles. In that way he accumulates a store of principles, with their applications, which will enable him to be of practical service when he is next called in consultation. In every case the local conditions and needs must be carefully studied so that the necessary adaptation may be made, for a brilliant success in one factory may be a dismal failure in another of the same kind, without a study of the local environment.

In the great problems of railway transportation, there is the question of administration, the purchase of the raw material to be worked into the finished product by the company itself, and the actual operation of the railway itself. Some of the large lines are maintaining pension funds, libraries, and various movements for recreation. Take the New York Central railroad by way of example. In the operation of the 10,453 miles of this system the services of an industrial army of 87,200 persons are required. Mr. Cornelius Vanderbilt had a building put up for the railroad branch of the Young Men's Christian association to be used by the employees of the line. This was practically a railroad man's club, for there were then no social secretaries who were trained for the all round management of such a club. This New York Railroad Man's club is typical of the many others established along the line of this one road. On entering the building, it is almost impossible for the newcomer to escape the observation of one of the officials, who are there for the express purpose of serving the newcomer in any way. It may be that he is seeking information about the club and its organization; if so, the necessary explanations are given, and he is made to feel at home. If he is a member, he has access to dining rooms, sleeping rooms, libraries, reading rooms, gymnasiums, and baths; religious services, lectures and recreations. Provision is made not only for the temporal and mental, but also for the spiritual welfare of the employed.

The widening care of the road for the employee is further evidenced by a system of hospitals along the lines for the sick and injured. Traveling hospitals, as they may be called, are maintained—that is, emergency boxes containing articles necessary for use in case of accident or injury, placed in cars, shops, and roundhouses, the men receiving instructions in first aid to the injured.

Closely allied to industrial betterment is social betterment, for every movement adding beauty, comfort, and satisfaction directly promotes a better communal feeling. In line with this thought, the engineering department of the same railway has established a system of horticultural gardens and greenhouses, from which plants and shrubs may be prepared for use at the various stations, and trailing vines are supplied for the purpose of covering up the bareness of fences, poles, and buildings, adding beauty by the subtraction of ugliness. This form of social betterment is not confined to the New York Central company. It can be extended still further, for there seems to be no reason why the employees of the road should not be supplied with the vines, plants, and shrubs for their own home adornment, at cost, and, under certain conditions, free, provided that they would agree to plant and care for a definite amount. By that means each employee becomes a missionary of beauty, bringing the delight and pleasure of the flowers not only to his own home, but to the community.

In preparing the programme for the great industrial betterment meeting which was held at New York by what is known as the Get Together club, employers of 258,000 employed told what was being done to improve the conditions of their people, looking towards self help and self advancement. Mr. George H. Daniels, of the New York Central railroad, in telling at this meeting why his road was doing all these things, said:

"First, those responsible for the management of the New York Central lines, believing in the fatherhood of God and the brotherhood of man, realize that a sacred duty devolves upon them to aid, in so far as it lies in their power, their employees, who are associated with and more or less dependent upon them. They are, in a sense, of our household, and it is our duty, as well as our pleasure, to assist them in living better, and, therefore, more useful lives.

"The second reason is a patriotic one. Those to whom is intrusted the management of these companies are impressed with their responsibility as citizens of this great republic, and are conscious of their duty to the state and national governments to set an example to their employees which shall be an incentive to them to become wiser and better citizens, and to enable them to perform those important services to the public that are a part of the duties of so many of the employees of transportation companies.

"The third reason is a business one. It is considered good business to surround our employees, so far as we possibly can, with healthful, helpful, homelike, temporal, as well as moral, influences. It is desirable, from a purely business standpoint, that every employee who is away from his home, on completing his work for the day or night, should have a regular resting place which he can call his own, and where for a reasonable outlay he can secure a comfortable bed, good, wholesome meals, good papers and books to read, and good companionship. We consider that there is no excuse for such employees to be found in improper places or in questionable company.

"The employee who is surrounded by such helpful influences is ready at any moment to perform the duties devolving upon him in a manner which contributes to the safety and comfort of all who serve and are served by the railways. The construction by the New York Central lines of buildings such as I have briefly referred to, which will bring within the reach of their employees all those aids to correct living, the attainment of higher ideals of life, and help in the formation of sterling character, which is so essential in railway employees, will go on from year to year, until eventually at every division point there will be means provided, through the co-operation of the companies and their employees, for all these helpful agencies."

VILLAGE COMMUNITIES OF THE FACTORY MACHINE WORKS, AND MINE.

BY CHARLES BUXTON GOING.

[Charles Buxton Going, managing editor of the Engineering Magazine; born Westchester, N. Y., April 5, 1863; educated at public and private schools and Columbia university; engaged in professional practice as an engineer and in industrial management after 1892–6; associate editor Engineering Magazine 1896–8 and managing editor since 1898. Author of a number of books and contributor for the magazines not only of technical articles but also of several short stories and poems. The following article is published from the Engineering Magazine by special arrangement.]

The years just past have been characterized above all by mechanical progress and, as its corollary, by centralization of industry. The factory system has drawn the working community toward foci, with ever increasing intensity. Economy of production—the great all controlling influence in the modern material world—requires the concentration of power in huge units, and about these cluster ever growing and ever denser swarms of machine tenders—workers of every grade. The movement goes on with almost unthinkable rapidity, but pace by pace with it move the conditions of labor, of life for the laborer, and of relations between workman and employer. Mechanical production—to use the accepted phrase —is working a revolution in economic affairs, in the distribution of industry, in the balances of trade, and in national politics and precedence. It is also working a revolution in social conditions and relations.

It is no wonder that many earnest minds shrink from the realization of this ceaseless onrush, and wish that it might be stayed. And yet it is not mere optimism to hold that the outcome is for good, and continually for the better. Viewed in the large, the last century has done more to free the body and the mind of labor—to reduce physical toil, increase its reward, enlarge opportunities, and open the way to a larger sharing in the higher things of life—than all the centuries which went before. The future may be most safely judged from the past. What the introduction of machinery began, the enlargement of its use will continue.

It needs time for so large an adjustment, and the period of adaptation to new conditions is a trying one. As, in the factory management, system and organization must take the place of proprietary oversight and direction, so between employer and employee a new basis of relation must be established. The close personal contact between proprietor and workman, which belonged to the domestic and semi-domestic era of manufacturing, must give way to something else—some counterpart suited to the new order. But that it should give way and nothing take its place, would be as fatal as that management should lapse into chaos, because the owner could no longer personally direct every detail of a mammoth plant. The complex human element in a great manufacturing works needs the more intelligent provision, in even greater degree, than its complex motive power and machinery need more skillful care than the little water wheel of the first factory. But modern civilization—at least in the enlightened industrial countries—rejects the paternalism of early days, even if modern conditions do not make it impracticable. Not the least characteristic result of the age of machinery has been the development of individuality in the worker. Enlightened self interest demands that the employer shall consider the welfare and comfort of his men, but reason, justice, and sympathetic comprehension must be the elements of the relations —not patronage on the one side, nor unmanly dependency on the other.

It must be admitted that the perception of the employer's interest in the well being of employee has been rather lately regained after a period of indifference to, or perhaps active rejection of, the idea that there should be—must be—such an interest. The cycle is swinging round again to a phase somewhat modified, possibly not always enough modified, from that displayed in the old days of proprietor and apprentice, when the physical and moral charge of the laborer was assumed by his master. Perhaps a prototype still closer, because on a scale more nearly equal, might be found in the great iron works of the early half of the nineteenth century. In the black country of England, and in the Ohio valley in the United States up to the time of the civil war, these great establish-

ments were the largest existing aggregations of manual workers
and heavy machinery. The very conditions of their being
marked them out for isolation and necessary self dependence.
The mine and the furnace created the community. The owner
of the plant was very generally, from the nature of the enterprise, owner of most of the adjoining land. He alone had
sufficient facilities for securing the distributing and needful
provisions and supplies. He was employer, landlord, health
officer, lawmaker, magistrate, merchant. The workman,
while separated from his employer by a wider gulf than now,
was more dependent upon him. The system was almost
patriarchal—quite feudal. The ironmaster was a petty lord
and a political power of no small importance; for while internal
conflict was by no means lacking, especially when the feudal
baron had not the wisdom to be beneficent, the community
was one in its interest in outside affairs. The often remote
situation and peculiar surrounding conditions of the mine,
together with the semi-military discipline which must characterize its conduct, favor the persistence of many of these
conditions to the present day. With the growth in importance
of factory plants, and their necessary location in outlying
situations where they may have room to grow and space
enough for their dependencies, there is a marked and rising
tendency toward the establishment of somewhat similar relations, modernized and improved, between the factory management and factory operatives. Wisely directed, it has vast
possibilities for bettering the surroundings of the working
classes and creating a strong, practical, concrete political
influence for sound economic legislation and the promotion
of national welfare.

There is no danger of the pendulum swinging back too
far. Twentieth century social ideas are sufficient to hold the
balance. The conceptions of constitutional and individual
liberty are too firmly planted and broadly branched to allow
paternalism to grow under their shadow. But it would be
unfortunate to see efforts, well conceived and meritorious in
the main, meet a check which would reflect on other budding
enterprises, simply because they did not sufficiently recognize
the boundary between healthy fostering care and encourage-

ment and an unwise even though benevolent bossism, or an intolerable attempt to control the man because he is a workman. Probably no more carefully devised or thoroughly worked out plans for a factory community were ever put into effect than those which took shape in the town of Pullman. Possibly the model was excellent. But individual lives cannot be stamped into uniform pattern nor made interchangeable, and the Pullman experiment, instead of preventing trouble, aggravated one of the worst strikes known in the history of America's labor wars. The way to a sound and healthy life in the factory community lies well between the two extremes of apathy and indifference of the management on the one side, and an over interest, coupled with chafing restrictions, on the other. But that the happy mean can be found, and when found will promote mutual satisfaction and prosperity, is amply shown by a rapidly increasing number of examples in the manufacturing world.

The most obvious step in protecting a factory community through the critical times which come with increased pressure of intensity on its life, is one whose simplicity puts it within range of every establishment, large or small. It is confined in its exercise within the factory, and is simple attention to those matters of hygiene and comfort which the workman can not provide for himself, but which are essential to physical well being (and hence to high efficiency) and to the promotion of good personal habits and self respect. Such matters are proper ventilation and heating, proper facilities for washing, provision for changing clothes, and decent sanitary arrangements. Coupled with these is the provision for bath time during working hours without loss of wages—a tacit recognition that conditions of employment which bring dirt and discomfort should provide also for its removal. Next come provisions for providing meals, or supplementing those which the workmen bring with the nourishing or appetizing things which can not be carried, or which the situation of the works or the shortness of the meal time make it difficult and unduly expensive to procure. Something can be done in this way, also, toward directing the employees' attention to more nutritious and wholesome dishes than they have been accustomed to provide for themselves. Beyond this again are the opportunities for mental improvement through the establishment of clubrooms, assembly rooms, lectures, libraries, and other means of education in the subjects most helpful in the men's work. All of these are well recognized and largely practiced.

But it is outside of the factory walls that the workman spends most of his life, and here the interest of the employer more rarely follows. This is an oversight all the more grave because, with the growth in size of individual plants and the increase in the number of works employing thousands of employees, the distinctly factory community is becoming a larger element in economic and political influence. If, by patient exercise of a due and consistent regard for the workman's welfare, the employer establishes a feeling of mutual regard and sympathy, much of the misunderstanding between capital and labor will be effaced and no demagogue will dare —or should he dare, will succeed—in playing upon the suspicions of one side to enable him to fleece or force the other. United, they will be an irresistible power for wise and stable economic legislation.

It is, therefore, to repeat, by a grave oversight that the manufacturer has not oftener considered the employee's interest parallel with his own in building up his works. Within city limits, this is perhaps hardly possible; but there general conditions govern the cost of living and the employer can scarcely, without meddling, enter into his employees' arrangements in that regard. But it is growing more and more common for large works to move, or to be established, in rural and semi-rural districts, where land and taxes are low and there is room to spread as the growth of business may demand. Under these conditions it has been altogether too common— at least in the United States—for the proprietor to make the best arrangements he could for himself and leave his workpeople to get what they could after his bargain was tightly closed. It is not at all uncommon for a factory site to be given to the owners of the business, free of any charge and often free of taxes for a period of years, in consideration of their locating in a certain place. The neighborhood gains from the increased population and the increased chance of employment for its own people; but the employees practically pay the bill for the site, for all ground nearby is advanced greatly in value, houses are built in certainty that they will be absolutely needed by the incoming army of workers, and local landlords and lodging house keepers put up their prices to the limit. I have known personally of men who made their living by dealing in factory sites—buying up or securing options on available properties, getting some large manufacturing plant, under good inducements, to take enough for their own purposes, and making their handsome profit out of the adjoining ground—the higher values being paid, immediately or indirectly, by the workingmen and their families.

In a case of this sort, where the men's interest is diffused and almost intangible—at least, incapable of being concentrated into a unit which can operate with the factory management to joint advantage—it certainly seems as if it would be only reasonable and just for the employers to act as trustee of the tacitly confided interest of their men, and to secure for them the same advantages they get for themselves. In this there would be no paternalism, but simply the regard which an active partner might show for an unrepresented one—simply the regard which, it is now recognized, a controlling stock interest should show the other shareholders. And here the question is not one of abstract principle but of practical relations, for the management and the employees must continue to work together, and everything that makes life fuller and more satisfying to the workman tends directly to the advantage of his work and of his employer.

The after adjustment might be determined as good judgment and the special conditions direct. The main point is that the development of the very desirable factory community spirit can not well be fostered by starting with a real estate deal in which capital takes a virtual profit at the expense of its co-operative element—labor. As Mr. Shuey says: "The experience of Pullman and similar efforts has not encouraged others to do much toward building towns owned and controlled by the company," though throughout the new cotton manufacturing district in the southern states this is at present the custom, as it is in some leading English examples—notably,

I believe, the Cadbury Brothers' village at Bourneville and the Lever Brothers' settlement at Port Sunlight. In New England are to be found some of the best established examples in the United States—those whose soundness of basis is evidenced by the length of their existence and their satisfactory results to both sides. One of the most clean cut and definite instances, perhaps, is the village of Ludlow, Mass. The company built the waterworks, gas works, electric light plant, churches, and schoolhouses. Their general policy with regard to the employees' residences can best be given in the words of Mr. J. E. Stevens, agent of the company:

"Our efforts have been to give every family a complete home, even if it has but four rooms, which is the smallest cottage we build. We avoid as far as possible building anything in the way of blocks, and what is known as the usual mill tenement block we have long since discarded. When we first began building the modern type of cottage, or about sixteen years ago, it was our policy to sell to any of our operatives who cared to buy, and as a matter of fact we did sell several cottages with lots of about one quarter acre. We sold the cottages for about the cost of building, calling the land nothing, and making easy terms of payment. This plan, however, did not work out successfully, for the reason that rules drawn up to promote the health and comfort of the community at large could not be enforced against individual holders. For this and kindred reasons we have ceased to sell cottages and, in fact, bought back at a premium those we sold. Our rents are made as low as can consistently be done, and are much lower than the prevailing rents in this neighborhood. It is our intention to offer prizes for the best kept homes and gardens, for while many tenants take an interest in their surroundings, others are wholly indifferent and can with difficulty be got to co-operate in the protection of shade trees. In designing our cottage homes, we have limited our study almost wholly to the inside; many of these we believe are models of comfort and convenience. We have not made an effort to obtain striking or even showy outside effects, but have rather adopted plain exteriors, with a view to minimum of expense for repairs and maintenance."

Another strikingly successful factory community in the state of Massachusetts is Hopedale—a small place of about 2,000 inhabitants, whose only industry is operated by the Draper company. It is, in fact, a typical example of the factory village. The tract of ground on which it stands was laid out at the company's instance by a prominent landscape architect, and sidewalks, sewers, and other improvements were put in. The principles governing the relations of the company to the community of its employees are thus defined by the assistant agent, Mr. F. I. Dutcher:

"We do not give special encouragement to our workmen to buy their own places. Hopedale is a very small town and our company operates its only industry. It is necessary for us to furnish tenements to a great many of our people, and, on the other hand, those employed by us owning their own places, in case they should leave our employment, are not as well situated as they would be in or near a large town or city if left with a piece of real estate on their hands. We do make an inducement in the way of rentals, in the fact that our rates are based upon an extremely low percentage of income, so low, in fact, that no outside parties build tenements for this purpose.

"To encourage care of the premises about the houses of our employees, we offer every year premiums covering the general outside conditions both of the front and back yards, and shall distribute $300 in this way. We have found after an experience of quite a number of years in this direction, that the average condition of the premises has greatly improved.

"Two boarding houses are owned by our company, and are operated independently by people who rent them, but we do reserve the right to limit the price to be charged for board and to keep a certain amount of supervision on the way in which things are run.

"The local government in Hopedale is the same as in any Massachusetts township. While our people interested in and owning the works of this company are in a way equally interested in the town, its boards and officers are elected by people having a right to vote, and without the least regard to property ownership.

"As far as the writer is aware, there is a good understanding between the employers and employees in this community. We have had absolutely no labor difficulties for many years, and none whatever that were at all serious."

The Peace Dale Manufacturing company, of Peace Dale, Rhode Island, is yet another New England example of the distinctive factory community, and one in which personal, family, business, and village interests have been linked together for nearly a century. The company built the town hall, library, and village church. The Hazard Memorial contains library, gymnasium, baths, class rooms and hall, and was built by the owners of the company for the use of the village. In this case, the treasurer of the company writes, the employers build houses for rent to the help, and also encourage them to build and own their own houses by loaning money and selling land on easy terms. In some cases operatives have not only acquired their own houses, but have secured additional houses and themselves become landlords.

One of the most characteristic of American industrial settlements is the co-operative village of Leclaire, connected with the factories of the N. O. Nelson company, near St. Louis, Mo. It would be impossible to set forth its constitution or its effects more forcibly than in Mr. Nelson's words:

"It is a wretched arrangement by which men are huddled together in ugly factories. We have tried to make the factories attractive as well as healthy. Our days are shortened by the fact that the homes and factories are close together; no time is lost in going and coming. Every home has about a third of an acre of ground attached, thus holding one foot on the sod and one in the factory.

"Leclaire was an outgrowth of the profit sharing system, which was adopted in 1886, and still continues. In the first ten years the dividends on wages amounted to 57 per cent. In the last four years there have been no dividends, the earnings being invested in additions and improvements. But much more important than cash dividends is the improved living, the co-operative spirit, unconsciously absorbed from the common benefits enjoyed out of the fund jointly created."

In answer to my special inquiry, Mr. Nelson writes the following fuller explanation of the policy and constitution of Leclaire:

"Leclaire is built upon a farm of 125 acres, platted into streets, blocks and lots. The land is owned by me as trustee for the Nelson Manufacturing company. The lots when sold are deeded in fee simple.

"There are no legal co-operative elements. Co-operation is entirely voluntary, as well in the social things as in the public things that are provided and maintained by the company. In that respect, the corporation acts as the agent for that associated number of men who do the work and who, with their families, want these public things.

"There are only two legal bodies: the business corporation, and the school and library association, which holds the endowment fund and manages the school library and looks after the village public affairs. The settlement is not at all restricted to employees. At first, we built the houses for the employees on plans agreed on with them, and they paid for them in monthly installments. Now, they build with their own money and loans from the outside, either from building associations in Edwardsville or private lenders. The company owns a few of the houses, but it has no intention of being a landlord. These few are mainly those that have been taken back from employees who left, and they are a convenience for newcomers until they get naturalized and conclude whether they are permanent residents or not.

"There are no ordinances or regulations for the village or its residents—none whatever. There is no local incorporation or authority except the county and township, and especially is there no boss. I live in the village myself, but no resident has ever been asked by me to do anything or refrain from doing anything. Every resident understands that he is as free as he would be on a farm.

"Very decidedly, Leclaire as an institution promotes sympathy and understanding between the work people and employers, and diminishes labor troubles to the vanishing point."

A somewhat less unusual policy is pursued by the Cleveland Cliffs Iron company, of Ishpeming, Mich., but a policy which nevertheless is addressed directly toward establishing a bond of sympathy to bind the community together by other ties than those of mere payment and receipt of wages. Its most characteristic feature is the stimulus to thrift and neatness, by means of prizes given annually for well kept premises and prettily planted gardens. The more general relations of the company with employees are thus explained by the agent, Mr. M. M. Duncan:

"The company owns some sixty houses, which it rents to its employees at a very nominal figure; in fact, about one-half of the rates prevailing on properties owned by individuals in the city. These houses were built many years ago to attract labor to this district. Up to this time we have leased ground to those wishing to build, the rent for which is from $12.00 to $15.00 a year, in some cases exempt from taxation and in some cases the lessee pays a nominal tax.

"Of the mine employees of this city, there are about 1,125 employed by our company, about 725 by the Lake Superior Iron company, and about 500 by the Pittsburgh & Lake Angeline Iron company. These all live within the city limits, and all take interest in municipal government. The company retains some influence in local government, but not to the extent of holding municipal offices. The municipal officials are made up from employees of some of the mining companies and business men, as is also the city council and the county board of supervisors."

The policy of fostering the employee's interest in his home and establishing a communal interest by co-operative and competitive effort in this direction, is pursued also by the National Cash Register company, of Dayton, Ohio. Their methods are thus defined:

"We simply stimulate and encourage our employees to beautify their homes. The company does not own or rent a single dwelling house, and does not believe in attempting to do so.

"Our work was started by organizing the South Park Improvement association, composed of residents of South Park interested in beautifying their homes, and while it is entirely independent of the factory, we encourage them in every way possible by loaning them stereopticon slides, letting them have the use of our hall, and all facilities. In our Sunday school, which might be termed a Sunday club, we teach the principles of landscape gardening, distribute free seeds, and offer $250 annually for the best results in home beautifying."

It is not coincidence that the concerns which take these views regarding the relations between employer and employee are conspicuously fortunate in their freedom from labor troubles. The list of such concerns is lengthening at a wonderful rate, but the millennium is still far off. There are yet workmen who are wholly indifferent and can with difficulty be got to co-operate. There are yet employers who look with disgust on what they call coddling the men. There are yet mine stores exacting so large profits on their compulsory sales that they more than support an unprofitable mine. Where these conditions persist, the factory community will hardly survive its second summer. But such instances serve as foils to set off the better way found in the better directed plants which are working toward fuller understanding and fuller co-operation between labor and capital. That this basis of mutual support should exist grows every year more vitally important. A larger and larger proportion of the nation is annually engaged in manufactures. With the increase in size of individual plants, waxes rapidly the possible damage, to the concern and the community, from the clashing of opposing parties. But organization, which was conceived, even by its promoters, to be an institution of war, is rapidly revealing itself as the most effective agency for stability and peace. When to the reciprocal understanding and tolerance which it is bringing about between capital and labor in the large, is added the community feeling, the sense of unified interest, and the esprit de corps induced by an enlightened policy in the individual works, the second summer of the working community will be safely passed, and the way be open to stable industrial peace and the enduring welfare of both employers and employed.

THE FACTORY AS AN ELEMENT IN SOCIAL LIFE.

BY CARROLL D. WRIGHT.

[Carroll Davidson Wright, United States commissioner of labor; born Dunbarton, N. H., July 25, 1840; educated at Dartsmouth, Wesleyan, and Clark universities; member of the Massachusetts senate, 1872–73; chief Massachusetts bureau of statistics of labor, 1873–88; United States commissioner of labor, 1885–1892 and 1893–97, professor of statistics and social economics, school of comparative jurisprudence and diplomacy, Columbian university, 1900; lecturer on wage statistics at Harvard, 1900–01. Author: The Factory System of the United States; Relation of Political Economy to the Labor Question; The Industrial Evolution of the United States; Outline of Practical Sociology; History and Growth of the United States Census, etc.]

A superficial study of the factory in almost any community leads to the conclusion that it has a deteriorating influence upon the operative as well as upon the population surrounding it, but this is only the superficial view. Years ago, before I began the investigation of social and economic conditions, I very naturally adopted the superficial view; but as my investigations proceeded, and as I studied the real relation of the factory to common, everyday life, I was obliged to change my attitude. It is only natural that this superficial view should obtain in the popular mind. Almost every writer, certainly with rare exceptions, adopts the view that the factory has been beneficial in a purely economic sense. Few are ready to adopt the idea that the factory has been of itself and through its own influence an element in civilization or an element in lifting up the social life of any of the people.

The latter view results from a superficial study, as I have said, and also from an inverted vision. The glamour which surrounded the factory in the early days of its establishment in this country has led to very many erroneous conclusions. Everyone has heard of the Lowell factory girls and the intellectual standard which they attained. Then, looking to the present textile factory operative in different parts of the country, the comparison becomes very sharp and the conclusion apparently decisive. In making this comparison, however, the real conditions of the factory in the early days at Lowell, when the factory girls edited their own literary magazine, which achieved high rank everywhere, are not clearly recognized. The then existing prejudice of England against the factory was well known here, and managers who built their factories in this country at that time were obliged, therefore, to offer attractive wages as well as attractive environment, and by such offers they drew into the eastern factories the daughters of the New England farmers and a high grade of English girls.

In speaking and writing of this period I have often called attention to my own recollections, and such recollections are just those which have led to false conclusions. My first teacher was a weaver in the factories at Lowell, Biddeford and Salem. She was a writer on the Lowell Offering, the factory girls' publication, and a contemporary of Lucy Larcom and the other noble women who worked in the cotton mills of those days.

A change came over the industrial condition, however, and the American and English girls were forced out of the factory through economic influences, but they were not forced downward in the scale of life. They were crowded out, but up into higher callings. They became the wives of foremen and superintendents, teachers in the common schools, clerks in stores and counting rooms, and they lost nothing whatever by their life and services in the factory. The lower grade of operatives that succeeded them brought the sharp comparison which led to the conclusion that the factory is in itself degrading. The women who came in then were very largely Irish girls, fresh and raw immigrants, coming from the ignorant and degraded localities of Ireland. Taking the places of the English and American girls in the eastern factories, they soon began to improve their condition, and the result was that they in turn were crowded out by another nationality. But the Irish girl did not retrograde; she progressed, as had her predecessor, and enlisted in higher occupations. The daughters of the original Irish factory operatives and scrub women who came to this country were no longer factory operatives and scrub women. They were to be found standing behind the counters of our great retail shops, well dressed, educated in our common schools, bright, active, and industrious and with a moral character equal to that of their predecessors.

The war period created the necessity of an increased number of factory operatives, and brought into our mills a great body of French Canadian women. The opposition in the New England states to the presence of the French Canadians was as great as it ever had been against the coming of the Irish. The opposition to the Irish had ceased; it was transferred to the French Canadians, but I venture to say that there never has been a nationality coming into the United States that has shown such great progress in the same period of time as have the French Canadians. They are now graduating from the factory, the Swedes, the Greeks, and others coming in, and the factory is performing the same civilizing operation for the new quotas that it has always performed for the others. It is reaching down and down to the lower strata of society and lifting them up to a higher standard of living.

Now we are in the presence of another experiment, or experience, rather, which teaches the soundness of the view I am trying to convey, and that experience is in the south. When the American girls left the factories of New England, foreigners took their places. The establishment of the textile factory in the south led to the employment of the body of native people, those born and bred in the south, popularly known as the poor whites, who up to the time of the erection of cotton factories had lived a precarious existence and always in antagonism to the colored people, looking upon work as rather degrading than otherwise, because of the peculiar institution of the south, and on the whole not constituting a very desirable element in southern population. To-day these people are furnishing the textile factories of the southern states with a class of operatives not surpassed in any part of the country. This is the testimony of the late Mr. Dingley in a speech in the house of representatives. It is the testimony of English manufacturers who have carefully studied the conditions in the south, and the testimony from all sources is to the effect that the poor whites of the south are entering the cotton mills as an opportunity which had never before been open to them. They are becoming industrious and saving in their habits, and, coming to the factory towns, they bring their families, and they are in turn brought into an

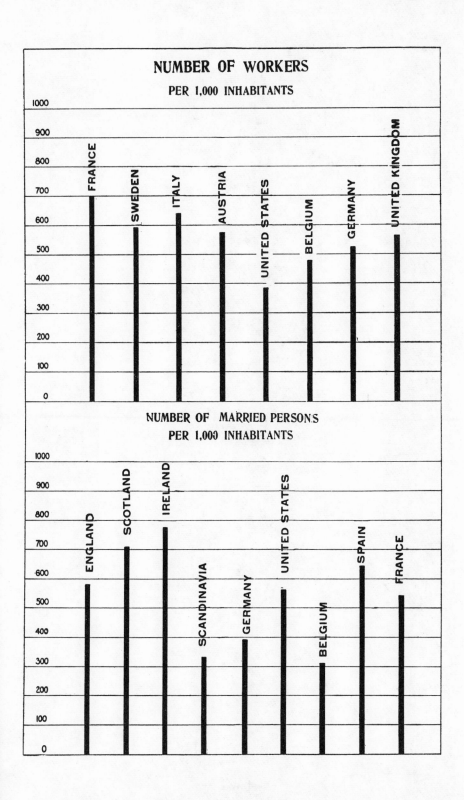

NUMBER OF WORKERS

PER 1,000 INHABITANTS

NUMBER OF MARRIED PERSONS

PER 1,000 INHABITANTS

environment entirely different from that under which they were reared. They are now able to educate their children, to bring them up in a way which was never possible to them before, and thus the poor whites of the south are gradually and with more or less rapidity becoming not only a desirable but a valuable element in southern population, on which the integrity and prosperity of a great industry largely depends.

The experience of the south is simply that of other localities, whether in this country or in England. The factory means education, enlightenment, and an intellectual development utterly impossible without it—I mean to a class of people who could not reach these things in any other way. It is an element in social life. By its educational influences it is constantly lifting the people from a lower to a higher grade.

When the textile factory was originally established in England it took into its employment the children of agricultural districts—paupers, charity boys and girls. Much was said about the degradation of the factory children. Parliamentary investigations and reports bewailed the conditions found, but it was forgotten in every instance that the factory really lifted these children out of a condition far worse than that in which parliamentary committees found them when employed in the factories. We have had no such conditions to contend with in this country, but we have this superficial idea with which to contend. The notion that the factory creates ignorance, vice and low tendencies is absolutely untrue. It does bring together a large body of comparatively ignorant persons; it congregates these persons into one community, and hence the results of ignorance and of lower standards of life become clearly apparent because of the concentration. Before the concentration the ignorance existed precisely the same, but was diffused and hence not apparent.

There is a class of writers who are very fond of drawing comparisons between conditions under the factory system and those which existed prior to its establishment. They refer to the halcyon days of England, and call attention to the Engglish operative working under hand methods as a happy, contented, well fed, moral person. History teaches just the reverse. Prior to the establishment of the factory the working classes of England lived in hovels and mud huts that would not be tolerated even in the worst coal mining districts in this country or in England to-day. The factory graduated all these people from the mud hut. But what was the old system? Degrading, crime breeding and productive of intemperance in the worst form as compared with the factory of to-day.

We hear a great deal about the sweating system, and the popular idea is that the sweating system is the product of modern industrial conditions. The fact is that it is a remnant of the old industrial system. It is the old hand system prior to the establishment of the factory, and has been projected into our time. Once universal, the sweating system is now limited to one or two industries, and is gradually being eliminated through the very system which is sometimes condemned. Just as fast as the sweatshops are developed into the factory and brought under the laws which relate to factory regulation, just so rapidly is the sweating system being eliminated. The only cure is to make of the sweatshop the factory. The social life of sweaters can be improved only by lifting them to the grade of factory operatives.

We sometimes hear of the immorality of factory operatives. I have no doubt that immorality exists among factory operatives, the same as it exists in Fifth avenue and everywhere else on earth where men and women are found, but I do not believe that it exists in any greater proportion in the factory than in any other walk of life. On the other hand, I believe that immoral lives are less frequent among the factory population than among any other class in the community, and investigations, and extensive ones at that, in this country and abroad teach the truth of this assertion.

Some years ago it was my good fortune to look over some of the great thread works in Paisley, Scotland, and this very question of immorality was discussed with the foreman of one of the works. One gentleman, who had been connected with the Coates factories for forty years, informed me that during that period he had known of but one girl who had departed from a strictly honest life, and she, as soon as her habits were known, was ostracized by the coldness of her associates. This I have found to be true in almost every factory I have ever visited. As soon as a girl loses her character her mates frown upon her and she is fairly driven from the field. Women in cotton mills and in all other factories are as careful of their characters as is any other class. The charge that the factory breeds immorality among women is not true, and cannot be sustained by any facts that have ever been collected. This one condition constitutes the factory an important element in social life, for the women who are there and are working for low wages—lower than any of us would like to have paid, but which are governed according to economic conditions and laws—are working honestly and faithfully and living honest and virtuous lives. It must be so. Women cannot work eight or ten or twelve or more hours in a cotton factory and live a dissolute life the rest of the day.

There is another supposition relative to the factory to which I wish to call attention. It is that the factory has a dwarfing influence upon skill; that skill is degraded to common labor. This supposition also arises from a superficial examination of modern establishments wherein a cheap and often an ignorant body of laborers is employed, the appearance being that skilled and intelligent workmen are replaced by unskilled and unintelligent workmen, the conclusion being that the modern system forces the skilled and intelligent workman downward in the scale of civilization. This is not the true sociological conclusion, which is that the modern system of industry gives the skilled and intelligent workman an opportunity to rise in the scale of employment, in intellectual development, in educational acquirements, in the grade of services rendered, and hence in his social standing in his community, while at the same time it enables what was an unskilled and unintelligent body of workers to be employed in such ways, under such conditions, and surrounded by such stimulating influences that they in turn become intelligent and skilled, and crowd upward into the positions formerly occupied by their predecessors, thus enabling them to secure the social standards which they desire. This conclusion, it seems to me, is the true one, and makes the discussion of the question whether the modern system of industry, the factory, really has a stimulating effect upon the intellectual growth of the people not only an interesting but a peculiarly appropriate one.

The whole matter of the consideration of the workingman to-day, then, becomes intellectual. He is carried onward and upward by the power of mental activity which comes from the factory, and cannot be treated separately as one of a class, as he could in the olden time, because in the olden time he was neither a social nor a political factor. Changed conditions in all directions have brought mankind to a new epoch, the distinguishing feature of which is the factory itself, or machinery, which makes it. This we see is true when we comprehend that machinery is constantly lifting men out of low into high grades of employment, constantly surrounding them with an intellectual atmosphere, rather than keeping them degraded in the sweatshop atmosphere of the olden time.

Of course we know that the condition of the worker is not the ideal one; we know that every employer who has the welfare of his race at heart, and who is guided by ethical as well as economic motives, would be glad to see his work people receiving higher pay and living in better houses, living in an environment which should increase rather than diminish their social force. At the same time, we recognize that the sanitary and hygienic condition of the factory is vastly superior to the sanitary and hygienic condition of the homes of the operatives in many cases. When the factory operative in his home reaches the same high grade that has been reached in the factory itself his social force and life will be increased and his standard raised to a much higher plane. All these things are matters of development, but when we understand that manufacturers in this country are obliged constantly to deal with a heterogeneous mass, so far as nationality is concerned, while those in other countries deal with a homogeneous mass of operatives, the wonder is that here we have kept the standard so high as it has been. In considering all these aspects, as briefly as they have been touched upon, we cannot but feel, as I have indicated, that the factory reaches down and lifts up; that it does not reach up and draw down those who have been raised to a higher standard. This is the real ethical mission of the factory everywhere.

Whether the new developments of concentrated industrial interests will lead to a still higher recognition of the ethical forces at work is a question which cannot at present be answered. My own belief is that the future developments of industry will be on this line, and that the relation of the employer and his employees will rest upon a sounder basis than heretofore.

The social condition of the workingman and his education, which we have insisted upon, have led him into the strike method as a means of asserting what he called his rights. He has in this adopted the worst examples set him by his employers in the past. Greater intelligence, a broader recognition of the necessity of higher social standards, will lead to a recognition of other principles that will enable him to avoid industrial war and his employer to recognize the intelligence which is willing to avoid it.

THE MINE WORKER'S LIFE AND AIMS.

BY JOHN MITCHELL.

[John Mitchell, president of United Mine Workers of America since September, 1898, born Braidwood, Will county, Ill., Feb. 4, 1869; from the age of six to ten years went to school at Braidwood; later education obtained by night study; studied law for a year; worked in coal mines in 1882; traveled in the west, mining coal, 1885–90; secretary-treasurer sub-district of United Mine Workers of America, 1895; organizer since 1897; national vice-president, 1898; acting national president, September, 1898; fourth vice-president American Federation of Labor, 1898–1900; second vice-president, 1900; national president United States Mine Workers, 1899–1903; directed the strikes of the anthracite mine workers in 1900 and 1902.]

Little is thought and less is known by the average man concerning the lives, surroundings and environment of those who produce the originating motor power, the power which moves the wheels òf commerce and industry and contributes so much to the civilization of the present day.

I refer to the four hundred thousand men and boys who delve in the bowels of the earth; removed from the sight of their fellow beings; obscured from the rays of the sun; with hundreds, oftentimes thousands, of feet of rock between them and all that is dear to them; in a place which teems with dampness and danger; where not a day goes by without recording the death, by falls of rock, coal or slate, of more than one unfortunate miner; and where, at frequent intervals, by the explosion of gases which are permitted to accumulate in the mines, there are accidents by which the nation is appalled, humble homes are made desolate, wives made widows and children orphaned. These are the men that dig the dusky diamonds whose reddening glow cheers the hearthstone of the poor and rich alike, the product of whose labor is so essential to the welfare and happiness of society and to the progress of the world.

If all the conditions surrounding the lives of this heroic class of sturdy workmen were understood by the justice loving American people, they would not be surprised at the numerous strikes and suspensions which have from time to time interfered with commerce and industry, and on more

than one occasion have threatened a complete paralyzation
of the nation's activities.

It is impossible to portray in intelligible terms the exact
conditions under which coal miners work and live, because
none but those who work in the mines can fully comprehend
or realize the physical conditions prevailing there, as only
those who work in them ever have opportunity for observation; and only those whose interests bring them into daily
contact with mine workers or who are close students of statistical reports on coal production are familiar with the startling truth that for every two hundred and seventy thousand
tons of coal brought to the surface of the mine one employee's
life is sacrificed, and five times that number are maimed
and injured. In other words, of every four hundred and
fifty men employed in the mines, one is killed and five are
injured each year. This makes a total of nine hundred persons who yield up their lives each year, and of forty five
hundred who suffer serious injury. In no other industry
in the United States are there so many fatalities in proportion
to the total number of employees. But, sad and distressing
as these facts may be, they are not the greatest source of
discontent or complaint of this army of workers, for whom
life holds few charms and offers few opportunities.

A peculiar feature of the mining industry, and one which
more than all others affects the interests of those employed
in the production of coal, is the fact that nearly one hundred
and fifty thousand more men are employed in the mines
than are required to produce all the coal which it is possible
for our nation to consume; that is to say that, while the consumption of coal at home and the export trade abroad amount,
in the most prosperous year, to two hundred and fifty million tons, this enormous production gave only two hundred
days' employment to the men and boys at work in the mines.
If the mines were worked three hundred days a year, they
would produce at least one hundred and twenty five million
tons of coal more than is consumed at home or sold abroad.
As a consequence of this abnormal condition, a miner is enabled to earn only about two thirds as much wages as he would
were he steadily employed; and as mining communities are,

with few exceptions, isolated from the centers of industry in other lines, opportunity is not afforded the mine worker to employ profitably the one hundred days of enforced idleness due to the non operation of the mine. Nor can any practical plan be adopted which would fully relieve the mining industry of this apparent surplus of labor, for the reason that a vastly greater amount of coal is consumed in the winter months than at other periods of the year, and as bituminous coal cannot be kept in stock without deteriorating in value and quality, it follows that more coal must be produced in the winter season than in the summer; and consequently during these months all the workers are steadily employed. That this overplus of labor has disastrously affected the earnings of mine workers goes without saying; in fact, for many years prior to 1897 the tendency of wages was downward.

The almost entire absence of combination or organization among the workers made it possible for employers to depress the earnings of their employees almost uninterruptedly each year until, in the summer of 1897, the conditions of employment became so unbearable and the spirit of unrest and resentment so general that the bituminous, or soft coal miners of the United States, having exhausted every peaceful measure at their command to secure redress for their wrongs, determined upon a suspension of operations in all of the states in which soft coal was mined. The date upon which the strike was to take effect was not even known to the miners themselves, they having instructed the officers of the then weak and struggling organization (at a convention held in the spring of that year) to order a cessation of work at whatever time the officers believed to be most opportune, and the possibilities of success most promising.

July 4, 1897, will be a day long remembered by the soft coal miners of our country. A few days prior to that date, from the office of the national union of the miners, a proclamation was issued calling upon all men employed in or about the mines in the states of Illinois, Indiana, Ohio, West Virginia, Kentucky, and the western part of Pennsylvania to cease work and remain in idleness on and after Independence day; and while the miners' organization at that time num-

LEGISLATION

Columns (states/territories): U.S., Ala., Alaska, Ariz., Ark., Cal., Colo., Conn., Del., D.C., Fla., Ga., Hawaii, Idaho, Ill., Ind., Iowa, Kans., Ky., La., Md., Mass., Mich., Minn., Miss., Mo., Mont., Nebr., Nev., N.H., N.J., N.Mex., N.Y., N.C., N.Dak., Ohio, Okla., Oreg., Pa., P.R., R.I., S.C., S.Dak., Tenn., Tex., Utah, Vt., Va., Wash., W.Va., Wis., Wy.

Mine inspection:
- Inspectors to be appointed
- Inspectors to be examined before appointment
- Accidents to be reported to inspectors
- Reports to be made to inspectors
- Miners' committees to be permitted to inspect
- Plans of mines to be filed with inspectors

Employment in mines:
- Employment of women prohibited
- Employment of children prohibited
- Hours of labor limited to 8 per day
- Certain employees to be examined
- Duties of certain employees defined

Health and safety of mine employees:
- Mines to have two openings from each seam
- Mines to be adequately ventilated
- Sufficient timber for props to be on hand
- Shaft openings to have safety gates or fences
- Cable drums to have brakes and flanges
- Cages or cars to have safety catches
- Cages for passengers to be covered
- Verbal communication between top and bottom required
- Signals for cage movements prescribed
- Traveling ways at bottom of shaft required
- Shelter holes in gangways required
- Machinery to be guarded
- Abandoned openings to be closed or fenced
- Steam boilers to be regularly inspected
- Number of persons on cage limited
- Passengers prohibited on cage carrying coal
- Kind of oil for lighting prescribed
- Handling of explosives regulated
- Mine rules to be posted

Mines generating fire damp:
- Daily inspection required
- Safety lamps to be owned and cared for by operators
- Bore holes to be made in advance of workings

Protection of rights of mine workers:
- Mines to have accurate coal scales
- Weighmen to take oath of office
- Employment of check weighmen to be permitted
- Coal to be weighed before screening

States and Territories having coal mines
States and Territories having metalliferous mines

bered less than eleven thousand members, one hundred and
ten thousand men employed in the states named above threw
down their tools, and the first great successful struggle for
higher wages began. The contest continued until September
10, at which time a conference between the representatives
of the United Mine Workers of America and the owners of coal
properties was held which resulted in a partial settlement advancing the earnings of the mine workers an average of twelve
per cent. The following January, the miners and mine owners
of the central competitive coal fields, which embraces Illinois,
Indiana, Ohio, and western Pennsylvania, met in delegate convention in the city of Chicago and agreed that thereafter all
disputes as to wages and conditions of employment should be
adjusted by joint conference and conciliation rather than by
resorting to the arbitrament of industrial war. The result
was that an agreement was reached increasing the earnings of
mine workers eighteen per cent, and reducing the hours of
labor from ten to eight in the states just mentioned.

The Chicago conference of 1898 was followed by conventions in Pittsburg in 1899, Indianapolis in 1900, and Columbus in 1901. At the first two, further advances in wages and
improved conditions of employment were secured for the mine
workers; and it is a pleasure to record the cordial relations
which now exist between these two forces, which were formerly
so antagonistic. Both operators and miners concede that the
adoption of this humane and business like method of adjusting
all differences affecting conditions of employment is preferable
to the old method of strikes and lockouts, with the consequent
bitter suffering and loss of profits.

During the period in which the bituminous coal miners and
operators were working out a solution of the labor problem,
the anthracite, or hard coal miners of Pennsylvania, one hundred and forty two thousand in number, were suffering and
chafing under the most humiliating conditions of employment
conceivable. Wages were so low and employment was so
irregular that parents were compelled to take their boys from
school, sometimes when they were less than ten years of age,
and put them to work in the breakers and the mines; and this,
too, in spite of the fact that the laws of the state of Pennsyl-

vania prohibit the employment of children at the mines until they have reached the age of twelve. For many years efforts had been made to organize the mine workers of the anthracite field, but owing to the struggle to establish equitable conditions of employment in the bituminous region, the miners' union was unable to concentrate a sufficient force in the anthracite district to bring about this result. During the years 1899 and 1900 further efforts were made in this direction, but the application of the blacklist, and the extreme poverty of the mine workers (which made it impossible for them to move to other fields should they be discharged), rendered the work discouragingly slow.

About this time it became obvious to the officers of the United Mine Workers of America that it would be necessary to inaugurate an aggressive movement in order to arouse from their lethargy the thoroughly subdued workers in the anthracite coal fields. With this object in view a large force of organizers was assigned to work among the anthracite miners; and by constantly mingling with them and addressing meetings, sought to revive their hopes and rekindle in their hearts the spirit of resistance which we feared would be put to the severest test before the close of the year 1900. While this agitation among the workers was in progress, efforts were also being put forth, through the United Mine Workers, to bring about a conference of representatives of the miners and the companies which operated the railroads and the coal mines of that field. But, to our dismay, the operators, feeling sanguine that their employees would not engage in a strike should one be attempted, received our overtures with ridicule and disdain. Having no alternative but to abandon the field or engage in a strike which, if participated in by all of the producers of anthracite coal, would seriously affect the industry and commerce of the eastern and New England states—provided it should be prolonged for a period of time sufficient to consume the several million tons of coal then held in reserve by the anthracite operators—we decided upon the latter course; and on September 17, the very eve of a presidential election, the most memorable struggle between capital and labor in the industrial history of our nation began.

With an organization of only eight thousand members in that field who were obligated to cease work upon the order of the miners' union; with a people the counterpart of which it would be difficult to find in any other section of this broad land—people differing widely in religious customs and observances, with racial characteristics and old world feuds dividing them—speaking so many languages and dialects that one half scarcely knew what the other half said; yet one hundred and twelve thousand men and boys responded on the first day to the call for the strike; and this number increased day by day until, when the call for resumption of work was issued, one hundred and forty thousand were idle. These men, heretofore, had never known what it was to strike in unison; one section always working while the other fought, thus making victory improbable because those remaining at work produced enough coal to supply the market and their idle brothers were ultimately starved into submission. But in this strike they seemed to be imbued with the single idea that in the struggle they must stand or fall together, and their devotion and loyalty to the organization and the principles it espoused were almost without a parallel.

No other industrial conflict of any magnitude has been characterized by such absence of rioting; it being a fact attested by the sheriffs of the several counties that fewer arrests for lawlessness were made during the weeks from September 17 to October 29, the day on which work was resumed, than for many months previous.

The successful prosecution and happy termination of this strike—the first ever won by the anthracite mine workers—secured for them an advance of ten per cent in wages; a reduction in the price of powder and other supplies; the semi-monthly payment of wages in cash, and tacit recognition of their right to organize. Since the resumption of work, many further concessions have been obtained and the conditions of employment materially improved through the instrumentality of their organization, which now embraces within its fold practically every man and boy employed in the mining industry in the anthracite region. And—what is, possibly, of greater concern and interest to the general public—hope

and promise are held out that the same system which prevails
in the bituminous fields, through which differences are adjusted without resorting to strikes, will also be adopted by
the operators and miners in the anthracite district.

Until a comparatively recent date a careful system of
espionage on the part of the company had made the mine
worker little more than an animate machine. Prior to 1874
the miners were paid, by many of the companies, with scrip,
which was exchangeable for provisions at the company store.
The use of scrip was discontinued in 1874, but many of the
companies still retained a system whereby payment was made
in cash should the miner be so fortunate as to have anything
coming to him after the house rent, the bills for coal, for the
grocer, the butcher and the doctor, had been deducted. The
company paid the doctor an annual salary, and added the
surplus collected from the miners to its profits. The general
store was owned and operated by the company, although
usually under another name than that by which the mining
enterprise was known. In almost all cases the miners were
compelled to choose between dismissal from employment and
dealing at the company store, where prices were usually higher
than at other establishments. By these means the men were
rendered absolutely dependent upon the companies, often not
receiving pay in cash from one year's end to another, and
being deprived of all liberty of action in regard to their personal
affairs. During the progress of the anthracite strike I was
personally informed by a number of miners that they had not
received one cent of their earnings in cash for over eleven
years. But, thanks to the work and the spirit of organization
among the workers, many changes for the better have been
made in this respect during the past few years; and, although
these abuses still exist, they are much less common than formerly.

A trip through a mining town is very interesting, particularly in the anthracite field. First, most conspicuous and
most important is the breaker, or tipple; next, one notices the
long rows of two or three roomed houses owned by the company or by some enterprising capitalist who finds the alluring
disparity between outlay and income an incentive for invest-

ment in property of this character. These houses are often unpainted, and blackened by coal dust and rains; but clean and shining within, the miners' wives being, as a rule, neat and tidy housekeepers. The only method of distinguishing one house from another is by the number placed above the door of each. In many of the towns these rows contain from ten to twelve houses and are built flush with the sidewalk, having a tiny back yard where there is, oftentimes, a vegetable garden. Usually, in the larger towns, particular localities contain rows of six or seven double houses set slightly back from the walk, with a small front, side and back yard for each house; and evidences of thrift are often noticed in the vines trained above the door or over the porch which has been built by the miner on idle days. Flower beds in front and side yards, and a garden in the back, make some of these places quite attractive. Again, rows of double houses are set down in bleak and barren spots where there is not the slightest trace of the verdure which clothes the side of the mountain near by. These houses are usually built two or three feet from the ground, and under them a shelter is afforded the chicken, the dog or the goat. Many of the non-English speaking miners in the anthracite region keep goats. In the bituminous regions the miners who are able to afford it usually keep a cow, but the nature of the country in the anthracite districts, where the ground is rendered uneven by numerous cave-ins, makes it extremely perilous for cows to run at large; the nimble goat, however, is better able to avoid these dangerous places, and this, I presume, accounts for so many families owning goats.

The interior of the house of the mine worker, while barren of decoration, is usually scrupulously clean; and the few cheap knickknacks which serve as bric-a-brac evidence the desire of the wife to make home as attractive as possible upon the small sum at her command. The casual visitor is struck not only by the poor and unlovely aspect of the typical mining towns themselves, the pitiful endeavor to make the homes cheerful and comfortable, but also by the stoicism written indelibly upon the faces of the men and women one finds there. Particularly is this true of the people of the anthracite field, where there are many who might well serve as models for Millet's famous French peasants; and more than one the hopeless dejection of whose countenance and bearing brings to mind Markham's touching poem—The Man With the Hoe.

Of course, it is said by many that the mine workers are a shiftless, intemperate, illiterate lot, who are without ambition, who have no high and noble aspirations; but the many who say so do not know these people as I do; they do not pause to consider that practically all of these men and women have begun a life of drudgery at a very early age—at an age, in fact, when the children of the average American citizen are considered scarcely more than babies; that they have worked alone, away from the civilizing influence of contact with their fellow beings, under such conditions and for such weary hours that neither thought nor time remained for recreation or for study. I know them to be as a class honorable and upright in the payment of their debts; I know that lack of honesty in matters of this kind means ostracism by their neighbors; I know that during strikes it is a common occurrence for one family to divide the last bit of bread in the house with a neighbor whose supply of provisions has become exhausted; and I know that the standard of morality among them will challenge comparison with that of any other class of people in our land. In my own experience I have many times witnessed acts of such heroism and self sacrifice among them as to make the valorous deeds of our soldiers at home and abroad pale into insignificance by comparison; there are innumerable instances that can be cited in which mine workers, in the cave-ins which every now and then befall, have knowingly and willingly surrendered their lives in an effort to rescue their entombed fellow workmen.

First, the boy of eight or ten is sent to the breaker to pick the slate and other impurities from the coal which has been brought up from the mine; from there he is promoted and becomes a door boy, working in the mine; as he grows older and stronger he is advanced to the position and given the pay of a laborer; there he gains the experience which secures him a place as a miner's helper; and as he acquires skill and strength he becomes, when in the height of his manhood and vigor, a full fledged miner. If he is fortunate enough to escape the

falls of rock and coal, he may retain this position as a miner
for a number of years; but as age creeps on and he is attacked
by some of the many diseases incident to work in the mines,
he makes way for those younger and more vigorous following
him up the ladder whose summit he has reached. He then
starts on the descent, going back to become a miner's helper,
then a mine laborer, now a door boy; and when old and
decrepit, he finally returns to the breaker where he started as
a child, earning the same wages as are received by the little
urchins who work at his side.

Thus, in these few words, is told the simple story of an
anthracite miner's life in its entire course from the cradle to
the grave.

There is no incentive for ambition in the average miner's
life. He cannot rise to places of eminence and wealth; only
one in five hundred can even be given place as a foreman or
superintendent, and these are positions which few miners care
to hold. The work at the mines is wholly in charge of managers or superintendents, the chief cause for whose retention
and promotion is their ability to produce coal cheaply; and
this has been usually accomplished by depressing the earnings
of their employees, or insisting upon the performance of more
work than men are physically able to do. I am of the opinion
that the men who own the mines, those who hold the stock
in the large companies and profit by this cheapness of production, do not know the means employed to secure it. They do
not know the dangers which make a miner's life a daily sacrifice; they do not realize, as they bask in the comfortable glow
of a coal fire, that oftentimes the hearth of the man whose
labor made their comfort possible is cold and cheerless because
he cannot afford to buy enough of the coal which he has mined
to keep his wife and babies warm.

As a people we are forgetful of the fact that every convenience we enjoy, every device that enhances our material
comfort and ease, is purchased at the cost of infinite pains,
and often of actual suffering, to others. We do not remember,
when, by touching a button, the house or office is lighted or
machinery is set in motion, that men have dug in darkness to
furnish the power for the operation. We are unmindful of

the fact, when the limited express or the ocean greyhound speeds us from ocean to ocean or from land to land, that those whose labor supplies the energy by which we are able to seek health or wealth or happiness in other climes, trudge from home to mine and from mine to home, year in and year out, too poor to avail themselves of the facilities their toil has supplied; that they work below ground, scarcely seeing even the daylight beauties of the home neighborhood, with no opportunity to grasp the means of culture and refinement brought to our very doors from the old and new world through their patient efforts.

If the great, sympathetic American public could see for itself, could know as I know the sorrows and the heartaches of those who spend their lives in the coal mines of our country, I am sure that they would give their unqualified support to every effort which is being made by the organizations of labor to ameliorate the conditions under which these men work, and to secure for them wages commensurate with their hazardous employment; thus enabling them to take the little boys from the breakers and mines and place them, for a few years at least, in our schools, where they properly belong, and where they may receive their birthright of education and enjoy the sunlight so needful to their physical development. To make this great movement a success we are bending our every effort, and we look with confidence to the American people for sympathy and support, for we are firm in the belief that any action which raises the standard of our citizenship confers upon our country a measureless blessing, the benefits of which will be increasingly apparent as the years go by.

A PRACTICAL VIEW OF AMERICAN MACHINE SHOP CONDITIONS.

BY M. COKELY.

[M. Cokely has for eleven years been engaged in systemizing and organizing the work of various American shops with a view to determining costs, stopping leaks, reducing expenses, and increasing output. He was engaged as inspector with the Edison company, and as superintendent under the receiver of the Mather Electric company; was with the Jeffrey Mfg. Co., Columbus, Ohio, introducing piecework and other advanced systems; with the Falls Rivet and Machine Co. during reorganization; with Clark Bros., as superintendent; with the C. W. Hunt Co., the Payne Engine Co., the Chicago Malleable Castings Co., and the Plano Mfg. Co., as expert and superintendent. He has made economical production a study, and has an intimate acquaintance with the practical work of the shop. The following is an article from the Engineering Magazine.]

In considering the relations which should exist between employer and employee in industrial establishments, it is necessary to take into account their records and surroundings and the influence these exercise on character. The energy which the American workman has exhibited has not been equaled in any other part of the globe. This is true not only of the native born but also of the naturalized foreigner. The latter soon becomes imbued with that all pervading spirit of activity which is a recognized national American characteristic. How that spirit originated I am not prepared to explain. It may be due to race intermixture, to political or climatic conditions, or to all three; but this is positive—that the commingled races of people who have made the United States famous have emigrated to pretty much every other quarter of the earth but in no place have they developed the same characteristics or produced the same results as they have within the boundaries of the United States. Suffice it to say that this peculiarity exists and that it is nurtured by the influence of example. It is a fact that the workman has been educated to a realization of the necessity of comfort and luxury. He is a witness of it and in touch with it nearly every hour of his life. In the mansion of his next door neighbor, in the streets and in the conveyances that traverse them, he is side by side with it. As he

357

travels through the country he sits in the midst of it, and throughout his whole existence affluence is constantly before his eyes. He sees the man with whom, perhaps, years before, he labored side by side as a workman, now in the possession of wealth and honor. He sees no barriers to the possession of wealth and position except those due to his own natural defects. There is no class distinction in America so clearly defined as to limit his ambition or efforts. Say what one may, there is a civilizing influence in luxury, judiciously enjoyed. The example has been set for him. On the record sheet of human ambition and honorable success he may place his mark at a point equal to the highest ever reached by man. The record sheet from that exalted point down to the bottom is covered by marks, clear and distinct, of varying degrees of success according to the ambition or ability of the individual or the circumstances under which he labored. That is the record of the American workingman. Amid such surroundings and with such incentives his heart must be imbued with a spirit which lifts him above the plane of a mere servant or that of the workman as it is understood in Europe. The position which has been productive of such results cannot be otherwise than dignified, and to maintain that dignity he must receive sufficient remuneration for his labor. In describing the record of the workman we have practically described that of his employer, the manufacturer, because the majority of the manufacturers are nothing more or less than successful American workingmen—men in whom that spirit of activity was intensified to such a degree that they became the employer instead of the employed. While, as a bedrock principle, the workman on account of his record is entitled to the highest remuneration for his service, the manufacturer is entitled to the highest possible returns from his investment. The manner in which he has benefited science by his fearless acceptance of new principles—the glory which he has secured for his country by his indefatigable efforts and the daring of his enterprise—all this and much more to his credit entitles him to every consideration and respect. But in addition to this he possesses one more virtue which shines clear and brilliant above all others; that is the generous spirit in which he reaches down and grasps the hand of the ambitious, thinking workman. There is the keynote to American industrial success. It is this spirit which has, to a great extent, nullified whatever evil there might be in the influence of overzealous labor unions. In using the brains of his workmen to aid him, he has stimulated their inventive genius, encouraged their ambition, and inspired them with that feeling of self reliance that brings to the surface that which is best in man.

While man's labor remains a purchasable commodity, there will always be conflicts between labor and capital, and for the person who can suggest some means by which these two elements can be brought sufficiently close together to prevent misunderstandings by viewing each other's contentions in the pure light of reason, there is no reward too great. In the pursuit of that object the employer should lead the way by managing his business in such a manner that he can afford to allow his workmen the highest remuneration for their labor. It is not a very pleasing sight, even for a workman, to see his employer's money squandered around the factory while he is pinched to supply it.

Looking at them as employer and employed, the manufacturer and his assistant, both animated by a spirit of justice and having in view one common ideal—that of national industrial success—let us follow them into the factory and see how it is possible to realize their ideal with the least amount of friction. The whole question of their relations hinges on the cost of production. As a result of their activity, the United States find themselves occupying a position in the industrial world to maintain which they must produce more cheaply than they have ever done before. Production has so far exceeded the requirements for home consumption that they are compelled to go into the foreign markets with their product and meet the foreign manufacturer on his own ground. Having once started in this direction they are compelled to continue or suffer an industrial depression. This is a point which should be brought home to the American workman so that he may understand the circumstances under which his employer is working and regulate his demands accordingly.

As before stated, the controlling question is simply one of cheap production, and the capitalist has very wisely decided to accomplish that object by curtailing expenses at the general expense end first. By the consolidation of business interests a much lower ratio of general expense results, consequently less necessity for reducing workmen's wages in order to meet competition successfully in foreign markets. Workers' wages should be the last thing to be touched unless they are glaringly out of proportion. Every item of general expense should be so classified as to permit of the closest scrutiny at all times in order to detect excessive waste and to determine whether changes in methods and systems cannot be effected and greater economy practiced.

The next question to receive attention is that of engineering. If the product is machinery, is the design such as will admit of the least amount of outlay in labor and material in its production? Can a cheaper grade of material be used in certain unimportant parts? Can it be arranged for a less amount of finished surface, a less number of operations, and a less amount of handling and transferring? Can it be reduced in weight? Can it be so designed as to permit of being finished on a more simple grade of machine tools? In a word, has everything possible been done in designing that machinery to permit of the lowest possible cost of production without impairing either its artistic value, its durability, or its general efficiency?

If so, then take up the question of tools, appliances, and facilities generally. Are the machine tools such as will give the greatest possible output, or will it pay to install special tools? If the product is a specialty, has the question of small special tools, such as jigs, templets, gauges, punches, dies, and attachments, by which production is promoted, been considered? Is the best quality of tool steel used for cutting tools? Is it such a grade as will stand the highest cutting speed, or is a cheap grade in use which will stand a speed of only thirty or forty feet per minute, while a steel can be bought in the open market that will stand eighty or a hundred, and in some cases more? Has the work been classified according to the skill required to perform it, and judiciously distributed among the tools on which it can be done by the cheaper grade of labor? Has the labor properly been classified according to the skill required on the work on which it is engaged, or are we using skilled mechanics on work that should be done by handy men or boys? There is hardly anything around a factory so destructive to profits as the employment of skilled mechanics on work that requires little more than muscular effort to perform; besides, it is an injustice to a large class of workmen who, perhaps through no fault of their own, have not had an opportunity to learn a trade and become skilled. It is my firm conviction that if a man has been skilled to that pitch of perfection where he considers himself above and beyond the reach of the common laborer, he should be employed, as far as possible, only on work worthy of his skill. We can appreciate the pride, if not the judgment of the moulders on this point when as a rule they refuse to operate moulding machines, considering it beneath their dignity.

Unfortunately, the same high sense of honor does not exist among the machinists. There is no reason why a laborer should not operate a machine tool so long as the work to be done requires little or no skill. It is not the machine a man operates that makes him a mechanic, but the skill required in the work that he performs. My sympathies are with the laborer who must live and be a respectable citizen on a dollar and a half or less a day. Fortunately, through the invention of automatic and semi-automatic machinery and the standardization and specialization of product, avenues have been created through which the common laborer of thirty or forty years ago has advanced himself to a higher position in the industrial world and what is left of the place he vacated is now occupied by what is considered an element of inferior ability from continental Europe. The common laborer of old is the handy man of to-day, and he is just as essential as the skilled mechanic. We can find him through most American factories doing much of the work once done by the old all around mechanic; and with the improved facilities which he uses he is doing it not only as well, but in greater abundance, thus elevating his own position as a workman and assisting his employer to bring his product within the reach of a greater number of consumers.

There is much to be gained by a judicious distribution of the work among the tools and a proper classification and organization of the help. Their movements also should receive close attention. In walking through a shop, it takes but a glance of the practiced eye to determine the actual condition of affairs in every department, and the amount that is being lost through apathy. Fortunate is the manager who from a superficial observation can detect this and see whether tools are operated to their full capacity or whether apparent activity is feigned. There is no mistaking the eager, active, animating spirit that is visible in a well governed factory—a factory in which every man knows his duty and understands that he will be held strictly responsible for the faithful performance of it.

It is unfortunate that there should be such a lack of uniformity in the task required for a day's work. What is considered a day's work in one place is frequently but a half day's work in another. This condition exists not only between different factories but often between departments of the same factory, thus producing a very bad influence on the help. While it seems impossible to improve this condition in so far as it relates to the different factories, with the more perfect organization of the manufacturers something might be done in that direction. In line with this comes the question of discipline and the observance of factory rules. Too often this refers to the shops only. No department should be exempt. Discipline, like charity, should begin at home and the office is the place to start it, as that department should serve as a model for all others. Rules of discipline should be as few as possible, but there should be a strict enforcement of those few. In some shops notices are posted at every turn notifying the help that unless they do, or do not do, so-and-so they will be immediately discharged. It is my experience that in places where notices carrying this terrifying threat are most numerous, discipline is most lax, because the threat is seldom carried out. A plain statement of what is required of employees and an example made of the first deliberate violation will be much more effective. Less threats and more dismissals will be much more beneficial, because the help will soon realize that when a rule is issued it is going to be enforced, and they will govern themselves accordingly. Discipline should not be administered so as to make men feel as though they were criminals by the enforcement of useless irritating restrictions, but rather to inspire them with a knowledge of that conduct which is necessary to the success of their employer's business.

Next in order is the prevention of waste in material, supplies, etc., and to govern this requires a knowledge of the most modern practice. What is frequently considered as waste in one factory is a source of revenue in another. Great care should be exercised not only in the purchase of material in such form, quantity, and quality, as will give the most economical results, but in the final disposition of the scrap and refuse generally. In the foundry, facilities for extracting the shot from the cupola dump have been made so complete that the operation is one of the best paying features about that department, and in tests which I witnessed when the shot thus secured was melted without any mixture of pig, a very desirable grade of iron was obtained. Still we find facilities for accomplishing this in very limited use. Refuse from all other departments should receive the same close attention. The use, or rather the abuse, of supplies is often the source of considerable leakage. In fact, leaks are likely to occur anywhere along the line, both in material and labor, and the best way to guard against them is to know where to look for them.

As an evidence of what can be accomplished in this direction I may cite a case in a factory with which I was connected. In the first department to receive attention on the lines indicated in the foregoing, after a very slight effort, and that under unfavorable circumstances, a reduction in the labor cost of the product amounting to nearly 18 per cent was realized, without any diminution in the average earnings of the help, but rather an increase. This was in a department which was considered modern in most respects, and as it employed several hundred men, largely mechanics earning good wages, it can be seen what such a saving amounted to in a year. All other departments were treated in the same manner and a saving realized according to the condition in which they were found. The means by which the minimum cost of production can be reached are numerous and depend largely, of course, on the line of manufacture in which one is engaged; but perfect system and organization backed by good executive ability are absolutely necessary. When the employer has got his business so arranged that all sources of profit or loss are under perfect control, he will be in a position to decide whether he can afford to grant a demand for an increase of wages, or must ask for a reduction. The chances are, however, that when his business is in that condition it will not be necessary to ask for a reduction in order to meet competition, excepting during periods of extreme industrial depression. In order to avoid the necessity of a reduction, the workman should not murmur if he is requested to produce a good day's work in order to insure a good day's pay. He must remember that he is no more entitled to extraordinary remuneration than his employer is to extraordinary profits, and his co-operation is necessary to the realization of both. If he follows the inclination of his union to measure his service by European standards, he must be prepared to accept European conditions; for he can no more expect an American day's pay for a European day's work than his employer can expect an American day's work for a European day's pay—and in order to insure that advantage to his employer by which he can accord him that substantial recognition to which his record and achievements entitles him he must, in the language of the shops, toe the mark in line and harmony with his employer.

MACHINERY AND LABOR.

BY HENRY WHITE.

[Henry White, general secretary United Garment Workers of America; born in Baltimore, May 21, 1866; graduated from the public schools in New York; served apprenticeship to trade of clothing cutter; journeyman at 18; organized a secession movement which resulted in the organization of the United Garment Workers of America, affiliated with the American Federation of Labor; general officer since organization, and general secretary since 1896; editor the Garment Worker, and writer of many articles on the labor question.]

This subject is one which involves the whole industrial problem. It is the complexity of conditions due to the introduction of machinery which has caused the wide differences of opinion upon the question of wealth distribution. Under the simpler methods of industry the manner in which the proceeds of labor were divided was readily understood; to-day, however, the system is so highly organized that there is much confusion as to its operation. The perplexity is so great that many who see in labor saving inventions some malign purpose, and others again who discern that any means which enhances the productiveness of labor must benefit mankind, are unable to comprehend the manner by which that result is effected. The habit of judging the operations of so complex a system by the effect upon special interests instead of viewing it as a whole, accounts for the common misconception regarding the function of machinery.

If people were to consider how meager would be the rewards of toil without the aid of machinery, how costly the necessities of life, and how small the purchasing power of the laborer, its uses would soon become apparent. The confusion is heightened by the dual relation which a person occupies as a producer and as a consumer. As a consumer he benefits almost at once by every saving in effort, while as a producer his means of a livelihood may in consequence be threatened. The laborers thrown out of work by a machine, or even the merchant forced out of business through some combination, cannot be expected to appreciate the beneficence of such economy. In both cases their horizon is limited to their own means of a livelihood.   When a person finds his occupation suddenly gone, it outweighs all other considerations; and unmindful of the benefits he may have received from similar economies in other trades, inventions to him seem a curse. The rewards of the particular invention which distresses him go to the body of consumers and he only shares indirectly as one of them.   In the case of the wage workers the gain is not evident, as it is with the manufacturer who first utilizes an invention, and consequently their views on the subject will differ correspondingly.   It is regrettable that even the temporary disadvantages of industrial progress should fall heavily upon some to the advantage of others, but it is as unavoidable as friction is to motion.   The suffering can be mitigated only in proportion as our knowledge of the methods of industry increases, by recognizing the inevitableness of the changes and preparing to meet them.

Economic laws, like the laws of nature, admit of no exceptions.   Were discriminations possible the consequences would make the present hardships seem nothing in comparison.   In fact, society would quickly disintegrate and revert to its primitive state.   If society had to wait for the sanction of every person before a forward step could be taken it would never start.   In the process of adjustment and readjustment which progress implies, it is unavoidable that some have to be forced out of old grooves and made to fit into new ones. It is this adaptability to change which characterizes modern enterprise; this willingness to suffer immediate discomforts for the achievement of larger ends.

The general confusion as to the service rendered by machinery is not strange considering the absurd notions which are rife regarding the rudiments of social economy. No distinction is usually made between useful and useless labor.   There is supposed to be only a given amount of work to be done, and hence the less each one does the more jobs there will be to go around.   If wealth be wasted or destroyed, it will in some mysterious manner be replaced.   The destruction of property by fire or flood is regarded with complacency by those not directly affected, upon the supposition that more work is thereby provided, without taking into account that the wealth required to replace it must be diverted from some productive use. The spending or circulating of money is equivalent to creating wealth. Luxury is looked upon with more favor than frugality, and it is even thought that gambling benefits a community as much as industry because the fortunate ones spend freely, and the misery which it begets is lost sight of in contemplation of the profits of a few. With such erroneous ideas entertained even by educated people, it is apparent why the complex operations of our industrial system are so slightly understood. The expansion of industry which follows labor saving devices, the creation of new industries and the consequent replacing of those displaced is unintelligible to all save those that comprehend economic principles. In addition to the popular misconceptions of the subject, there are historic causes which have created this antipathy to machinery. During the transition from the domestic to the factory system in England, machinery became a club to subjugate the laborer. Untutored, unorganized, without any resisting power, the former independent artisan, now a factory hand, was placed in brutal competition with his fellows, and every invention only served to add to his helplessness. The plight of the English laborers at that time abundantly shows that there are circumstances in which the wealth of a nation may increase tremendously, the productive power of labor multiply many fold, while the workers on the other hand become impoverished and brutalized. Mill was of the opinion that machinery had not benefited the working class, but happily, since the time in which he wrote, education and organization, two indispensable factors in their advancement, have come to their aid. An upward trend has in consequence taken place, and the stimulus which it has given will make a relapse, owing to the advances in sanitary science, as improbable as another visitation of a plague. Where the workers have succeeded in acquiring some independence, in raising their standard of living, machinery, despite the drawbacks described, has undoubtedly become a potent factor in the elevation of their class.

Under a collective system the immediate benefits which would be derived by each individual through labor saving inventions are its chief merit, but to compare the good features of an imaginary social system with the disadvantages of the existing one is not an easy task. It can, however, be shown that this desired co-operative principle actually does work out at the present time in a rough way by the distribution of the benefits of inventions throughout society and that there are possibilities for a more perfect application of it.

As to the workers' share in production, Karl Marx in his incisive analysis comes to the conclusion that the value of commodities is based upon the labor cost plus the profits of the capitalist and in that he is in accord with the authorities upon social science since Adam Smith. He deduces from that, that labor alone represents the actual wealth which is exploited for profit by the capitalist and that the very capital invested was previously appropriated from the laborer. Granting this conclusion, Marx should have made allowance for the competition between capitalists by which the price of commodities is kept within certain limits and the benefits of cheaper production are given to the consumers. In the cases Marx deals with, cheaper production unfortunately did not only mean more economical methods, but lower wages and long hours and the sacrifice of the worker, while the consumer represented someone else than the operative, who barely subsisted on his pittance. Without the ability to purchase the goods he produced, England had to dispose of in foreign markets that which should have been consumed at home, always the best market. Her chief dependence being upon outside markets, everything had to be subordinated to cheaper production, no matter how obtained.

Concerning the attitude of trades unions upon the question of machinery, the membership being composed of men with the usual abilities, their views do not materially differ from others. Having, however, the benefits of an education derived from a close study of economic problems and an experience which has helped them form broader opinions, they are gradually reconciling themselves to machinery. As for example the action taken at the convention of the American Federation of Labor held at Scranton. In a resolution introduced by the delegates of the Cigar Makers' International union requesting that a certain firm be declared unfair, there was reference to a cigar making machine used in the shop of this employer. Although the machine was mentioned as an evidence only of the inferiority of the product of the concern, a vigorous objection was at once raised by the delegates against any mention of the use of machinery by the firm. In the debate which followed, it was argued that the convention could not afford to go on record as against labor saving devices and that any attempt to oppose them would prove futile. The objectionable words were stricken out by a decisive vote. As to what action the convention would have taken if the delegates had thought it possible to suppress the machine is a question. The decision of the convention however, has brought the movement to a point in which the members will be enabled to take a more liberal and complete view of the subject, and realize that the limitation of work is not only impolitic, but that by increasing their capacities the opportunity is afforded for them to insist upon a fair share in the larger product. The British unions have not advanced in that respect as far as the American unions because the habits of the working people there are more set, but circumstances have also changed very much their attitude toward machinery.

The Typographical union is a notable example of a union which accepted a revolutionizing invention as being inevitable, and thus succeeded in securing a rate of wages for the operators considerably in excess of that received by the hand compositors. An officer of the New York union estimates that each linotype machine introduced into the newspaper offices displaced three men, and that within three years, owing to the increase in the size of the newspapers and the larger demand for printed matter which it encouraged, the men laid off have been re-employed, and that to-day the pay rolls even exceed the former figure. This machine has also had the effect of elevating the standards of the craft, owing to the higher skill and education required. The competition among the employers is such that profits are reduced to a minimum, the public therefore receiving the full benefit of the improvement.

In the building trades, similar results are also noted. Improved methods have led to a prodigious expansion in building operations. The laborer's work is now largely done by mechanical means, and parts of a structure, such as the trimmings, are made in factories and are only fitted together upon the premises. The subdividing of the work is carried on to an extent that a number of contractors, each performing a distinct function, co-operate in the completion of a single building. When this specializing began and the ingenious hod-hoisting device made it unnecessary for men to make beasts of burden of themselves, a general alarm was created over the prospect of great numbers of workmen being thrown out of employment. To-day a far greater number of men are steadily employed in this fundamental industry than at any time in its history.

Examples of this kind can be cited indefinitely to demonstrate the larger results which flow from greater economy in effort. Allowances are seldom made for the enterprises which could not be carried on at all were it not for labor saving methods.

The lowering of the cost of commodities enables the average person to indulge in what were formerly considered luxuries, and by this encourages the development of new industries. The tendency under the influence of machinery is for industry to spread out fan shape, ever widening as the distance from the starting point increases. Were it not for the limitations set by the purchasing capacity of the people and the periodical disarrangements or panics which occur as a result of what is conveniently termed overproduction, there would be no check. To fear a surfeit of wealth seems absurd considering the needs of the average person. What is meant by overproduction is the inability to buy what has been produced.

Russia with her immense population is unable to consume the products of her few mills, while in the United States, where the efficiency of labor is higher than anywhere else and is being increased at a marvelous rate, not to speak of the half million aliens absorbed every year, the percentage of unemployed is lower than it has been for years, and even less than during the earlier part of our history when manufacturing was in its infancy.

To increase the purchasing capacity of the people either by higher wages or cheaper products is to reduce the surplus and maintain an equilibrium, hence the economic value of higher standards of living. Production cannot be greater than the ability of the average person to consume, any more than water can rise higher than its source, therefore increased production must be accompanied by the same increase in consumption, if normal conditions are to be maintained. No matter to what extent machinery, division of labor or economy in management may be perfected theoretically, the demand for labor ought not to be diminished. The eight hour work is advocated by many, not because of the personal benefit to the workman, but upon the same grounds that they would favor the curtailment of production, in the belief that it would increase the number of the employed. By decreasing the average amount of work done in order that it may be distributed more evenly may accomplish that object temporarily, but if generally practiced would decrease the demand for work through the increase of the price of the commodity.

It is doubtful if workmen in a particular craft have ever succeeded for a length of time in erecting a wall around themselves and preventing as many extra men as could be employed from getting in if the emoluments were sufficient. So even if it were possible to so restrict work as to create a scarcity of workmen, this pressure from without would prove irresistible and the normal level would be maintained. If on the contrary a lack of work would make a number of workmen superfluous, there would be a tendency for them to find their way into growing occupations. Union regulations, such as apprenticeship rules, can and do prevent undue crowding into a trade owing to a sudden and temporary demand which would prove highly injurious unless checked, for it would serve to break down standards upheld by the union. Through such means an assimilation of those entering the trade is gradually accomplished.

Unions have been frequently charged with trying to restrict output. The same accusation has also with equal effect been made against industrial combinations for seeking to create an artificial scarcity. In many cases where unions endeavor to prevent rush or driving work injurious to the worker, they have been accused of limiting work. Such restrictions can be easily defended. That labor organizations have in some instances attempted to prevent the use of labor saving appliances there can be no question considering the prevailing ideas on the subject, and organized workmen can give force to their opposition, but that such is the policy of labor movement is far from fact as I have just illustrated. The opposition to labor saving methods is not confined to workmen alone, for employers will rail against competitors able to give better service for less cost. The same resentment at being forced out of a settled occupation is entertained by all.

The actual injury done by machinery is caused by the suddenness of the changes that result. Since there could be no way of regulating inventive genius, and the incentives for using improvements will remain as great, the rational and the only way to meet them is by preparation. The working class suffers most because it is less able to accommodate itself to new situations. The rising generation should be better equipped with a general knowledge of mechanics, and taught how to handle tools with skill. Such a training would undoubtedly relieve the difficulty and it could only be adequately supplied by the public schools. The results would be to increase the independence of workmen, as they would not then rely upon a small division of a trade or upon a single employer. Independence and higher wages go together. Unskilled laborers in some cases learn more than skilled mechanics for the reason that workmen trained only in one craft are usually unfitted for other work, while those accustomed to being thrown upon their own resources are more adaptable.

In the case of the aged workman the situation is especially hard, as he cannot find any place in an industrial system in which alertness counts for more than skill. He cannot profit by accumulated experiences as others do. It is the tragic side of the question, this grievous predicament of the worker who has spent his energies adding to the nation's wealth. It can and ought to be overcome, not by any system of alms giving which must always prove inadequate, not by retiring him to idleness, but by keeping him employed at such work as his long training and peculiar abilities fit him for. As his earning power declines at a certain period, some system of insurance could supply the deficiency.

In respect to the material advantages of machinery, it surely has enlarged the capacities of the people and multiplied their opportunities. The possibilities are such as to make the mind tremble in anticipation. It is the agency which alone can raise wages, reduce the working time and enhance the buying power of money—a threefold gain.

The feeling against machinery will not cease until the workman profits more directly as a producer as well as a consumer, until he is treated as a human being and not as a mere animated tool, until he becomes more than a tender, an incident in production. The human element must become more evident and the toiler made to feel his partnership. The true mission of machinery would then be revealed to all as the only means which liberate man from drudgery, increase his control over nature and provide the leisure essential to a higher culture.

One of the acknowledged evils of machinery is the exploitation of child labor which usually follows its introduction. Such was the case in England, and we find it repeated to-day in the new industrial districts of the south. In such industries where the repetition of a small mechanical process enables child labor to be employed, the temptation to take advantage of the opportunity is great; for children have no rights to assert, no wage scale to uphold or working time to protect. In that respect child labor is akin to slave labor. It must be added for fairness that the capitalists utilizing such opportunities are not alone to blame, for shortsighted and grasping parents often drive their children into the mills because of the paltry sum which can be added to the family income, and in time they get into the habit of depending upon the pittance purchased at so terrible a price.

The inducement of a plentiful supply of cheap labor is also held out to capitalists by small communities as a means of persuading them to locate factories in their neighborhood. These are the two chief obstacles in the way of reform. In course of time, however, as the consequences become more evident and the exultation over the establishment of a new factory wears off, the public conscience revolts against this debasement of the helpless children and the law is eventually evoked to suppress the evil. The strenuous efforts being made in the south upon the part of the labor organizations and sympathizers to enact protective laws lead us to hope that we will at least be spared the dreadful experiences of England during the first half century of the factory system.

WOMAN'S PLACE IN INDUSTRIAL AND LABOR ORGANIZATIONS.

BY SOPHIE YUDELSON.

[Sophie Yudelson, labor leader and charity worker; has had a prominent part in the organization of the women of New York city into labor unions, especially the garment workers; latterly she has been engaged as a charity worker with the various societies of organized charity in New York; her experience has been such as make her views as expressed below worthy of consideration.]

Woman's status throughout the civilized world is different now from what it has been. This difference is not due to the special physical or mental merits suddenly discovered in her. And it is not because of her so-called increased industrial activity. From time immemorial woman has been an industrial producer. We have no accounts of the battles she has fought and won, no record of her inventions, discoveries, or the creation of new ideas and ideals, but nearly every parent industry calls her mother. As far as primitive history can be reconstructed, it was she who originated and fostered the peaceful arts of life. She it was who discovered the ability of labor. She, the slave before the slave existed, laid the foundation of civilization, but, as regards her present industrial contributions, she compares most favorably with the woman of old. In savage or barbarian society as food bringer, weaver, shin dresser, potter, and burden bearer, she was the acknowledged economic factor. In the words of a Chippewayan chief, "Women are made to labor, one of them can carry or haul as much as two men can do. They also pitch our tents, make and mend our clothing. . . . and in fact, there is no such thing as traveling any considerable distance in this country without their assistance."

In Greece and Rome woman's function as slave or supervisor of slaves was generally recognized. This is true all through the mediæval ages. Her duties were so manifold that a conscientious housewife had to be at her post from early in the morning till late at night to fulfill them, and even then it was only possible to do so with the help of her daughters. She had to spin, weave, and bleach, to make all the linen and clothes, to boil soap and make candles and brew beer. In addition to these occupations she frequently had to work in the fields and in the garden and to attend to the poultry and cattle. In short, she was a veritable Cinderella, and her solitary recreation was going to church on Sunday.

While woman's labor was thus very much in demand hitherto, at present, when organized industry displaces domestic work, men would only be too glad to do away with her industrial activity altogether. They claim the ability to produce all the necessaries of life conducive even to a higher standard of living than is possible at a time when women competitors crowd the factories, shops, offices, schools, and so forth.

Woman's present status is not due to her increased physical, mental, or industrial importance as compared with that of man. Is it due to his increased chivalry, charity, generosity, liberality, or effeminacy? Perhaps. But the majority of men, whom we cannot by any means deny to be possessed of most of those attributes, are sincerely and intensely hostile to the so-called woman's movement. They do all they possibly can to check and hinder her advance. They give, also, very plausible reasons why woman should not go beyond her sphere, determined by natural instincts, traditional, and universal custom, etc. And yet, whether or not men's claims and protests are fair, just, and expedient, the fact is that they are being respectfully ignored.

Within the last century woman has almost revolutionized society, as far as it concerns herself individually. As late as 1789 the situation of woman in France reaffirmed the triumph of the traditional idea of her inferiority and the necessary subordination. Rich or poor, women were equally removed from all public life, equally deprived of all the means to cultivate their intelligence. Those who had to earn their livelihood found it impossible, because of their ignorance. In England, the publication of the Vindication of the Rights of Woman (1792), brought upon the author torrents of the vilest abuse. She was denounced as a social outcast. A philoso-

PROPORTION OF MALES AND FEMALES IN EACH CLASS OF OCCUPATIONS
AND IN CERTAIN OCCUPATION GROUP

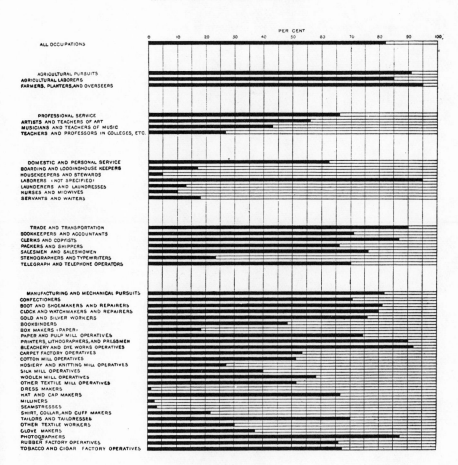

PER CENT

0   10   20   30   40   50   60   70   80   90   100

ALL OCCUPATIONS

AGRICULTURAL PURSUITS
AGRICULTURAL LABORERS
FARMERS, PLANTERS,AND OVERSEERS

PROFESSIONAL SERVICE
ARTISTS AND TEACHERS OF ART
MUSICIANS AND TEACHERS OF MUSIC
TEACHERS AND PROFESSORS IN COLLEGES, ETC.

DOMESTIC AND PERSONAL SERVICE
BOARDING AND LODGINGHOUSE KEEPERS
HOUSEKEEPERS AND STEWARDS
LABORERS (NOT SPECIFIED)
LAUNDERERS AND LAUNDRESSES
NURSES AND MIDWIVES
SERVANTS AND WAITERS

TRADE AND TRANSPORTATION
BOOKKEEPERS AND ACCOUNTANTS
CLERKS AND COPYISTS
PACKERS AND SHIPPERS
SALESMEN AND SALESWOMEN
STENOGRAPHERS AND TYPEWRITERS
TELEGRAPH AND TELEPHONE OPERATORS

MANUFACTURING AND MECHANICAL PURSUITS
CONFECTIONERS
BOOT AND SHOEMAKERS AND REPAIRERS
CLOCK AND WATCHMAKERS AND REPAIRERS
GOLD AND SILVER WORKERS
BOOKBINDERS
BOX MAKERS (PAPER)
PAPER AND PULP MILL OPERATIVES
PRINTERS, LITHOGRAPHERS,AND PRESSMEN
BLEACHERY AND DYE WORKS OPERATIVES
CARPET FACTORY OPERATIVES
COTTON MILL OPERATIVES
HOSIERY AND KNITTING MILL OPERATIVES
SILK MILL OPERATIVES
WOOLEN MILL OPERATIVES
OTHER TEXTILE MILL OPERATIVES
DRESS MAKERS
HAT AND CAP MAKERS
MILLINERS
SEAMSTRESSES
SHIRT, COLLAR,AND CUFF MAKERS
TAILORS AND TAILORESSES
OTHER TEXTILE WORKERS
GLOVE MAKERS
PHOTOGRAPHERS
RUBBER FACTORY OPERATIVES
TOBACCO AND CIGAR FACTORY OPERATIVES

▓ MALES   ▢ FEMALES

phizing serpent, Horace Walpole politely called her. In the United States up to 1848 the condition of married women under the law was nearly as degraded as that of the slave on the plantation. To-day, the industrial, educational, professional, social, legal, every one except the political, status of woman in those countries is surprisingly high.

This great and rapid change cannot, of course, be accounted for by any single reason. Ages of human experience in theory and practice were necessary to enable both men and women not only to develop, but also to accept, the new condition. As in all other movements in human history, the various influences and causes leading to a great social upheaval combine ultimately into one great force or principle, which becomes the moving spirit in transforming an entire social system, so in the woman's movement the same law prevailed. Woman had early learned to labor and to wait. But when the time had come for the recognition of the feminine element in the progress of civilization, without concert of action, unknown to each other in every civilized country, she began, directly or indirectly, to demand a broader sphere, direct representation in society and the state. Lady Montague, Abigail Smith Adams, Mary Wolstoncraft, Harriet Martineau, Madame de Staël, Madame Rolland, George Sand, Mme. D'Herricourt, Margaret Fuller, Elizabeth C. Stanton, and others, in as many different ways, demanded the same thing. Aware of the necessity and the rightness of this demand, woman has taken her cause in her own hands. And, whether or not men approve of it, whether or not her personal happiness is thereby increased, woman is bound to demand her rights, and public opinion must sanction it. The condition in the modern organization of society makes it unavoidable.

The argument for a woman's sphere may continue to be advocated by a certain type of men and women, too, but the question itself becomes less important as society conceives its raison d'être to be neither military nor religious, nor any other purpose but the well being of its constituent, individual members. In a democratic society of this kind, where individuals have their choice in selecting vocations and the power to determine social values, they will naturally demand and receive their desired place in society. We see this idea realizing itself in the growing demands and gains of men since they became independent individuals, instead of being the property of or belonging to a state, an individual or a group of individuals. As long as men fought or worked for a chief, a king, an emperor, a lord on earth, or served professionally a king in heaven, they also stood in successive grades of subordination. For it was not society, including themselves, that determined men's position in the world. L'état, c'est moi is the well known motto of kings, and the same is carried out in the hierarchy of the church. By the grace of the Lord, the king is a man, high or low. Similar was the case of woman, but, of course, in a more complex form, since she was a subject's subject as well as an object of his emotions. As long as the father or husband was the sole employer, there could be no question of social remuneration. A woman worked for a private man who paid her in kind, according to the dictates of his caprice, finer sentiments, or reasonableness. There was practically no society or state for her apart from the man she happened to belong to. She did not work for society, and, therefore, had no place in it, except as a man's property or protégé. In the exceptional cases, where she was supposed to serve the state, as in Sparta, and in Plato's republic, she was given a very high position.

But as soon as woman entered the factory, she became not only a social producer, but also an independent worker, i.e., her work had to be paid for at a definite rate, otherwise she could leave one employer for another. She now came into contact, moreover, with a new order of man, the strange employer who was emotionally indifferent to her, who had no claims over her, either as a father, husband, or master, except as a wage payer. He had no special reason to suppress or subject her. Individual skill had to be acknowledged. Of course, he met a very humble, submissive, ignorant, non-resisting creature, and he took full advantage of these feminine virtues in cutting down her wages to the lowest point possible. The mass of women had neither power nor wish to protest, and thus the few traces we find of their earliest connection with labor show us that they accepted a bare subsistence as all to which they were entitled, and were grateful if they escaped the beating which the lower order of Englishmen still regards it as his right to give. The employers' cruel treatment of women and their followers, the children, the conflict between the employers and the workingmen over woman's employment, and the fact that women were now social producers, forced society to interfere in their behalf by means of legislation.

On the other hand, since the industrial revolution has taken place, the state, in the progressive countries, is ever more assuming the characteristics of an industrial organization. We may call it a limited monarchy, a republic, or a political democracy; but its essential, its dominant interests are industry, and its concomitants, trade and commerce on an international scale. In their external relations the leading modern states are bent upon extending their economic activities through treaty right and acquisition of territory as markets. Internally their legislatures are largely busying themselves with the adjustment or the regulation of economic interests. The past twenty five years has been a period of incessant activity by legislatures and courts in prescribing the duties and limiting the powers and privileges of railway and express companies, telegraph companies, industrial combinations, and trusts. The warrior and the clergyman are still present. But military force is a last resort, when other diplomatic means fail to secure commercial privileges; whereas, the church, incorporated religion, is a private affair, which may or may not be supported by individuals or groups of individuals. The captain of industry and the ethical teacher are gradually taking the place of the soldier and the theological teacher, respectively.

Both have a place for woman's activity. One has given her a chance to become economically independent, the other, the moral motive that makes for largeness of conscious life, the belief that many things can be made better than they are at present, and that life in many ways can be made more desirable.

The conditions in modern society favorable to a rise of woman's status are chiefly these: The opportunities for eco-

nomic independence and direct service to society; the chances
that man, the educator, the employer, and the legislator, may
judge her rationally instead of emotionally, as heretofore the
father and the husband did; the decreasing importance of
man as a military power, thus in a sense equalizing the social
value of men and women; and the modern ethics advocating
an increase of human happiness in this world rather than in
some other one. Here woman is especially fit to do something.

Economic writers generally explain woman's entrance
into industry as a wonder of the age. Machinery, necessity,
starvation, or its extreme opposite, love of luxury, are given
as chief causes. The fact that woman is only following her
old pursuits while sharing in the general expansion of industry,
is rarely, if ever, emphasized. She is regarded as usurping
man's place, whereas, in reality, the spirit of the living creature in the wheels of machinery is the genius of industrialism,
originated and fostered by women. What this industrial age
has effected is not woman's entrance into industry, but the
social recognition that woman is an independent economic
factor as distinguished from a domestic worker. Writes
Carroll D. Wright: "It cannot be said that women and children constituted an economic factor during the colonial days.
Their labor was not in demand, except in a domestic sense,
to any great extent. But their (women's) more extended
employment as independent wage workers dates practically
from the period between 1815 to 1830.

"They followed the textile industries from the household
into the factories, and the consolidation of industry in large
establishments instead of small individual shops, broadened
the field and gave women opportunities of entering independently in the gainful pursuits . . . . which they gladly embraced." Under the new conditions, "It is evident," says John
A. Hobson, "that many forces are at work which tend to equalize the productivity of men and women in industry, the evolution of machinery adapted to the weaker physique of women;
the breakdown of customs excluding women from many occupations; the growth of restrictions upon male adult labor
with regard to their working day, etc., correspondent with

those placed upon women; improved mobility of woman's labor by cheaper and more facile transport in large cities; the recognition of a growing number of women that matrimony is not the only livelihood open to them, but that an industrial life is preferable and possible."

The proof of the economic value of woman's economic productivity is undoubtedly given by the fact that their numbers in all industries are steadily increasing. If their work did not pay, employers would certainly not admit them. In England, according to Mr. Hobson, during the half century 1841 and 1891, the number of women engaged in manufactures has increased by 221 per cent, while that of men increased by 53 per cent. But the movement, he adds, is by no means peculiar to the textile and dress industries, which may appear specially adapted to the faculties of women. Wherever women have got a firm footing in a manufacture, a similar movement is traceable; the relative rate of increase in the employment of women exceeds that of men, even where the numbers of the latter do not show an absolute decline. Such industries are wood, furniture, and carriages; painting and bookbinding; paper, floor cloths, feathers, leather, glues; food, drink, smoking; earthenware, machinery, tools. Women have also obtained employment in connection with other industries, which are still in the main male industries, and in which no women, or very few, were engaged in 1841. Such are fuel, gas, chemicals; watches, instruments, toys. The only group of machine industries in which their numbers have not increased more rapidly than those of men since 1851, are the metal industries. Over some of these, however, they are obtaining an increased hold. In the more mechanical portions of the growing cycle of industry, hollow ware, and in certain departments of the watchmaking trade, they are ousting male labor, executing with machinery the work formerly done by male hand workers.

The following table, taken from the twelfth census of the United States, shows the general progress of American women in all gainful occupations, since 1880, as compared with that of men:

	Number.	Per Cent.	Number.	Per Cent.	Number.	Per Cent.
All Occupations.						
Males......................	23,754,205	100	18,821,090	100	14,744,942	100
Females....................	5,319,912	100	3,914,571	100	2,647,157	100
Agricultural Pursuits.						
Males......................	9,404,429	39.6	7,887,842	41.9	7,119,365	48.3
Females...................	977,336	18.4	678,884	17.3	594,510	22.5
Professional Service.						
Males......................	828,163	3.5	632,646	3.4	425,947	2.9
Females....................	430,576	8.1	311,687	8.0	177,255	6.7
Domestic and Personal Service.						
Males	3,485,208	14.7	2,553,161	13.6	2,242,309	15.2
Females	2,895,449	39.4	1,667,651	42.6	1,181,506	44.6
Trade Transportation.						
Males.....................	4,263,617	17.9	3,097,701	16.4	1,803,629	12.2
Females...................	503,397	9.4	228,421	5.8	62,852	2.4
Manuf. and Mechan. Pursuits.						
Males......................	5,772,788	24.3	4,650,540	24.7	3,153,692	21.4
Females....................	1,313,204	24.7	1,027,928	26.3	631,834	23.8

In the least female occupation, trade and transportation, the percentage for women has increased from 2.4 vs. 12.2 for men in 1880 to 9.4 vs. 17.9 for men in 1900; while the percentage in the leading female occupation, domestic and personal service, is gradually decreasing from 44.6 in 1880 to 42.6 in 1890, to 39.4 in 1900. "All the industries in the United States, and their variety is practically unlimited, were assigned," says Mr. Wright, "to one of three hundred and sixty nine groups at the census of 1890. An examination of the totals of these groups discloses the fact that in only nine of them are no women and children employed. Their employment, therefore, either as clerks, operatives, or apprentices, may be considered universal. The apparent number of vocations in which women cannot engage is constantly diminishing, and is now, relatively, very small." This statement may be compared with one made in 1840 by Harriet Martineau, who found only seven employments open to women: teaching, needlework, keeping boarders, working in cotton mills, typesetting, bookbinding, and domestic service.

The growing appreciation of woman's work is indicated by a relative rise in wages. The greatest percentage of gain in average wages in the cotton industries is in favor of the female employees. The average weekly earnings in cotton factories of New England for women in 1831 ranged from

$2.20 to $2.60, and for men, $9.05. In the same industry for the entire United States the average weekly wage for women in 1890 was $5.53, ranging from $5.17 to $10.44. In 1831 men's wage was twice as great as women's; in 1880 it was less than one third greater. Between 1831 and 1880 men's wages had increased 38 per cent; women's, 149 per cent. . . . A careful examination of the actual earnings of women discloses the fact that in many industries their average earnings equal or exceed the earnings of men. This is especially true of the pieceworkers. In general, however, it must be said that woman's wages as compared with man's is considerably lower. But this is easily explained, when we consider the fact that she has stepped out of industrial subjection and come into the industrial system as an entirely new economic factor. If there were no other reasons this alone would be sufficient to keep her wages low and prevent their very rapid increase.

Professor Mason, in his book on Woman's Share in Primitive Culture, devotes a chapter to woman as a jack-at-all-trades, and remarks that in the entire course of human history the combination of abilities in one woman stands in sharp contrast with the co-operation of many individuals at one duty or activity among men. "In co-operation," he says, "women have always been weak. There are few duties that they have in common. Even as beasts of burden they seldom worked in pairs." Unless we can realize what must be the effect of centuries of isolated work, we can hardly explain the ill success of women's trade unionism, nor appreciate the progress already made by women in co-operating with one another for various other purposes. "In industry, women, as a class, are just beginning to understand the power and the force which come from organization," says Mr. Wright. This is true; but woman's entrance into labor unions took place before she became conscious of her class.

The employers' persistence in keeping women at the trades, wherever wages could be saved, and the workingmen's conviction that they must either leave their trades or admit women to their unions was the real cause of women's first connection with unionism. There was, of course, a strong opposition. The eighteenth century trade clubs of hatters, basket makers, or compositors would have instantly struck against any attempt to put a woman to any part of their craft. The intensity of resentment or abhorrence with which the average workingman regards the idea of woman entering his trade equals that displayed by the medical practitioner of the last generation. The Lancashire weavers alone never made any sex distinctions. The various organizations of weavers have from the introduction of the power loom included women on the same terms as men.

The typical status of woman in the male occupations may be illustrated by the following resolution adopted by the London society of compositors, 1886: "While strongly of opinion that women are not physically capable of performing the duties of a compositor, this conference recommends their admission to membership of the various typographical unions upon the same conditions as journeymen, provided always, the females are paid strictly in accordance with scale." The standard rate practically excludes sex competition, while it does not debar a woman from a man's work, provided she wins her way by capacity, and not by underbidding.

In Germany, the workingmen for a long time believed that the employment of women could be restricted. But, in spite of all efforts of restriction, the employment of women increased constantly, until five and a half millions, according to the census of 1882, were wage earners. Then only did the workingmen realize that women workers were no longer a factor to be neglected, and that equal duties toward society gave them equal rights. At their parteitag, or annual congress, held at Halle in 1890, the social democrats, therefore, passed a resolution demanding the full equality of the sexes in the state and society; and the next year at Brussels, the International Socialists' congress adopted the same resolution unanimously. After 1892 women were permitted to choose delegates to the annual congress, and now the members of the working women's association are an integral factor of the social democratic party.

In the United States, the Knights of Labor and the granger associations of the western farmers formulated (1870) a principle that no grange should be organized or exist without women. The more conservative men, too, began about 1884 to receive women in their unions. The rapid advance here made is evident in the United Garment Workers' union. In its establishment (1891) women bore no part, either directly or indirectly, says Miss Hurd. In April, 1902, the union was composed of 179 local bodies, of which 83 admitted men only, while 96 were made up either exclusively of women or of both men and women. Their number of delegates at the conventions increased from 2 out of 53 in 1894 to 18 out of 56 in 1900 and 23 out of 88 in 1901. "An interesting phase of the changing attitude of women toward unions is revealed," says John Mitchell, "by the action of the Chicago Federation of Teachers. The teachers of Chicago, recognizing that they were wage earners and realizing the similarity of their aims and ideals with those of the great body of trade unionists, threw their fortunes in with their fellow workers and became affiliated with the Chicago Federation of Labor." That woman as a factor in organized labor is considered important, the words of the most prominent labor leader of to-day amply testifies: "The future will undoubtedly show a vast strengthening of the labor movement through the compact organization of the women employed in American industries."

THE EVOLUTION OF NEGRO LABOR.

BY CARL KELSEY.

[Carl Kelsey, sociologist; born Grinnell, Iowa, September 2, 1870; educated at Iowa college, Andover Theological seminary, University of Gottingen and University of Pennsylvania; is assistant professor of sociology in the University of Pennsylvania and assistant director of the New York school of philanthropy. Author, The Negro Farmer.]

Few questions now before the American people are of more general interest than that which relates to the rôle the negro is to play in the great industrial advance of the southern states. That there is much in existing conditions both of encouragement and discouragement is patent to every careful observer. Unfortunately most of those discussing the questions close their eyes to one or the other set of facts and are wildly optimistic or pessimistic accordingly. As everyone has his standpoint, let me say that I agree with Dr. J. L. M. Curry, who states: "I have very little respect for the intelligence or the patriotism of the man who doubts the capacity of the negro for improvement or usefulness." The civilization of a race has taken place many times in the history of the world. How long it may take for any given people, or whether the development may be stopped by unpropitious conditions, no one can tell. It took the Germans hundreds of years to absorb the Roman culture, and the immoralities of the May days were the despair of the Puritans almost a thousand years later. One trouble regarding the negro is that we have no standard for comparison. It may be that if we knew the rate of progress of other primitive peoples we should find his progress remarkable.

We know comparatively little about the ancestry of the American negroes. They came, originally, from the west coast of Africa, but it is not known how far into the interior the slave trade had extended. Western Africa was inhabited by many tribes, some of which were much superior to others. It is certain that Semitic blood had been infused into the more

386

northern tribes. All these tribal distinctions, however, have been hopelessly lost in America and to increase the confusion no small amount of white blood has been added. The number and relative position of negroes as contrasted with mulattoes, etc., no one knows, and the census does not attempt to ascertain. The traveler through the south is impressed by the fact that the leaders in industry and education are not pure negroes. It should be remembered that a black skin is no guarantee of the pure negro. Crossing with the whites may show itself in shape of skull and features as well as in color. While ethnologists may not yet predict the results of race mixture, it is safe to say that it is unscientific to use the achievements of a score of half breeds as an index of what may be immediately expected of the original stock.

In Africa the negroes had established no enduring state. At the time when the slave trade was at its height the strong hill tribes of the east had been crowding the weaker tribes to the low west coast; slavery in its worst forms was universal and slave raids were known long before the advent of Europeans. Cannibalism was prevalent; religion a mass of grossest superstition, with power of life and death in the hands of the priests of the mystic rites of the Voodoo and Obea. The sexual passions were strongly developed. Marriage was a living together for a longer or shorter time. Life and property were in subjection to the chiefs, consequently very insecure. Wild animals were dangerous. The damp tropical climate made great provisions for the future unnecessary, not to say impossible, while social conditions did not favor the accumulation of property.

The transfer to America made a sharp break with the past. Simple dialects were exchanged for a complex language. Physical health was carefully safeguarded; life became more secure. An emphasis previously unknown was placed upon the permanence of marital relations. In return the negro, for the first time, was made to work. Admitting, as all do, that slavery was an economic mistake, from the negro's standpoint it conferred a great benefit by teaching him to work. Booker T. Washington has said: "American slavery was a great curse to both races and I would be the last to apologize for it; but, in the presence of God, I believe that slavery laid the foundation for the solution of the problem that is now before us in the south. During slavery, the negro was taught every trade, every industry, that constitutes the foundation for making a living." Dr. H. B. Frissell of Hampton has borne the same testimony. "The southern plantation was really a great trade school, where thousands received instruction in mechanic arts, in agriculture, in cooking, sewing and other domestic occupations. Although it may be said that all this instruction was given from selfish motives, yet the fact remains that the slaves on many plantations had good industrial training, and all honor is due to the conscientious men and still more to the noble women of the south, who in slavery times helped to prepare the way for the better days that were to come." Work is the foundation of human progress. The people which has learned to work and which lives where work brings proportionate results has made a great start toward civilization. The advantages of the discipline of slavery are seen when the negro and the Indian are contrasted. Dr. Frissell says of this comparison: "When the children of these two races are placed side by side as they are in the schoolrooms and workshops, and on the farms, at Hampton, it is not difficult to perceive that the training which the black had under slavery was far more valuable as a preparation for civilized life than the freedom from training and service enjoyed by the Indian on the western reservations. For while slavery taught the colored man to work, the reservation pauperized the Indian with free rations; while slavery brought the black into the closest relations with the white race and its ways of life, the reservation shut the Indian away from his white brothers and gave him little knowledge of their civilization, language or religion."

Under slavery three general fields of service opened to the blacks. The first, of the quickest and brightest, was that of the house and body servants. These were constantly in the houses and with their masters and absorbed, as did the next class, no small amount of learning. The second class, consisting of men alone, comprised the artisans, carpenters, masons, blacksmiths and the like. In large parts of the south these had practical monopoly of the trades. In technical knowledge, they, of course, soon outstripped their masters and became, as compared with other slaves, independent and self reliant. The significance of this training appeared in the generation after freedom was declared. The third and largest class embraced the field hands. To this class were naturally consigned the dullest as well as those whose services were not elsewhere needed. Some of these became foremen, but the vast majority worked on tasks directly under the eye of over-seers. As a rule, the methods of agriculture were crude; tools, usually heavy clumsy hoes, were of the simplest; even plows were unknown in some districts until long after the war.

I recently have seen grass being cut with hoes. The soil was cultivated for a time then abandoned for new land. Corn, cotton and in a few districts rice, were the chief crops, although each plantation raised its own fruit and vegetables and about the cabins in the quarters were often little garden patches. Slavery, however, like Africa, gave the negro little training in independence, in responsibility for propriety, in thrift and foresight for the morrow. All things were the master's and he had to replace old tools, furnish a sufficiency of food and clothes, and be responsible for the whole. Thus, neither Africa nor America had trained the bulk of the negroes to any sense of personal responsibility away from the eye of the manager. Moreover, there had been nothing of home life with all that this means in the development of a race.

Freedom came, a second sharp break with old economic conditions. There was now no one to provide the necessities of life. But the negro can labor and the white must employ his labor. Gradually new relationships are worked out.

It is often assumed that slavery laid a black deposit of equal depth over the south. This assumption is incorrect. There are sections of the south where the whites knew and know as little about the blacks as do the average northerners. The economic causes which made slavery unprofitable at the north fixed its location in the south. The center of slavery moved, therefore, south and west. Even before the war, Kentucky and Virginia had become largely breeding states and slave labor less and less profitable. The least desirable slaves were sold south, the best retained even when economically unprofitable, because of family pride. For this reason, perhaps, the Virginia negroes have often been considered the best of the race. At the outbreak of the war the alluvial districts of the lower Mississippi were probably the most prosperous of the slave regions. Since the war other causes, such as the attraction of northern cities, have conspired to make the rate of increase among negroes in the northern slave states lower than that of the whites. What this means to the economic life of a state is seen when we learn that in 1860 negroes were in a majority in five counties of Maryland, in but two in 1900; in forty three counties of Virginia in 1860, and thirty five in 1900, while sixty counties out of the one hundred showed an actual decrease of negro population between 1890–1900. In North Carolina in 1860 nineteen counties were black, fifteen in 1900.

Along the Tennessee there are many negro farmers. In two counties, Winston and Collman, the census records only twenty eight negroes. The explanation is that negroes are not allowed there and it is interesting to note that in this district the dominant element is that of Germans, who emigrated from Ohio since the war. The records show that six counties in north Alabama lost in negro population and two others were stationary during the last decade, while in the black belt the whites have decreased in four counties and are stationary in two others. The negroes are in a minority in the pine flats district. This is true in other states. From 1890–1900 the negroes lost relatively in the metamorphic and sand hills districts, were stationary in the prairie and gained slightly in the oak hills, and more heavily in the pine woods. This statement is based on an examination of five or six typical counties lying almost wholly within each of the regions named.

This segregation of the negroes is found in all the states in a more or less marked degree. With a fairly dense population on the immediate seacoast of the Atlantic, the bulk is found from southeastern Virginia through eastern Mississippi, along the line of the pine hills and black prairie of Alabama, swinging north with this prairie as it enters Mississippi. Only the border of the metaphoric region is encroached upon. The

negroes are again in the majority in the alluvial districts of
the Mississippi and Red rivers. In Texas, though seldom
preponderating, they are located chiefly in the oak and hickory
lands, which run from the northeast corner, southwest through
the center of the state.

Wherever in the south a heavy negro population is found
outside of what we may call the black belt, it may be accounted
for by the presence of some city or by the development of
some local industry giving employment to numbers of unskilled
laborers. Thus, the counties in Virginia which are gaining
heavily in negro population are those about Norfolk, Newport
News and Richmond. In Mississippi the delta is the seat of
an increasing black population. In many sections the negroes
are leaving the hills for the more fertile bottom lands. Previous
to 1884, only the lands immediately adjacent to the rivers in
this district could be cultivated, now the railroads are pene-
trating every part of it. Meantime the levee system is lessening the danger of floods. Arkansas shows a similar, but slower
development. Oklahoma and the Indian Territory in the
west and Florida in the east have attracted many negroes.
Numbers have also gone to the coal field of West Virginia.
The trend to northern cities has been mentioned.

The significance of this geographical segregation and the
movement of the negro population is often overlooked, and
this may lead to very great misconceptions regarding actual
conditions. On page 419 of volume VI., Census 1900, we
learn that the negro landowner and cash tenant produced
almost as much cotton per acre as did white owners and tenants and that in Mississippi the negro tenants actually produced more per acre than white tenants. Are we to infer that
they are better farmers than the whites, or do these facts
denote remarkable progress, as the census informs us? By
no means. In Mississippi the whites farm the hill country,
the delta is cultivated only by negroes and the delta land will
raise twice as much cotton per acre as the hills. No wonder
the negroes' crops are larger. Moreover, the negro owner
and cash tenant are not independent of the white man.
Nearly all of them receive advances from white factors, who
personally or through their riders visit their debtors and give

instructions as to the cultivation of the crops. If these instructions are not followed the advances stop. If we are to base our estimates of the negro upon such facts we may as well argue that the negro owners are poorer farmers than negro tenants, for the same table shows that in nearly every state the tenants raise more per acre than do the owners. The explanation, in part at least, is that the tenants are probably under closer supervision of the white planter.

This segregation brings up other questions. Why does Dr. Paul Barringer, of Virginia, find that race hostility is increasing, while Mr. A. H. Stone, of Greenville, Mississippi, says that their problem is how to get more negroes? What is the significance of the fact that there is least race friction in districts in which the negro is relatively most numerous? Why do lynchings and assaults upon white women seem largely confined to regions in which the negro is least numerous? What does this segregation mean for the future of the negro? Professor DuBois has noted a difference in cities. Savannah is an old city, where the class of masters among the whites and of trained and confidential slaves among the negroes formed an exceptionally large part of the population. The result has been unusual good feeling between the races and the entrance of negroes into all walks of industrial life with little or no opposition. Atlanta, on the other hand, is quite opposite in character. Here the poor whites from north Georgia, who neither owned slaves nor had any acquaintance with negro character, have come into contact and severe competition with the blacks. The result has been intense race feeling. What does it signify that the prosperous section of Alabama is the north, in which whites predominate, while in Mississippi power seems to be concentrating in the alluvial regions in which the negroes are in the majority? Yet again, the manufactories which are springing up in the south are moving westward along the hills of the Piedmont and have scarcely affected the life of the negro. Is he to have no part in this save as an unskilled laborer? Certainly here is a field for study which has as yet been little worked. The influence which this segregation has upon the school opportunities of the negro should not be overlooked.

This geographical segregation naturally has greatest significance for the farmers, who comprise some 85 per cent of the negro men in productive pursuits and 44 per cent of the women, for city conditions are everywhere more or less similar. The land occupied by negro farmers may be divided into several districts: (1) Virginia and Kentucky north of the line of profitable cotton culture; (2) the Atlantic coast; (3) the pine flats and hills which sweep westward around the Piedmont to central Mississippi; the black prairie of Alabama and eastern Mississippi and the oak woods of Alabama and Mississippi; (4) the alluvial regions of the Mississippi and Red rivers; (5) prairies of Texas.

1. In Kentucky, negroes cultivate only about 4.8 per cent of the farms and in Virginia only 26.7. As has been noted, there seems to be an exodus from these farming sections. Cotton is no longer profitable and the tobacco industry seems to be concentrating in the hands of the whites. These Virginia lands have been greatly reduced in value in recent years and many have passed into the hands of negroes, perhaps because no one else wanted them. Farm hands get from six to ten dollars per month.

2. The seacoast region offers peculiar facilities for gaining an easy livlihood. In the northern section (Virginia) there has been a great development of the oyster industry, the negro oystermen making about $8 a month and families occupied in shucking oysters earning up to $400 a year, three fourths gaining less than $250. Berry picking occupies much time in the early summer. The work is not continuous as on the farm and is accordingly preferred. In the southern portion along the islands of Carolina and Georgia the streams abound in fish and crabs. The climate is warm. There are some rice plantations and cotton is of the Sea Island variety. The day laborer gets from $0.35 to $0.50 on the farm; $0.75 or so in the phosphate industry. This latter is declining and the negroes who left the farms to go into it are drifting to the cities. Land is abundant and cheap. In some places a negro can rent all he wants for $10 a year, it being taken for granted that he will not use more than ten acres and $1 being a general rent. The farmer gets advances of from $35 to $50 a

year. The rice planters say it is harder and harder to get laborers.

3. In this section are grouped several different soils, but they are about equally adapted to cotton, the prairie soil being the best, probably, and are under similar conditions of rainfall. The soils are light and easily tilled. They wash badly and have suffered greatly from improper tillage. The introduction of artificial fertilizers has enabled them to keep up a competition with the newer and better soils of the west. On the whole, however, it seems to be a losing game for the negro. To produce cotton successfully requires an expenditure of $1.75 to $2 an acre for fertilizer and this the negro often fails to appreciate. The result is that in most of this district the negroes are not progressing as they might. Professor DuBois says: "A good season with good prices regularly sent a number out of debt and made them peasant proprietors; a bad season either in weather or prices still means the ruin of a thousand black homes. The industrial awakening of Georgia has tended to send up the rent of the farming lands, while at the same time the crop lien system, being especially suited to a non perishable crop like cotton, checks and often absolutely forbids diversity in agriculture, and thus gives the unearned increment almost entirely to the whites." Professor DuBois gives the record of a year for 271 families as follows:

Bankrupt and sold out..	3
$100 or more in debt...	61
$25 to $100 in debt..	54
$1 to $25 in debt..	47
Cleared nothing..	53
Cleared $1 to $25..	27
Cleared $25 to $100..	21
Cleared $100	5
	271

In this district one-mule farms, i.e., thirty to forty acres, prevail, the rent ranging from $2 to $4 an acre. The average amount of advances secured is from $50 to $75, a good profit being paid on all goods and high interest on the total advanced. In 1900 a typical family of three adults and three children, owning a mule and two cows, leasing fifty acres of land, not all in cultivation, secured the following advances:

Balance, January 1, 1900	$0 50
Cash	9 00
Clothing	9 79
Feed for stock	11 50
Provisions	13 48
Tobacco	80
Tools	40
Interest and recording fee ($1 00)	5 77
	$51 24

Advances are based on number of working hands. They begin about February and stop in August. The family must get along as best it can in the interim.

The remainder of his money was spent elsewhere and he must have come out about even, as on January 1, 1901, he owed the planter about $4. The plow and hoes, etc., needed by the farmer cost not to exceed $3. Really a large part of the interest should be charged to wages of superintendence, as the merchant has learned that if he wants his money he must himself, or by men called riders, keep in constant touch with his debtors to see that the crops are cultivated. The negro knows how to raise cotton, but he may neglect to plow his field unless reminded. As is well known, the crop is mortgaged in advance, for few negroes are able to advance themselves. A dishonest creditor will manage to get about all the crop. This fact, combined with the necessity for raising cotton to meet the mortgage requirements and the lower price of cotton, has done much to discourage the farmer in this district and to drive the young people away from the farm. To these causes should be added the fact that few negroes raise their own supply of vegetables, and are, therefore, compelled to buy. All plant gardens but few take care of them. The last catalogue of Tuskegee states: "If they have any garden at all it is apt to be choked with weeds and other noxious growths. With every advantage of soil and climate, and with a steady market, if they live near any city or large town, few of the colored farmers get any benefit from this, one of the most profitable of all industries." In a word, in the great trucking industry, the negroes bear little part. Field hands get about $0.50 per day and find themselves. A diversified agriculture would greatly improve the situation, but for this he is not prepared. In poor years large numbers seek temporary work on the railroads or in the cities. The planters say the old men, women, and girls are their most steady workers.

4. The alluvial lands. These may be subdivided into the cotton in the north and the cane districts in the south. In the cotton district we come upon a very different condition of affairs. The cabins are better. Land rents from $5 to $8 per acre, and the average amount tilled by a family does not exceed twenty acres. The average advances range from $100 to $150 a year. They are continued as long as is necessary. Wages range from $0.60 to $0.75 a day, and during cotton picking time $1.50 upward is often made. In 1900 a family of five adults and two children (under fourteen) came into the delta of Mississippi. They had nothing, not even decent clothing. In 1901 they cultivated thirty acres of land on which they raised twenty seven bales of cotton. They now own a wagon and farm implements, two mules, pigs, and chickens. Their plantation account in 1901 was as follows:

DEBIT.		CREDIT.	
Doctor	$35 35	Cotton	$1,091 28
Clothes and rations	284 10	Cotton seed	196 00
Mule	77 00		
Feed	5 00		
Extra labor (on their place)	67 60		
Ginning	101 25		
Rent	175 50		
Cash	290 00		
	$1,035 80		$1,287 28

This left them a balance of nearly $250. This family is composed of good workers, but they are by no means exceptional. I wish I could add that the negroes in this district were saving their money, but I fear most of them waste their earnings. In fact they often squander as much as families in the eastern districts earn. Of course there are many exceptions. Yet in spite of the opportunities planters find it difficult to get all the cotton picked. The average family can pick all they raise, but they do not—hence a heavy charge for extra labor, and this labor is often hard to get. The work must be carefully watched if it is to be well done. If the attempt is made to improve the cotton by taking special pains to secure certain seed, as like as not it will develop that some enterprising renter has mixed in a lot of poor stuff obtained elsewhere. In this region also wood is free and tenants often have free pasturage for stock.

The situation varies in the cane and rice country as here the planters pay cash wages for all labor. Houses with garden plots, firewood, etc., are furnished. The wages run from $0.40 per day for women to $0.70 for men, during cultivation, rising during the grinding season to $0.75 for women and $1 to $1.25 for men, children, of course, receiving less. On cane plantations there is work the year round, but there is great difficulty in getting regular labor. All work is done under careful supervision of overseers. The average yearly returns seem to be less than in the cotton country. One family of which I have record, the working force consisting of father and son (with a little assistance from two small children) earned, in 1901, $382.54. The man owns a horse and buggy, lives and dresses well and has money stored away. Wages are usually paid by an order on the store, which must be cashed if negro has no account. The men seldom work more than five and one half days per week, hence arose the custom of paying off every eleven days. The planter never knows how many laborers he will have on Monday, and it is said to be difficult to get extra work done even at higher wages. On one plantation, in 1901, an effort was made to get the cane cut at so much per ton. Higher wages were offered and the men could make $1.15, women $1 per day. After a week or so the hands asked to return to the gang at $1 and $0.75 per day, as they disliked the extra exertion. Negroes have had little to do with the development of the rice industry of southern Louisiana. Along the river some rice is raised, usually in connection with other crops. The rice season is short and other labor must be found if this is the sole crop.

The last district is found in the prairie regions of Texas. I have never visited this district and can get only hearsay evidence, which tends to show that the negroes are more prosperous than in most sections of the east. I make, therefore, no special mention of this state.

These six regions offer very diverse opportunities. The development is bound to be varied. We may, therefore, reasonably expect that the progress of the negro will not be at equal rate in the different sections, and will follow very different lines. Enough has been said to indicate that in some districts the present situation is not specially favorable, while in others a surplus results from present labors. It is not in place to discuss the crop lien system, etc., at length, but it may be said in passing that this system, bad as many of its features are, offers to the poor man an opportunity to at once start in and receive his supplies until the crop is made. He pays a big interest but the security is not good and it must be remembered that the white man pays big interest at the south and gets his money only under onerous conditions. The necessity of receiving advances greatly handicaps any development of diversified farming. In all sections the great criticism on the farm laborer may be summed up in unreliability. Mr. Alfred Holt Stone says: "One of the traits which militates most against the negro here is his unreliability. His mental processes are past finding out and he cannot be counted on to do or not to do a given thing under given circumstances. There is scarcely a planter in all this territory who would not gladly make substantial concessions for an assured tenantry." Agriculture is becoming more and more scientific. The lessening price of the great staple, whose culture the negro understands, makes more necessary the practice of small economies. Is he in a position to exercise these? Regarding the negro farmer let me quote a bulletin of the Farmers' Improvement society of Texas: "Very many (colored farmers) in the first place do not try to make their supplies at home. Very often much is lost by bad fences. Lots of them don't know where their hoes, plows, singletrees, etc., are this minute. Lots of them buy butter, peas, beans, lard, meat, and hay . . . well really, to sum up, if there's anything like scientific methods among the vast majority of our people I don't know it. . . . I venture to say that not one negro farmer in a hundred ever saw the back of one of these bulletins (agricultural), much less the inside." The need of some instruction which will enable the negro to take advan-

tage of his agricultural environment and get the most out of it
is apparent.   In the opinion of many observers, the negro has
a better chance on the farm than in any other occupation.
The opportunity is almost endless.   The south is not densely
populated and thousands of acres of land lie idle either because of lack of workers or lack of intelligence to make them
yield good returns.   The negro has every opportunity to
secure these lands, either at fair price or rental, and because
of the system of advances may get a start when the white
man at the north must work for a long time at wages to save
enough to do his own advancing.   I can but feel personally
that the farm offers the mass of the negroes their opportunity,
although for years to come it may be that their work must be
under the close supervision of the white man.   That appreciation of the value of constant labor and of the necessity for
that reliability already mentioned as lacking, will be gained
here if anywhere.   But I am anticipating.

   We have seen that besides being taught agriculture, the
slave was trained in domestic service and in the mechanic arts.
What is the situation a generation after freedom?   In domestic service the negro has maintained a monopoly in the districts in which he is numerous and in most of the towns and
cities.   Fifty two per cent of the women in productive employments are servants.   The average servant (female) receives from $4 to $8 per month and board, good cooks occasionally getting $12 to $15.   The servant never sleeps in the
house but lodges either in a small separate cabin or, more
often, at home.   The development of the towns has brought
large numbers of girls from the country to act as servants.
The practice of sleeping outside the houses where they are
employed during the day subjects them to many temptations
and is an unfortunate element of the situation.   The quality
of the service, judging from the almost unanimous consensus
of opinion, is deteriorating.   The children are not trained in
the home and do not get elsewhere the training they received
under slavery.   The evil is, again, unreliability.   Their com-
petence is often unquestioned after a period of service; but
little reliance can be placed in them.   It is interesting to note
that northern women who go south filled with the idea that

the negro is abused usually have very great difficulty in keeping any servants at all during the first year or so of their stay.

The old custom of slavery, that whatever is left from the master's table goes to the cabins, is still adhered to and every housewife expects to feed the family of the servant. Those engaging two servants often try to get them from one family for obvious reasons. A friend of the writer in Philadelphia discovered that her girl's husband was being regularly fed from her larder. The servants come in the morning, leave in the afternoon and in some places will not return to get supper. When this is the custom the housewife is helpless unless extra wages solve the difficulty. During the summer, when there is a chance to get odd sums by picking berries and the like, servants are hard to obtain, "Ise restin' " being the response to would-be employers. Writing of Virginia conditions Professor DuBois has said: "There is considerable dissatisfaction over the state of domestic service. The negroes are coming to regard the work as a relic of slavery and as degrading, and only enter it from sheer necessity and then as a temporary makeshift. The servants receiving less than they think they ought are often careful to render as little for it as possible. They grow to despise the menial work they do, partly because their employers themselves despise it and teach their daughters to do the same. Employers, on the other hand, find an increasing number of careless and impudent young people, who neglect their work and in some cases show vicious tendencies and demoralize the children of the family. . . . One result of this situation is the wholesale emigration of the better class of servants to the north." Male servants get from $8 to $15 a month. The old body servants naturally became barbers, waiters, restaurant keepers, etc., under the new régime.

The negro artisan, as we have seen, had control of the situation in 1865. It must be admitted that this is no longer the case. Bruce says: "Indeed, one of the most discouraging features in the character of the negroes who have grown up since the war is their extreme aversion to the mechanical trades. . . . The explanation of this antipathy on their part is easily found: such pursuit constrains them to conform more closely than they like to a steady routine of work, which is more arduous and trying on the whole. . . . Above all, the laborer is not tied down to one spot; if he grows weary of one locality he can find occupation elsewhere. But this is not the position of the young mechanic; his success is largely dependent upon his remaining in one place; he secures patronage by winning a reputation for assiduity and skill in his trade, and it is not possible to earn such a reputation as long as he yields to his inclination to wander."

Booker T. Washington, than whom none could give more valuable testimony, says in The Future of the American Negro: "The place made vacant by the old colored man, who was trained as a carpenter during slavery, and who, since the war, had been the leading contractor and builder in the southern town, had to be filled. No young colored carpenter, capable of filling his place, could be found. The result was that his place was filled by a white mechanic from the north. or from Europe or from elsewhere. What is true of carpentry and house building in this case is true, in a degree, in every skilled occupation; and it is becoming true of common labor. I do not mean to say that all skilled labor has been taken out of the negroes' hands; but I do mean to say that in no part of the south is he so strong in the matter of skilled labor as he was twenty years ago, except possibly in the country districts and the smaller towns. In the more northern of the southern cities, such as Richmond and Baltimore, the change is most apparent; and it is being felt in every southern city. Whenever the negro has lost ground industrially in the south, it is not because there is a prejudice against him as a skilled laborer on the part of the native southern white man. The southern white man generally prefers to do business with the negro mechanic rather than with a white one, because he is accustomed to do business with the negro in this respect. There is almost no prejudice against the negro in the south in the matter of business, so far as the native whites are concerned; and here is the entering wedge for the solution of the negro problem. But too often, where the white mechanic or factory operative from the north gets a hold, the trades union soon follows, and the negro is crowded to the wall." Quotations and observations to the same effect might be multiplied indefinitely. As a rule the negro works for less wages than the white in the same trade. His standard of life is also lower. Negro carpenters and bricklayers receive from $1 to $2.50 per day, with an average, perhaps, of $1.50. The quality of the work is generally inferior in common estimation. The negro working under white direction usually does better work than one alone. A man who has been intimately associated with negroes all his life, Rev. J. L. Tucker, Baton Rouge, La., writes as follows on this point: "A large schoolhouse was recently built here . . . all the digging and preparation of ground was done by gangs of negro men under white bosses. The mortar was mixed, lime and sand and brick hauled by negroes. A white man gave to negroes the exact proportions of ingredients for the cement, cement mortar and mortar for the different parts of the building, watched it done for a while, then went his way and the negro did that work, but the white man came back every now and then to make sure. That negro has been mixing mortar for many years, yet could not be entirely trusted. On the walls of the building were white men and negroes side by side, laying brick; but every piece of nice work was done by the white men. Straight work done by line and plumb the negroes could do, but the arches were turned, pilasters, sills, window recesses, etc., done by white men or quadroons; they could not be trusted to negroes. Let a negro build you a chimney and your house will probably burn down unless you stand over him and make him fill all the cracks with mortar. He may have been told a hundred times; he may have seen a house burn down by his faulty chimney, yet he will not do his work as it ought to be done and as he knows how unless you stand over him. . . . Negroes nailed up the lathing without much supervision. Negroes did the plastering, but white men laid on the hard finish. In my own house in one room the white plaster finish has largely peeled off from the mortar plastering underneath. A couple of negroes were left to finish that room. They knew how, that is, they had worked side by side with white men all their lives and had been told, and been made to do it, a white man prompting, hundreds of times; yet, left alone, did it wrong. . . . They are good helpers, usually docile, proud of their work, and doing good work when

told each separate thing, and told again each time it is done."
If it be said that testimony from southern whites is preju-
diced, a quotation from a letter of a northern man now resident
in the south and employing negro labor may be cited: "I am
convinced of one thing, and that is, that there is no dependence
to be put in 90 per cent of the negro laborers, if left to themselves and out of an overseer's sight." In my own observation
I saw little discrimination because of color, much because of
inability to get competent negroes.

As was suggested in the quotation from Mr. Bruce, the
trades and the farm have been dropped for all sorts of unskilled
labor, particularly in the cities, not only because of greater
opportunities but for the social advantages. In every town
the ranks of the unskilled are overflowing. Thus has arisen
the problem of the negro criminal from this mass of semi-idle
men. Many indeed are supported by wives or mistresses and
spend their time lookin' for a job. Yet objection to work, to
hard work under trying conditions, if it be not the steady day
in and day out grind, the negro has little. America cannot
show a happier, more cheerful body of laborers than these
blacks doing odd jobs about the city, diving for phosphate
rocks in the rivers of South Carolina, unloading fruit steamers
at Mobile, working on the levees of the Mississippi, lumbering
in the pine woods of south Alabama, or digging coal about
Birmingham. Free and easy, careless of the morrow, with
tempers of children, angry in a moment yet cherishing no
revenge; sullen and surly if they feel abused; working for ten
to fifteen cents per hour, seventy five cents to a dollar a day;
preferring to work three days and play four; the last cent
gambled if opportunity offers—an aimless, drifting life with
nothing saved for old age—they are the typical unskilled laborer of the south. The cotton of the best lands often is wasted
because of lack of pickers. On the wharves of Mobile there is
never any scarcity of laborers—the magic of the city which
has caused trouble in some northern agricultural districts.

I am not arguing the question whether this oft mentioned
unreliability is the result of a lowering of the negro's standard
or the rising standard of the white. It may be that in this
respect, in quality of workmanship, in knowledge and self

control, there has really been progress. I have simply tried
to show that, judged by the needs and demands of the present,
the negro is still decidedly lacking. Personally, I am not surprised at this. I should be astonished if conditions were
otherwise. The trouble is that most of us at the north are
unable to disabuse ourselves of the idea that the negro is a
Yankee with a dark skin. Therefore, we think that if all is
not as it should be that some one must be keeping him back,
some force restraining him. We accuse the southern white
man, attribute the trouble to slavery. Something is keeping
him back but it is his inheritance from thousands of years in
Africa, not the southern white man nor slavery. It is my
observation that the southern white in the negro belt will
deal with the negro more patiently and gently and endure far
more of shiftless methods than the average northerner would
tolerate for a day. Of course, there are exceptions—few in
number—who say, as did a lumberman in Alabama last summer: "I never have any trouble with the negro. Have
worked them for twenty years. Why—I haven't had to kill
one yet, tho' I did shoot one once, but I used fine shot and it
didn't hurt him much." On the other hand I have seen men
enduring and taking for granted a quality of service which
made me writhe in agony. We have attempted to hasten
natural progress and are impatient at the seeming meagerness
of results. Compare the negro of to-day with the negro in
Africa, and what a contrast there is!

Judging the average negro by our standards we find him
suffering under some serious disabilities. Gross immorality
—indulgence in which is seldom a bar to active church membership—bigamy, adultery, and similar offences seldom are
heard in the courts; venereal disease widespread. Marriage,
a mating of more or less permanence, often without any cere-
mony, while divorce is equally informal. Crime and insanity
increasing. Home life primitive—no regular meals nor common family interests. Children allowed to grow, receiving
neither at home nor in the average school any training in
neatness, punctuality, obedience, and industry. A people to
whom time is no object. A church service advertised at
11:00 may begin at 12:30. Great lack of foresight; as econo-

mists say, an over appreciation of present goods. Lack of thrift—the list is too long already. To his credit we find a personal devotion to one whom he trusts which is faithfulness itself. During war time the families of the soldiers were well cared for. One of the most disastrous results of the years following the war was the alienation to so large a degree of the former masters and slaves. The negro respects and trusts the white as he does not a fellow negro. It would be a happy day for the negro if the white woman of the south should again take a personal interest in his welfare. Greatly to his credit also is the willingness to work, and work hard under white leadership. Slavery taught him to work, but as a race he is not yet ready to work alone and get the best results. In his favor also is that friendliness on the part of the white man, which leads him to prefer the negro as a workman under ordinary conditions. It must be remembered that the succeeding generations will be less moved by this sentiment and will base their preferences on quality of workmanship.

Another factor in the problem which is growing in importance is that of white immigration. Into many southern communities is setting a tide of immigration from the north. White barbers, carpenters, masons, cooks, are making their presence felt. In agriculture the negro has experienced little competition. Yet the rice industry of Louisiana has been revolutionized within a decade. In The Cotton Plant, Mr. Harry Hammond states that in thirty nine counties of Texas in the black prairie region in which whites predominate, the average value of land per acre is $12.19, as against $6.40 per acre in twelve counties of similar soil in Alabama in which negroes are in a majority. He says further: "The number and variety of implements recently introduced in cotton culture here, especially in the prairies of Texas, is very much greater than elsewhere in the cotton belt." What will be the result when the white farmer seeking cheap land discovers (as he is slowly) that he can live and work in the richest soil in the country, perhaps—the alluvial regions of the Mississippi river? To-day over 80 per cent of the population is negro; will he be fit to hold his own or must he either surrender the best land or take a subordinate position?

As Dr. Curry has said: "It may be assumed that the industrial problem lies at the heart of the whole situation which confronts us. Into our public and other schools should be incorporated industrial training. If to regularity, punctuality, silence, obedience to authority, there be systematically added instruction in mechanical arts, the results would be astounding." The question of classical education does not now concern us. The absolutely essential thing for the negro now is that he learn to work regularly and intelligently. The lesson begun in slavery must be fully mastered. As Dr. E. G. Murphy puts it: "The industrial training supplied by that school (slavery) is now denied to him. The capacity, the equipment, and the necessity for work which slavery provided are the direct causes of the moral superiority of the old time darky. Is freedom to have no substitute for the ancient school? . . . The demand of the situation is not less education but more education of the right sort."

A great trouble with the mass of schools for negroes is that they have not fitted their pupils to teach the things upon which the negro's progress depends. Hampton and Tuskegee are attempts in the right direction. That they are being duplicated on smaller scales in many districts is a hopeful sign. The state institutions, such as the school at Westside, Miss., and Normal, Ala., are not to be forgotten.

If agriculture offer the best field for the negro, it is a matter of regret that greater headway is not being made in the training of farmers. The training on the average farm is not sufficient, particularly in those districts where a departure from the traditional crops seems to be imperative. Even Tuskegee is not doing as much in this line as generally supposed, in spite of the emphasis I know is being laid upon it. In examining their catalogue I find only sixteen graduates who are farming and of these thirteen have other occupations —principally teaching. Three others are introducing cotton raising in Africa under the German government. From the industrial department nine have received certificates in agriculture and six in dairying, but their present occupations are not given. Asking a prominent man at the Tuskegee institute for the reason he exclaimed, rather disgustedly, that they didn't like to work and preferred teaching. Tuskegee is wielding great influence through its yearly Farmers' conference and the small local association which meets monthly. There is a similar organization at Calhoun, Ala., which has held fairs, the exhibitors being negro farmers. At both Calhoun and Tuskegee and a few other places land has been purchased in large tracts and is being sold to the negroes at reasonable terms. It is too early to judge of the results of these experiments. In Texas there is an interesting organization, The Farmers' Improvement society, which is composed of negroes. The aim is to stimulate the members to improve their homes, buy land, overcome the custom of receiving advances and to have a distributing co-operative society. A fair is held each year. From the Galveston News of October 12, 1902, I learn that the society has about 3,000 members and that they own 50,000 acres of land, more than 8,000 head of cattle, and 7,000 head of cattle and mules. If the figures are correct they indicate progress. The Hampton Building and Loan association has been very successful and pays its stockholders 7 per cent dividends.

Mr. Joseph A. Tillinghast in closing his chapter on Industrial Progress (The Negro in Africa and America) sums up as follows: "The general conclusion we reach, then, is to this effect, that an overwhelming majority of the race in its new struggle for existence under the exacting conditions of American industry is seriously handicapped by inherited characteristics. Economic freedom has not developed a sense of responsibility and a persistent ambition to rise, as many hoped to see. As a race the negroes are still wanting in energy, purpose, and stability; they are giving away before the able competition of whites in the skilled and better paid occupations, and they fail to husband resources so as to establish economic safety." I think this a fair statement of the facts of the case. If I have indicated some of the lines along which there has been development and the conditions limiting further progress, I am content. Regarding the future, I am hopeful.

AMERICAN LABOR'S DEBT TO RAILROADS.

BY GUY MORRISON WALKER.

[Guy Morrison Walker, student and traveler; was called in consultation by President McKinley during the last Chinese war, and his article on "China, the Sphinx of the Twentieth Century" has been regarded as a little classic; Mr. Walker is much interested in financial and transportation problems, and his contributions are sought by the best of American magazines, and his articles invariably set men thinking, and often along new lines. He is a native of Indiana, a graduate of De Pauw university.]

It is a well known fact, though one that we seldom stop to recall, that the price of the finished product in the markets of the world is made up of the cost of manufacture plus the cost of transportation. Reduced to its lowest analysis, the cost of every manufactured product is simply the cost of labor to produce it, for the cost of raw material is simply the cost of labor to obtain it, whether it be by digging ore from the mines, gathering ivory in the forests of Africa, or shearing wool from the backs of sheep.

Under primitive conditions even transportation is simply labor, and the cost of transportation is simply the cost of the human labor necessary to carry the finished product to market. This condition is still to be seen in Oriental countries, particularly in China, where the greater part of the tea crop is borne to the waterways on the backs of men, and in Africa, where strings of negroes still bear to the coast the ivory gathered in the forests of the interior.

By the development of modern means of transportation labor in civilized communities has been relieved of the burden of transporting its manufactured products to market by the costly and laborious methods that still prevail in less favored communities. The farmer of Kansas and Nebraska sells his great surplus of wheat and corn at a good profit in the markets of Europe because American railroads transport his grain from the farm, 1,500 miles in the interior, down to the coast at a cost of approximately one third of 1 cent per ton per mile. The province of Honan, in China, lying about 600 miles inland from the coast, with an area about equal to that of the state of New York, but with a population of over 22,000,000, has a foreign commerce that aggregates only about $500,000 a year. The province of Szechuan, with an area of 200,000 square miles and a population almost equal to that of the United States, is practically an unknown world, because almost its only means of communication is by the small boats that descend the Yangtze river and the returning boatmen, who trudge into the interior carrying on their backs such small bundles as they are able to bear. Although the men engaged in this traffic are paid only about 8 cents a day for their work, and they board themselves out of that pittance, this method of transportation costs about 10 cents per ton per mile, or nearly fifteen times the average freight charge of American railroads, and more than thirty times what American railroads charge for the transportation of grain.

The value of every commodity depends upon the breadth of the market for it, and particularly is this true of the value of labor, for labor necessarily depends for its value on the facilities which exist for transporting its products to market. Thus we see that in China, where the facilities for transportation are the poorest in the world, we find the cheapest labor— cheap because it is confined for a market for its products to the territory immediately surrounding it and is cut off from the markets of the world by the high cost of reaching them. In all China there is in operation less than 1,000 miles of railroad. The following table gives the population, total miles of railroad, and the miles of railroad for each 10,000 of population in the leading industrial countries of the world:

Country.	Population.	Miles of road.	Miles per 10,000.
Great Britain	41,454,578	21,855	5.27
France	38,641,000	26,234	6.78
Germany	56,343,000	31,392	5.57
Austria	47,102,000	22,545	4.78
Italy	32,449,000	9,772	3.01
Russia	128,932,000	28,589	2.21
United States	76,303,000	202,000	26.47

It will be seen from this table that the average man in America is four times better served with railroad transportation facilities than the average Frenchman, who, next to ourselves, are the best served by their railroads of any people in the world; while the average American is five times better served in this respect than is the average inhabitant of Great Britain or Germany, who are our chief industrial rivals. From this it is easy to see how much greater is the opportunity of the average American to market the products of his labor, and how much wider is the market which these products may reach.

Transportation rates are not only governed by the methods of transportation employed, but in civilized countries where practically the same methods of transportation prevail, they are governed by skill in operation and by the fixed charges that are necessary to build up the transportation systems. Nowhere else in the world has railroad operation been reduced to the science that it has in this country, where our train loads average almost double those of Europe, and our ton mile rates are not only the lowest, but are scarcely one third those of our nearest competitors. In all this the American laborer has a great advantage over the laborer in any other part of the world.

The average capitalization per mile of American railroads is only $61,884, while the average capitalization of the railroads of Europe is almost twice that sum, amounting to $113,-880 per mile, and the railroads of Great Britain and Ireland are capitalized at $268,051 per mile. This means that the charge of American railroads upon the products of labor for transporting them to market, necessary to pay the fixed charge upon the investment in the roads, is only one half as much as European railroads must tax the product of their labor in order to place that product in the market, and only one fourth as much as English railroads are forced to tax the products of English labor in order to pay their fixed charges or the interest upon the sum invested in them.

While the market for any given product is controlled by that nation which can combine the lowest cost of manufacture together with the lowest cost of transportation to market, the price of that product in the market is governed by the next to the lowest possible combination of these two elements —or, in other words, by the cost to the nearest competitor.

The nation which makes cheapest and reaches the market cheapest need not sell its product as cheap as they can be made and delivered in order to control the market, but only to sell a little cheaper than its nearest competitor can make and deliver. When one of the competitors for a market has secured control of it by reducing the sum of his cost of making and delivering below that of his nearest rival, he may thereafter, by the reduction of one of the elements of cost, be able to increase his profit without danger to his control of the market. He may even reduce one element of cost so much as to be enabled to increase the other element of cost and still make the combined cost less than it was before.

In other words, when one country has secured control of the market for any given commodity by being able to make and deliver it cheaper than it can be done by any industrial rival, that country may, by reducing its cost of transportation to market, greatly increase its profit and still control the market without in any manner reducing the price of its wages. It may, in fact, so materially reduce the cost of transportation that wages in that country may be materially increased without endangering its control of the markets of the world. It is just this that American railroads have enabled us to do in the markets of the world, and what this means to American labor is shown by the following table, which gives the cost of transportation per ton mile and the average wage per day that is paid to labor in the leading countries of the world:

Country.	Cost of transportation per ton-mile.	Wages per day.
China	$0.10	$0.10
Japan	.05	.23
Russia	.022	.34
Italy	.024	.26
Austria	.0225	.50
Germany	.015	.90
France	.019	.80
England	.026	1.04
United States	.0069	2.60

From this it will be seen that in China, where the cost of transportation amounts to 10 cents per ton per mile, wages average only 10 cents per day. In Japan, which, by reason of a small railroad system and fair means of water communication, has reduced its average cost of transportation to 5 cents per ton per mile, the wages are about 23 cents per day. In Russia and Italy, which of the civilized countries have the lowest railroad mileage in proportion to population and a high average cost per ton per mile for transportation, the average wage is only 34 and 26 cents per day, respectively. In Germany, France, and England, which approximate each other in the average cost of transportation per ton per mile and in their average mileage of railroad in proportion to their population, there is a fair approximation in the average wage, while in our own country, where we have the greatest railroad mileage in proportion to our population and the lowest cost of transportation, we have the highest average wage to be found in the world—the highest wage in fact of which there is any record in history.

In the face of these figures it is impossible to escape the conclusion that there is a definite, fixed relation between wages and the facilities and cost of transportation; that in the absence of transportation facilities and in the presence of a high cost or rate of transportation, industry languishes, labor finds little to do, and wages remain low. While as transportation facilities increase and transportation rates grow lower and cheaper, industry thrives, markets widen, commerce grows, and wages increase by leaps and bounds.

The industrial development of America, the great demand for labor, and the high wages that exist in our country to-day are due primarily to our wonderful railroad development and to the wonderful cheapness of our transportation rates. It is a mistake to imagine that manufactures can thrive or agriculture flourish in advance of adequate transportation facilities. Were the farmers of Kansas and Minnesota compelled to pay such transportation charges as the farmer of China, it would cost them $150 a ton to ship wheat from their farms to New York, or $4,500 for a 30-ton carload of 1,100 bushels. In other words, their wheat worth only 60 cents a bushel on the farm would cost $5 a bushel delivered at tide water.

Were the steel mills of Pittsburg compelled to pay only as much as the manufacturer of Japan for the transportation of their products to market, it would cost them $25 a ton to deliver steel rails on board ship. Pittsburg rails costing $25 a ton at the mill would cost $50 a ton in New York, while Chicago rails facing a transportation charge of $50 a ton would have to be manufactured for nothing in order to compete with Pittsburg rails in the Atlantic coast market.

Neither the products of the farm nor of the factory can pay such charges for transportation to market. It is easy to see that industrial development in competition with conditions as we know them in America is impossible in a country like China, where coal mined by cheap Chinese labor at a cost of only 25 cents per ton at the mouth of the mine is raised by the mere cost of transportation to $8 per ton when transported a distance of less than 40 miles. Under such conditions the consumption of coal is naturally limited to a small radius around each mine, and it is impossible to develop any mining industry. The miners of this country should recognize the fact that were it not for the wonderfully cheap rates made by our American railroads for the transportation of coal, not one mine in one hundred would be open to-day, and most of them would be seeking employment, as are the inhabitants of most other countries, at wages averaging about one fourth of what they are earning to-day.

In contrast with the labor conditions that exist in China, the recent railroad development in Japan has resulted in a wonderful rise in wages. Wages have increased within the last twenty years from an average of 8, 10, and 12 cents per day to 20, 30, and 40 cents per day, according as the labor is skilled or unskilled, while her exports to foreign countries have increased over 800 per cent.

Wages have always been low in those parts of the country far ahead of or removed from railroad facilities, and to-day the lowest wages found in the United States are in those states which have the poorest railroad facilities. Whenever the railroads come into a new community wages are almost immediately doubled. The following table, showing the cost of transportation per ton per mile for each decade of the last fifty years and the average wage of American labor at the same time, shows what the increase of our transportation facilities and the reduction of our railroad rates have done for American labor:

Year.	Cost of transportation per ton-mile.	Wages per day.
1850	$0.035	$1.23
1860	.0274	1.50
1870	.0199	1.97
1880	.0126	2.13
1890	.0092	2.50
1900	.0069	2.60

It will be seen that as our transportation rates have steadily fallen the wages of labor have steadily risen, and that, too, in an almost constant proportion. In the last fifty years our railroad mileage has grown from a few thousand miles of scattered and disconnected links into a great railroad system of over 200,000 miles, every mile of which is in connection with every other mile, equalizing labor conditions and leveling prices throughout the whole country, preventing either local famine or local waste of surpluses. This and the reduction during the same period of our railroad rates from 3½ cents per ton per mile to 6.9 mills, or less than one fifth what they were fifty years ago, has enabled us to accomplish the greatest miracle that the world has ever seen.

During those fifty years our population has grown from 23,000,000 to over 76,000,000, and over 18,000,000 foreigners have immigrated to our shores. Yet in the face of this great supply of labor, and most of it extremely cheap labor, that has poured in upon us, we have been enabled to develop our industries and create such a demand for labor that we have more than doubled our own average wage and at the same time delivered our finished products in Europe so cheaply that that country, even after shipping its surplus supply of labor to us, has been unable to bring about any material increase in its own wages.

The reason that the iron mills of Saxony have been idle has been because German railroad rates to the coast have been more than the combined charge of American railroad rates from interior points to our seacoast and the added cost of transportation across the seas. Why do the industries of Germany languish? It is because the government control of German railroads has abolished competition and maintained German freight rates at figures nearly three times greater than those fixed by private competition here in America. In America the necessity for lower rates forced many roads into receiverships, but this resulted in a scaling of their debts and their reorganization on a basis which lower rates were able to support. This relief, however, is impossible to the government owned railroads of Europe, for the attempt to reduce railroad rates based upon the present capitalization or cost of those roads to their governments would impair at once the security of government investments; and so the German laborer must struggle for a wage scarcely more than one third that paid to the American laborer, in order to equalize this difference which prevails in the freight rates of the two countries.

Of what use was it to discover that California could raise fruit for the whole world when that state had but a population of 1,500,000 to consume it? But this fact becomes of great importance when it is known that by reason of our fast freights and cheap railroad rates California apples are shipped across the continent, then across the Atlantic, and sold in London so cheap that Scottish apples, paying English railroad rates for a distance of only 600 miles, are unable to compete with them. There is no question but that the high standard of American wages has been brought about and made possible by our low transportation charges. Our wages have, in fact, continued to advance until the standard is so high that in many branches of industry it is becoming difficult to maintain our command of the world's market, the struggle for which is growing fiercer with each day. Europe, still thirty years behind us in transportation rates, which she has heretofore equalized by low wages, is reaching after us, and a better development of transportation facilities is going on in all her different countries.

There is but one possible way of maintaining our domina-
tion of the world's markets, and that is either by a reduction
of wages or by a still further reduction of the cost of transportation. Our laboring people must therefore recognize that
their only hope not only of better pay, but even of maintaining
their present industrial position, depends upon the ability of
our railroads to continue as they do to-day to deliver our
manufactured products at a cost which defies competition;
that every imposition laid upon our transportation systems
is an imposition upon labor itself; that every advantage taken
from these transportation facilities robs the labor that benefits
by low railroad rates; that every tax and burden laid upon our
transportation facilities is doubly a tax and a burden upon
labor, which is at the mercy of these same transportation
facilities to find a market for its products.

Every obstacle placed in the way of cheapening the cost
of transportation prevents and makes impossible any rise in
wages. It is surprising, when our attention is called to the
manner in which we have hampered and burdened our railroads, that we have succeeded as we have. It is time for
laboring men to recognize that their future is inseparably
bound up with that of the railroads of this country. It is
these railroads that have enabled our workingmen and mechanics to fatten off the work that they are doing for the whole
world while foreign workmen are idle and all Europe is wildly
protesting against the American invasion. If our railroad
rates were doubled, at which figure they would still be lower
than those of any other country in the world, it would close
almost every mill and factory in our country away from tide
water.

In order to maintain our position railroad rates will doubtless become even cheaper than they are to-day. But it is to
be hoped that this will not be accomplished by the reduction
of the wages of railroad laborers to the standard of Germany,
whose railroads only pay their engineers and firemen a wage
ranging from eight to ten cents per hour for a ten-hour day
and whose laborers work for a pittance of from five to seven
cents per hour.

Our whole people should join in securing every reasonable immunity from taxation or oppressive regulations for our great transportation systems, so that as we have used them to attain our present position in the industrial world, we may by removing all obstacles from their way, make them the means of maintaining American wages at their present high standard and at the same time securing for American labor its rightful heritage—the markets of the world and the industrial supremacy of the earth.

MANUAL TRAINING IN THE PUBLIC SCHOOLS.

BY HARRY E. BACK.

[Harry E. Back, lawyer and statistician; born Union, Conn; graduated Brimfield academy, Boston university, and law school of latter university; member Connecticut legislature, 1897: prosecuting agent, Windham county, 1897–9; commissioner of the bureau of labor statistics, Conn., 1899–1903: judge town court, Killingly,1903; has taken much interest in manual training and has done much to encourage it in Connecticut.]

Of recent years much has been written about manual training. The educators of this and other countries have discussed the matter in all its bearings upon the intellectual, ethical, and practical development of students. There has been much debate as to whether manual training, with the object of teaching some trade, should be made of prime importance in the study of a school boy arrived at the age of 14 years, or thereabouts, or whether it should be co-ordinated with other branches of learning in the interest of a comprehensive, well balanced educational system. The first method, which was favored by practical men, meant the conversion of ordinary schools into trade or technical schools. The second method meant only the addition of general dexterity and mechanical knowledge to the fund of information acquired by grammar and high school scholars. This second method was opposed on the ground that it gave only a smattering and fitted the student for nothing. As time went on, the people, not the educators, settled the question. It was found that boys from the schools where manual training had only a relative value soon surpassed those who had been fitted only for some particular trade. They stepped into higher positions requiring executive ability and the general knowledge in which they had been drilled. Consequently, the schools with the broad educational ideals met with public favor and developed and multiplied throughout the land. The advantages of this system were recognized even by the practical trade and technical school directors, who have repeatedly raised the standard of general educational requirements for admission to their schools.

Manual training means to-day, then, the training of the hand and eye together with the mind in ordinary schools of general culture for the better development of all the faculties. It assumes that the pupils in the grammar and high schools are not old enough to know their innate possibilities or the compass and limitations of the various trades and professions. By its introduction and co-ordination with other branches of learning, the pupil learns the relation of his theoretical knowledge to the practical affairs of life. He learns how to apply his book knowledge to affairs of human concern, and in so doing develops an interest and ardor which animate him in all his study. The drudgery of abstract learning is turned into the pleasure of learning by the creation of something concrete and original. All this means indelible impressions upon the minds of the pupils and a rounding out of characters and developing of talents and energies which make shrewd, careful, well poised workmen and masters. Yet the end of the school life finds the young man's career open at the top. He has not been forced to learn some particular trade to the exclusion of all other knowledge. He stands at the threshold of his career with a general training, knowledge and dexterity which enable him to make an intelligent choice of his life work and to achieve successful results in whatever field he may wish to enter. If the young man enters the mechanical field he is not humiliated or compelled to lose time in learning the rudiments of, and the general dexterity required in, this industry. He takes his place with others of his own age, but with greater intelligence and understanding, which makes his work more valuable and causes speedy promotion. If, on the other hand, he enters an office, or takes some executive position in business, his knowledge of mechanics and understanding of manufacturing processes give him a weight and importance which comparatively few business executives possess. He is alike competent as superintendent and manager.

The modern manual training is of recent growth and flourishes to best advantage in this country. It is distinctively American in recognizing the pre-eminence of the individual. In England and on the continent individual interests are subordinated to commercialism and industrialism. There

trade schools and technical schools exist, not to offer alternative higher educational courses, but to mould the young
boys and girls into industrial machines. Our manual training schools are the result of the great revolution in thought,
sentiment and methods, which has changed the whole fabric
of the American republic in every department of life and given
us the world's leadership in two decades. Dissatisfaction
with the old methods and a healthy desire for progress were
the causes of this revolution in educational as well as business
methods. There came a demand for the application of scientific principles to all matters, for the development of a broader
and more liberal culture and the correlation of all man's
faculties and energies. This was seen in the demand not only
for manual training, but for physical culture, for the study
of sciences and for elastic high school and college courses. The
day of manual training was hastened by the remarkable success in all walks of life of boys born and bred in the country
or rural districts, and by the marked failure of city boys to
qualify for the important positions of life. The country bred
boy possessed a general aptitude and fund of practical information which made him a commanding genius wherever he
went. He had breadth of character and soundness of sense
acquired by daily contact with, and practice in, the numerous
routine affairs of the rural sections. As the cities increased
their populations at the expense of the country districts, the
pre-eminence of the citizens from the farms and villages was
still more marked. How to overcome the disadvantages of
city life and education and how to make industrious and useful citizens of the children of the uneducated foreigners became pressing problems.

Manual training seemed to furnish a solution, and the
results of its introduction have exceeded the highest hopes
of its sponsors. One of the best arguments for manual training has been advanced by Edward C. Vanderpoole, a New
York teacher. It was made in answer to the statement of
the Rev. Dr. Hillis that "a canvass of a large eastern city
showed that ninety four per cent of its leading men were
brought up on the farm. Of one hundred representative commercial and professional men of Chicago, eighty five were

reared in the country. A census of the students of four colleges and seminaries showed that the rural districts furnished eighty five per cent. The leaders are quickly succeeded by men from the country. They always have been, they always will be."

Mr. Vanderpoole takes up the cudgels at this point. Is this latter statement true? he asks. Will not the constantly enlarging influence of manual training tend to give city boys the tests so often imposed upon country boys by the varying duties of life on a farm? The country boy learns early that he can and must do something; he is constantly meeting emergencies. Dr. G. Stanley Hall declared that the farmer boy had to know about seventy different industries, and must daily meet and overcome the severest tests of industry and skill. He must think, and act while thinking, which makes him resourceful as well as self reliant. All this is education, and fits him for leadership; but manual training does all this and more.

There are now hundreds of schools throughout the country with manual training courses of varying kinds. For many years in Boston, and in several other cities, some form of manual training, as sewing, drawing or clay modeling, has been taught. The first real manual training school of the world, however, was opened in St. Louis, in 1880. Its history and progress have been remarkable and the methods have been copied the world over. Its success completely answered the various objections to the modern manual training system and furnished an incentive to progressive thinkers, educators and philanthropists everywhere. All the large and growing schools of this character embody the successful ideas of the St. Louis school and an outline of its work will indicate very nearly what is being done elsewhere. The newer schools are different only in admitting girls and arranging lines of work particularly adapted to them. The St. Louis school is not a free school. It is an adjunct to Washington university. It takes boys at the age of 14 or 15 years and is planned to cover the period of general development in a boy's life that is ordinarily passed in the high school. While the amount and thoroughness of the manual training and mechanical work are surprising, the general culture work and mental discipline do not suffer. So much greater interest and energy is manifested by the pupils that the graduates are able to do the additional work without hardship or nervous strain. They possess all the intellectual qualities of the ordinary high school graduate, besides the magnificent equipment for the practical affairs of life. An outline of the three years' course of studies of the St. Louis school, follows:

First year. Algebra, through simple equations; review arithmetic; English language, the structure and use; history of England; Latin, French, or German grammar and reader may be taken in place of English and history; American classics; commercial geography; elementary physics; botany; drawing, instrumental and freehand from objects; penmanship; joinery; wood carving; wood turning.

Second year. Algebra, through quadratics and radicals; plane geometry; chemistry, theoretical and practical; English composition and literature; rhetoric; English or French history; Latin (Cæsar), French, or German may be taken in place of rhetoric and history; British classics; bookkeeping; drawing, line shading and tinting; forging; patternmaking; moulding; casting with plaster; soldering and brazing; military drill.

Third year. Geometry continued through plane and solid; review in mathematics; mensuration; English composition and literature; civics and political economy; general history; French or German may be taken in place of English and history, or in place of the science study; physiology; elements of physics, with laboratory practice; drawing, brush shading, geometrical, machine, and architectural; metal work with hand and machine tools; filing, chipping, fitting, turning, drilling, planing, screw cutting, etc.; execution of projects; military drill.

Says Professor C. M. Woodward, to whom a large share of the St. Louis school's success is due: "The manual training school has many windows through which all of the great professional and industrial fields may shine in upon the students, and where the student may look out upon all the activities of modern American life; and the school has many doors, through one of which the graduate may step out into the field of his final and deliberate choice."

More than 800 graduates have gone forth from the St. Louis Manual Training school and, almost without exception, the effect upon their careers has been very marked. Prof. Woodward, the director of the school, says the demand for the graduates is always in excess of the supply. As the boys have equal knowledge and skill with woodworking, forging, and machine tools, and with drawing instruments, those who want work scatter according to taste and opportunity in all directions.

Professor Woodward told the American association of officials of bureaus of labor statistics at St. Louis that his graduates earned before the end of the year from $30.00 to $75.00 per month, that they received higher wages than other apprentices from the beginning, and that they were in general demand for draftsmen, electrical workers, inspectors, apprentices, clerks, foremen and assistant superintendents. The number who remained long as machinists was small, he said, because their general versatility and executive ability earned speedy promotion. About one third of the graduates from this school go directly into the higher scientific and technical schools, where they attain the highest rank.

Pages might be written showing the growth of similar schools all over the country. In Chicago, Brooklyn, New York, Philadelphia, Baltimore, Boston, Worcester and other cities are manual training schools with equally good records. Their development has been one continuous story of triumph for the individual and society, as well as for American educational and industrial ideals, in the training of self reliant, self supporting, broad minded, vigorous and useful American citizens. Indeed, manual training has furnished the solution of a great sociological problem. It has long been noted by criminologists that most crime is committed by men who are uneducated in industrial pursuits. It has also been found by the penologists that criminals may be reclaimed as useful citizens by teaching them some trade at which they may earn a livelihood. Hence, the attention of the reformers has been turned to the establishment of manual training and trade schools in the state prisons for the cultivation of the hands and minds and for the development of all the faculties of the inmates. The great Elmira reformatory in New York is the principal one of its kind in the country. It has accomplished a most beneficent work. The employment of the hands and the acquirement of a trade have given stability of character, moral appreciation, a due sense of responsibility and of the value of society and an elevated tone to hundreds of the fallen.

Because manual training has been found so efficacious in the reclamation of criminals, it has been urged as a preventive of crime by its introduction into the public schools. The amount of manual training now practiced in the city schools will show, it is believed, a greatly reduced percentage of criminals in a few years. The value in which this training is held as a preventive of crime is nowhere better illustrated than at the Catholic Protectory, Van Nest, New York, where two thousand incorrigible boys are sent for the reform which reforms. The Catholic Protectory is, in reality, a great school. Its system of education is now largely manual; and the effect upon the boys is astonishing. The idea here takes a highly developed form. The extensive shops are both educational and productive. In all the schools where manual training is in operation, it has been found that a boy's interest is keener, that he learns more rapidly, and that he retains what he learns more thoroughly, when he is constructing a workbench, or making the tools he is to use. At the protectory this principle is so clearly demonstrated that no one can see and question. For four hours every day the two thousand boys are as busy as the workers in any commercial factory. They are not kept at one monotonous task, but are taken from one stage to another, learning as they go. All the work about the buildings is done by the boys. They run the engines, and have charge of the dynamos. They have wired the buildings and fitted them with electric lights. There are squads of masons, painters, plumbers, some still wearing knickerbockers, who are as competent as many journeymen. I have presented some of the arguments of the advocates of manual training but, it seems to me, none is more convincing than the simple statement of the director of the protectory, Brother Leonine:

"I have come to believe," he said to me, "that there are no bad boys. We have here but a handful of the Brothers, in charge of almost two thousand of the worst specimens New York can send us. I would not ask for better friends than anyone can have in those boys, if he really wishes their friendship. They are generous and tender hearted. That they are exceptionally active and intelligent goes without saying. That is, at bottom, the reason why they are here. Most of them came to trouble because they were too eager in their blind scrambling in a strange world that did not know how to treat them."

Manual training, without reference whatever to any practical use, is taught more or less in most of the primary and grammar schools of to-day. Kindergarten schools are devoted almost entirely to manual training, because the hands and eyes of young children can be trained and disciplined much easier than the minds. The grammar schools have introduced clay modeling, wood carving, drawing, paper cutting and other simple exercises designed to vary the monotony of the older methods and to teach those habits of carefulness, accuracy, neatness and application which are essential in the acquirement of all education.

CONSANGUINITY OF LABOR AND EDUCATION.

BY WILLIAM J. TUCKER.

[William Jewett Tucker, president Dartmouth college since 1893; born Griswold, Conn., July 13, 1839; graduated from Dartmouth in 1861; ordained Congregational minister, and has been the pastor of Franklin street church, Manchester, N. H., Madison Square church, New York; professor Andover theological seminary; founder of the Andover house, Boston; editor Andover Review. Author: The Making and the Unmaking of the Preacher; From Liberty to Unity.]

What I have to say is in the nature of some reflections upon the mind of the wage earner—an expression which I borrow from the opening sentence of the book by John Mitchell on organized labor: "The average wage earner has made up his mind that he must remain a wage earner." I would not take this generalization in any unqualified way. The author has himself qualified it by the use of the word average. But when reduced to its lowest terms, it is, I think, the most serious statement which has been made of late concerning the social life of the country, for it purports to be the statement of a mental fact. If Mr. Mitchell had said that in his opinion the conditions affecting the wage earner were becoming fixed conditions, that would have been a statement of grave import, but quite different from the one made. Here is an interpretation of the mind of the wage earner, from one well qualified to give an interpretation of it, to the effect that the average wage earner has reached a state of mind in which he accepts the fixity of his condition. Having reached this state of mind, the best thing which can be done is to organize the wage earner into a system through which he may gain the greatest advantage possible within his accepted limitations. I am not disposed to take issue with the conclusion of the argument (I am a firm believer in trade unions), but I do not like the major premise of the argument. I should be sorry to believe that it was altogether true. And in so far as it is true —in so far, that is, as we are confronted by this mental fact—I believe that we should address ourselves to it quite as definitely as to the physical facts which enter into the labor problem.

If the average wage earner has made up his mind that he must remain a wage earner, we have a new type of solidarity, new at least to this country. No other man amongst us has made up his mind to accept his condition. The majority of men are accepting the conditions of their daily work, but it is not an enforced acceptance. This is true of the great body of people engaged in farming, in mercantile pursuits, and in most of the underpaid professional employments.

In the social order, one of two things must be present to create a solidarity—pride or a grievance. An aristocracy of birth is welded together by pride. It perpetuates itself through the increasing pride of each new generation. An aristocracy is an inheritance, not of wealth, for some families are very poor, but of an assured state of mind. An aristocrat does not have to make up his mind; it has been made up for him. An aristocracy is in this respect entirely different from a plutocracy. A plutocracy is at any given time merely an aggregation of wealth. People are struggling to get into it and are continually falling out of it. There is no mental repose in a plutocracy. It is a restless, struggling, disintegrating mass. It has no inherent solidarity.

Next to pride, the chief source of solidarity is a grievance. The solidarity may be transient or permanent. It lasts as long as the sense of grievance lasts. Sometimes the sense of grievance is worn out; then you have to invent some other term than solidarity to express the deplorable condition into which a mass of people may fall. But whenever the sense of dissatisfaction is widespread and permanent it deepens into a grievance which creates solidarity. The human element involved is at work to intensify and to perpetuate itself.

Now, when it is said that the average wage earner has made up his mind that he must remain a wage earner, the saying assumes unwillingness on his part, the sense of necessity, and therefore a grievance which, as it is communicated from man to man, creates a solidarity. If you can eliminate the grievance, you break up the solidarity. The wage earner then becomes, like the farmer, the trader, the schoolmaster, a man of a given occupation. The fact of the great number of wage earners signifies nothing in a social sense, unless they are bound together by a grievance, unless they have made up their mind to some conclusion which separates them from the community at large or the body politic.

We have come, it seems to me, to the most advanced question concerning labor, as we find ourselves in the presence of this mental fact which Mr. Mitchell asserts. What can be done to so affect the mind of the wage earner that it will not work toward that kind of solidarity which will be of injury to him and to society?

It is, of course, entirely obvious that a greater freedom of mind on the part of the wage earner may be expected to follow the betterment of his condition. This betterment of condition is the one and final object of the trade union. I doubt if one half of that which the trade union has gained for the wage earner could have been gained in any other way. I doubt if one quarter of the gain would have been reached in any other way. Trade unionism is the business method of effecting the betterment of the wage earner under the highly organized conditions of the modern industrial world. But trade unionism at its best must do its work within two clear limitations.

In the first place, every advance that trade unionism tries to make in behalf of the wage earner as such finds a natural limit. The principle of exclusiveness, of separate advantage, is a limited principle. At a given point, now here, now there, it is sure to react upon itself, or to be turned back. Organization meets opposing organization. Public interests become involved. Moral issues are raised. The co-operating sympathy of men, which can always be counted upon in any fair appeal to it, turns at once into rebuke and restraint if it is abused. The wage earner in a democracy will never be allowed to get far beyond the average man through any exclusive advantages which he may attempt through organization.

In the second place, trade unionism can deal with the wage earner only as a wage earner, and he is more than a wage earner. There comes a time when he cannot be satisfied with wages. The betterment of his condition creates wants beyond which it satisfies. The growing mind of the wage earner, like anybody's growing mind, seeks to widen its environment. It wants contact with other kinds of minds. When once it becomes aware of its provincialism it tries to escape from it—a fact which is clearly attested in the broadening social and political relations of the stronger labor leaders.

But while I believe that trade unionism is the business method of enlarging the mind of the wage earner through the betterment of his condition, I think that the time has come for the use or adaptation of other means which may give it freedom and expansion. One means of preventing a narrow and exclusive solidarity of wage earners is greater identification on their part with the community through the acquisition of local property. Mobility is, in the earlier stages of the development of the wage earner, the source of his strength. He can easily change to his interest. No advantage can be taken of his fixity. He can put himself without loss into the open market. He can avail himself at once of the highest market price, provided his change of place does not affect injuriously his fellow workers in the union—an exception of growing concern.

But in the more advanced stages of labor the wage earner gains the privilege of localizing himself, and in so doing he takes a long step in the direction of full and free citizenship. A good deposit in a savings bank adds to his social value, but that value is greatly enhanced by exchanging it for a good house.

I am aware that in advancing the acquisition of local property I touch upon the large and as yet undetermined question of the decentralization of labor. If the great cities are to be the home of the industries, then this idea can be realized in only a partial degree through suburban homes. But if the industries are to seek out or establish smaller centers, then the wage earner has the opportunity to become more distinctly and more conspicuously a citizen.

Another means of giving freedom and expansion to the wage earning population in place of a narrow and exclusive solidarity is by giving to it ready access to the higher education. There is no reason why the former experience of the New England farmer and the present experience of the western farmer should not be repeated in the family of the intelligent wage earner. The sons of the New England farmer who were sent to college identified their families with the state and church and with all public interests. They lifted the family horizon. I have said that this experience may be repeated in the families of the wage earner. It is being repeated. Let me give you an illustration with which I am familiar. The students at Dartmouth are divided about as follows, according to the occupation of their fathers: Thirty per cent are the sons of business men, twenty five per cent of professional men, fifteen per cent of farmers; of the remaining thirty per cent, more than half are the sons of wage earners. The per cent from the shops now nearly equals that from the farm. I have no doubt that this proportion will hold in most of our eastern colleges and universities. The home of the wage earner is becoming a recruiting ground for higher education which no college can afford to overlook. As Professor Marshall, the English economist, has said, since the manual labor classes are four or five times as numerous as all other classes put together, it is not unlikely that more than half of the best natural genius that is born into the country belongs to them. And from this statement he goes on to draw the conclusion that there is no extravagance more prejudicial to the growth of the national wealth than that wasteful negligence which allows genius which happens to be born of lowly parentage to expend itself in lowly work. So much for the necessity of fresh, virile and self supporting stock to the higher education, if it is to discharge its obligation to society. Virility is as necessary to educational progress as it is to industrial progress. I am in the habit of saying that, from an educational point of view, it is on the whole easier to make blue blood out of red blood than it is to make red blood out of blue blood. The reaction from the higher education upon the family of the wage earner is yet to be seen, but no one can doubt its broadening influence. As the representatives of these families become more numerous in our colleges and universities, and as they have time to make a place for themselves in all the great callings, they will of necessity lift those whom they represent toward their own level. Some of them will become captains of industry. I believe that in that capacity they will also become leaders of labor. For, as it seems to me, the settlement of the relation of capital and labor is to be more and more, not in the hands of men who have been trained away from one another, but in the hands of men who have been trained toward one another. The industrial world is becoming a great school in which men must learn to practice the industrial virtues. And among these virtues I put, next to honesty in work and in the wage of work, and absolute fidelity in keeping agreements at any cost, that sense of justice which comes of the ability to put one's self in another's place. When we have capitalists and leaders of labor, it must be both at one and the same time, who are really able to reason together, we shall have industrial peace. This will mean arbitration at first hand.

I mention another source of freedom and breadth and power to the wage earner—a source which is common to all —namely, satisfaction in his work. The wage is not and never can be the sufficient reward of labor. This is just as true of the salary as of the wage. The difference at present lies in the fact that the person on a low salary is apt to take more satisfaction in his work than the person on a high wage —the school teacher on $800 or $1,000 a year, in distinction from the mechanic on four or six dollars a day. The present ambition of the high wage earner seems to incline more to the pecuniary rewards of his work than to the work itself. Doubtless this tendency is due in no slight degree to the fact that the wage earner is brought into constant and immediate contact with the money making class. He sees that the value of the industry is measured chiefly by its profits. Sometimes the profits are flaunted in his face. At all times the thing most in evidence to him is money. I deprecate this constant comparison between the capitalist and the laborer. The comparisons were far better taken between the workman and the other men whose chief reward is not money. The old time professions still live and maintain their position through a certain detachment from pecuniary rewards. The exceptional doctor may receive large fees, but his profession forbids him to make a dollar out of any discovery which he may make in medicine. The exceptional minister may receive a large salary, but his profession puts the premium upon self denying work. Even the law is more distinctively represented by the moderate salary of the average judge than by the retainer of the counsel for a wealthy corporation. The skilled workman, the artisan, belongs with these men, not with the money makers. In allowing himself to be commercialized he enters upon a cheap and unsatisfying competition. His work is an art, and he has the possible reward of the artist. Under mediæ-valism the guild and the university were not far apart. I should like to see the relation restored and extended.

I am not speaking in this connection of the unskilled laborer. There is a point below which it is impossible to idealize labor. The man who works in ceaseless and petty monotony, and under physical discomfort and danger, cannot do anything more than to earn an honest livelihood, if, indeed, he receives the living wage. But he is as far removed from the advanced wage earner of our day as he is from any of the well supported and well rewarded classes. For him we are all bound to work, and to act, and to think—not as an object of our charity, but as a part of our industrial brotherhood; and whenever a great labor leader, be he John Burns or John Mitchell, goes to his relief and tries to give him self supporting and self respecting standing, we should count it not a duty but an honor to follow the leading; but equally do I hold it to be a duty and an honor that, as the wage earner advances in intelligence, in pecuniary reward, and in position, he should take his place without any reservation whatever among those who are trying to meet the responsibilities which attach to citizenship in a democracy.

But viewing the present disposition and purpose of the best intentioned leaders in the ranks of organized labor, I am convinced that their avowed object is not commensurate with their opportunity. I am convinced that the interpretation put upon the mind of the wage earner, if it represents a present fact, ought to suggest a duty toward the mind of labor. That duty is to give it freedom, breadth, expansion; to incorporate it into the common mind of aspiration and hope, the American type of mind. In saying this I do not overlook or minimize the imperative duty of raising the lowest wage earner to the highest place to which he can be lifted, and of giving a future to his children and to his children's children. I would urge, in the full apostolic sense, the old apostolic injunction— We that are strong ought to bear the infirmities of the weak. But I would not stop with this duty. I would make the wage earner, as he grows strong, a helper all round; a partner in all the serious work of the republic; an active power in that commonwealth which draws no line within the wants or hopes of man.